The

COMPLETE BOOK
OF INTERNATIONAL
ADOPTION

Previous page, clockwise from top:

Carlos was born in Guatemala on July 13, 2002, and joined his forever family in March 2003.

Kylen was born in Novosibirsk, Russia, on August 13, 2002, and joined her forever family in April 2004.

Luke was born in Russia on December 9, 2002, and joined his forever family in June 2003.

Kiah ZiPing was born in China on July 22, 2002, and joined her forever family in March 2003.

Jacob Ivan was born in Tyumen, Russia, on August 9, 2004, and joined his forever family in June 2005.

Emilie was born in China on June 13, 2002, and joined her forever family in September 2003.

Karin (center photo) was born in China on January 5, 2004, and joined her forever family in November 2005.

The

COMPLETE BOOK
OF INTERNATIONAL
ADOPTION

A Step-by-Step Guide to Finding Your Child

DAWN DAVENPORT

Broadway Books

BROADWAY

PRINTED IN THE UNITED STATES OF AMERICA

BROADWAY BOOKS and its logo, a letter B bisected on the diagonal, are trademarks of Random House, Inc.

Visit our website at www.broadwaybooks.com

First edition published 2006.

Book design by Chris Welch

Cataloging-in-Publication Data is on file with the Library of Congress.

ISBN-13: 978-0-7679-2520-4

ISBN-10: 0-7679-2520-3

3 5 7 9 10 8 6 4 2

To Cait, who believed in this book and in me, and frequently showed her pride in both.

To Hays, who taught me how fun the teen years can be for a parent (and teen) and who periodically came out of his world long enough to ask about The Book.

To Wells, who has taught me much about strength, overcoming, and patience.

To Leah, who is a joy beyond belief and the fulfillment of a dream.

and

To Peter, the love of my life and my partner throughout.

———

To all the parents who have found their child and to those who are still looking.

To those children who have found their forever families, and especially to those who have not.

CONTENTS

My Prayer for All Children

I pray that all children will be loved for who they are, for no reason other than that they are.

I pray that all children will be loved as first best, not second best; that they will be loved with an intensity that can move mountains, because life will present plenty of mountains that will need to be moved.

I pray that all children will have someone who will . . .

- seek them, and only them, out of the crowd on the stage;
- push them to reach for their goals and discover their unique gifts;
- hold them accountable for their actions with love and dignity;
- advocate for them through this maze called life;
- explain the unexplainable; and
- smile when they walk into the room, just because they did.

Mostly I pray that all children will have someone who knows them well enough and loves them deeply enough to see the divine spark that is unique in them.

I pray that this be the birthright of all children throughout the world. And since this birthright can only be fulfilled by parents, I pray that each child, regardless of the circumstances of their birth, finds their parent and each parent finds their child.

Thanks, God.

Amen.

ACKNOWLEDGMENTS

Although I chose it, I will admit that the title of this book is a bit ostentatious . . . *The **Complete** Book of International Adoption.* The title sounded good (albeit mundane); it sounded like what was needed, but trying to live up to such a title was often overwhelming and always humbling. Fortunately, many in the adoption community rallied around to support and guide me with their knowledge and wisdom. Without their very gracious help, this book would more aptly be titled *The Incomplete Book of International Adoption.*

First and foremost, I want to thank the many families who shared the story of their adoption journey with me. I value the trust they placed in me to honor their experience and treat it gently. Many of these people shared intensely personal stories for no reason other than to help others feel less alone if they found themselves in a similar position. They are my heroes, and their wisdom is the heart of this book.

Thank you to my agent, Katharine Sands of the Sarah Jane Freymann Agency, for her belief in this book and in me long before there was evidence to warrant either, and her tireless efforts to find us the right home.

Thanks to Trish Medved for her editorial help in fine- (and not so fine) tuning this material.

Many professionals in the field of adoption and international adoption medicine shared their time, knowledge, and support to make this book better. These folks took time from their already busy schedules with nothing to gain other than helping me and, through me, helping prospective adopting parents. Although I talked with many, any errors and all opinions are my own.

Maren Brose
Alice Laeger Doyle
Rebecca Hackworth

Jynger Roberts
Rhonda Runnells
Sue Ellison
Nicky Losse
Janiece Wieschhaus
Margi Miller
Janice Simon
Alexa Ricciardi
Debra Dreyer
Carol Wahl
Jill Taylor
Hue Pham
Debra Harder
Katherine Holliday
Mimi Huminski
Susan Soon-keum Cox
Laurel E. Anderson
Carol Nelson
Anita Thomas
Joan McNamara
Dr. Arthur Becker-Weidman
Doris Marshall
Jennifer Yang-Kwait
Jane Aronson, M.D.
Patrick Mason, M.D., Ph.D.
Jennifer Ladage, M.D.
Dana E. Johnson, M.D., Ph.D.
Julian Davies, M.D.
Laurie Miller, M.D.
Jerri Ann Jenista, M.D.
Deborah A. Borchers, M.D., F.A.A.P.
Gail Farber, M.D.
I especially want to thank Carol Nelson, Maren Brose, Margi Miller, and
Joan McNamara for help above and beyond the call of duty (especially since
there was no *duty* whatsoever). Their prompt, cheerful responses truly sus-
tained me in the last crazy days of getting this book to print.
    I also owe a special dept of gratitude to Dr. Gail Farber, Dr. Patrick Mason,
and Dr. Dana Johnson for their time and patience as I tried to untangle the
best way to present the often confusing and contradictory medical informa-

tion. I am especially indebted to Dr. Farber for listening and for the helpful distinction between cabdrivers and doctors (you hire one and consult the other, but I still get confused on which is which). After her gentle chastisement of my incorrect verb choice, I wasted a good thirty minutes playing my own version of Jeff Foxworthy's *You Know You're a Redneck When . . .* ("You know you're a cabdriver, not a doctor, when . . .").

Thanks to Janet Henderson and Anne and Bill Bond for providing me with a place to escape to for uninterrupted writing time.

Thanks to Anne Bullard and Belinda Roberts for our morning talks and walks (notice the order) and for always asking how the book was coming along even when they were tired of hearing about it.

Thanks to my lovely daughter, Cait Johnson, for her excellent review of Chapter 10. Her edit was insightful and thorough, even if she did use the words *chunky* and *clumsy* to describe my writing more often than I thought absolutely necessary.

Thanks to my mom, Sadye Davenport, and my late dad, Dave Davenport, for their support and encouragement and for giving me wings.

Thanks to the *Wall Street Journal* for including recipes in their *Weekend Journal.* They transformed my husband into a gourmet cook and I have never eaten better.

And last, but certainly not least, my everlasting thanks to Peter, husband and dad extraordinaire, for embarking on both the parenting and writing journey with me. Words cannot express my gratitude for both his emotional support as well as the practical support that he unfailingly gave day in and day out to keep our house and family running while I devoted myself to our fifth child—this book. I truly couldn't have done it without him, and I certainly wouldn't have had as much fun along the way.

INTRODUCTION

My husband remarked the other day that no one ever reads Introductions. As I pondered his comment, I realized he had a point—I seldom read Introductions. Preferring a straight road over a meandering path, I like to jump straight to the meat of the matter, which I reason is not in the Introduction. But now that the shoe is on the other foot, or pen in the other hand, I regret my lifetime of haste. Introductions set the stage for the book by providing context and background information; they allow the author a little more leeway in shaping the material. I hope you will indulge me and keep reading.

I have attempted to break from the deadly serious mold of most of the adoption literature available. I don't believe respect and humor are mutually exclusive, and the lighter tone makes it more likely that you'll actually read the book through and learn something that may help you. Although the book is written following the adoption journey from beginning to end, information that will help you at the beginning can be found throughout, so I strongly suggest that you read the book through at first and then focus on the chapter pertaining to the stage you are in. You can find updates and other information at my Web site, www.findingyourchild.com.

I always knew I wanted to adopt. In high school and college, when I was allowed my choice on topics for a paper, I always chose to write on adoption. My husband, Peter, claims I broached the subject on our first date, right after I asked him his favorite baby name. (That we had a second date after that conversation tells you something about the state of his hormones.) I now have four children, through birth and adoption, and am living my dream. We adopted from Korea, primarily because at the time it was one of the few countries that were open and would accept a family with three children. Times have definitely changed.

I am an attorney and researcher by training, and although I have relied on that training in researching and writing this book, my real qualification is being an adoptive mom. I have been on the adoptive parenting journey for some time and have shared with you what I've learned. I have added to my experience the voice of the many families I have interviewed who are also on this path. I interviewed these families in person, online, by phone, and every combination of the above. Some people were interviewed several times throughout their adoption process to show the progression of their feelings and experiences at different stages. I promised them anonymity to ensure their privacy and also to encourage them to speak frankly. They did.

The story at the beginning of each chapter is either my story at that stage or is a combined story of several families to make it more representative. The stories at the end of the chapters come directly from the interviews. There are as many experiences as there are families adopting, and the stories selected reflect this diversity. My criterion for selection was the experience expressed rather than the country involved, since most of the experiences are universal regardless of the country. Families who have adopted from a country often feel intensely loyal to that country and take offense at anything that casts a negative light on adopting from that country. Inclusion of a "negative" story from one country should not be taken as my preference for one country over another. I am well aware that good and bad experiences can be had in any country. I should add that I do not necessarily agree with the opinion of the parents who shared their stories and inclusion of a story is not intended as an endorsement. This is especially true in Chapters 1, 2, and 3.

I have studied the published research in the field of adoption and adoption medicine and have interviewed many professionals who have devoted their lives to bringing kids home and helping them and their families once they are here. Information and wisdom from both have been included throughout, and a more complete list of the research can be found in the References at the back of the book.

This book is intended to prepare you for all the possibilities in international adoption, but there is a fine line between preparing you for the possible problems and scaring you needlessly. I heard frequently in my interviews that parents dreaded and often avoided reading adoption books or preparation material because they were "all so negative." I remember having these feelings myself. There is some truth in what these families say. Much of what is available for adoption education was written specifically to focus on a *problem* (attachment, neurological disorders, etc.), and it was never the author's intent to present the whole picture. These books are wonderful resources for families living that experience, but most families at the beginning of the adoption process lack the proper context to keep them in perspective. But a book that ignores the potential problems or does not address them thoroughly at the beginning would do a disservice to prospective adoptive parents and to the children they adopt.

It is my fervent hope that this book paints the whole picture—complete with the possible problems and the likely successes. I want parents to understand the risks in international adoption so they can make good choices and can be prepared. There are big risks, but there are also big rewards. Anything in life worth doing has risks, and anything involving love is especially risky.

Yes, your kid may have some problems or delays; they may be temporary or permanent; they may be inconsequential or life-altering. This book points out things you can do to reduce the chance of your child having the more serious of these problems, but no matter how your children come to be yours, you can never eliminate the risk entirely. Since you are their parent, their problems will become yours. Most of the time the best response to that is "So what, that's life." But this response comes easier if you are prepared going in. My advice is the same as your grandmother's: Prepare for the worst and hope for the best.

International adoption has brought me great joy and I am one of its biggest supporters, but international adoption is not the best solution for orphaned children throughout the world. Oh, don't get me wrong—I believe it is good for that particular child at this particular time, but it does little to address the fundamental problems that cause children to need to find homes outside their birth family and birth country in the first place. And it does little for the thousands of children who won't be adopted because of their age, gender, or health. I believe adoptive parents, as a community of people whose lives have been enriched by this process, have an obligation to help. We can support efforts to address the problems of extreme poverty or social instability in our children's birth countries that contribute to the disintegration of families, we can choose agencies that give back to the children who remain, and we can support organizations that help orphaned children throughout the world. I pray that someday there is no need for international adoption, but until that time I believe it is a wonderful option for the children who need a forever home and can't find one in their country of birth.

The adoption community can be a mighty exacting crowd where words must be chosen with care. I find it all a bit wearying—birth vs. biological; birth country vs. foreign country; children with special needs vs. waiting children; and heaven help the person who accidentally says they adopted a pet for the family. I understand that words matter—I make my living with words—

but too much focus on saying everything just right will simply result in less talking about adoption in general, and I think we need more, not less, discussion on these issues. Without a doubt, some words are better than others, but I suggest we spend more time trying to understand the meaning behind the words rather than focusing on the words themselves. Nonetheless, I have attempted to use the least offensive language throughout this book. No doubt I have only partially succeeded.

When talking about something as diverse as international adoption, you have to generalize to communicate. I understand that not all adoptive parents are white, not all parents are married, not all parents faced infertility, not all adoptions are transracial, not all children will have health issues, and not all children will come from orphanages. But qualifying each sentence for all possibilities was too cumbersome and, quite frankly, too boring. I have faith that you can read around the words to gain the kernel of truth and information that applies to your circumstances and disregard the rest.

Adoptive families aren't perfect families; we are real families with the beauty and warts of all families. But, fundamentally, adoption works. It works because it's good for kids and good for parents—it's the ultimate win/win. You get the joy (and pain) of parenting, and a child, your child, gets the security and love of a family.

As I was finishing the manuscript for this book, I had just announced that I was again going to hole up in my office for the week to try to get some more done on The Book. Most of the parenting responsibility that week would fall once again on Peter. Shortly thereafter, as we were cleaning up from dinner, my husband and youngest daughter were engaged in their favorite pastime—teasing. She was screaming, he was laughing, her sister was commiserating, and her brothers were egging it on. In the midst of all the noise, Peter looked at me and said, "You take all the time you need to write that book. People need to adopt. It's too much fun to miss." He's right.

The

COMPLETE BOOK

OF INTERNATIONAL

ADOPTION

CHAPTER 1

IS INTERNATIONAL ADOPTION RIGHT FOR YOU?

Where DO Babies Come From?

Gabriel was born in Guatemala on March 14, 2005, and joined his forever family in August 2005.

After three doctors, two surgeries, and three failed in vitro fertilizations, Elizabeth and John were running short of time, money, and patience. John in particular was tired of the infertility merry-go-round and their life being defined by infertility. He felt their money and energy would be better spent on a surer bet. Elizabeth wasn't ready to give up her dream. "The tension between us was building and I knew our relationship needed a break from infertility, but it was still something I had to process at my own speed," she recalls. After six more months of talking and continued treatments, Elizabeth began to get excited about the possibility of becoming a mom even if she couldn't become pregnant. Elizabeth and John are now the proud parents of Emily and Lia, both adopted from China as babies. "I truly wonder now why we didn't do this much sooner," says Elizabeth. "I couldn't possibly love them more or feel more like a mom if they had been born to me."

People come to adoption from many different places. Single women adopt when they want to be a mom, but haven't found the elusive Mr. Right and think a sperm bank is silly when kids are already out there who need a mom. A growing number of couples with one or two kids consider adoption because there are kids who need homes and they believe they could be just that home. Many people, however, turn to adoption because biology failed them. We are a "pull yourself up by the bootstraps" nation; anything can be conquered with grit, determination, and money. Not so infertility. What was supposed to be as simple as buying a bottle of wine, lighting the candles, and ditching the condoms becomes a medical ordeal that sometimes no amount of money or perseverance can overcome.

Some couples caught up on the medical treadmill that is infertility are so focused on getting a child that they jump immediately onto the adoption treadmill. It is important to slow down and give yourself time to grieve the losses of infertility before you assume that adoption is the right path to parenthood for you. Parenting through adoption is different from parenting through birth—not worse, not second best, just different. Your child, regardless of how she joins your family, deserves parents who want her for who she is, not because she is all they can get. Take the time to make sure you are that parent.

IS ADOPTION FOR YOU?

Answer the following questions honestly. No one is going to see your answers, so forget about political correctness and answer how you really feel.

1. Do you spend time imagining the child of your dreams—the perfect (or not so perfect) combination of you and your spouse's genes?
____ Frequently   ____ Sometimes   ____ Seldom

2. Do you long to be pregnant or see your spouse pregnant?
____ Frequently   ____ Sometimes   ____ Seldom

3. Does it bother you that future generations of your family will not be related by blood to you and your ancestors?
____ Frequently   ____ Sometimes   ____ Seldom

4. Does it hurt you to see a pregnant woman or nursing mother?
____ Frequently   ____ Sometimes   ____ Seldom

5. Do you find it hard to talk about your infertility without crying or intense emotions, or do you avoid talking about your infertility at all?
____ Frequently ____ Sometimes ____ Seldom

6. Are you furious at God for afflicting you with infertility? (Why not boils or locusts, for goodness' sakes!)
____ Frequently ____ Sometimes ____ Seldom

7. Do you feel like you are less of a woman or man because you can't biologically have a child?
____ Frequently ____ Sometimes ____ Seldom

8. Do you feel pressured to hurry up and get past infertility and get on with adoption and the rest of your life?
____ Frequently ____ Sometimes ____ Seldom

9. Do you get angry at the thought of having to prove yourself worthy to adopt?
____ Frequently ____ Sometimes ____ Seldom

10. Do you wish you could skip all the adoption education and just jump straight to the part where a child is in your home?
____ Frequently ____ Sometimes ____ Seldom

Adoption professionals and psychologists strongly recommend that infertile couples resolve their infertility issues before they adopt. Coming to terms with infertility takes time. If you answered "frequently" to more than a few questions, you need more time to grieve.

Infertility robs you of more than just the opportunity to parent. It also takes away your dreams of pregnancy, your dreams of childbirth and breast-feeding, your dreams of biologically continuing your family line, and your dreams of your perfect child. Infertility also affects your sex life (privacy and spontaneity are the first victims) and your finances. I've included this litany of woes not to add fuel to your pity bonfire, but to help you see that adoption addresses only one of the many losses associated with infertility—the loss of raising a child.

Take the time you need. The decision to adopt, or not, is a process, not an event. Join Resolve, a national infertility support group. Read some of the infertility books and magazines listed in the Resource Guide at the end of this book, especially *Adopting after Infertility* by Patricia Irwin Johnston. Ask your local Resolve group or your infertility doctor for a referral to a therapist who is familiar with infertility.

Resolution does not necessarily mean that the grief entirely goes away, but it's a matter of degrees. Many parents I interviewed said they knew they were ready to adopt when they wanted to parent more than they wanted to be pregnant. When you can answer sometimes and seldom to the adoption quiz questions, then it is time to go forward and find *your* child through adoption.

ADOPTION FACTS VS. MYTHS

Adoption is often misunderstood, even though it has been around since the beginning of time. Even if you don't believe these myths, others do, so it helps to address them at the beginning of your adoption journey.

Myth #1: Adopted kids grow up to have lots of problems.

Life experience should dispel this myth. Ask around and you'll be surprised by the number of well-adjusted people who have been adopted. Fortunately, we have more than just anecdotal reports; longitudinal studies have found that adoptees fare well in adolescence and adulthood (Bohman and Sigvardsson, 1990; Kelly et al., 1998).

Myth #2: You can't really love an adopted child as much as you could love your "own" child.

Oh yes you can! Love is not limited to biology. I love my husband more than life itself and he is not biologically related to me. Love for your children, by birth or adoption, grows from parenting, from nurturing, and from sharing your life. Your child is *yours* regardless of how he joined your family. Shortly after we adopted our daughter, a neighbor said to me that she couldn't really love someone else's child. Without realizing that she was inelegantly making a reference to our adoption, I replied wholeheartedly that I couldn't either. All of my children are my own, and I love them each with a passion that sometimes scares me and often annoys them.

Myth #3: Your adopted child will never really consider you her real parents.

This is the flip side of myth #2. Real parents are the ones who stay up until the wee hours with a sick child and then a few years later are up in those same wee

---

FAMOUS ADOPTEES

Families have been formed by adoption since the beginning of time. Alexander the Great was adopted, as was Moses. Although not all the following were adopted outside their extended family, they all were touched by adoption.

- Edward Albee—playwright
- Maya Angelou—author
- John J. Audubon—naturalist
- Tallulah Bankhead—actor
- Les Brown—motivational speaker
- Surya Bonaly—Olympic figure skater
- Peter and Kitty Carruthers—Olympic figure skaters
- George Washington Carver—inventor
- Lynnette Cole—Miss USA 2000
- Faith Daniels—news anchor
- Toby Dawson—Olympic skier
- Larry Ellison—chairman and CEO of Oracle Corporation
- Ella Fitzgerald—singer
- Jamie Foxx—actor
- Melissa Gilbert—actor
- Scott Hamilton—Olympic figure skater
- Deborah Harry—singer
- Faith Hill—singer
- Langston Hughes—author
- Steve Jobs—CEO of Apple Computer and of Pixar Animation Studios
- Eartha Kitt—singer
- Greg Louganis—Olympic diver
- Steve McQueen—actor
- Sarah McLachlan—singer
- Tom Monaghan—founder and CEO of Domino's Pizza
- Lucy Maud Montgomery—author
- James Michener—author
- Dan O'Brien—Olympic decathlete
- Jim Palmer—baseball player
- Edgar Allan Poe—author
- Michael Reagan—talk-show host
- Buffy Sainte-Marie—musician
- Dave Thomas—founder of Wendy's International
- Leo Tolstoy—author

---

hours waiting for her to get home from a date. Real parents limit TV and candy and push educational games and vegetables. Real parents have gray hairs from worry and laugh lines from joy. Yes, adopted children have two sets of parents: one set who gave them life and one who raised them. But I know of no adopted child who considers their adoptive family any less than their real family, and this feeling is not lessened if they later decide to search for their birth family.

Myth #4: The kids adopted from _____ (choose one: Russia, China, Guatemala, Vietnam, India, etc.) have all kinds of problems.

There are no guarantees in parenting—or in life, for that matter. Birth children and adopted children can have health, learning, or behavioral issues. Possible problems are discussed at length in Chapters 2 and 8, but research over many years of adoption has shown that the vast majority of internationally adopted kids thrive. Early-life experiences do matter, but you can lower the risks of adopting a child with health or emotional problems by following the steps laid out in this book.

Myth #5: Adopting a child of another race or ethnicity is bound to cause problems for the child.

International adoptions began with American families adopting Korean War orphans in the 1950s. More than fifty years of research on these transracial/transcultural adoptions, as well as research on African American children adopted by Caucasian parents, disproves this myth. Transracially adopted children usually adjust well, with strong racial identity, self-esteem, and attachment to their family. This does not mean that transracial adoption is for everyone or that transracial adoptees don't have issues to face as they mature, but ultimately transracial adoptions can work. Refer to Chapters 2 and 10 for a complete discussion on the issues to consider.

Myth #6: Adopted children should/will feel grateful to their adoptive parents.

Sorry to burst your bubble, but gratitude is not inherent in the nature of most children. I will get an occasional spontaneous "thank you," a few more when demanded, and even more when they want something, but usually my children take what I offer as their due, which in fact, I suppose, it is. This is the case regardless of whether your kid becomes yours through birth or adoption. I am told that this changes once they are adults, but I'm still waiting. If you are adopting thinking of undying gratitude for rescuing a child, you likely won't get it and no child deserves that pressure. You are adopting because you want to be a parent. It's an added bonus that your child will get a home and a great family.

Myth #7: You are more likely to get pregnant after you adopt.

Adoptive children do not cast a fertility spell on their parents. If relaxation were all it took to get pregnant, you would have been pregnant the first six months you tried. The reason that you hear stories of Aunt Ida's cousin's hairdresser conceiving after adoption is that this is the exception that stands out because of its uniqueness. Do not adopt if your motivation is to increase your odds of getting pregnant. It won't work and it is not fair to your child. Every

---

ADOPTION LANGUAGE

Using the right words to talk about adoption is more than just political correctness. Word choice can express subtle negative meanings reflecting either ignorance or prejudice. I certainly feel very much like my daughter's real and natural mother, although I am not her birth or biological mother. Above all, she is my real child; she is my own. Although I think that some in the adoption community are a little too sensitive and quick to take offense at word choice, it is a good idea to know and use positive adoption language.

Accurate Language	*Inaccurate Language*
Birth parent/ Biological parent	Real parent/ Real mother/ Natural parent
Birth relative	Blood relative
My child	Adopted child
Birth child	Own child
Parent	Adoptive parent
Making an adoption plan	Giving up your child/ Putting up for adoption
Born to unmarried parents or unwed mother	Illegitimate
Child placed for adoption	Unwanted child
Deciding to parent	Keeping your baby
Terminate parental rights/ Consent to adoption/relinquish	Take away/Give up
International or intercountry adoption	Foreign adoption
Child born in another country	Foreign child
Child with special needs/ Waiting child	Handicapped child/ Hard to place
Was adopted	Is adopted
Search	Track down parents
Finding a pet	Adopting a pet

---

child deserves to be the one you really want, not the one that keeps the dream of your perfect child alive.

INTERNATIONAL ADOPTION VS. DOMESTIC ADOPTION

International and domestic adoption appeal to different people for different reasons. Neither is inherently better than the other, although one or the other may be better for you. I hate the competition that sometimes surfaces between proponents of either domestic or international adoption, with each side attempting to scare prospective families away from the other choice. Anytime a family finds a child and a child finds a family, regardless of whether that child is from Beijing or Boston, the world is a better place.

I didn't write this book to discourage families from considering domestic adoption. I wrote this book to help you decide between these options and, if international adoption is the right choice for you, to guide you in the process. In my experience, most people will instinctively feel more comfortable with one type of adoption, depending on their priorities.

- The top priority for parents who are drawn to domestic private adoption is getting a child as young as possible with as much health information as possible.
- The top priority for parents who are drawn to the public foster-care system is providing a home for a child who really needs them.
- The top priorities for parents who are drawn to international adoption are the predictability of knowing that they will get a baby or toddler within a set period of time and a discomfort with the domestic adoption process (for example, the amount of time a birth parent has to revoke their consent to adopt or open adoption post-placement).

It helps to have a basic idea of how domestic and international adoptions differ. If you decide that domestic adoption is for you, look at the Resource Guide for suggestions on how to proceed.

Domestic Adoption

Domestic adoption covers both private adoptions (usually of infants) and public adoptions from the foster-care system (usually of older children).

Private domestic adoptions

Private domestic adoptions are about evenly divided between agency adoptions and independent adoptions, with the distinction being whether the birth parents place the infant with the adoptive parents through an adoption agency or independently (usually with the help of an attorney or facilitator). If you don't work through an agency, you must hire an adoption attorney to handle the legal aspects of the adoption. Most private domestic adoptions are of newborns and gender selection is usually either prohibited or strongly discouraged. In almost all domestic adoptions, the birth parents (usually the birth mother) choose the adoptive parents based on pictures, biographical information, and meetings.

Adoption is governed by state law and a great deal of variation exists between the states, but in every state birth parents must either consent to the adoption through relinquishment of parental rights or have their parental rights terminated. In most private domestic adoptions, birth mothers relinquish their parental rights through consent. In most states, a parent must wait a set period of time after birth (ranging from one day to fifteen days) before they can consent to the adoption, and up until this time, they can change their mind. Estimates are that up to 50 percent of birth mothers who start the adoption process change their mind during the process and decide to parent their child. They can change their mind before or after selecting an adoptive family, before or after their expenses are paid by the adoptive family, and before or after birth. The parental rights of unknown birth fathers present a special problem, and each state handles this situation differently. You should consult an experienced agency or attorney for advice.

Many states also give birth parents a set period of time after they have signed the relinquishment papers and placed the baby with the adoptive parents to change their mind (range is from 0 to 180 days). Although this is a nail-biting period for adoptive parents who are parenting the child during this time, it is required to make sure the birth parents are truly committed to the adoption. Once this legal time period has passed, it is extremely rare for a birth parent to successfully challenge the adoption. A good adoption attorney knows how to reduce this possibility. The media tend to focus on these cases since they are unusual and sensational, just as they focus on the unusual and sensational plane crashes while ignoring the millions of safe landings. Crashes, whether of planes or adoptions, are always going to get more attention, but you shouldn't make the decision to fly or adopt based on them.

Finding birth mothers who want to make an adoption plan for their child is key to private domestic adoptions, and there are many more families who want to adopt than birth mothers who want to place. How adoptive parents find birth mothers depends on the agency or attorney/facilitator. With some agencies, adoptive parents need only apply; the agency finds the birth mother and shows her biographical information on prospective adoptive families. She meets with several and then chooses one to parent her child. The waiting time to be selected varies greatly, depending on how flexible the adoptive parents are on health, race, and prenatal risks and how attractive their profile is to birth parents. Serendipity plays a role as well. To speed up the process, many facilitators and some agencies require adoptive parents to independently look for birth mothers. Print and Internet advertisements and toll-free telephone numbers are the norm. Usually independent adoptions with the proactive approach are faster and more expensive than agency adoptions, again depending on the flexibility of the adoptive parents.

Adoptive parents may be required to pay reasonable living, legal, counseling, and medical expenses (including prenatal care and birth expenses) of the birth mother. What can be paid differs by state. These fees may not be refundable if the birth mother changes her mind and decides to parent her child.

Today, most domestic private adoptions are *open,* which is adoptionese for ongoing contact between birth parents (and sometimes their extended family) and the adoptive family after the adoption is finalized. The degree of openness varies from sending pictures and letters annually, to occasional meetings, to regular contact. Birth mothers usually let adoptive parents know the amount of openness they want during the selection process, with the trend being toward more contact after placement. Many adoption professionals believe openness is helpful for the child because it removes the mystery surrounding adoption. As he matures, the child can ask his birth mother questions about why she decided on adoption and he has access to the medical history of his birth family.

Public adoption from state foster-care systems

Every state has children who have been removed from their birth parents' care for a variety of reasons, including abuse, neglect, parental substance abuse, or incarceration. Children can be placed directly through the state social services department or through a private agency authorized by the state to place foster children. Almost one quarter of these children are eligible for adoption, and there is always a need for adoptive families. The first goal of the foster system is to reunite the child with her birth parents or extended family. Only after the state determines that this goal is not in the best interest of the child will they seek to terminate parental rights.

Most of the younger children placed for adoption from the foster-care system are first placed with the prospective adoptive family as foster children, because their birth parents' parental rights have not been terminated and they are not legally free for adoption. Under this foster-to-adopt system (also known as fost/adopt), the foster parents/prospective adoptive parents must accept the risk that the child may be returned to his birth parents. Most states consider the likelihood of reunification before they place the child in a foster-to-adopt home. There are always children, usually school age, who are legally free for adoption and ready for placement. Here are some facts to consider:

- Approximately 64 percent of the waiting U.S. children are over six years of age and the median age is eight and a half years.
- Many sibling groups are available for adoption.
- Forty percent of children available for adoption are black, 37 percent are white, and 14 percent are Hispanic.
- About even numbers of boys and girls are available and gender preference is allowed.

The foster-to-adopt process is fairly straightforward. Contact your local Department of Social Services, complete a home study, attend foster parenting classes (usually six to twelve weeks), and wait for a child or children to be matched with your family. You are the foster parent for the child while you wait for him to become legally free for adoption. If he becomes free, you adopt; if not, the child is reunited with his birth parents or extended birth family and you can have another child placed in your home to foster/adopt. Public adoptions cost very little, and often adoption assistance (sometimes in the form of a monthly subsidy) and health care coverage are available from the state.

International Adoption

This book is devoted to a thorough (if I do say so myself) explanation of international adoption; however, for the purposes of comparison here is a quick overview. International adoption is open to a wide variety of parents regardless of age and marital status. The children, mostly babies or toddlers, are usually adopted through adoption agencies. Families choose a country and then apply to an agency that places children from that country, or families choose an agency first and then select from that agency's country programs. A significant amount of paperwork, including the home study that is required for domestic adoptions, is required to comply with the legal requirements of the state government, U.S. government (for immigration), and foreign government. The paperwork is compiled, sent to the birth country, and a child is referred to the family, although with some countries the family goes to the country to select a child. Families either travel to the birth country to pick up their child and complete the adoption or, with some countries, the child can be escorted to the parents in the United States. Contact with birth parents either before or after the adoption is uncommon, although possible in a few countries. See the box at the end of the chapter for a comparison of the three major types of adoption.

> ### INTERNATIONAL ADOPTION IS RIGHT FOR YOU IF . . .
>
> - You want a fairly predictable process with few surprises or disappointments.
> - You want to choose the gender of your child.
> - Adopting a newborn is not your top priority.
> - You worry about birth parents changing their mind.
> - You don't like the idea of having to market yourself and win the approval of a birth mother.
> - You don't think you look as good on paper compared to other families that a birth mother has to choose from.
> - You are comfortable with having minimal contact with the birth family.
> - You are comfortable with the idea of traveling to another country.
> - You are excited about providing a home for a child who may otherwise not have a family.

A RELUCTANT SPOUSE

When I hear adoption professionals say that you shouldn't consider adoption unless both partners are 100 percent on board, I wonder what planet they are living on. From my interviews with many adopting couples, I have found that in the beginning almost always one partner is more interested in adoption than the other.

I don't think this situation is unique to adoption, which may be why there are so many "accidental" pregnancies with married couples in this day of effective birth control. Fortunately—or unfortunately, depending on how you look at it—it is impossible to accidentally adopt, so a spouse's reluctance must be fully considered.

There aren't easy answers on what to do when one spouse wants to adopt and the other does not. This decision will alter both of your lives forever. Peter and I had always planned on adopting, but we hadn't necessarily planned on having four children. After our third child was born, I still felt a very strong pull to adopt. Peter did not. His resistance had nothing to do with adoption and everything to do with being the father of four. He wondered whether he had the time for another child, whether his work would suffer with more kids, or whether his guilt would increase over the time he devoted to work. Would this child have needs that demanded even more time and money? Wasn't he too old to have another child? After all, he had not planned on paying college tuition in his sixties. The whole idea of adopting seemed risky and he didn't feel the need to take the risk. I did.

I don't have any magic answers. What worked for us may not work for you. We kept the lines of communication open, talking about it more than he wanted but less than I wanted. I asked his permission to share my research with him. I tried to understand his concerns more than I tried to convince him. After about a year, Peter became more comfortable with the time and financial commitment. He loved me enough and valued my happiness enough to take the risk. We compromised on what special needs or disabilities we were willing to consider. And we slowly moved forward. For what it's worth, our daughter has been the apple of his eye from the moment he first held her, and he says he has never regretted his decision for one minute.

It is very important to understand why your partner is hesitant to adopt. Don't assume you know. He or she could be thinking any of the following:

- Can I love a child that is not biologically related?
- Can we afford to adopt?
- Do I want to be a parent at all, especially if it's not going to happen the old-fashioned way?
- Am I ready to stop infertility treatments and give up all hope of having a birth child?
- Will I feel like a failure if I can't biologically have a child?
- Am I too old to become a parent?
- Do I have the time or do I want to devote the time to being a parent?
- How will my parents or older children react?
- What type of medical or emotional problems may this child have?
- We already have birth children—why complicate things?

You've reached an impasse. You want to adopt, but your partner doesn't. What do you do? Therapists and other parents suggest that you keep talking. Don't assume that if it isn't said, it isn't felt. If the reluctant partner feels that this is all you talk about, agree to a set time each week to talk about this subject. When he is speaking, really listen rather than planning your rebuttal. Seek to understand more than convince. As strange as this may seem, share your own fears about adopting. You know you have them. The relationship dynamic of some couples is to balance each other out. Yin and yang are great for philosophical discussions, but lousy for decision making if one partner is stuck at yin while the other is clinging to yang for dear life. Talk about what each of your hopes and dreams are from parenting in general.

Let him know that you want to start getting educated on adoption, and ask his permission to share the information with him as you go along. Ask him to read specific sections or chapters in this book that address his concerns. Don't expect him to be as enthusiastic as you.

Join an online adoption support group for people considering adoption. Encourage your partner to participate as well. Talking with others who have similar concerns can be helpful. Introduce a thread on reluctant spouses. You'll be surprised at how many people have had this experience.

Take a break from infertility treatments for a set period of time, with the agreement that you can resume if you still want to once the break is over. Spend time enjoying your life as a couple. Remember why you married each other in the first place.

Attend an "in person" support group for adoptive families or an informational meeting at an adoption agency, with the promise that this does not mean a commitment to adopt. Spending time with families formed by adoption is amazingly helpful to normalize the process and to provide an opportunity to ask questions. If your spouse feels it is too soon to do this, agree to revisit this option at a set time in the future. Visit a therapist to help with communication, and if applicable, choose one that understands infertility issues. Ask your fertility doctor or infertility support group for recommendations.

As hard as it may be, give your partner time. Each of us has a different speed and style for processing grief and making decisions. If you are totally committed to him regardless of whether you ever become parents, tell him. If not, talk with a therapist before you issue an ultimatum.

Ultimately, you should not force (or coerce or guilt) your spouse into something as major as becoming a parent. It likely won't be effective, since during the home study the social worker will delve into each of your reasons for wanting to adopt. And though it can be faked during the interview with the social worker, every child deserves to be truly wanted by both parents.

TELLING FAMILY AND FRIENDS

When to Tell

Some adoption professionals will tell you that an unwillingness to tell others of your adoption plans is a sign of unresolved infertility issues. I disagree. There can be any number of reasons why someone waits to tell, and unresolved grief (as if grief is ever totally resolved!) is only one.

Some parents tell everyone at the beginning, while others prefer to wait until later in the process. When deciding when to tell, ask the following questions:

HOW OLD IS TOO OLD TO ADOPT?

With international adoption, it is usually possible to adopt when you are older, but should you? The answer depends more on your attitude and health than on your age, but don't kid yourself—age is more than just a number. As an older parent, you will likely have less energy for the high-maintenance "T" years (toddlers and teens). You will have to save for college costs at a time when retirement is looming ever closer. You run a greater risk of having to care for an aging parent at the same time you are caring for a young child. Your child may not know his grandparents, and you may not know your grandchildren. But, on the plus side, older parents are usually more financially and professionally secure. They have more time to give and often more patience. Life experience allows them to truly believe, rather than hope and pray, that "this too shall pass" when their little darling is not so darling. Many older parents report savoring each moment of their child's childhood because they understand that it won't last forever. The bottom line for all adoption questions is to ask what is in the best interest of the child. So ask yourself if it is better for the child to be raised by you, given your health and age, than to remain in her birth country.

The good news is that if you adopt you will not be the only one with gray hairs at the preschool parents' meeting or chaperoning the middle school dance. More of the over-forty crowd than ever are having and adopting children. AARP even has a guide for older parents (www.aarpmagazine.org). See the Resource Guide for other resources for older parents. And, although I truly believe that kids help keep you young, you have an obligation to your child to live a healthy lifestyle and exercise regularly.

- How supportive will your family and friends be of your decision?
- What is your tolerance for unsolicited advice?
- How often can you hear "Any word yet?" before you want to scream?
- How sacred is your privacy?

Keep in mind that you can tell different people at different times. You may want to have the support of your close family and friends at the beginning but tell your hairdresser later on. You will be required to have references for your home study, so at least a few people have to be told at the beginning. The number of references required and their relationship to you varies by state and your child's birth country. If you choose to tell different people at different times, be careful. I've found that friends and family may not care when they were told but are hurt if they find out that others were told before them.

This is what I hear from people who decided to tell at the beginning:

- "I was so excited that I couldn't wait to tell."
- "Our families had been a part of our infertility struggles, so we wanted to share the adoption process with them as well."
- "I figured I'd tell people if I was pregnant, and since this is like my pregnancy, I told everyone now."
- "It has taken me a while to get used to the idea of stopping infertility treatments and to go forward with adopting, so I thought I should also give my family some time to adjust to the idea before our child comes."
- "We told everyone at the very beginning since most people knew we were in treatment for infertility. We wanted to stop the 'are you pregnant yet' line of questions."
- "I'm glad we told everyone—and I mean absolutely everyone—early, because we found our agency and country by word of mouth."
- "I wanted everyone's prayers to be with me through the whole process."
- "After we told people, we were surprised by the positive feedback and by the number of people who either were adopted or had adopted. This information helped me when I was scared during the process."
- "Not to sound like a money grubber, but adoption is expensive and we are hoping that some of our family will offer to help us out financially, so we told them of our plans and the cost."

Families who wait awhile say the following:

- "I knew that I didn't want to have to answer questions and explain the adoption process over and over, so we told only those we had to tell until we were close to getting a child referred to us."
- "We didn't think that my parents would be supportive and we didn't want to listen to them try to talk us out of it. We figured once it was a done deal, they would be less likely to try."
- "We had been through so many losses in trying to start a family that we just wanted to protect ourselves for a little while until it seemed like it would really happen."
- "I know this sounds silly, but it felt like telling everyone before we were close would tempt fate."
- "We thought that if we told people at the beginning, the actual arrival of the baby would be anticlimactic."
- "I told everyone at the beginning, but next time I'll wait until further

along, because after the initial flush of wanting to talk about it with anyone, I went through a private phase."
- "We just wanted to share our excitement and fears between ourselves for a
while before we shared with others. This was a real bonding time for us."
- "We wanted to feel more settled and less fearful before we told the world."

As long as you are not avoiding telling people because you still feel sad or
ashamed or second best, it doesn't matter when you tell. Peter and I told only
the people we were using for references at the beginning of the process. I have
a low tolerance for unsolicited advice, and we thought that both of our families might try to talk us out of our decision. We waited until after all the paperwork was submitted and we were close to having a child assigned before we
told them, but we made sure to tell them before we told the rest of the world.
Once they got over the shock, mostly of our having four kids, they were very
supportive and have been crazy about our daughter from the beginning.

I also have a low tolerance for "have you heard anything?"–type questions
(do you see a pattern here?), so we told other friends and acquaintances after
we were assigned a child and we knew about when she would be coming
home. We believe we made the right choice for us, but each family has to look
at their circumstances when deciding when to tell family and friends.

Telling at Work

When you tell your employer depends on the details of when you need time
off, how much time you want, and whether you will be returning to work. You
will have a general idea of the timing once you decide on a country and then
you can decide when to tell at work. Although you should be fair to your
employer and coworkers, you don't want impending parenthood to unnecessarily affect promotions or assignments. Keep in mind that if you have the
option of working overtime to help finance the adoption, you may want to tell
as soon as possible.

How to Tell

There is no bad way to tell your close family and friends if you are expecting an
enthusiastic response. Chapter 7 makes suggestions for winning over less-than-
enthusiastic relatives. If you are uncertain of the response, consider writing a
letter. Peter used this approach with his parents. They like to think about things
and discuss it between themselves before talking with others, so a letter gave

them this opportunity before we spoke with them. A letter is also a great way to broadcast your news to lots of people at the same time. Include information from this book on the adoption process so that you will have fewer questions to answer. Better yet (here comes a shameless plug), encourage them to buy a copy of this book so they will understand what is happening at each stage.

What to Tell

The when and how questions are quite different from the what question. How much information to share about your new child is discussed in Chapters 8 and 10. But for now consider that it may be best to share just the basics, such as name, country, age, and, of course, the picture. Personal background information on your child or her birth parents may not be anyone else's business.

FUAQs (FREQUENTLY UNASKED QUESTIONS)

I was diagnosed with cancer two years ago. I was treated and have been cancer-free for a year and a half. Will I be able to adopt?

Most countries and agencies (and parents, for that matter) view adoption as finding a forever family for a child. Good adoption practice is child focused, not parent focused. As a result, agencies and countries are looking for a parent who will be around to raise this child for the long haul. They are not looking to fulfill a parent's burning desire to parent regardless of their physical or mental capabilities.

Agencies and countries differ on how this philosophy applies to major illnesses. Some require that applicants be free from any significant medical condition (including cancer and substance abuse) for five years and that mental illness be stable for five years with drug therapy or other treatment. Others have less stringent time requirements or require only a statement from a doctor that you have a good prognosis and that the illness or condition will not interfere with your ability to parent. Address the issue up front with your agency and get their advice. If you have a good prognosis from your doctor but the agency is not flexible, shop around.

Is adopting internationally faster and easier than adopting domestically?

This is an impossible question to answer with a "yes" or "no." The speed of the international adoption is usually more predictable but may not necessarily be faster, depending on how *appealing* you are to domestic birth parents, how hard you work at finding a birth mother, what race and risk factors you are open to, and just plain old luck. With international adoption you will have a good idea when you apply how long you will have to wait until you have your child. The waiting time depends on the country but is usually less than one to one and a half years. See Appendix 1: Country Charts. Which type of adoption is easier depends on what you find easy. For example, international adoption requires more paperwork. For some this may be excruciatingly hard, while others may view it as something tangible they can do to get their child home. International and domestic adoption are two different processes, with neither one being the fastest, easiest or best for everyone. See the chart at the end of this chapter to help you decide which one appeals to you.

Can we continue infertility treatments while we are going through the adoption process? We very much want a child, and we figure this will increase our odds of getting a child one way or the other.

Adoption experts and therapists are divided about the advisability of continuing to pursue infertility treatment and adoption at the same time. Those that oppose pursuing both are concerned that you will consider adoption second best. They view continuing treatment as a red flag that you have not come to terms with your infertility losses and may have trouble bonding with your adopted child. The financial drain of pursuing both may also put undue stress on the family.

Others do not think pursuing infertility treatment and adoption are mutually exclusive and that it is possible to pursue both without lessening your commitment to either. You must be completely honest with yourself on whether you have truly addressed your infertility grief. No child deserves to be anything but first in his parents' eyes. If you decide to pursue both, consider talking with a therapist who specializes in infertility to make sure you are really ready to parent an adopted child.

Regardless of what the experts say, most adoption agencies do not want their prospective parents to be in treatment for infertility, and many require that parents withdraw their application if they become pregnant. They believe that the couple will not remain committed to sticking out the ups and downs of adoption or will back out of the adoption if they become pregnant. They also worry that the couple will still be actively grieving the loss of their birth child when the adopted child joins the family, which could interfere with bonding. If continuing treatment is important to you, shop around for an agency that will not object and be prepared to address this issue carefully in your home study.

My husband and I have one son but have been unable to conceive again. We are thinking seriously about adoption but are concerned about combining adopted and birth children. My mother thinks it would not be good for our son or the child we might adopt.

First, let me tell you that I have never talked to anyone who combined adopted and birth children who didn't worry before the adoption about "ruining" or somehow messing up what they had. I certainly had my share of these concerns before we adopted. Adding a child to your family changes your family, and change is scary. Just knowing that your concerns are extremely common may help.

Combining children by birth and adoption is common, whether because of secondary infertility, not wanting to go through invasive infertility treatments again, a surprise pregnancy after adoption, or because a fertile couple with birth children wants to adopt. Although many parents choose to have only one child, others want to provide a sibling relationship for their child, knowing that this bond may well be the longest-lasting bond a person will ever have. And rest assured, your son will see the next child as his brother or sister no matter how he or she joined the family. Children form sibling bonds before they realize the significance of adoption or birth.

However, there are some real issues to think about. At the risk of stating the obvious, all children are different and the odds that you will have a child with different looks, personality, and talents are greater when you adopt. If you choose to combine adopted and birth children, you must commit to creating a family atmosphere where differences are valued and celebrated. You are all family regardless of whether you joined through birth, adoption, or marriage. You are all family regardless of whether you are good at school, band, football, or bird watching. You are all family regardless of whether you have dark straight hair, tight black curls, or blond waves.

Research supports my personal experience that combining adopted and birth children can work well for all. Although many factors can influence the adjustment of birth and adopted children, including personality, age at adoption, prior life experiences, and parental attitudes, research has shown that combining children through birth and adoption does not adversely affect either (Brodzinsky and Brodzinsky, 1992; Boer et al., 1994).

When combining adopted and birth children, parents should look for ways to create family unity and a sense of family identity. Have fun creating family traditions. Point out ways you are all similar (love to read, eat Italian food, and travel). We have a standing family joke that everyone in our family is always late, always blames other family members for being late, and never admits to losing at any board game.

If you are adopting transracially, be sensitive that your son may not like the extra attention your family will receive. Some children bask in the attention, while others dread it. My eldest loved the attention and always wanted to be the one carrying our youngest so she could share the spotlight. Seek out other families that are formed through adoption, and if you are adopting transracially, find other families that have adopted transracially as well.

Most siblings have some degree of rivalry, and you'll likely not avoid this. Parenting techniques can minimize these squabbles, but they need not be specific to siblings created through adoption. However, if your children think playing the adoption card will get a rise out of you to their advantage, they will use it. It's up to you whether it works.

You can share this information with your mother to ease her concerns, but don't be surprised if her underlying concern is really whether she can love an adopted child as much as she loves your son. See Chapter 7 for a discussion of this issue.

FOR EVERY ADOPTION, A DIFFERENT STORY . . .

These are the responses I received in interviews when I asked why the family pursued international adoption. By inclusion here, I am not endorsing their reasoning or attempting to sway someone away from private domestic or foster-care adoption.

The decision to adopt was not an easy one for us. But after seven IVFs, two surgeries, three doctors, and every alternative treatment known to man, including acupuncture, massage, Chinese herbs, and wheat grass, we had reached the point when my nightly prayer was for guidance to know when to stop. I am a driven person and it is not easy for me to give up. Just when I would get ready to throw in the towel, I would hear a "one in a million" story and I was back in treatment. Finally, we knew we had reached the point where we had to decide between donor eggs, embryo adoption, regular adoption, or a child-free life.

The big speed bump for me was always biology—I wanted to have a biological connection to my child. Donor eggs and embryo adoption didn't get me there. With donor eggs, I wasn't sure how I would feel about a child who was related to my husband but not to me. The biological connection wasn't that big a deal to him. Basically, it all boiled down to thinking that it made no sense to use donor eggs or to adopt an embryo when there were so many kids already in the world who needed parents. I wasn't going to be biologically connected in either case, but I thought that somewhere out there is a baby who needs me and I need him or her. After we made the decision, I felt a huge weight off my shoulders. I still grieve; I think I will always grieve for the biological child I did not have. But while I still hope to get pregnant, I no longer pray for it.

We looked into domestic adoption, but we didn't like the way it worked. Our ages worked against us, we knew we would be devastated if a birth mother changed her mind even within the allowed time, and we didn't want an ongoing relationship with the birth parents. International adoption was the better choice for us. —RM, *Virginia*

We had been in infertility treatment for six years. Physically and mentally I had reached a very dark place. When I got the call saying the last pregnancy test was negative, something just snapped. I prayed for help because I didn't know how to continue. The next morning, I knew that I was ready to stop all the poking and prodding and was ready to adopt. Before I had wanted a biological child; now I just wanted a child. My husband was not there yet. He wasn't sure he could love a child that was not his. I told him I was going to research adoption, but I wouldn't push him.

At first I only considered domestic adoption, because I had heard negative things about international adoption. But the more I researched, the less comfortable I felt about domestic adoption. In our state, the birth mom has thirty days after birth to change her mind. After six years of trying, I couldn't live with the unknown. You have to find what works for you.

Once I settled on Russia, I started e-mailing my husband pictures of Russian children. Slowly he came around and has loved our son completely from the first day. I know this will be hard for people just beginning this process to believe, but I can honestly say I don't want to be pregnant now. Infertility was the worst thing that has happened to me, but it has given me the best thing in my life. I got what I really wanted. —SH, *Virginia*

My husband and I started trying for children eleven years ago. We went through two IVF procedures as well as all the miscellaneous infertility treatments that they try before IVF. We just finished our last IVF nine months before our daughter was born in Colombia! We kind of look at this like God intended her to be ours, just not from our bodies.

We first tried to adopt domestically and had three failed tries. Our last domestic adoption fell through when the birth mother changed her mind one hour before we were to bring our daughter home from the hospital. We had already named her and spent time with her at the hospital. We were devastated and switched to international adoption because we just couldn't go through this experience again. —RO, New York

We are very research-oriented people, so when we began considering adoption we did a lot of information gathering. We had children by birth and were adopting by choice. Our decision to adopt internationally rather than domestically was based on a number of reasons. International adoption often involves children who were orphaned or relinquished based on poverty (Guatemala), war, AIDS (Ethiopia), or strict family laws (China). They were children (from very young to older) who, through circumstances of birth, could not be cared for by their birth families. Our state foster system did not have many children under the age of six. We were not comfortable with the amount of contact with birth families that the state system offered through foster/adopt because we did not want to manage potentially challenging relations with birth families throughout our child's childhood. We were not interested in spending years mired in expensive private adoption for a white infant since race or ethnicity was not a concern of ours, and at no point did we learn about healthy available African American children in the information we read (although I have since learned that many are available for adoption).

Anecdotally, we know people who have adopted internationally (primarily from China), and although they've had some challenges, their experiences have been overwhelmingly positive. In all honesty, by contrast, friends who have adopted domestically seem to have encountered many more challenging issues and dealt with more psychological and learning difficulties with their children. This perception may or may not be accurate, but still, it did affect our decision, so it is worth mentioning. —SS, New York

⌒

We tried for a long time to get pregnant, but never felt the need to go the infertility treatment route. Maybe because I was adopted, I felt very comfortable considering adoption as a way to have children. We never even considered domestic adoption, even though I am a domestic adoptee. Mine was a closed domestic adoption, and I do not like the concept of open adoptions. Also, I have an aunt who was on a domestic waiting list for over ten years and was never selected by a birth mother. Domestic was just never an option for us. —LL, *Washington*

⌒

We have decided to start the adoption process because we have finally hit the wall emotionally, and neither of us can take the ups and downs and grief of infertility any longer. We are just so tired of loss and pain. I want my life back. Adoption is a positive thing instead of all the negatives with infertility, and, most important, it is a sure thing. With adoption we have hope again; we have control again. I think we finally transitioned to wanting to parent more than wanting to be pregnant.

I worry with adoption about the lack of control I will have over my baby's uterine environment. I worry about the health issues of children adopted internationally, but I worry more about a birth mother changing her mind with domestic adoption. I honestly don't think I could go through that loss. Also, because of our ages, I think we might have to wait a long time to be selected, especially for a healthy baby. —SM, *Virginia*

⌒

We chose international adoption for several reasons. My husband and I realized that in domestic adoptions you can choose an infant through private adoption or an older child through our foster-care system. Neither option seemed to work for us. We are not particularly interested in an infant, but don't want the child to be too old because of the potential emotional problems they may have from abuse and neglect. I have worked as a counselor, social worker, and now psychology postdoc, and have seen a lot. While I do this for a living, I don't know if I could handle it at home too. I have also known two couples who adopted children from foster care who then had to deal with biological family problems. I know I can't handle that. International adoption seemed to be a better option for us to get a child under five. I should add that I was adopted so I am in no way against domestic adoption, but it was not right for us. —GD, *Texas*

———

Our struggle with infertility was made harder by the inability of the doctors to find anything wrong with either of us. But after four failed IUIs and three failed IVFs, I was getting depressed. I had to get back to my core values. I was obsessing on pregnancy, birth, nursing, and biology in general. One day I realized that it was all about me: *I* wanted to be pregnant, *I* wanted to give birth, *I* wanted to nurse. I felt very selfish. It wasn't about me, it was about parenting. From this perspective the decision against donor eggs or more extensive fertility treatment and toward adoption became easier.

But still I have been the reluctant spouse. My husband has been the one doing the research and all the legwork. I think I'm still grieving, but I realize I need to get more involved now since our agency is questioning my lack of involvement. —RM, *Maryland*

———

We tried the domestic adoption route first. After waiting a long time, a birth mother finally asked to meet us, but she selected another couple. When we were finally picked we were thrilled, but two weeks before her due date, the birth mother said that if the baby was a girl she was going to parent, if it was a boy she would place him with us. She had a girl. At this point we just wanted to be parents. We switched to international adoption, chose a country that had a short referral time, and adopted two children within the year. —MG, *Virginia*

———

When we were first looking into adoption, we thought it would be with a domestic adoption agency. We hadn't considered international. The more we researched, the more we became aware of the new trend in open adoptions. We were told by some private agencies that they weren't accepting new clients due to the already long waiting lists. We didn't want to wait a long time, we didn't want to try to convince a birth mother to pick us, and we were more comfortable with a closed adoption. We had the local DSS do our home study, not knowing yet where we would choose to adopt from. We were researching countries when we got a call from a county just a couple hours away saying that we had been chosen to adopt a newborn relinquished at birth to Social Services. We were ecstatic. When we were ready to adopt again, we wanted the guarantee that we would get a child. With domestic adoptions, the birth parents usually choose who gets their child. If you don't get picked, then you don't get a child. With international adoption, you are on a waiting list and when your name comes up, you will get a child. We also like the closure of knowing that there wouldn't be the chance of birth parents changing their mind. International, even with the possible health risks and getting a baby sight unseen, felt like more of a sure thing. —CH, North Carolina

After four IUIs and two IVFs, I was ready to adopt, but my husband was not. We went round and round on this issue and finally went into counseling. In counseling we agreed to compromise: I agreed to do one more IVF, but my husband had to agree that this was absolutely the last one. It was either "third one's the charm" or "three strikes you're out." It took him a while to agree to this compromise. It turned out that the third time was charmed and our son was conceived. When we were ready for our next child, we were disappointed to find out that our frozen embryos had disintegrated. There was never any thought about going back into infertility treatment. I was forty-two and I just wanted to get on with life. We briefly looked into domestic adoption, but we both felt more comfortable with international adoption, primarily because we wanted to select the gender of the child so that we could have one of both. Also, at our age we didn't want to wait too long and adopting from Guatemala was fast. Compared with the three years of infertility treatment, everything about adoption was a breeze. Our daughter arrived home when she was four and a half months old and she is perfect. —SG, Washington, D.C.

Our older two children were adopted from foster care—we've always felt strongly about adopting children who really need us—but the foster/adopt system is inherently risky. When it was only our hearts that would be broken if the child/children were returned to their birth family we were willing to take the risk, but our older children have experienced enough loss in their young lives that we didn't want to put them through losing a child they thought of as a brother or sister. With international adoption, by the time our older children met their brother, the risk was over. —*HMJ, California*

⌒

Adoption was my husband's idea and he drove the process. Even though at our last try at IVF I didn't produce enough eggs for retrieval, I was still committed to "having my own child." Intellectually, I knew that there is no perfect child, but in my heart I thought that the child we conceived would be pretty close. My husband, on the other hand, was ready to move on and suggested as a compromise that we proceed on both fronts—continue infertility treatment and start the adoption process. I was adamant about not doing both, because I felt that we would not really be giving fair attention to either and that adoption would be second best. That didn't seem fair to the child we might adopt.

My husband went alone to an adoption conference just to listen and get information. He came home ready to stop infertility and start adoption. What really impressed him was the panel of adoptive parents. He couldn't get over how happy these people were, and after all our struggles with infertility, he was ready to be happy. I agreed—reluctantly—for him to start getting more information, but my heart was still on getting pregnant. So while he was pursuing adoption, I was pursuing yet another opinion from yet another infertility doctor. The more information he got, the more afraid I got. I didn't know if I could love a child who wasn't mine.

I was ready to try anything. Looking back I realize that fertility patients can become very selfish very quickly. My prevailing thought at that time was *I want my baby now!* We looked into donor eggs and embryo adoption, but these were just other forms of adoption, and they seemed weird to me when there were children already born who needed adoption. Besides, I wasn't sure my emotional state could take it if I lost the pregnancy.

Meanwhile, my husband was networking and researching and basically dragging me along the adoption path. What finally changed my attitude was meeting an adoption agency director who I immediately "clicked with." She called seventeen days later and told me she had a baby girl for us. At that second, I knew there was a child, my child, that was waiting for me and I had the overwhelming realization of how much I wanted to be a mother to this child and how much love I had to give. Our adoption moved very quickly, and I was struck over and over again by how easy adoption was by comparison to infertility.

We decided against domestic adoption because we didn't want ongoing contact with the birth family. We were afraid that the child would never really be ours. Now that I am an adoptive mom, I feel differently. I think about my children's birth mothers and wish I could let them know that their children are doing fine. —*MS, Virginia*

I wish all prospective adoptive parents could meet my two wonderful girls—they have given me a part of myself that I did not even know was missing. They love without boundaries, they tease without malice, they interact without prejudice. They were conceived in my heart out of the love that I share with my husband. They were born into our family when they were handed to us in crowded uncomfortable conference rooms half a world away. Two couples created the perfection that is our daughters. Two women nurtured these precious beings in their bodies and endured the pain of childbirth to bring them life. Countless people, from caregivers to bureaucrats, cared for, nurtured, and finally brought us together with these two priceless blessings. I am humbled to be given the responsibility of their care. I am fearful that I will not be able to rise to the challenge. But I know that my life was not complete until I looked into their eyes, saw their souls, and swore to be the one, unique thing each needed—their mother. —*NA, Indiana*

QUICK COMPARISON OF ADOPTION TYPES			
	International	*Domestic Private*	*Domestic Public*
Age of child	Mostly babies and toddlers; youngest is 4 to 6 months, depending on country. Older children are also available.	Primarily new-borns.	Majority are over age 6; some younger children available but often in sibling groups and most placed with foster-to-adopt families before they are legally free for adoption.
Current health information on child	Varies by country, but all countries give a current assessment on health and some are quite extensive.	Complete.	Complete.
Prenatal care and habits of birth mother	Prenatal care varies by country; if child is relinquished rather than abandoned, birth mothers are usually asked about prenatal care and habits.	Prenatal care varies; birth mothers are asked about prenatal care and habits.	Varies greatly.
Birth family medical history	Very little with most countries.	Usually detailed questionnaires are asked of birth mother and birth father (if known).	Varies.
Select gender and age?	Usually yes.	Usually no.	Yes, but few infants or toddlers are available that are not part of sibling group.
Paperwork	Lots.	Minimal by comparison.	Minimal by comparison.

QUICK COMPARISON OF ADOPTION TYPES (CONT.)		
	International	*Domestic Private*	*Domestic Public*
Possibility of birth parent changing mind	In most countries, there is little possibility by the time the child is referred.	States require that birth parent must wait from 1 to 15 days after birth to consent to the adoption. States allow 0 to 180 days for birth parent to revoke their consent. After that time period, there is little risk.	It depends on where the child is in the process. The goal of the foster system is family reunification when possible. When this is not in the best interest of the child, the state seeks to terminate parental rights. Parents can legally contest the termination. There are children available, usually school age, whose parental rights have already been terminated and there is no possibility of the parents regaining parental rights.
Waiting time until child is home	6 to 24 months, depending on country and gender; time is usually predictable.	Varies greatly, depending on how appealing your biography is to a birth mother; how much you can afford to spend on advertising and applying to different facilitators and agencies; and health, race, and risk factors of the child you are willing to consider.	Varies greatly, depending on your flexibility.
Contact with birth parents	No, although it may be possible in some countries for child to find birth	Yes, with trend toward increased contact after adoption.	Varies; in foster-to-adopt, often contact with birth family, at least

QUICK COMPARISON OF ADOPTION TYPES (CONT.)		
	International	*Domestic Private*	*Domestic Public*
Contact with birth parents (cont.)	parents if they choose to search.		initially; after adoption contact with birth siblings or extended family members is sometimes requested.
Age of parents	25 to 55	Most states have no legal restrictions; agencies often have age requirements; even where agency or attorney have no requirement, parents over 40 or younger than 25 are selected less often by birth parents.	No restrictions, depending on what is in the best interest of the child.
Marital status	Many countries accept singles.	Most states have no legal restrictions, but single applicants are selected less often by birth parents.	No restrictions, depending on needs of child.
Travel	Usually; some countries allow the child to be escorted to the United States.	Adoptive parents usually must travel to where the birth mother resides.	Only if adopting a child in another state.
Cost	$13,000–$35,000	$10,000–$40,000	Minimal (ongoing subsidies sometimes available).
Predictability of cost	Fairly predictable.	Can vary greatly, but more predictable with agency adoption.	Predictable.

CHAPTER 2

DECIDING ON A COUNTRY

Do I Have to Be Able to Spell Kazakhstan?

Marina was born in Novokuznetsk, Russia, on July 11, 2004, and joined her forever family in July 2005.

eth and Bill were totally overwhelmed at the thought of selecting a country. Not knowing where to begin, they found themselves paralyzed at this step. "There is a whole world to choose from, so how in the world are we supposed to decide?" says Bill. Breaking the process down into steps was the key to getting moving again. They were too old for some countries and hadn't been married long enough for others. Beth's top priority was adopting a young baby girl, and Bill's top priority was adopting as healthy a child as they could. They both wanted as short a wait as possible since they didn't want to be buying Depends and Pampers at the same time. "When we analyzed what we were looking for, the world got a lot smaller," says Bill.

I am analytical by nature and training. With graduate degrees in science and law, I like to think that research and reason rule my decision making. In reality, intuition plays a part, but I like my intuition flavored by facts. When faced with a big decision, I immediately shift into research mode. I will continue to investigate and collect information until the *right* answer becomes apparent. I have friends who prefer the gut-feel approach to decision making; trusting their instincts, they have little use for facts. Both approaches have a place when choosing a country, but I can't ignore who I am, so I've included as much hard data as are available. Just remember that having children, regardless of whether they come into your family through birth, high-tech infertility treatment, domestic adoption, or international adoption, is a leap of faith; you will never have all the information you want until you hold your child, and then all the facts in the world are irrelevant.

Selecting a country from which to adopt is a little like choosing a college. Colleges have specific entrance criteria that students must meet (certain GPA and SAT scores), while students have their own list of preferences (majors offered and nearness to ski slopes). Students must consider both the college's criteria and their own preferences when deciding on a school. The same is true for choosing a country for adoption. Countries place criteria that parents must meet and then each family has specific preferences for the child they can best parent.

Each country has certain restrictions that families should look at first, since these restrictions may make them ineligible to adopt from that country. The restricting criteria are parental age, length of marriage, prior divorces, number of children already in the family, marital status, and sexual orientation. If a country does not want to place a child with parents above the age of forty-five and you are a spry forty-seven, cross that country off your list and move on to consider another country. The beauty of international adoption is that there is almost always a country for every family.

Be aware: Countries aren't the only ones that place restrictions on adoptive parents—agencies do as well. Agencies may have more stringent limits on length of marriage, number of divorces, parental age, and religion than do the countries. For example, China imposes no requirement on length of marriage (if married), number of previous divorces, or religion, but I found the following variation in agency requirements.

- Length of marriage: 1 year; 2 years; 2½ years (?); 3 years; 5 years; 3 years if this was a second marriage for either spouse; 5 years if this was a second marriage for either spouse

- Previous divorces: 1 divorce each; no more than 2 divorces per couple; no more than 3 divorces per couple
- Religion: No requirement; must be Christian or Jewish; must sign a statement of Christian faith attesting to a personal relationship with Jesus

Agencies seldom highlight the distinction between these two sources of restrictions; in fact, in my interviews I found that many agency personnel don't know which of the restrictions are imposed by their agency rather than the country. The Country Charts appendix includes the country restrictions and makes note where agencies might have additional restrictions.

It should be noted that agencies impose these additional requirements because they believe it is in the best interest of the child or because their experience in that country has shown that families who meet these requirements have an easier time adopting. Nevertheless, if you do not meet the agency-imposed restrictions and are still interested in adopting from that country, shop around—you can almost always find a reputable agency that will not have more stringent criteria than the country. Specifically ask the new agency if they have successfully placed children of the age and health that you want with families that have the specific limitation of concern. For example, have they placed young healthy babies from that country with families where one parent is over fifty or with couples that have been married only one year? See Chapter 3 for a more detailed discussion on finding the right agency.

RESTRICTING CRITERIA

U.S. Citizenship: The U.S. government requires that at least one parent is a U.S. citizen. If you and your spouse are not U.S. citizens, you must comply with the adoption and immigration laws of your country.

Parental Age: A major advantage of international adoption is that older parents can adopt. In a refreshing change to our youth-obsessed culture, some countries actually view age as an advantage, at least when it comes to parenting. Many countries accept parents up to age fifty-five.

Some countries simply state a parental age range. Others require no more than a set number of years between the age of the youngest parent and the age of the child. And then there is India. (You'll want to get out your calculator for this one.) To adopt from India the oldest parent can be no more than forty-five years older than the child. Simple enough, right? But they're not finished yet. In addition, the combined ages of the parents can be no more than eighty-

---

SPECIAL-NEEDS AND WAITING CHILDREN

Children with "special needs" are simply children who have needs that are outside the ordinary and may make parenting more challenging. "Waiting children" refers to those children who wait for a family because of their special need. Special needs can include:

- Age
- Sibling group
- Correctable/curable medical problems (such as cleft lip or palate, clubfoot, repairable heart defect, or tuberculosis)
- Noncorrectable/incurable physical or medical condition (such as missing limbs or length discrepancy, albinism, limited vision or hearing, obvious birthmark or scar, hepatitis B)
- Emotional or behavioral problems (such as attachment issues or mental illness)
- Premature birth or low birth weight
- Prenatal risk factors (such as alcohol exposure or malnutrition)

Online support groups exist for every type of special need and can provide information on treatments and what it is really like living day to day with this condition. Talk with an international adoption doctor or your pediatrician about any hidden condition or problems that may typically accompany the special needs.

---

three years older than the child. (How they came up with the magical number *eighty-three*, I'll never know.) And to further confound your calculations, neither parent may be older than fifty-five.

Keep in mind that even countries that have an upper age limit may be flexible if one parent fits within their restrictions, especially if that parent is the mother. Also, most countries have more flexible requirements for families adopting children who are harder to place because of special needs (see box). It may take some flexibility on your part and some shopping around, but gray hairs, even lots of them, don't preclude adoption.

Length of Marriage: As with other restricting criteria, countries are all over the board on how long they want prospective adoptive parents to have been married. Most countries do not have a restriction, but others require couples to have been married up to five years. Years lived together before marriage may count toward the total for some countries.

Previous Divorce: Having been divorced is not an impediment to international adoption with most countries. This is especially true if each spouse has been divorced only once. Even with those countries that have no specific restrictions on number of divorces, couples with multiple prior divorces should be prepared in the home study to explain why this marriage is stable.

Children in the Family: Few countries have restrictions on families that have biological or adopted kids living in the home. Even countries that do have restrictions usually make exceptions for families adopting children with special needs.

Singles: Most countries allow adoption by single women, and a few allow adoption by single men. Singles may have to jump through a few more hoops, such as submitting a letter from their chosen guardian in case they die before the child is eighteen, but usually nothing too onerous. With some countries, the wait is longer for singles, and for all countries, single applicants should be prepared in their home study to demonstrate that they have a strong support network, the ability to financially provide for the child, and a plan to provide opposite-gender role models.

Sexual Orientation: Most countries do not have regulations specifically prohibiting homosexuals from adopting (except China), but in practice none of the major placing countries will knowingly place a child with a homosexual. This means they will not accept an application from an openly homosexual couple. Many countries, however, will accept applicants from singles; therefore, the real issue is whether the agency or country questions the sexual orientation of single applicants. China requires single applicants to sign a statement stating that they are heterosexual. For other countries, the process is less clear.

The issue of sexual orientation is addressed, if at all, in the home study and each agency and country requires something different. See Chapter 5 for a discussion of the home-study process. Most agencies want to respect the desires of the placing country, but on the issue of sexual orientation there is no consensus on how best to do this. Some of these differences are based on the values of the agency, and some are based on the agency's experience placing children from that country.

Some agencies require that the home study address the sexual orientation of all single applicants regardless of whether they are living with someone or alone. Others ask only if they have reason to believe that the applicant is homosexual, and still others follow the "don't ask, don't tell" policy unless specifically required to ask by the country. Keep in mind that all adults living in the home must go through the required background checks even if they are not applicants to adopt.

PARENTAL PREFERENCES

Once you determine which countries want you, the next step is to figure out which countries have children that you want to adopt. Each family has preferences and limits on the type of child they want to parent. Nothing is wrong with this. It is perfectly acceptable to want as young a child as you can get; it is reasonable to want as healthy a child as you can get. You should run, not walk, away from an agency that pressures you to accept a child that you do not feel capable of parenting. However, wonderful children are available that might not match your first idea of perfection, so it pays to keep an open mind, educate yourself, and remain flexible. Magic is sometimes in the unexpected.

Children Available: The age of the child when she arrives home in the United States generally depends on the adoption laws in the country of origin. These laws govern how long a child must be in state care before they are eligible for foreign adoption, how the court process works, and how children are referred— all factors that affect the age of children available. You must specify an acceptable range of ages you will accept rather than a specific age. See the discussion later in this chapter for issues to consider when selecting an age range. Most countries also have children with special needs (toddlers and older children, sibling groups, and children with medical problems) available for adoption. (See box.)

Ethnicity: When adopting internationally, parents can decide whether they want to adopt a child of a different race or their same race, and both choices are acceptable. If, however, you are hesitant to adopt a child of a different race because you think that "it won't work out," then think again.

International adoption across cultural and racial lines in the United States began after the Korean War, when many Korean orphans, some fathered by U.S. soldiers, were adopted by U.S. families. Since then, transracial international adoptions held steady until they began to increase significantly about ten years ago. Researchers have been able to study how these adoptions and transracial domestic adoptions have worked out from the parents' and children's perspective for over fifty years, and the evidence is that transracially adopted kids do fine and compare favorably with same race adoptees (Simon et al., 1994; Bagley, 1993; Andujo, 1988; McRoy et al., 1982). As a rule, they are attached to their families, succeed academically and socially, and grow up to be productive, happy adults. Of course, there are exceptions to this general success story, just as there are exceptions to the overall success of same-race adoptions and birth children. See Chapter 10 for a discussion of becoming a multiracial family.

IN PRAISE OF OLDER KIDS

While many parents go into adoption thinking they want the youngest child available, all countries have older children available for adoption, and "older" often means older than the age of two. There are challenges to adopting a child with a past, but there are advantages, too.

- You will have more information about the child's personality and interests and can choose a child that will fit well with your family.
- You will probably have more medical and developmental information on the child, enabling an international adoption doctor to give you a more realistic picture of her health risks.
- The child will be able to take care of herself better than a younger child.
- The child will be able to fit into your lifestyle sooner (for example: go skiing, go to movies, garden, and help with chores).
- You still get to experience lots of firsts: first taste of ice cream, first Christmas with presents, first bike ride, and so on.
- Your child may be able to share his past with you—the good, the bad, and the ugly—allowing you to help him integrate his past into his present.

If you are thinking about adopting a school-age child, consider the many school-age children in U.S. foster care that are legally free for adoption and just waiting for a family. It is a myth that older kids adopted from abroad will have fewer emotional and educational issues than kids in our foster system. The potential challenges are the same, but you usually have more information on U.S. foster children, and the adoption is free. Monthly adoption assistance may even be available to help with living expenses until the child is eighteen. There are wonderful older children available both here and abroad, so check out both. To see some of the U.S. children in foster care, go to www.adoptuskids.org.

But even though adopting across racial lines can be successful, it is not for everyone. You are changing not just your immediate family but your extended family as well, both now and for generations to come. Your family will stand out as a family formed by adoption, and you won't be able to pass for just the average biologically formed family. It is crucial that you think past the cute little baby and toddler stage to what your attitudes are toward teens and adults of that race. You will also have to commit the time to finding same-race role models for your child as he grows. See the box for questions to ask yourself before you adopt transracially.

SHOULD YOU ADOPT A CHILD OF A DIFFERENT RACE?

Becoming a transracial family is not something to take lightly, regardless of whether the child you are considering is Asian, African, or Latin American. Think about the following before you make the decision:

- Does it matter to you or your family that your extended family will be inter-racial for generations to come?
- Will the obvious and subtle stares of strangers bother you?
- Are you comfortable that your family will stand out as a family formed through adoption? Interracial families get more adoption-related questions. See Chapter 10 for a discussion of this topic.
- How would you feel if your birth child married a person of this race?
- How will your extended family treat a child of this race?
- Will you care if someone seeing you alone with your child assumes you are married to a person of your child's race?
- Are members of this race within your circle of friends? Within your school district? Within your community?
- Can you find role models of this race for your child?
- What stereotypes do you have of people of this race (Asians are quiet, Africans are superior athletes, black male teens are dangerous, Latinos are shiftless)?
- What are your feelings about the child's birth country and culture?
- Would you enjoy learning more about your child's birth culture?

Gender: One of the major advantages of international adoption is that you can usually select the gender of your child. Based on interviews with adoption agencies, 75 to 80 percent of parents request girls, so for every country, except China and India, the wait is shorter for families that will adopt a boy. Nothing is inherently wrong with preferring to adopt a girl, but I encourage you to think carefully about your reasons for this preference.

SNIPS AND SNAILS VS. SUGAR AND SPICE

Women are usually the drivers in the adoption process, and many women pre-fer to parent girls. As with most issues of the heart, the reasons aren't entirely clear. Maybe they want to enjoy the same gender-specific activities and toys of their childhood, or they hope they have a better handle on how to raise girls, having been one themselves. But I think the reason may be deeper. I believe many women are afraid of raising boys, assuming that boys are more active, disruptive, loud, and dirty, and that teenage boys will engage in more risky or challenging behavior.

The matriarchal nature of our society may also play a role. It is more often the daughters that are the keepers of the family traditions, planners of the family reunions, and schedulers of the grandparent visits. Parents may subconsciously be trying to position themselves on the inside track with their adult child's family.

Daughters are also more likely to be the caregivers for aging parents. As my husband, Peter, so inelegantly tells our kids, "In a couple of years, I'm going to need someone to wipe the drool off my chin and one of you will be the lucky one." (He says this to both our sons and daughters, who are equally disgusted at the thought.) We all know exceptions to this generalization, and we expect that our son will be one of these exceptions; but, perhaps on a subconscious level, parents may think daughters are a surer bet for being old-age drool wipers.

There is also what I call the "China doll" effect. Girls, especially Asian and Latino girls, are sometimes perceived as pretty little dolls to be dressed up and admired. They often receive attention for their looks, and parents may enjoy the reflected glory. Don't misunderstand me: Life is undoubtedly easier for the attractive, and enjoying your child's beauty and the compliments they receive is fine. I think, however, it helps to acknowledge it, if this is part of the motivation for wanting a girl, since not all girls gracefully fit this stereotype. You may get one of the rough-and-tumble, nose-picking variety. Even if your daughter fits the bill, you will have the added challenge of helping her understand that she is more than her looks; she is also smart, strong, and capable.

The family name has traditionally been passed through the males of a family, and some families are less willing to have a male outside their bloodline carry the name into future generations. Most liberated modern folks don't consciously subscribe to this belief, but on an unconscious level you may be vulnerable or you may believe that this will concern your extended family.

As the mother of two sons and two daughters, I would never deny that differences exist, but my experience and research show that there are more differences within a gender than there are between the genders. While the loudest of my children is a boy, the second loudest is a girl. The calmest of my children is a boy, and all of my children are slobs. Undeniably, girls are more fun to dress until they develop a fashion sense of their own (and I use the word "fashion" quite loosely), which usually hits around the age of five. From that point on, they are both harder and more expensive to dress.

From my experience, it is truly a blessing to have children of both genders. Parents often say that the ideal family is a boy first and then a girl. Since the adoption wait for a boy is shorter, you might consider going for a boy first.

Adopting More Than One at a Time: Most countries have sibling groups that need homes; however, some parents are interested in adopting more than one unrelated child of similar ages at the same time, sometimes called "artificial twinning." While adoption professionals try to place sibling groups together whenever possible, many are strongly against the practice of adopting two unrelated children at the same time, especially two children of similar age. When adopting siblings, most adoption professionals believe that the benefit of keeping siblings together outweighs the disadvantages of adopting two children at once. Artificial twinning does not have these benefits. Some countries prohibit the practice, and some agencies do not allow it even with countries that do. It's not surprising that both sides to this controversy have well-thought-out arguments.

Pros	Cons
More quickly reach family size you want. This is especially helpful for older parents.	Each child deserves to be the center of his parents' attention for at least nine months, and some child development experts recommend two to three years.
Having another child going through the same thing at the same time may help the children adjust.	Each child deserves to establish himself in the home as an individual, not as a member of a group.
The children will have a built-in playmate and will have someone from their birth country with whom to identify.	It is very difficult to avoid comparing children of similar ages with each other. Even if parents are determined not to compare, teachers, friends, and—perhaps most important—the children themselves will. This is especially difficult for a child who may not be as good as his sibling athletically, academically, or socially. A few months' difference in age can make a big difference developmentally.
Saves money on home study, dossier preparation, travel, post-placement reports, and sometimes on agency fees.	It is a huge adjustment in time, laundry, and cooking for parents to add two kids at once. This much change can make the adjustment to parenting much rougher than necessary.
More efficient use of time since you do the paperwork only once.	The emotional needs of two children who are both adjusting to the change of everything they know can overwhelm the family.

Pros	Cons
Two children coming into the home at the same time may reduce sibling rivalry, since neither child is displacing the other child's position in the family.	It is harder for parents to establish a special relationship with each child as an individual.
Don't have to worry about what to do with the first child when you travel to adopt the second.	Adoption agencies report that they see more disruptions in families adopting more than one unrelated child at the same time.
Minimizes the time one parent needs to be out of the workforce since the parent needs to take off from work only once for both children.	Parents will have age-related expenses, such as college tuitions, hit at the same time.
These kids need homes, and it is better for the child to be adopted, even if two are adopted at the same time, rather than remain in an orphanage.	If the children are in the same grade, they will have to explain often that they are not twins and that they are adopted. Some kids don't want to stand out as different.

Each family must look at themselves and their resources in making the decision. If cost savings is your primary reason, most families I interviewed did not save much money by adopting two at once. You can take the adoption tax credit for both, but depending on how much tax you pay, you may not be able to use the full credit within the specified time limit, and many employers do not double their adoption benefit when two are adopted at the same time. (See Chapter 4.) Before you decide, visit in person with families who have adopted more than one at the same time and ask lots of questions. Ask about the advantages and disadvantages on your favorite Internet adoption forum. Most families I talked to, even those who recommend the practice, acknowledged that the first six months after adopting two were very hard.

If you decide to adopt more than one unrelated child at the same time, consider the following advice from families who have been down that road. It is very important for one parent to stay at home for at least a year, if at all possible. For the first three to six months at home, get help with housework. Treat each child as an individual with her own strengths and needs, and spend the time necessary to develop a special relationship with each child. As with all decisions in adoption, focus on what is best for the child rather than what is best for the parent.

Travel in Country: Parental opinions on adoption travel vary from considering it an adventure to a costly hassle. Most agencies encourage families to travel even if it is not required so that they will experience their child's culture and can talk with her caregivers. No doubt your travel stories will become a part of your child's history, to be told again and again as she grows, and will form her first impression of her birth country.

If international travel is about as appealing to you as a root canal or is a problem for other reasons, consider adopting from South Korea, Guatemala, India, Taiwan, or some African countries that allow the child to be escorted to you. You will pay an escort fee, usually $1,500 to $2,500, and the child will be brought to the nearest entry airport. You may be able to have the child escorted to the airport nearest to you for an extra fee.

If your hesitancy about travel is the amount of time required, look for a country that requires one short trip, such as Guatemala, South Korea, Haiti, Taiwan, or the Philippines. If the problem with travel applies to only one member of a couple, check the Country Charts for those countries that require only one parent to travel. You will have to readopt the child in the United States if only one parent travels, but many families choose to do this anyway. (See Chapter 10.)

If you're hesitant about traveling because you are a little intimidated about the foreignness of the whole thing, consider adopting from a country such as China, where families usually travel in groups and have an English-speaking guide for the entire trip. Although less common, it may be possible to travel in groups with some other countries as well. Check the Country Charts. An added bonus is the possibility of lifelong friendships for parents, and later their children, that may be forged on these trips. In many countries, even if you are not traveling in a group, part of your adoption fee pays for an English-speaking facilitator while you are in the country.

Method of Referral: The process of presenting information on a child for prospective parents to consider is called a referral. Chapter 8 discusses the referral process in detail, but generally speaking, countries refer children in three ways.

- Standard: Parents receive medical information and a picture of the child and decide whether to accept or reject the referral before they travel to pick up the child or have her escorted to them. Either the child is *matched* with a family by the orphanage or governmental agency in the birth country, or the referral is sent to the adoption agency in the United States, which matches the referral to a family on its waiting list. It is harder to generalize about waiting times if the agency matches the child to a family on its list, since agencies can have vastly different numbers of applicants waiting.

- Blind: Parents travel to the country without a specific child referred and are presented with information on a child or several children while they are in country. They accept or reject the referral after they have met and spent some time with the child.
- Semi-blind: Parents receive very limited information on a specific child, such as age and gender, but do not receive medical and background information until they travel to the country to meet this child. They do not officially accept or reject the referral until they have met the child.

Read Chapter 8 for more information and think about which method you will feel more comfortable with.

The Wait: The wait is really two waits: first the wait for a referral and then the wait to travel to get your child. See Chapters 7 and 8 for more detail. I've included times on the charts, but times vary greatly from year to year and sometimes season to season, so call a few agencies and ask for the current waiting times pre- and post-referral. With countries closer to the United States, such as Guatemala, Mexico, and Haiti, it may be possible and affordable to visit your child during the wait.

Cost: The costs included in the Country Charts appendix are estimates of total costs for everything associated with completing the adoption except for travel, and are included only for a rough comparison of costs between countries. The range reflects not only the variations in adoption agency fees but also the difference in the cost of your home study and dossier preparation, which can vary widely depending on where you live. When you are choosing an agency, you will get a more exact cost, and I have included a cost-comparison chart in Chapter 3 to guide you.

HEALTH

Parents should think about health issues at two stages in the adoption process: when choosing a country and when evaluating a referral. Once you have a referral, you will have medical and background information on a specific child and will be in a better position to assess the health risks for that particular child, which, after all, is what you really care about. But it is equally important to consider health issues when you are choosing a country, in order to increase the odds of finding a child with health risks you can accept.

Unfortunately, at this stage I can only give you generalizations, which by their very nature are problematic. Healthy children can be adopted from all countries, and the same can be said for unhealthy children. Mark Twain's quip that "all generalizations are false, including this one" holds true, since some generalizations are indeed correct. But even if true, sweeping statements are of limited usefulness when you try to extrapolate from the general to the specific. For example, saying that the incidence of fetal alcohol syndrome (FAS) is higher for children adopted from countries of the former Soviet Union than from many other countries is true, but it is not true that most children adopted from Russia have FAS or that your child adopted from Russia will necessarily have FAS. Unfortunately, at this stage in the adoption process, I know of no other way to help you assess the health risks of adopting from a particular country. If generalizations offend you or bring out your argumentative side, skip this section and read the discussion in Chapter 8 on evaluating the health issues for a specific child.

For this discussion to have any relevance, you must think of health in the broadest sense. Health, as I use the term, has physical, emotional, and cognitive aspects. Pre-adoptive parents tend to focus on the physical and cognitive, but in the long run, it's the emotional disabilities that cause parents the most stress. A distinction can also be made between the current health of the child and the prognosis for future health. Research shows that children can make spectacular growth and developmental progress after adoption, but some problems are for life.

Before we get too far into a discussion of the health issues of internationally adopted kids, I need to add a disclaimer. When writing about health issues, there is a danger of focusing too much attention on the potential problems of adoption rather than on the more likely successes. Most children adopted internationally are thriving, having recovered from their early-life deprivation once placed in "stable, loving, and economically resourceful" homes (Judge, 2004; Ryan and Groza, 2004). Most are succeeding behaviorally, academically, and socially (Tan and Marfo, 2006; International Adoption Project, 2002). Adoption does have risks, but so do most things in life. The key is knowing how much risk you are willing to take and preparing yourself beforehand. It also helps to remember that the likelihood of adopting a child with problems so severe that you will regret your decision is very small. A large long-term study of families that adopted children from Romania showed that 90 percent of the parents had a positive view of their adoptions even though these children came from some of the most horrific orphanage conditions ever seen and arrived home with very significant physical, emotional, and cognitive problems (Ryan and Groza, 2004).

The first step in thinking about health from a countrywide perspective is identifying what factors influence a child's chances for a long healthy life. For the greatest chance of health, a baby should be born to a well-nourished mother who abstained from alcohol, drugs, and smoking during her pregnancy and received good prenatal care. The baby should be born full term and of average height, weight, and head circumference. After birth, the baby should have a caring, consistent caregiver who feeds, diapers, cuddles, caresses, and interacts verbally with him in a stimulating environment. Obviously, he should not be abused. The picture I just painted of a child with a very low probability for physical, emotional, or cognitive problems is not often found in the world of adoption. All children placed for adoption (be it international or domestic) are at some risk, and parents who are extremely risk-averse should not consider adoption.

But based on this scenario of a low-risk child, we can conclude that the following factors increase the risk of a child having health issues. These factors are cumulative, meaning that each additional insult increases the probability of problems.

- Time in an orphanage (with risk increasing with time)
- Low birth weight with full-term pregnancy
- Premature birth
- Prenatal exposure to alcohol, drugs, or tobacco
- Poor-quality postnatal care (many children per caregiver, high turnover among staff, neglect, physical or sexual abuse)

No one country can guarantee you a child that will have none of these risk factors. It is also not possible to rank countries based on these factors, since some countries do a good job on one but not another. Nonetheless, given these factors, it is fair to say that in order to reduce your odds of adopting a child with health problems, look for a country with a lower incidence of drinking in pregnant women, where children are in foster care and are placed for adoption at a young age.

Many families decide after reviewing the Country Charts and working through the parental preference worksheets that they are willing to assume greater health risks because of their other preferences. That is a perfectly valid choice. Every country has children in need of homes, and children with potential health issues are certainly just as deserving of a forever family. Without a doubt, these kids are better off with you than remaining in an orphanage, and many of these potential problems will never come to pass. It is not my intent to steer you toward any one country, but rather to help you choose a country with the greatest likelihood of finding your child.

The following country-specific factors can influence the health of the children being placed for adoption.

Age at Adoption: Research is mixed on the importance of age at adoption in predicting future health problems, but it is at least one factor to consider (Fensbo, 2004; Tan and Marfo, 2006). It stands to reason that children placed for adoption at a younger age will have spent less time in an orphanage. Adoption laws of the country determine the age of the child at placement and differ by country. Generally speaking, risk increases with age, with those children adopted before six months showing few impacts (International Adoption Project Newsletter, 2002; Bledsoe and Johnston, 2004).

Age at placement can cut both ways. Although the youngest children may well have fewer developmental delays, they are harder to evaluate for these delays, since fewer developmental milestones have been reached and the earliest milestones can be met by all but the most seriously impaired children. Further, the characteristic facial features for fetal alcohol syndrome may be easier to detect after age two. The child's basic personality traits and how well he would fit into your family are also more apparent as he ages. Also note that age at adoption does not necessarily correlate to length of time in an orphanage, since not all children come into the orphanage at birth. See the later discussion on reasons why children enter governmental care.

Orphanage vs. Foster Care: *Orphanage* is the general term I use to cover institutional care and includes social welfare institutions, group homes, or baby houses. No matter what the name, orphanages are lousy places to raise children. Every child deserves prompt consistent care, lots of verbal and physical stimulation, and love. In short, children need parents, not shift workers. The quality of care varies greatly by country, region, and even within the same orphanage, but even in the best of situations, communal living is not conducive to providing the degree of care infants and children need. This fact alone is why some families choose a country where children are in orphanages in order to provide a home to a child who really needs it.

While most children available for foreign adoption live in orphanages, foster care is available in some countries, most notably Korea and Guatemala. Other countries, such as China, are making some progress in placing children in foster homes rather than institutions. Unfortunately, foster care does not automatically guarantee quality care, but it increases the odds.

Dr. Dana Johnson, from the University of Minnesota International Adoption Clinic, says that the chance that a child adopted from an orphanage will be completely normal (whatever that means) when she first arrives home is essentially zero. Growth and development will both be delayed. For growth delays, the rule of thumb is that a child will lose one month of linear growth for every three months in an institution. In a study comparing Guatemalan children in foster care and orphanage care, the children who had resided in an orphanage before adoption were significantly smaller in height, weight, and head circumference (Miller et al., 2005). Similar growth delays were also found in Chinese and Russian orphans adopted from institutions (Miller and Hendrie, 2000; Albers et al., 1997).

Developmental delays are also common for children who lived in an orphanage before adoption. A large study of children adopted from China showed "gross motor delays in 55% of the children, fine motor delays in 49%, cognitive delays in 32%, language delays in 43%, social emotional delays in 28%, and delays in activities of daily living in 30%" (Miller and Hendrie, 2000). Forty-four percent had delays in three or more of these areas. Interviews with international adoption (IA) doctors and research reveal that developmental delays were common for children who resided in orphanages in other countries as well (Albers et al., 1997).

Most parents accept that their child will arrive home with growth and developmental delays, but their burning question is will their child make up these delays with loving care. Research clearly indicates that love and nutrition do wonders for a child's physical and developmental growth. The gains made in this area post-adoption have been described as miraculous (Ryan and Groza, 2004; Bledsoe and Johnston, 2004; Judge, 2004). Motor skill delays are often the first to improve, while language and social skills may lag behind, especially for children who spent more time in an institution. The younger the child, the greater the chance that he will make up any growth and developmental delays, but whether your child will completely catch up is impossible to tell. One researcher, Dr. Victor Groza, categorized the children adopted from Romania several years post-adoption as follows: "the resilient rascal" (20 percent) showed little long-term effects of orphanage life; "the wounded wonders" (60 percent) were making good progress but had some delays; and "the challenged children" (20 percent) continued to struggle. These children came from extreme deprivation and arrived home significantly delayed, but other researchers have seen similar results in other countries. Dr. Dana Johnson said in an interview, "With love, 70–80 percent of the children adopted from orphanages will do quite well; unfortunately, it is impossible to pick out in advance with certainty the ones who won't."

Better orphanages have the following:

- Consistent care (low turnover among caregivers, caregiver assigned to care for the same children each day)
- Fewer children per caregiver
- Adequate nutrition and medical care

It is impossible to generalize about orphanage care for an entire country, but once you have selected an agency you can ask specific questions about the quality of care in the institutions they work with. You can talk with other parents who have adopted from the same region of the country, and it may be possible to find parents who adopted from the same orphanage. Your agency may be able to give you names, and yahoo.com has some groups formed around certain regions. And remember, institutionalization is not an automatic sentence to physical, cognitive, or emotional health problems; many children come home and thrive despite having spent their first years in an orphanage.

Reasons Why Children Are in Government Care: Children come into government care through abandonment, relinquishment, or removal from their homes. Little is known about the reasons children are abandoned, since birth parents aren't around to ask. In some countries, such as China, parents are not allowed to legally relinquish a child; therefore, most children available for international adoption are abandoned. The assumption, supported by some research, is that Chinese children are abandoned due to societal pressure for a boy combined with governmental population-control policies (Johnson, 2002; Johnson, 1996). In essence, most were a wanted pregnancy but an unwanted gender. The reasons may be changing somewhat, since more healthy baby boys are being placed from China, with the assumption being that these are sons of unwed mothers.

The reasons for relinquishment are varied, but some combination of poverty and unwed motherhood is usually involved, and with some countries, such as India, gender preference plays a role in relinquishment just as in abandonment. More information on birth family, prenatal care, and birth history is usually available when children are relinquished.

Children are removed from homes by governments the world over for much the same reasons: neglect or abuse. These children are at the greatest risk for short- and long-term physical, emotional, and cognitive problems. Children can be removed in all countries, but the availability of these children for international adoption is more common in some.

Prevalence of Fetal Alcohol Spectrum Disorders (FASD): Prenatal habits are a concern for all types of adoption, since they are mostly unknown and out of the control of prospective adoptive parents. Alcohol is of particular concern because it is so common and can cause such devastating health problems in children whose birth mothers drank excessively during pregnancy. See Chapter 8 for a complete discussion of FASD and the most severe of these disorders, fetal alcohol syndrome (FAS).

Data on the rate of FAS per country are not available. Information on the drinking habits of women of childbearing age is available for some countries but is not very useful for comparing countries for prevalence of FAS. The World Health Organization compiles country-generated reports on drinking habits, but there is little uniformity in the data collected by each country, the definitions used, and the accuracy of reporting. Furthermore, a great deal of variation is present between population groups within a country, with those in lower socioeconomic levels being more at risk (Abel, 1995). The most relevant information would be drinking rates for that segment of the population most likely to place their children for adoption; unfortunately, these facts are not available on a countrywide basis for any country.

Also, interestingly, the prevalence of alcohol consumption does not correlate well with the incidence of FAS when known. For example, American and Canadian women have a lower drinking rate than European women, but the United States and Canada have a higher rate of FAS than does Western Europe. Researchers speculate that this is due to factors such as public education on the dangers of drinking while pregnant and cultural differences in consumption patterns (moderate daily consumption with meals versus binge drinking) (Kyskan and Moore, 2005).

International adoption doctors are in a good position to assess the current prevalence of FAS in adopted children, since they review a large number of medical and background records pre-adoption and examine many children post-adoption. Unfortunately, their assessment is hampered by the lack of information on the drinking habits of the birth mothers, the difficulty of identifying babies and young children with FAS, and the difficulty of distinguishing prenatal alcohol exposure from the other causes for delays in internationally adopted kids, such as institutionalized care, multiple placements, malnutrition, and premature birth. Also, some of the less-impaired kids will not show symptoms of alcohol exposure until they are in school and are not being seen regularly by IA doctors. Nevertheless, interviews with a number of leading IA doctors revealed a consistent assessment of which countries were referring children with a higher risk for FAS, and that information has been included in the Country Charts appendix.

Adequacy of Medical Reports: Each country provides parents with medical and background information in order to help them assess the health risks of the child that has been referred to them. The thoroughness and accuracy of these reports vary greatly by country. The medical evaluations are fairly good at identifying the current health of the child, although unidentified problems do occur. In studies of children adopted from China, Guatemala, and Eastern

Europe, researchers found that 18 percent, 14 percent, and 20 percent of the children, respectively, had medical problems that were not discovered until the children arrived home (Miller and Hendrie, 2000; Miller et al., 2005; Albers et al., 1997). Research on the accuracy of the medical reports from other countries is not available; however, IA doctors are in a good position to assess the accuracy, since they review the medical information pre-adoption and then evaluate many of these same children post-adoption. The results of my interviews are included in the Country Charts.

Keep in mind that when you are evaluating a referral of a specific child, you can hire an international adoption doctor to help you assess this child's risk for current and future health problems and you can ask your agency to get additional information if needed. In some countries, you may be able to hire a doctor to examine the child in person and report back to you or your IA doctor. The availability of additional information is influenced by both the willingness of the country and agency to get additional information, and the capability of the country to provide this information. A CAT scan may be very helpful in ruling out some problems, but even the most willing orphanage director and regional administrator can't get one if the only machine is a thousand miles away.

INTANGIBLES

Your head and your heart have to work together when choosing a country from which to adopt. The intangibles have to be factored in as well.

Program Stability: How do you cope with uncertainty and delays? The countries I have rated as stable are more likely to proceed at a predictable pace with fewer unanticipated delays. Not surprisingly, the stable programs tend to be the older programs. These ratings are subjective and you could have a smooth, predictable experience with a less-stable country and encounter unexpected surprises with a stable country, but as with most of the factors we've discussed, it is a matter of playing the odds. If stability is not your top priority, you shouldn't necessarily shy away from a country rated less than stable, but I would suggest asking lots of questions of the agency about what the exact waiting times have been in the last year for the regions and orphanages they work with for the age and health you are seeking.

Number of Children and Program Growth: The number of children being placed in the last four years from that country and whether the program is growing or declining influences predictability. Generally, the more kids being placed, the more information there is on the program and the timing. Another advantage of choosing a country that is placing a lot of children in the United

States is the ready access to country-specific support groups, culture programs, camps, and language schools for you and your child both now and in the future.

Affinity for a Country: Don't discount an interest, love, or connection to a particular country, because once you adopt a child your family will have a permanent connection to his birth country. Do you feel drawn to a country because of travel, heritage, or just general interest? As your child ages, you will likely read folk tales from that country, make yearly presentations on that country to his class, and learn to cook traditional dishes from that country. It helps to really like the country, since you are going to be spending so much time learning about it.

Post-Adoption Reports: Countries differ greatly on what reporting they require agencies and parents to submit after the adoption. Some want only a few reports in the first year after adoption prepared by the home-study agency on how the child and family are adjusting; others want these social worker–prepared reports for a few years; and others want parents to submit annual reports until the child turns eighteen. The amount of cost and time varies depending on what the country requires, so before you choose a country, carefully consider their requirements. After the first year or two, preparing these reports will be a hassle, but if you choose a country that requires years of reporting, you have a legal and moral obligation to submit them on time. Countries have closed to international adoption because of lack of compliance with post-adoption reporting requirements, preventing other families from adopting, but more important, dooming thousands of children to a life without a family.

Agencies often require post-adoption reports even when the country does not, in order to provide evidence to government officials, judges, and orphanage directors on how the children are doing once they are home. Your state of residence may also have additional post-adoption reporting requirements.

Hague Treaty on Intercountry Adoption: The Hague Convention on Protection of Children and Co-operation in Respect of Intercountry Adoption (commonly known in adoption circles as the Hague Treaty) was drafted in 1993 to protect children, birth parents, and adopted parents and to prevent child trafficking and other abuses. To join, a country must sign the treaty and then comply with its laws in order to implement the treaty, also known as becoming a party or member to the treaty. The treaty is not in force in the country until these steps are taken. The United States signed the treaty in 1994 and is slowly taking the necessary steps to implement it. The first step was passing the Intercountry Adoption Act (IAA) in 2000. The last significant step was issuing the regulations that put meat on the bones of the IAA in February

2006. Exactly when the treaty will be in force in the United States is unclear, but it will likely not be until late 2007 at the earliest. To check the status, go to www.travel.state.gov, click on Children & Family, then click on either Hague Convention or Hague Implementation.

Countries are not required to join the Hague Treaty in order to place children for international adoption, and even though the treaty will soon be in force in the United States, you can adopt from a country that is not a party to the Hague Treaty. The rules of the Hague Treaty apply only if both the placing and receiving country are members; therefore, if you adopt from a nonmember country, the protections offered by the Hague Treaty are not in effect.

Once the United States is a party to the Hague Treaty, all agencies placing children between the United States and another Hague country must be accredited or approved according to U.S. Department of State regulations. This accreditation provides protection for parents by requiring agencies to meet specific standards for ethical adoption practices and by providing complaint procedures and a complaint registry. (See Chapter 3.) By choosing a Hague country, the agency you work with (after the United States fully implements the Hague Treaty) must meet these standards, but any agency can become accredited even if they place children from countries not a party to the Hague Treaty.

HOW TO DECIDE

Use the following process to decide on the best country for you:

1. Go through the Country Charts appendix and cross off those countries where you do not meet the restricting criteria. The Country Charts are organized with the restricting criteria first. Note that I only provided charts for the top seventeen countries placing children in the United States. Other countries place children as well, just in smaller numbers. If you are interested in one of these countries, call at least two agencies that place from this country and make your own chart.
2. You and your spouse read the parental preference section of this chapter. It is best if you both read Chapter 8 as well.
3. Make a copy of the parental preference worksheet for you and your spouse, and fill them out separately.
4. Compare and discuss the parental preference sheets. Note not only the answer but also the weighting that each of you gave each preference. The weighting allows you to say how strongly you feel about this issue.

5. Agree to a priority ranking of the parental preferences, including equal rankings on the same line. Take your time with this step.
6. With your priorities in mind, look at the countries you have not already crossed out and narrow them to one or a few.
7. Read Chapter 3 to find an agency that places children from these countries.

FUAQs (FREQUENTLY UNASKED QUESTIONS)

My husband and I have fallen in love with a child whose picture we found on an Internet photolisting Web site. Everything I read is telling me to avoid adopting off a photolist, but I don't understand why. It seems like a good way to find a child that is perfect for our family.

A *photolist* is adoptionese for a collection of pictures, usually posted on the Internet, of children supposedly available for adoption. Limited information on the child is available, and an agency is listed for you to contact for more information.

Absolutely nothing is wrong with finding a picture and information about a child, falling in love, and then adopting. So long as it is allowed by the country of birth (and not all do), it makes sense in many ways. After all, the child is the most important piece to this whole adoption business. Right? It isn't very different from the standard way of receiving a referral (apply to an agency, then receive a picture and medical information on the child).

The reason photolists are used is that they work. They follow the basic principle of advertising—pictures sell; or to put it more poetically, "A picture is worth a thousand words." When it is used to find homes for children with special needs (older, sibling groups, medical issues), the hope is that potential parents will see the child first and the special need second. In fact, this approach has been used for years by state foster-care systems in the United States.

But it is true that photolistings have a bad reputation. They are effective because potential parents fall in love, but they are potentially dangerous for the same reason. After seeing the picture of a child, prospective parents start thinking of him or her as *their* child, and the way to get their child is to sign on with the agency that is listed. All thoughts of researching the agency are replaced by thoughts of getting/rescuing this child as soon as possible. A sense of urgency is created. "My child is _____ (waiting, getting older without us, needs me)." These thoughts can wipe out all common sense, or at least all business sense, and people who are eager to become parents are particularly vulnerable.

Photolistings have been used by less-than-scrupulous adoption agencies to lure parents into the agency. Once in the door and money has changed hands, that particular child may not be available either because she was never available for adoption or because she was offered to numerous parents at the same time and other parents were ready to adopt sooner than you. Once you are on board, another child will be offered as a substitute. This may be fine with you, but either way, the agency used the picture of the first child to get you in the door and paying money.

Be extremely cautious of an agency that offers to "hold" a child for you unless you have completed your home study and have all your paperwork ready. If you think about it, it's not fair to the child to wait for you to get ready when he could be adopted sooner by another family. If you feel hurried or pushed to act quickly, run the other way. Perhaps the biggest warning sign of all is if the agency is not requiring you to become educated about potential issues with international adoption.

If you decide to throw caution to the wind, at the very least don't check your brain at the door (or, more accurately, "at the homepage").

- Make a commitment to hold off emotionally attaching to the child before you have thoroughly investigated the agency. This is much easier said than done.
- Be very cautious about when money is due and realize that getting a complete or even partial refund if things go south may be impossible.
- Keep in mind the very real possibility that the child you fell in love with will not be the child that is ultimately available for you to adopt.
- Get all the medical information that is available to thoroughly assess the child, and ask for more if needed. Have this medical information reviewed by an international adoption medical specialist.
- Read Chapters 8 and 10 for a better understanding of some of the challenges of adoption. Also read books on this subject listed in the Resource Guide.

I saw news reports on an earthquake in another country and would like to adopt one of the children who were orphaned. How do I go about doing this?

It is hard not to be moved by the pictures on the nightly news of children orphaned by war or natural disaster. While the desire to come to the aid of orphans is wonderful, it is usually not possible to adopt these children, at least not in the immediate aftermath of the disaster. Adoption is not the first solution considered for these children for several reasons.

- Right after a natural disaster or war, it is surprisingly hard to determine if a child is truly an orphan or just temporarily separated from his family.

Countries need to move slowly to allow immediate and extended family members to find each other. U.S. law supports this by requiring that all children adopted by U.S. citizens meet the strict legal definition of *orphan*.

- Once a child is determined to be an orphan, the first step is to try to find members of his extended family or community to adopt him. This effort takes time.
- Orphans of war or natural disaster have been traumatized, and moving to a new home, with new parents, new language, and a new culture may not be in the child's best interest even if they cannot be adopted in their birth country.
- From a practical standpoint, a country torn apart by war or natural disaster may not have the infrastructure in place to process adoptions legally. Even if the government is functioning, processing adoptions should not be the top priority of the government and legal system.
- Travel to these countries may not be safe.
- Some countries do not have a program for international adoption established, and immediately after a war or natural disaster is not the best time to develop such a program. Also, some countries, such as those that follow Islamic law, do not allow adoption.

Literally thousands of children worldwide are ready and waiting for a permanent home. Consider adopting one of these.

FOR EVERY ADOPTION, A DIFFERENT STORY . . .

Inclusion of these stories should not be read as an endorsement of the opinions expressed or as an encouragement to adopt from a specific country. These were the responses I received when I asked why a family chose the country they did. Read these to understand the diversity of what parents consider important when choosing a country.

The parental preference worksheet really helped us focus on what was important to each of us. Before we completed the worksheet, we were just agreeing with each other on everything without clearly defining what was important to each of us. For instance, my husband gave the highest weight to not adopting an infant and adopting only one. And while I would love to adopt a baby and a sibling group, neither was my top priority, so we are looking for a single preschool-age child. Interestingly, we found out that we are both open to special needs, but we differ on which ones. We are in the process of talking about what we are comfortable with and getting more information so we can make the best decision on the type of special need we should look for. —*GD, Texas*

The decision to adopt from Russia was easy for us. We wanted a child that was as young as possible and who would look like us. My drive to have a biological connection to my child was what kept me in fertility treatment for so long, and I wanted a child who would not make our family stand out. I see no reason to advertise our infertility. Life has enough challenges, and having a child that looks different from us would add additional challenges for our child and for us. —*RM, Virginia*

Guatemala made the most sense given who I am and what I want. I am an over-forty single woman and my top priority was adopting an infant. My second priority was adopting as healthy a child as I could, and in Guatemala the children are in foster care, which improves the odds that they will be healthy. I also really liked the idea that Guatemala was close enough that I can afford to take my daughter to visit more than just once. Spanish is an easier language for me to expose her to as well. —*MM, Virginia*

When I started to research international adoption, we quickly eliminated many countries, or more accurately, many countries eliminated us. I was only twenty-eight, so China was out. The stay in country was too long for us to afford for Ukraine and Kazakhstan. Vietnam and Cambodia were closed. When I started reading about Russia, it felt right. I want to say that it was divine intervention, but who knows. People assume it is because we want a white child, but that is not important to us; I just felt that my child was in Russia. It bothers me that it is so unpredictable, but we are going for it anyway based on our faith and belief that this is what we should do. —*LL, Washington*

We chose Kazakhstan because we thought there would be less risk of FAS and the orphanages had a higher caregiver-to-child ratio. We really liked the idea that we would be able to complete the adoption in one trip, because I knew that once I met my daughter, I would never want to leave her.

A real negative about Kazakhstan at the beginning was that they did not give you a referral before you travel. I wanted a picture of our child before we left—almost like a guarantee that there would be this child waiting for us. We were scared that we would show up and be told, "I'm sorry, but we don't have any children that match what you are looking for. Go home." The other advantages to Kazakhstan outweighed this concern, and now, after traveling blind, I would never want to do a standard referral. In making a decision this important, it is crucial to meet the child in person first and not rely on a paper record. The picture of our daughter that we would have been given if they had given us a referral was terrible. Her tongue was hanging out and her face was expressionless. I probably would have been terrified to accept a child who looked like that. When we met her, she was nothing like her picture. —*AG, Texas*

I was drawn to adopt from China because of the large numbers of Americans adopting from there. There is a wonderful support network both pre- and post-adoption for parents of Chinese girls. I also liked the idea that my daughter would have a cohort of fellow adoptees with a story similar to hers. It is such a weird story to most Americans, but at least my daughter is not so alone in having been abandoned, cared for in an orphanage, adopted by parents from another country, and finding a home halfway around the world from her birthplace. She will have many others to share the transracial Chinese adoption experience.

Also, we happened to know a fair number of people who had adopted from China, which added to our comfort level. Finally, the idea of traveling in a group was very appealing—comforting actually. Funny, because I've never been keen on traveling in groups before, but especially since we would be first-time parents, we liked the idea of having support from other families. —*MM, Michigan*

I received information from about twenty-five different agencies that service many different countries, and as I read the information they sent I began to get a feel for the requirements, laws, and differences of each country. From this reading I narrowed our choice down to either

Guatemala or Colombia. We respected and liked both countries and cultures and felt like we could embrace either wholeheartedly in order to share with our child in a positive way. From here I began to look more into the length of wait for referral, travel requirements, and in-country time. The biggest selling point for us was the likelihood that the birth mother could/would change her mind. We had three failed domestic adoption attempts and didn't want to go through that again. One of the primary reasons we chose Colombia was that they do not let you know about the child until the mother has signed off totally. We also liked that you received your child shortly after arriving in the country and were able to spend the time in country bonding with your new child. Since Colombia does the paperwork after you arrive, the wait time between referral and travel is dependent on how quickly you can get your visas. (We traveled in three weeks because of work issues, but I have heard of a couple who traveled in five days!) —*RO, New York*

We chose China partly because of our age, but also because we really liked the Chinese adoption system, which is an administrative system versus a judicial system that is used in some countries. An administrative system is a cleaner process—if you cross your *t*'s and dot your *i*'s, you will come out at the other end with a child. The rules are very clear, and there is no question of what is required. With a judicial system, the judges in the country have a lot of say into what is required and they can change their mind. They can also blackmail agencies into paying bribes. This simply doesn't happen in China. —*JF, Florida*

I viewed adopting a child transracially [from Guatemala] as a plus. We had a birth son two years older, and having them look so different is a good way to remind us not to compare them. Choosing a different ethnicity has made it fun. I should add that we live in a diverse neighborhood and we "fit in" just fine. —*SG, Washington, D.C.*

We like to travel to South and Central America, so we first considered Guatemala since it is the largest placing country from that part of the world. This may sound weird, but what eventually turned me off is the

Guatemalan way of doing adoption. It just feels very money driven. We have decided on a less popular country—Peru—for a couple of reasons. What tipped the scales for us was that we really liked the idea of traveling to Peru. Also, agencies and adoptive parents have told us that they really try to match the parent and the child. Peru is a surprising choice, since we are not generally "the road less traveled" kind of people, but it feels right. —*GD, Texas*

We adopted from Ukraine for several reasons. The agency we were interested in using had a Ukranian program. My husband's great-grandfather was from Ukraine, so we would share the same cultural background with our child. We wanted to adopt a toddler, and Ukraine had toddlers. It was important to us to be able to bring along our bio daughter, which was not a problem in Ukraine. We also like the fact we would be in the country for a few weeks, so that we would get to know the culture of our child. —*AC, Ohio*

We were both interested in adopting from Asia. We thought about China, but I was younger than their age limit. When we learned about Korea, we liked the idea that the babies were in private foster care rather than orphanages and that they were so young. Our first daughter came home at three months. When we were ready to adopt again, the agency that placed from Korea in our state would not allow us to request the sex of the new baby. We wanted another girl because we still had all our girl clothes and because we wanted a sister for our first daughter. China seemed like the logical choice. I was old enough now and we had always had an interest in adopting from China ever since we saw a documentary on Chinese orphans many years ago. Also, at the time, the wait was just six to eight months. From the very first meeting with the agency until we got our baby was just under a year. —*CH, North Carolina*

We wanted to adopt a special-needs preschooler because we wanted to provide a home for a child who really needed it. We have good health insurance, so we figured "why not us." We have three bio kids (twenty-one, twenty, and eighteen) and we had the love and energy to start over.

The referral process for special-needs adoptions is very fast, much faster than we had anticipated. We adopted a three-year-old boy with a partially repaired cleft lip and palate. We were educated beforehand on the range of reactions common with toddler adoptions, and our son certainly had the full range. He cried nonstop for a while and it has taken a year for him to totally adjust. It has been a rewarding experience for us all, and we hope to adopt a preschool-age sister for him soon. —*MD, Florida*

The choice of China was easy for us. We wanted a girl and we wanted a stable program. We've had enough surprises on our road to parenthood and we didn't want any more. —*WM, New York*

You have to consider your circumstances as well as what you want when you pick a country. We are both under thirty, fertile, have been married one year, and want to adopt an infant. We didn't want to travel more than once or be in the country longer than two weeks. We wanted to adopt a child from an undeveloped country that really needed us. We considered Guatemala and the former Soviet republics, but the more research I did, the more I thought that Ethiopia was a good fit. When I brought it up to my husband, he was skeptical. His image of Ethiopia was the all-too-common one of the 1980s—starving children with distended bellies living in a dustbowl. I checked out books and a travel movie on Ethiopia and we began learning more. We met someone who had been to Ethiopia for work and he told us of the country's beauty, the friendliness of the people, and how amazing the food was. It may not be logical, but all of these things played a role in our decision. The fact that Ethiopia is cheaper than some of the other countries was a nice perk, but it didn't really factor into our decision. Twenty thousand is still a lot of money, no matter how you look at it. —*DM, Colorado*

Why we chose Ethiopia is a hard question to answer. Honestly, our decision was strictly a heart decision. We knew we were ready for another child and felt drawn to Ethiopia. After much prayer and discussion, we simply knew our child was waiting for us in Ethiopia. However, for those who are more systematic in their approach to choosing a country, there are many logical reasons to choose Ethiopia: the tremendous need (there are an estimated 3 to 5 million orphans), the relatively short wait time (from submitting paperwork to having him home took four months), and the relatively reasonable cost. The children are largely well cared for and loved in their families and communities before tragedy brings them to an orphanage, and the quality of care in the orphanage is quite good, so they are much less likely to have significant attachment issues. The availability of infants and young toddlers is another plus. —*HMJ, California*

We have five children, three of whom are adopted from Korea. We chose Korea for several reasons, but primarily because we didn't want to travel. We didn't want to leave our older children for a week. Also, we were a little unsure about traveling abroad since we had never done it before and didn't know what to expect. Other factors that influenced our decision were that Korea had a lower income requirement for adoptive families, very detailed medical reports, and background information on the birth family. The funny thing is that after we got a referral for twin baby girls, we decided to go to Korea to pick them up. It was actually cheaper for us to fly there than to pay two escort fees, but this was not the main reason we changed our mind. We learned more and felt it would be an amazing opportunity to experience their culture and understand where they were living. It was a great experience. Our experience with Korea was so good that we only considered Korea for our next adoption of a little boy with special needs. —*RM, Pennsylvania*

We went back and forth trying to decide whether to adopt two at once. We finally decided to adopt just one since we already have a two- and three-year-old. Our new guy has been home one month, and I am so glad that we only adopted one. I see now for our family it wouldn't have worked; I would have gone crazy with two. I already feel so torn between the three of them, and sometimes guilty that I can't do all the things I want to do for them. My older two are adjusting, our new child is adjusting, and when they all go into meltdown mode at the same time it's pretty tough. Also, I can't imagine trying to bond the way that I am with my little guy if we had adopted two. I'm really glad I can just hold and kiss him and that he gets all my attention as the new baby in the family without having to share too much. —*KB, Arizona*

⌐⌐⌐

We adopted two unrelated boys from Russia two years ago when they were eight and fifteen months old. One of the reasons we chose Russia is that this was an option. We knew we wanted a couple of kids and we were concerned that the country would shut down, so adopting two made sense. Also, we were able to save a little money by adopting two at once rather than going through the process twice. And after all the years of wanting and waiting, we were ready to have a family.

Knowing what I know now, I don't know whether I would adopt two so close in age. We went in thinking we would get a baby and an older toddler, but we were referred two that were only seven months apart. They are constantly being compared, and developmentally they are very different. I'm asked all the time if they are twins. While I am proud that they are adopted, I don't necessarily think the guy at the grocery store needs to know that. I just tell people they are close in age, or if pressed I'll lie and say they are ten months apart to avoid the discussion. I imagine when they get in school they will be asked this question even more.

The first months home were very stressful for us as first-time parents with two kids. We all had so much to adjust to. Just the logistics of going to the grocery store were overwhelming. What helped was setting up a schedule and sticking to it. Now that they are three and three and a half, we are seeing some of the benefits since they play so well together. —*MG, Virginia*

⌐⌐⌐

We adopted two unrelated children, a boy and a girl, when they were six and a half months old—their birthdays are one day apart. I have zero regrets now about our decision to adopt two at the same time, but the first six or so months were hard. The advantage of adopting two at the same time is that we felt complete as a family after wanting this for so long; we had a son and a daughter—an instant family. This made up for the lost years of trying to have a family. They are the best of buddies and always have a playmate. They learn so much from each other. I think adopting two made their adjustment easier. Also, I feel like I got one more child out of a bad environment.

But adopting two at once is exhausting! We were first-time parents and it really stretched our parenting skills, especially at first. There is only one of me and two of them, and I have felt inadequate to calm or control them at times. My skills have grown with them, and it is less of a problem now that they are toddlers. Finding babysitters for two babies or young toddlers is also hard. Two children close in age definitely draws attention, and we have less privacy in public. People often ask if they are twins, and I usually just say yes. —MS, *Virginia*

We started out looking at Russia. While that program was appealing to us at first, the more research we did, the more uncomfortable we became. The two-trip process bothered me a lot. I couldn't imagine going to Russia, meeting our child, and then leaving. That just seemed too heart-wrenching to me. China was out because we wanted a boy. Guatemala was just too expensive and too unpredictable. By a process of elimination, India seemed like a good match for us. The children are young, and we wanted one as young as possible. We liked the short stay in the country (about a week), the length of the entire process (eighteen to twenty-four months), and the cost. We also considered the low child-to-caregiver ratio and the overall health of the children and the availability of good medical care. —NC, *Oklahoma*

Our top priority, health, led us to select China. Why the children are placed for adoption affects the health of the children available. In China, most of the children in the orphanages are from an intended pregnancy, and we believe that increases the probability of the birth mother taking good care of herself during her pregnancy. Adopting across racial and ethnic lines did not concern us. Our families are pretty "white bread," but they have had no problem with the idea of a Chinese grandchild. In fact, they seem to think the whole idea is *cool*. —SM, *Virginia*

PARENTAL PREFERENCE WORKSHEET

Directions:

1. Make a copy for each spouse.
2. Answer questions honestly. Do not answer the way you think your spouse wants you to answer or the way you think you should answer. Adoption is for life, so think about what you are able to handle and what you want to be a part of your life.
3. Weigh each answer on a scale of 1 to 4 for how strongly you feel about this issue, with 1 meaning "I don't care that much" to 4 meaning "This could be a deal breaker."
4. Compare worksheets with your spouse and develop a priority list based on your combined answers.

Criteria	Questions	Answer	Weight
Children available	1. I want a child as young as possible.		
	2. I want or can accept a child under 2.		
	3. I want or can accept a child between 2 and 3.		
	4. I want or can accept a 3- to 5-year-old.		
	5. I want or can accept a child 6 to 9.		
	6. I want or can accept a child 10 to 12.		
	7. I want or can accept a teenage child.		
	8. I want a child as healthy as possible.		
	9. I can adopt a child with a correctable/curable medical condition.		
	10. I can adopt a child with a noncorrectable/incurable medical condition.		
	11. I can adopt a child with correctable physical problems.		
	12. I can adopt a child with noncorrectable physical problems.		
	13. I can adopt a child born prematurely or with low birth weight.		

Criteria	Questions	Answer	Weight
	14. I can adopt a child with minor developmental delays.		
	15. I can adopt a child with moderate developmental delays.		
	16. I can adopt a child with severe developmental delays.		
	17. I can adopt a child with known psychological or emotional problems.		
	18. I can adopt a child whose birth family has a history of mental illness.		
	19. I can adopt a child who was removed from her birth family due to neglect or abuse.		
	20. I can accept a child with unknown prenatal and early life history.		
	21. I can adopt a child whose birth mother drank alcohol during her pregnancy.		
Ethnicity	22. It is important that my child and I share the same race.		
	23. I can adopt an Asian child.		
	24. I can adopt a Latin American child.		
	25. I can adopt a black child.		
Gender	26. I want to adopt a girl.		
	27. I want to adopt a boy.		
	28. I prefer a specific gender, but I can accept either gender.		
	29. I don't care about gender.		
Adopting more than one at a time	30. I want to adopt two unrelated children of similar ages at the same time.		
	31. I would consider adopting two unrelated children of different ages at the same time.		
	32. I want to adopt a sibling group of two.		

Criteria	Questions	Answer	Weight
	33. I want to adopt a sibling group of more than two.		
Travel	34. I do not want to travel.		
	35. I want only one trip of one week or less.		
	36. I want one trip of 2 weeks or less.		
	37. I don't care about the amount of travel.		
	38. I would prefer to travel in a group with other adopting parents.		
Referral method	39. I prefer the standard referral method.		
	40. I prefer the blind or semi-blind referral method.		
	41. I don't care which referral method is used.		
Waiting time	42. I want a child as soon as possible.		
	43. I would prefer to not wait more than one year.		
	44. I won't let the waiting time influence what country I choose.		
Cost	45. Cost is one of the most important factors to consider.		
	46. I care about cost, but other factors are more important.		
Medical records	47. I want as thorough and reliable medical records as I can get.		
	48. I can live with sketchy medical records.		
Orphanage/ Foster care	49. I prefer or can accept a child living in an orphanage.		
	50. I prefer a child living in foster care.		
	51. I don't care whether the child is living in an orphanage or foster care.		
Stability	52. I can handle a fair amount of uncertainty.		

Criteria	Questions	Answer	Weight
	53. I need to know waiting times and travel times with a fair amount of certainty.		
	54. I would go nuts if this adoption didn't proceed according to plan.		
Post-adoption reports	55. I would prefer the fewest number of post-adoption reports.		
	56. I would be willing to submit a post-adoption report annually until my child is 18.		
	57. The number of post-adoption reports is not a deciding factor for me.		
Affinity	58. There is a country that has always fascinated me. (Write name of country.)		
	59. There is a country that I would love to travel to. (Write name of country.)		
	60. There is a country that I would love to learn about. (Write name of country.)		
	61. I love the food of a particular country. (Write name of country.)		

CHAPTER 3

DECIDING ON AN AGENCY

Eeny, Meeny, Miney, Moe?

Grace was born in Russia on August 3, 2004, and joined her forever family in July 2005.

Jennifer and Bruce wanted it all: a local agency large enough to process lots of adoptions from their first-choice country, but not so large that they would feel like a number. Oh, and they also wanted great references and a flawless background check. "I didn't want to prioritize because all these factors seemed important," says Jennifer. Unfortunately, they had to make some choices. The closest agency had just started a program in their first-choice country. They had to weigh how important it was to talk to someone in person and to be able to attend the various functions pre- and post-adoption offered by the agency for local families against years of experience in placing kids from this country. In the end, they decided to go with a medium-size agency that was located several states away that had been placing children from their preferred country for over ten years. "There are disadvantages to not using a local agency, but we finally decided that for us expertise trumps all," notes Bruce.

While less fun than decorating the nursery or shopping at Baby Gap, the business end of adoption is a necessary evil and you must do your homework. Choosing an agency is the second-most-important decision in the adoption process, ranking second only to deciding whether to accept the referral of a child. It's tempting at the beginning to focus exclusively on the quickest way to fill your waiting arms with a warm, damp bundle. I urge you to slow down and spend the necessary time selecting an agency. Money, time, and emotion rest on this decision. Adoption is stressful enough without adding a bad working relationship, incompetence, or outright fraud to the mix.

There is no such thing as the one best agency. Finding an agency is a little like dating, without the sloppy-kiss anxiety. The agency that is best for me may not be the best for you, and by necessity the selection process is part objective and part subjective.

NATURE OF THE RELATIONSHIP

When you select an agency you are in essence hiring this agency to help you, guide you, advise you, educate you, and advocate for you throughout the adoption process and to be available post-adoption to help you raise your child. Even if they are nonprofit, they are in the business of providing a service for a fee (and a hefty fee at that). You are the client and you are in charge, but in the best case, adoptive parents and the adoption agency form a partnership rather than an employer/employee relationship. It is similar to the relationship you have with your doctor. I firmly believe that I, not my doctor, am in charge of my health care and medical decisions. However, I view my doctor as my trusted partner in making these decisions. The same should be true with your adoption agency.

AGENCY OR FACILITATOR OR INDEPENDENT

The vast majority of international adoptions are through adoption agencies, but a few countries still allow independent adoptions (adopting a child without using an agency). Depending on the country, both independent and agency adoptions may use a *facilitator* in the country to locate the child, coordinate the placement, and assist with the legal proceedings. Adoption facilitators can be employed by an agency or can subcontract with one or more agencies or can work only for individuals. There is nothing wrong with using a facilitator, but the U.S. State Department reports a number of complaints against foreign facilitators alleging fraud, lying, and other unscrupulous acts. Regulation, or lack thereof, of adoption facilitators working in the birth country is controlled by the foreign government, with some countries doing a good job and others not. U.S. State Department regulations implementing the Hague Treaty on Intercountry Adoptions require accredited agencies to be responsible for the actions of their foreign facilitators, but these regulations apply only once the Hague Treaty is ratified in the United States and then only in adoptions from a country that is also a member of the Hague Treaty. (See Chapter 2.) Responsible agencies should oversee and assume responsibility for their facilitators regardless of whether they are accredited under the Hague Treaty regulations. With independent adoptions, the responsibility of working with the foreign government and facilitator is all on your shoulders, and you have no one to fall back on if things go south.

If you are thinking of going solo, first make sure it is legal in your country of choice. Second, talk with as many people as you can who have successfully completed an independent adoption in this country in the last year. You must assume the responsibility to educate yourself thoroughly on the potential health issues of children who are adopted internationally. See Chapters 2 and 8 as well as the Resource Guide. Go in with your eyes wide open and your hands guarding your wallet.

CHOOSING COUNTRY OR AGENCY FIRST

Most people start the adoption process with no idea which country they want to adopt from or which agency they want to use. In my experience, parents will have more preferences for the type of child they want to adopt than for the agency they want to use. For this reason, I recommend that you first work through the country-choosing method described in Chapter 2, select one or a couple of countries, and then look for agencies that place children from these countries.

This order was not handed down from Moses and is therefore not etched in stone. If you already have a relationship with an agency or have heard of an agency that you want to use, then by all means use them *if* they have country programs that will accept you and that you will accept. This is obviously easier for families that don't run into problems with the restricting criteria and have more flexibility in their child preferences. Since these issues are explained in Chapter 2, even if you think you know the agency you want to use, at least read through Chapter 2 first.

You should do some basic reading on the country you are thinking about before you choose an agency. Look at "Additional Information" and "Useful Links" in the Country Charts appendix.

MATCHING AN AGENCY WITH A COUNTRY

Once you've narrowed the world down to a couple of countries from which you want to adopt, how in the world do you find an agency that places children from that country?

Parent Support Groups: Other parents are your best source of information on selecting an agency, and support groups are the best place to find these parents. Support groups exist for each of the major placing countries. You can either attend meetings or go online. Although I'm a big believer in actual human-to-human contact, for finding agencies that handle adoptions from a country, online forums are just as good.

U.S. Department of State: For countries that require agencies to be licensed or authorized, the State Department Web site is a good place to start. (See the Country Charts appendix for which countries require licensing.) To access the State Department information, go to www.travel.state.gov and click on Children & Family Services; under International Adoption click on Country-Specific Information and select the country. Licensed agencies are usually listed in the discussion section. This site is not always current.

Internet: Adoption Web sites can also help you find agencies that place children from a specific country.

- **www.jcics.org** The Joint Council on International Children's Services is a membership organization of agencies that agree to abide by a set of ethical practices in international adoption. See the discussion later in this chapter. Their Web site lists member agencies under all the major placing countries. This is a great place to begin.
- **www.adoptivefamilies.com** *Adoptive Families* magazine has a searchable database by country. To access the database, look under search tools and click on Adoption Program. I like this database because it allows you to specify certain search criteria, such as number of years the agency has been licensed, the number of annual adoptions, and the largest country program for that agency. But at this stage it is most helpful to just include your state and the country as the search criteria.
- **www.rainbowkids.com** Rainbow Kids lists all agencies in their database that place from a country. They have a nice feature that allows you to e-mail all listed agencies to request information.

As a last resort, you can also do a simple search in your favorite search engine: "adoption agency (country)" (for example: "adoption agency Chile"). You'll get lots of junk, but you will also find agencies. If you are interested in a local agency, or at least one nearby, add the name of your state and nearby states to the search. You should always be extremely careful to evaluate any information you get over the Internet, but at this stage you are simply collecting agency names.

THE FIRST CUT

You should now have a list of agencies that place children from the country or countries you are most interested in. You need to narrow that list to save your time and sanity, both of which may be in short supply. In this first cut, you will reduce your list by deciding on your preference for agency size, location, and specialty, and you will make sure that any agency that makes it past the first cut has at least a minimum level of expertise placing kids from your country of choice.

This first cut will be made by reviewing Web sites and written materials, rather than by interviewing. E-mail or call the agencies and ask for material to be sent. Store the information in a multipocketed expandable file folder. (See Chapter 9 for the type I suggest for traveling, and save money by buying only one and use it at this stage and for traveling.) Each agency will have a labeled slot for any written information you receive. File all material you receive as well as your later interview notes under the agency. If nothing else, this organizational system will keep your desk (or dining room table or living room floor) somewhat clean and will give you the illusion of control.

Large vs. Small

Country-specific expertise is important, and an agency that processes more adoptions from a country will have more expertise in that country. Larger agencies will have staff in the United States that deal with only that country and will likely have staff in the country itself. This in-country staff will have a "finger on the local pulse" of adoptions from that country and can provide good support for you when you travel. These larger agencies should be able to give you a fairly good prediction of current waiting times, travel, and age and health of children being placed. Larger agencies have more support staff, thereby freeing up other staff to process adoptions. Many larger agencies work in different regions of the same country, and some parents (and larger agencies) claim this shortens waiting time for referrals. Note that an agency with programs in more than one country can be large for one country and small for another.

On the other hand, there is always the risk that you will be just a number in a larger agency without the handholding or individual attention you want. A smaller agency can still process enough adoptions to be able to guide you, but not so many that it feels like an assembly line. Some directors of smaller agencies have spent years establishing a personal relationship with folks in the country and travel frequently to the country.

National vs. Local Agency

Another decision you will have to make is whether to use a local agency or a national agency. Most national agencies are fairly large, so many of the issues are the same as discussed in the previous section. The large national agencies usually place many kids and have well-established procedures, but you will do most, if not all, of your communication by phone, e-mail, or regular mail. With a local agency, you can sit across the desk from the person and look them in the eye. This is more important to some people than to others. Most agencies provide opportunities for prospective adoptive parents to get together for social events and for adoption education. If the agency is not local or doesn't have a local branch, you won't be able to attend.

If you choose an adoption agency that is not licensed in your state or does not have social workers licensed in your state, you will need to hire a separate agency to perform your home study. (See Chapter 5 for how to choose a home-study agency.) This is done all the time and is not necessarily a problem; however, you may run into communication issues between the social worker doing your home study and the placing agency. Usually local agencies do the home study for their families and know exactly what they are looking for in the home study.

Right now you are focused on finding your child and likely have not given much thought to what happens after you find her. Good agencies provide post-adoption support for their families five, ten, and twenty years down the road. This support runs the gamut from annual picnics, to summer culture camps, to continuing education, to counseling on adoption issues, to tours of her birth country. The farther you are from the agency, the harder it will be for you to access these services.

The decision is easy if a local agency has the expertise and philosophy/personality that you are looking for or clearly does not. The hard decision is when the local agency seems good but not quite as good as a national agency.

Generalist vs. Specialist

Some agencies specialize primarily or exclusively in placing children from one country, while other agencies have programs in numerous countries. Some families know exactly what country they want to adopt from and want an agency that specializes in that country only. Other families have more than one country they are interested in or want the option of changing programs if problems arise. Both options have advantages. However, if you select a country whose international adoption program is unstable, you risk losing time and money changing agencies if adoptions slow down or halt in your first-choice country.

Expertise

You will get more information on the agency's expertise during the interview, but at this stage you need to be sure that any agency that makes the first cut

---

BEWARE OF AGENCIES THAT:

- **Request a large amount of money up front.** Most agencies require the money to be paid as the services are rendered.
- **Pressure parents to act quickly.** You don't want to hear "You need to adopt this child before":
  - ~ she is transferred to another/worse orphanage,
  - ~ someone else adopts her, or
  - ~ she dies.
- **Are seldom available by phone.**
- **Use the words "faster," "easier," "cheaper".**
- **Give any type of guarantee (quick referral, healthy child).**
- **Downplay the possibility of problems,** especially when adopting an older child or toddler who has spent much time in an orphanage. You don't want to hear:
  - ~ "All they need is love."
  - ~ "None of the children from _____ [pick a country] have attachment issues."
  - ~ "None of our kids have fetal alcohol syndrome."
- **Discourage you from getting an independent review of the referral by an international adoption medical specialist.**
- **Don't require adoption education.**
- **Don't have post-adoption services,** such as education and counseling.
- **Have costs or waiting times that are too good to be true.**

has an above-average knowledge about adoptions from your country. How long have they had a program in this country? How many adoptions did they complete from this country in the last couple of years? Do they have staff in the country? Do they have ongoing humanitarian work in that country to aid the kids who are not adopted? This information should be available from their written material or Web site.

THE SECOND CUT

You should now have a shorter list based on your preference for size, location, and specialty, and all of your choices should have a high degree of expertise. Now you get to the nitty-gritty—the interview. You are interviewing for information as well as for the *feel* of the agency. Don't discount the feel part. Agencies, and the people who work there, have distinct personalities. Think back to the dating analogy. A date can look great on paper and in person, but if there is no chemistry there is no future. While an agency will not likely make your heart flutter, you should enjoy working with them. This is obviously an inexact science.

The list of questions I have included at the end of this chapter is long and detailed because this decision deserves this degree of attention. Some parents will spend more time deciding on a stroller than deciding on an agency. I want you to rise above the stroller aficionados and take charge of your adoption. You will notice, however, that some of the questions will not pertain to your situation or country, some of the questions you already know the answers to from the written material, and some of the questions are different ways of getting the same information. Use your discretion on what to ask.

Do not e-mail this list to the agencies you are considering. These questions are to focus your conversation, but it is from the conversation part that you will pick up on the personality and philosophy of this agency. Remember, it's that chemistry thing.

I know that you may feel nervous and judged when you call adoption agencies. After all, you may reason, these people are the guarders of the gate behind which is your child. But agencies want to help you adopt; in fact, they are in the business of opening the gate for people, not closing it.

If you feel awkward asking some of the more detailed questions, you can blame me. "Well, you know, I bought this book and that ridiculous author made a big deal about all these questions, so while I have you on the line . . ." This makes me sound pushy, suspicious, and obsessive rather than you.

The questions are grouped by those that focus on country expertise, general agency information, and agency services. There is also a section to remind you to ask for specific documents to be sent. When you have finished the interview, take the time right then to analyze if you would enjoy working with this agency. What was their attitude and how helpful were they?

These interviews will take time, and it is only fair that you make an appointment so the agency can have the right person speak with you and that person will have allocated enough time. This is a courtesy you should extend regardless of whether you will be conducting the interview in person or on the phone. Your first preference is to talk with someone in the country program, but some agencies have one person handle all information calls to save the time of the country-specific case manager.

When you interview an agency, take notes and label them according to the question you are asking. For example, in the left-hand margin jot down the number of the question when you ask it and then take notes. When you ask the next question, write that number in the margin and continue. This helps to organize your notes and makes it easier to find information later. It's not perfect, since you hope this will be a conversation and not a series of questions and answers, but it will help give your notes some order and will keep you focused on going through the list. File your notes by agency in the expandable folder.

THE FINAL CUT

Based on the results of your interviews, you should have narrowed your list to just a very few for which you will need to check background and reputation.

Background Check

A bit of detective work is necessary to find out how your prospective agency looks on paper and if there is any record of complaints against them. You'll be glad you have only a few to check, since this really is a pain in the . . . neck.

Licensing in the United States

Adoption agencies are licensed by the states in which they operate, although a few states do not issue licenses. In order to be licensed, most states require that the agency meet certain minimum standards. Most states also record complaints on agencies they license, and you should check for complaints in each state the agency has a license. The contact for each state is listed at the Child Welfare Information Gateway (formerly the National Adoption Information Clearinghouse); web site (www.childwelfare.gov; use the National Adoption Directory

Search). You will ask if the agency is currently licensed, if there have been any complaints filed against them, and if they been sanctioned or disciplined.

Accreditation in the United States

Hague Treaty Accreditation. If state licensing establishes the minimum standards that are acceptable, Hague Treaty accreditation or approval seeks to establish the best. See Chapter 2 for more information on the Hague Treaty, but the main provision of interest to adoptive parents is the requirement that all agencies that place children for international adoption between two countries that are both members of the Hague Treaty must be accredited or approved under the Hague standards. (*Accredited* and *approved* are slightly different, but this distinction is likely not important to you.) In order to be accredited/approved, they must abide by very specific operating standards. Accreditation/approval is not a guarantee of ethical behavior or no problems, but it increases the odds in your favor and provides recourse if the agency does not abide by the standards.

Several organizations are authorized to accredit/approve international adoption agencies using the standards set out in the regulations. See www.travel.state.gov (click on Children & Family, then click on Hague Convention or Hague Implementation) for a list of these accrediting entities. Once the treaty is in force in the United States (not likely until late 2007 at the earliest), accredited agencies will be listed at the U.S. State Department Web site. Before that time, you will have to ask the agency if they are seeking accreditation.

Adoption agencies are only required to become accredited or approved under the Hague Treaty regulations if they are placing children from countries that are also parties to the Hague Treaty. See the Country Charts appendix for those countries that are parties to the treaty, or go to www.travel.state.gov, click on Children & Family, then click on Hague Convention. If the country you are interested in is not a party to the Hague Treaty, then your agency need not be accredited or approved. But even if not required, agencies may choose to be accredited or approved under the Hague Treaty, and it is something to look for when choosing an agency, since it sets standards that will protect you and your child in the adoption process. Also, as time goes by, more and more countries will ratify the treaty, so this accreditation/approval will become increasingly important.

Council on Accreditation. COA develops standards of practice and accredits human services organizations, including adoption agencies. It is expected that COA will be the primary accrediting entity authorized under the Hague regulations to accredit international adoption agencies, but even before the Hague

Treaty, COA was accrediting adoption agencies. Once the Hague Treaty is implemented, it will be possible for adoption agencies to get two types of accreditations from the COA—a standard COA accreditation, which shows that an agency complies with the COA standards of practice for adoption, and a Hague Treaty accreditation, which shows that the international adoption agency complies with the U.S. government regulations on international adoption. The standard COA accreditation is voluntary, but the Hague accreditation is required if an agency is placing children from a country that is a party to the Hague Treaty. Accredited agencies for the standard COA accreditation are listed at the COA Web site, www.coanet.org, and accredited/approved agencies under the Hague regulations will be listed at the State Department Web site, www.travel.state.gov.

Foreign Licensing or Accreditation

Some countries have their own licensing or accrediting requirements for agencies that want to place their children. To determine if accreditation or licensing is required, check the additional information section of the Country Charts, as well as the U.S. State Department site, www.travel.state.gov (click on Children & Family, click on Intercountry Adoption, click on Country-Specific Information). Agencies that are licensed advertise it well in their printed material and on their Web sites. To confirm this information, check the State Department Web site and the country's embassy Web site (or call their embassy in Washington, D.C.). The U.S. Department of State, www.state.gov, lists the URLs of the foreign embassies in the United States, but this list is hard to find on their Web site. If you have trouble, search for "foreign embassies in the U.S." in your favorite search engine and you'll find the U.S. State Department list. It is easy to link to the embassy Web site off this list.

Membership

The Joint Council on International Children's Services. This is a voluntary membership organization of international adoption agencies with the mission of promoting ethical practices in international adoption. To become a member, agencies must sign an agreement to abide by JCICS's standards of practice. Theoretically, membership can be revoked if an agency violates these standards, but JCICS is a membership-based organization with no investigative or enforcement power. Membership in JCICS is at least an indication that the agency believes it is important to operate by ethical standards, but it is not a guarantee that they actually do so. JCICS members are listed at their Web site at www.jcics.org.

National Council for Adoption. This is a voluntary membership advocacy and education organization for all types of adoption, not just international adoption. To join, agencies must agree with the general goals of NCFA and provide references verifying its qualifications. As with the JCICS, membership is not a guarantee of ethical practices, only an indication. Members are listed at www.adoptioncouncil.org by country program.

Complaints Against Agencies

Complaints can be made against agencies officially through the proper channels or unofficially through electronic or verbal word of mouth. Reputation and unofficial complaints are covered later in this chapter.

Adoptive parents are often encouraged to check the official complaint history of agencies prior to selection, and indeed, I am encouraging you to do so right here. Although great advice, I wish it were as useful as it sounds. There is no one place for families to file complaints; therefore, finding them is a hit-or-miss process. And just knowing that a complaint has been filed is less helpful than knowing if it was substantiated or how it was resolved, information that is often not available. Nonetheless, you should try.

The regulations implementing the Hague Treaty will make it easier to check for complaints once the United States is a party (not likely until late 2007 or later). The U.S. Department of State (www.travel.state.gov) will maintain a Complaint Registry where complaints can be filed against accredited or approved agencies and will prepare reports tracking history and patterns of substantiated complaints. The accrediting entities will have the power to investigate and respond to complaints about accredited and approved agencies and to take disciplinary action. However, as noted earlier, the Hague regulations apply only to adoptions where both the placing and receiving countries are members of the Hague Treaty. (See Chapter 2.)

Even after the Hague Regulation Complaint Registry is in place, prospective adoptive parents need to conduct their own search for complaint history if they are adopting from a country that is not a member of the Hague Treaty. Also, when the Registry is first open, any previous complaints will not be registered.

The first place to check for any complaints that might have been filed against an agency is with the state licensing bodies. Get their telephone numbers from the Web sites listed under the appropriate sections earlier in this chapter. State licensing boards may be able to tell you if a complaint has been filed, but they may not keep those records unless the complaint has been substantiated.

Complaints can also be filed with the Better Business Bureau in the cities where the agency operates. The BBB Web site, www.bbb.org, lists the telephone numbers and Web sites for the local BBB, and complaint information is available by phone and online.

Some disgruntled adoptive parents may file a complaint with the attorney general of the states in which the agency operates or with the state Office of Consumer Affairs. Call the attorney general's office and ask where complaints would be filed. The National Association of Attorneys General lists the telephone number and e-mail address for the attorney general of each state at their Web site, www.naag.org.

The foreign-country's embassy in the United States or the U.S. embassy in the country you are considering are also potential sources of information about the complaint history of adoption agencies. The U.S. Department of State, www.state.gov, lists the telephone number and e-mail address of both the foreign embassies in the United States as well as the U.S. embassies in the country you are interested in. As mentioned, the list of foreign embassies in the United States is hard to find on the Department of State Web site, so search for "foreign embassies in the U.S." in your favorite search engine and you'll find the U.S. State Department list.

Although you should do your research, don't overreact to one complaint. Adoption is an emotional business, and adoptive parents sometimes blame agencies unfairly for problems. Many excellent agencies have had a complaint or two filed against them. Good agencies try hard to resolve all complaints. Ask the agency about any complaints you uncover. It may be unethical for them to give you specifics, but they can address generally how they would handle a similar issue. Problems happen in adoption, and it's unreasonable to expect otherwise. It is reasonable, however, to expect every attempt to be made to resolve the problem. If you find a pattern of complaints or if you don't think the agency made all attempts to resolve a problem, cross them off your list.

Financial Records

You want an agency that is financially stable, since you will lose money and time and tears if they go out of business during your adoption. How long they have been in business is one sign of stability, and more information can be found in their audited financial statements that you requested in your interview. An agency may not have a financial audit every year; therefore, in addition to their last audited report, also review their latest internal financial report. Review these statements for any indication of a "going concern" problem. Ask a CPA to review if you have no idea what you are looking for.

Reputation

How an agency looks on paper is far less important than its reputation with other adoptive parents. You should not only check the references given by the agency but also ask parent support groups in person or online. First make sure that questions about agencies are allowed on the forum. Some forums prohibit this type of question entirely, some allow the question but require replies to be by private e-mail, and some encourage the discussion on the general forum. Some forums are devoted entirely to agency research and evaluation, such as the Yahoo Adoption Agency Research group. I've included a list of questions to ask references.

I've noticed that general "Whom do you recommend?"–type questions get fewer responses than those that ask about a specific agency and country. Make certain the reference has personal experience with the agency and that they adopted recently from the same country you are considering. Also search the archives for any previous discussion of this agency, but focus only on the most recent. You will get more responses if you include a personal e-mail address, since some parents will share more freely outside the forum.

QUESTIONS FOR REFERENCES

1. What country did you adopt from?
2. When was your adoption completed?
3. What was the age and health status of the child you were seeking?
4. How closely did the child you were referred match what you were seeking?
5. How accurate were the cost and time estimates that the agency gave you?
6. Were there any hidden charges?
7. What was the total cost of your adoption?
8. Was the agency up front about all possible medical issues? Did they help you get additional information?
9. Did you have any problems with the agency? If so, how were they resolved?
10. Did the agency seem impatient with your questions or anxiety?
11. How promptly did they return phone calls and send requested material?
12. Was the agency helpful when you were traveling?
13. Would you use this agency again?
14. Can you give me the names of others who used this agency for the same country and region?

You should also check Internet adoption agency evaluation Web sites. One of the best is the Inter-Country Adoption Registry (ICAR), at www.adopt-achild.org. The intent of this registry is to provide objective information on adoption agencies provided by parents who have used them. Parents supply the following type of information: agency; age of child at referral; gender; waiting time for referral; waiting time for child to come home; country, region, and city of origin; where family lives; e-mail address (optional); and how long since the adoption has been completed. This information is included in a handy chart format, with a section for parents to make comments. My only complaint with this site is that there are not enough entries, and many of them are dated and therefore of limited usefulness to the current crop of prospective adoptive parents. I suppose in the excitement of new parenthood it is hard to find the time to post an entry. Make a commitment right now to file a report after you find your child and bring him home, to help others coming after you.

As with all communication over the Internet, there is no way to verify whom you are communicating with or the truth of what is said. It may be a glowing post by someone working for the agency or a slanderous post by an irrational adoptive parent. Be wise and try to critically assess what you are hearing. Decide for yourself if the parent is being reasonable. Not all are. Are

---

WORDS OF WARNING ABOUT INTERNET FORUMS

Each Internet adoption forum has a personality reflecting the moderator, the participants, or more likely a combination of both. Something about the faceless nature of the Internet brings out the worst in some people. If you find that the people on a particular forum are quick to take offense or are not supportive, change forums. Life is too short to spend with jerks—in person or online.

Take care in your own communications that you are not inadvertently one of those jerks. Without the nonverbal signs we use when communicating in person, jokes, teasing, and sarcasm are often lost in transmission. Although I find the cute icons a little cheesy, I grudgingly admit to their usefulness in communicating nuances online.

The burden of having to type conversations compels some people to use every acronym they know and make up a few along the way. Internet-speak is like another language designed either to confuse the uninitiated or to prevent carpal tunnel syndrome. Agencies are usually referred to by initials and frequently used words are always abbreviated. A list of commonly used adoption acronyms is included in the Glossary at the back of the book. My approach: If it is not obvious, ask.

they basing their opinion on personal experience or what they've heard from others? Do they seem to have a vendetta? Finally, don't overreact to one bad reference. It would be hard to find any agency that has been in business for a while that bats 1.000 all the time or hasn't had the misfortune of a hard-to-please client.

How to Compare Total Costs

Cost can be a touchy issue when talking about adoption. It makes some people uncomfortable because it feels like they are putting a price on a child. They may want to take the "money is no object" approach; but, let's face it, money can be an object and is a factor some families must consider.

When comparing agency fees, it is important to make sure that the same services and costs are included. Some agencies are very careful to include all costs when they quote a fee, while others just hit the high points and add the "incidentals" as they go along. If you are told an amount that is substantially below the norm, be very careful that all costs are included. It's easy to be nickel-and-dimed (or, more likely, $1,000-to-$2,000ed) to death. On the other hand, a high cost does not necessarily ensure high quality and reliability. By using the Cost Comparison Chart at the end of this chapter, you will be able to see where your money is going and exactly what services are included. Also make note when the money is due.

Copy and fill out the Cost Comparison Chart for each agency that you are seriously considering. You will have to ask them if these services are included in their fees. Don't panic when you see the length of this table. Not all these costs will apply for each country, and many of these costs/services will be included in agency or country fees. Some of these costs, such as dossier preparation, are never included in the agency fee, but the agency should be able to give you an idea of how much their families usually spend on preparing the dossier for your specific country so that you can calculate a total cost.

Parting Words

Before you sign any contract or pay any money, have an attorney review the contract you will be required to sign. And remember, good agencies are child focused; they are more interested in finding homes for children than children for homes. Good agencies come in all sizes and flavors, but in my opinion and experience, they share the following traits: They fully educate prospective adoptive parents about all the ups and downs of international adoption and

adopting institutionalized children, they have ongoing programs in the placing countries to help the kids who will never be adopted, they try to find
homes for children with special needs, and they make a lifetime commitment
to you and your child. A good agency looks more like a child-welfare agency
than an adoption agency. It's worth the time to find that type of agency.

FUAQs

*The agency I am most seriously considering requires parents to sign an "Internet
Confidentiality Agreement." What is it and should I sign?*

Some agencies require their applicants to sign an agreement prohibiting
them from communicating certain things on the Internet. Carefully read
the agreement to see what it prohibits. Some of the agreements restrict only
the sharing of medical and social information about the referral, which
seems reasonable to me. After all, the child is not legally yours at that stage
and it is not really your place to share medical and birth-family information about a specific child. It also seems reasonable that you shouldn't
post overly negative information about officials or the adoption process in
another country, since this could negatively impact international adoptions
in general. (Whether I would feel comfortable being contractually bound
to this is another matter.)

However, many of these agreements go much further by requiring that
you not talk about waiting times and adoption costs online. Some attempt
to restrict you from spreading "gossip," whatever that means. Some may go
so far as to prohibit you from even posting your e-mail address on adoption
forums, perhaps to keep you from sharing information outside the forum.

Obviously, only you can decide how comfortable you are with contrac-
tual limits on your communications and only the agency can decide how
comfortable they are with your decision. It is certainly within their rights to
refuse you as a client if you don't sign. Before you pay any money, find out
if your agency requires an Internet Confidentiality Agreement and have it,
as well as the agency contract, reviewed by an attorney. If it doesn't bother
you, then go ahead and sign. Just keep in mind that there are plenty of
agencies that do not require these agreements. In fact, many agencies
encourage their parents to go online for support and education and trust
your discretion on what information to share.

*After years of infertility, we are ready to adopt. We are not getting any younger
and want to speed up the process as much as possible. We have also heard about*

countries closing down and we don't want to lose time by starting over with another country. Should we apply to two agencies at the same time to increase our odds of becoming parents soon?

There are both legal and monetary issues to consider. First, read both contracts carefully to make sure that both agencies allow parents to apply to more than one agency. Applying to more than one agency at a time is expensive. Some of the fees may be refundable if you get a referral faster from the other agency, but some will not be. You will also have the cost of compiling the paperwork for two dossiers.

If you decide to go forward with two agencies, let both know up front to avoid the problem of both agencies submitting your dossier at the same time to the same government. You should think through what you will do if you get two referrals close to the same time. What is the country's policy on this, what are the agencies' policies, and most important, what is in the best interest of the children?

To avoid some of the problems but still give you some peace of mind, consider an agency that places children from different countries. They may allow you to apply to two country programs at the same time, or at the very least allow you to switch programs without a financial penalty.

Finally, remember that adoption is a process that requires a certain amount of time. It's not a race to get the child as fast as possible. Allow yourself the time to become educated on international adoption and to prepare for your child.

FOR EVERY ADOPTION, A DIFFERENT STORY . . .

We had a great experience with our agency from beginning to end. Communication was important to us and we made sure our agency had a policy on returning phone calls or e-mails within twenty-four hours. They always honored that policy, and I think that set the tone for our adoption experience. Adoption is expensive, and we looked for an agency that gave us detailed itemized expenses up front. We had no cost or time-frame surprises. I liked that they strongly encouraged us to get an independent medical evaluation, because again, it showed their commitment to us having all the information we might possibly need. We knew we wanted a local agency because we needed to be able to talk to the people in person. Another advantage of a local agency is that we could attend their monthly waiting-parents meetings, which we found helpful. When selecting, I suggest that people select an agency that is a good balance between professional and nurturing. —*IL, Virginia*

———

Looking back from an almost disastrous adoption experience, I realize that our agency did very little to prepare us for adoption. They required only a minimal amount of adoption education. After we were having trouble, they suggested that we read a book, but we really needed the education before we started, not once we were in the middle of a bad situation. That would be my top warning sign to tell other parents to look for when choosing an agency. —*RH, New York*

———

Our number-one priority when choosing an agency was experience with adoptions in China. We didn't care about the size of the agency or where they were located, so long as they had been placing children from China for a long time. We educated ourselves about adoption from China before we selected an agency, and that helped us weed out the flakes. Some agencies implied that they had political connections in China that "could make things happen" or they guaranteed us a child that was six months old since we wanted one as young as possible. That's a load of bunk; political connections don't work in China, and an agency has nothing to do with the child that you are matched with. We also crossed off agencies whose staff was not professional on the phone or not responsive to us. After we had a list of agencies that met these criteria, we looked to see what they were doing to give back to the children of China. This narrowed the list to just a few, and then we called references and decided. We chose a large agency across the country from us. —*SM, Virginia*

———

It was important to me to have a local agency. I'm the type of person who likes to talk with someone in person rather than over the phone. Also, I knew that I would trust references more if I actually knew them, and I knew people who had used the local agency. It didn't take much research for us to choose the local agency that had placed the most children in our area. —*JF, Florida*

———

Research, research, and then research some more. Go in with a list of questions, and don't put off your questions because the information isn't necessary yet or because you are embarrassed by how many questions you have. Join Internet forums for the country you are thinking about and forums for researching agencies. Call the references and ask them questions. And finally, I personally avoided new agencies since I didn't want to be anyone's guinea pig. —*WM, New York*

The mark of a good agency is one who will be with you for the long haul. Post-adoption services are more important than you think. We adopted almost twenty years ago from Korea and our agency is still helping us out. They are committed to providing services for their adoptees as they age. Last summer they sponsored both my son and daughter at a language program at a Korean university. Spending the summer in Korea was an invaluable experience for both my kids. The social workers at the placing agency in Korea acted as translators for my kids and were available to help them whenever needed. My son was hit by an ambulance while there (banged up, but otherwise fine), and the social worker went with him to the hospital in the middle of the night. Talk about post-adoption services! —*ES, Texas*

At first we thought we wanted a smaller agency, because we didn't want to get lost in the shuffle and I knew I needed a lot of handholding. Much to my surprise, we ended up selecting a very large agency far away because we decided that the most important thing was to have a real expert in adoptions from our country. I never felt like a number, because they had one person assigned to us and that is who I primarily dealt with. I felt an instant connection to this person, and she never rushed me off the phone even when (especially when!) I was just seeking reassurance. When I did my background check, I found that they had one lawsuit against them, but we didn't hold that against them and our experience was great. —*SH, Virginia*

Reputation was the main criterion we had for choosing an agency. We spoke with lots of families and asked why they liked or did not like their agency, and we always asked the big question, "Would you use this agency again?" The answer to that one question speaks volumes. For us it was important that the agency have a permanent location or headquarters. Some agencies we looked at seemed to be patchwork quilts of different individuals working in different locations. We briefly dealt with one agency that had about five different people with different responsibilities who worked from their homes. It was extremely confusing, and communication within the organization seemed problematic. I would also be careful with agencies that are quickly expanding into new countries, since they may not have the best contacts or systems in place. Again, we experienced this with a "highly reputable agency" that tried to recruit us for a pilot program in a new country. As it turns out, there is a reason other agencies are not working in that country. The whole program bombed, and many people wasted time and money needlessly. —*SS, New York*

When choosing an agency, do your research. I felt embarrassed by my long list of questions, but I had to get over that, because it is really important to ask all of your questions up front before you sign the contract and start paying money. It's important to talk with people who have used this agency, but don't just talk with the references the agency gives you. Also ask about them online at country Yahoo groups and agency research groups. I also checked the background and complaint history of the finalists. I've concluded that you can't research too much. —*LL, Washington*

Even though we would have preferred a local agency, we went with one on the opposite coast, because we decided that our number-one priority was a demonstrated experience with Indian adoptions. India is a hard country to break into, and we wanted an agency that had a good reputation in India so their voice could be heard. We also checked to see how much humanitarian aid they give to the orphans who will remain in the country. —*RM, Maryland*

We chose the country we were interested in first, and then, via e-mail, we requested information packets from all the agencies licensed to place children from there. We learned a lot about agencies through this process, since some acted like they were too swamped to provide this information. Once we got the packets, we looked through them and read everything they sent. We realized we might have a problem since we had just married, but we had been together for eight continuous years before our marriage and met all the common-law marriage requirements of our state. When we spoke with the agencies about this, some were sympathetic and tried to help us, some blew us off, and some were rude. As a result, we were able to narrow it down to two agencies and we made the final decision on gut feel. We think we made the right decision, since our agency's willingness to work with us and help us has continued. —*DM, Colorado*

We decided to go with an agency within driving distance, because we wanted to be able to get the paperwork to them in person and not worry about losing documents in the mail. We also wanted the same agency that was placing the child to do our home study. It helped that they had programs in several countries so that we have the option of changing countries if we need to. —*BS, Kentucky*

We wanted an agency with a well-established program in the country we were looking at. We found an agency that is closely associated with the orphanage that we will be adopting from. That gave us confidence. They are not local, but we were more interested in their experience than in their location. We not only called the references they gave us, we also checked out their reputation on adoption forums. They got great reviews, and we have felt very comfortable with our decision. —*KF, Penn*

I found two agencies that seemed pretty equal—one was local and one was not. I knew the local agency could offer me a support group close to home and that was tempting, but in the end I settled on the agency that was not local. They were a Christian organization and placed a high value on humanitarian work in the countries they work in. I was impressed that many people called me to share how much they loved working with this agency, including a call from the head of the agency herself. Their close humanitarian ties with the orphanage were the deciding factor for me. Although at the time I thought of this as good for the kids, I now realize that I benefited as well because their facilitator knew the kids in the orphanage well and was able to do a good job of matching me to my child. I am using the same agency again for my second adoption. —*SR, North Carolina*

—

Although we did our research, nothing stood out with any of the agencies that made us want to use one over the other. We knew we had found the right agency for us when the person I was speaking to suggested several times that we pray on our decision and see where God directed us. I knew immediately that was the sign I was looking for. It is important to have the same belief and value system for a relationship this important. —*DF, Florida*

—

Choosing an agency was a long process for us. I did lots of research and requested information from forty-eight different adoption agencies all across the country. The factor that eventually distinguished the agency we chose from the others was their post-placement service. It was important to us that our relationship with them not end when our child got home. Also, from all the references we talked to, they are an incredibly ethical agency. —*NC, Oklahoma*

—

We ended up firing our first agency because we had so many problems with them and there were so many promises they didn't keep. It was a large agency with a good reputation, but we were adopting from a less stable country and their program was new in this country. We called references before we signed on, but the references had not used the agency for the country we were considering. That was a mistake. With the new agency, we made sure to talk with people who had gone through our country program recently. —*JN, Virginia*

—

I surprised myself by choosing a small agency halfway across the country, even though there are many good agencies in our area. For a decision this important, we thought it was worth the time and expense to fly to their office to meet in person. I'm glad we did, because the director of the agency and I had an instant rapport. I also was able to check out the offices and staff—sort of give it the sniff test. Communication was important to us, and the director stressed that we could call her at any time for any reason and even gave us her cell number. It was reassuring to know that she was always available. She was very forthright on costs, which added to our sense of comfort. Ultimately, we decided that the personality fit was worth the inconvenience of their location. I have never regretted our decision.

The thing you have to realize going in is that all agencies put on a good "dog-and-pony show" when you are interviewing them, so the most important factor to consider is the references. Other adoptive parents who have used this agency have no reason to lie, and in my experience they will be brutally honest with you about their experience. I could tell when I spoke with the references for the agency we chose that they felt a personal connection to the director and they wanted to talk. Even though the references for the other agency were positive, there was just a difference in how our agency's references spoke about their experience. When you find the right agency, you will know. —MS, Virginia

INTERVIEW QUESTIONS FOR ADOPTION AGENCIES

_____

(name of agency)

Country specific:

1. How long have you been placing children from the country I am considering?

2. Are you licensed/accredited in the country I am considering? (Check the Country Charts appendix for those countries that require licensing.)

3. How many children did you place from this country last year? The year before?

4. How many children of the age and general health I am looking for did you place last year? The year before?

5. How many regions within the country do you work in? Or, how many baby homes or orphanages within the country do you work in? (This question is not applicable to China and some other countries.)

6. Do you have someone on staff who is fluent in the language of the country?

7. How are the children cared for in the country prior to adoption?

8. If foster care, do foster parents receive any training and oversight?

9. What are the conditions in the orphanages? How many children per caregiver?

10. Does someone from your agency personally visit the orphanages from which you place children? (This is not allowed in all countries.) If not, how are you informed about the quality of care?

11. If birth mothers are identified, what services are provided to the birth mother? Counseling?

12. Do you have staff in the country I am considering? Do you have subcontractors?

13. Do you use facilitators? What services does the facilitator provide? How often do you communicate with the facilitator? How much supervision do you provide? Is the facilitator paid a fee for services or paid on a contingency basis per child referred or adoption completed? (The Hague Treaty prohibits contingency-based fees, but this legal prohibition only applies when both the United States and the birth country have ratified the treaty.) How long have you been using this facilitator? What are the names of the in-country facilitators? (Not all agencies reveal the names.)

14. What humanitarian services do you provide in this country?

15. How are children identified for adoption?

16. What is the average length of time for a referral of the age, gender, and health of the child we are seeking? What is the longest you have experienced within the last year?

17. What happens if we decline a referral that is offered? How soon can we expect to get another referral?

18. What is the average length of time after referral before I would likely travel to pick up my child? What is the longest you have experienced within the last year?

19. If this is a two-trip country, what's the average length of time between trips? What is the longest you have experienced within the past year?

20. What was the average length of time families were in country last year? What was the longest you have experienced recently?

21. If we decline a referral once we are in the country, what happens? What are the chances of getting another referral while we are in country that meets our requirements? (This only applies to certain countries; see Chapter 8 and the Country Charts appendix.)

22. How often do you send dossiers (collection of documents fulfilling the governmental requirements for adoption) to the country? Once a week? Once a month? (This is only applicable to certain countries, such as China.)

23. What has been your experience with placing children from this country with parents who have been treated for depression or alcoholism or who have an arrest record?

24. What is the total estimated cost of adopting from this country (not just fees paid to the agency, but the total out-of-pocket costs at the end of the adoption)?

25. If cash payments are required in country, do you have a mechanism for transferring funds to the country rather than have parents carry large amounts of cash?

Agency specific:

26. What state or states are you licensed in?

27. How long have you been in business?

28. How many full-time staff do you have? How many part-time staff or subcontractors?

29. How long has the staff been with the agency? Ask specific to the program you will be using.

30. If it is a very small organization, what are the plans if one of the key personnel is unavailable for a period of time?

31. How do you communicate with prospective adoptive parents?

32. What are your office hours?

33. Whom would we contact when we have questions? Will one person be assigned to us? How many cases/clients does this person handle?

34. Do you have a policy to return phone calls within a set period of time? How long should I expect to wait for a reply from an e-mail or phone message?

35. Are you seeking or do you have Hague Treaty accreditation or approval?

36. Do you have restrictions on age, marital status, gender selection, religion, or family size that are not part of the country's requirements? (Keep in mind that this is not necessarily a bad thing, but if you are excluded because of an agency-imposed restriction, you want to know that up front so you can choose a different agency or country.)

37. How much medical, social, and psychological information will we receive on the child? Can additional information be obtained? What steps do you usually take to get additional information?

38. Do you encourage families to get an independent review of the medical records and pictures or videos (if available) by a pediatrician or an international adoption medical specialist?

39. How long do we have to decide on a referral? (See Chapter 8 for a discussion of what is reasonable.)

40. Do you ask clients to sign an Internet Confidentiality Agreement?

41. What is your refund policy at different stages in the process?

42. What is your policy on adopting two unrelated children at the same time? (If applicable.)

43. What is your policy on continuing infertility treatments while pursuing an adoption? What is your policy if we become pregnant? (If applicable.)

44. Have you ever been disciplined or sanctioned by a government or legal entity?

45. How many of your placements in the last three years have fallen apart either before or after the adoption was finalized? (This statistic is one indication of how well an agency prepares families for adoption.)

Services:

46. How much help do you provide with the dossier (paperwork) preparation? (See Chapter 6.)

47. What travel arrangements do you make in country? To and from the country?

48. Do your families travel in groups to the country I am considering?

49. Who supports the families when they are in country? Are they employees of the agency? Subcontractors? How long have these people worked for your agency?

50. Do you have pre-adoption and post-adoption support groups for parents either in person or online?

51. How many hours of parental education do you require? How is it offered? Do I have to attend classes in person? (Remember, you want an agency that wants to educate you.)

52. What post-adoption services do you offer? Counseling for adoption-related issues? Heritage camps/programs? Reunions? Parenting classes?

53. What type of support do you offer for families in the first six months home?

Please send:

1. An itemized list of all costs, fees, or expenses and when they are due. Make sure to include estimates for costs that are paid to others outside the agency (e.g., home study, document preparation, etc.).

2. The latest audited financial statements and the internal financial report for last year.

3. Contracts, liability waivers, confidentiality agreements, or other paperwork that we will need to sign.

4. References (name, telephone number, and e-mail address) of families that adopted from the same country last year and adopted a child similar in age and health to what we are seeking.

Evaluation of feel:

1. How thorough and honest were their answers?

2. How easy was it to talk with the agency contact?

3. Did I feel rushed?

4. Did I speak with the person I will primarily be working with?

5. How knowledgeable did they seem about adoption in general and adoptions from my country of choice?

6. Did it seem like they were more interested in my understanding what to expect, or were they trying to sell me on their program by glossing over potential problems?

7. How clear was information on cost and waiting times? Did I have to dig to get this information?

8. How courteous were all the staff I spoke with?

9. How promptly were materials mailed and phone calls returned?

COST COMPARISON CHART

Item	Cost Due	When Due
Application fee	$	
Agency placement fee		
Placement fee for siblings (if applicable)		
Placement fee for special-needs child (if applicable)		
Placement fee for additional child if unrelated (if applicable)		
Home study		
Review fee for home study (if charged)		
Adoption education costs (may be included in agency fee)		
Dossier preparation costs:		
Will not be included in agency fee, but agency should give you an estimate of what you will spend for obtaining documents, authentication, translations, copies, medical evaluation, psychological evaluation, and postage.		
International fee or country fee:		
Specifically ask if these services have been included. If not included, add the charges.		
· Dossier processing in country		
· Foster care (usually included, but worth checking)		
· Medical report and pictures/video (some agencies charge for duplicating or mailing)		
· Orphanage donation/contribution		
· Translations of documents		
· Car and driver		
· Legal representative in country		
· Court costs		
· Interpreter		
· Guide (may also be interpreter)		
· Sightseeing tours		
International fee for siblings (if applicable)		
International fee for special-needs child (if applicable)		

Item	Cost Due	When Due
International fee for additional unrelated child (if applicable)		
Postage—express or regular for paperwork		
Photocopying		
DNA testing (may be included in country fee)		
U.S. Citizenship and Immigration Service (USCIS) fees		
Fingerprints		
Passports for parents		
Visa for entering child's country (if required)		
Airfare for each trip to country		
Airfare or other transportation costs in country		
Lodging in country		
Food in country		
Souvenirs/gifts		
Child's passport/visa fees		
Child's medical exam		
Post-placement supervisory reports:		
Since these are prorated over several or many years, you may decide not to include at this time.		
Finalization of adoption in the United States (for India and Korea)		
TOTAL	$	
Possible additional charges:		
Medical care of birth mother (only applies to certain countries)		
Medical care of child after referral		
International medicine specialist		
Readoption		
TOTAL	$	

CHAPTER 4

AFFORDING ADOPTION

Getting Blood Out of a Stone

Makenna was born in Guatemala on February 15, 2004, and joined her forever family in July 2004.

Noah and Lisa's insurance did not cover their last IVF attempt, so they paid out of savings. When it failed, they were ready to try adoption but had little savings left. The cost of adoption seemed prohibitive. "It had taken us a long time to get to this place and it seemed so discouraging to be facing yet another obstacle," says Lisa. Because the waiting time for their preferred country was about one year, they decided to start the process before they had the money saved. Between working more hours, spending less, forgoing a vacation, and taking out a home equity line of credit, the costs have all been surprisingly manageable. They intend to pay back the home equity loan with the tax credit. "I've actually been surprised by how the money end of things has worked out," notes Noah. "I'm not usually into the whole tight budget thing, but a kid at the other end is a real motivator."

No matter how you dice it, adoption, especially the adoption of a healthy young child, is expensive. International adoption is a complicated business involving the services of numerous people at home and abroad. Costs vary by country and can be attributed to any number of factors, including child support and travel expenses. It's a fact of life that adoption is a business, and you pay accordingly. See the Country Charts appendix for cost estimates by country and Chapter 3 for a breakdown of the costs. Railing against the injustice of it all will only take you so far. This chapter will take you the rest of the way with suggestions and stories of how others have done it. Obviously, your sacrifices to afford adoption should not be mentioned in later years to your child in a negative way. And for the record, I've never interviewed anyone who regretted the expense once they had their child.

Most people who adopt do not have the money sitting in the bank before they start. The typical family cobbles together the money from a variety of sources, including savings, employee benefits, grants, loans, second mortgages, fund-raising, scrimping, extra work, and best of all, tax benefits. And remember, the money is not all due at once. One of the red flags for an unscrupulous agency is asking for most of the money before you accept a referral. I'll spare you the cliché about long journeys and single steps, but the bottom line is to take it one cost at a time rather than looking at the total sum.

FEDERAL TAX BENEFITS

The federal government gives a tax credit of $10,630 for the cost of adopting a child. The credit amount is adjusted annually for inflation, so consult IRS Publication 17 for the current amount (www.irs.gov). A tax credit is better than a tax deduction, since it comes directly off any federal income tax you owe; in other words, for every one dollar of qualified adoption expense, you will pay the federal government one dollar less in taxes. You can take up to five years to use up the credit. Most of your adoption expenses, including travel, are eligible for this credit. There are income limits, but if your family makes less than $159,450 you can take the full credit and only those families that make more than $199,450 are excluded entirely. (These figures are also adjusted annually, so check the current year's income limits.)

For international adoptions, this credit is available only once the adoption is finalized. The adoption may be finalized when you are in the birth country, or you may have to finalize once you get back to the United States. Basically, if both parents (or the only parent if single) see the child before the adoption is finalized in the birth country, then the adoption is final at that time and you are eligible for the tax credit. If both parents don't see the child or the birth country's international adoption laws do not provide for finalizing the adoption in country, then you will need to readopt once you are back home to be eligible for the tax credit. Read the box on readoption in Chapter 10 for a more thorough discussion. The important point for this stage is that you will not receive the credit until after you pay most of your expenses; therefore, the tax credit is best used as a method of refunding your savings or repaying your loans.

In addition to the federal tax credit, you can also exclude from your gross income any payments or reimbursements your employer makes for qualifying adoption expenses under the employer's adoption-assistance program. An adoption-assistance program must be a separate written plan to offer assistance for employees adopting a child.

There is "fine print," of course—after all, it is the IRS—but the IRS has provided helpful publications. Go to www.irs.gov and search within forms and publications for Publication 17 *(Your Federal Income Tax)*, Chapter 37 (Other Credits). Tax Topic 607 gives further details on the adoption tax benefits. (Search for the word "adoption" and scroll to find topic 607.) During the years that you are seeking this credit, you should consult a tax professional.

Remember that you will receive tax benefits in the future unrelated to adoption since you can claim this child as a dependent and can also get the child tax credit. Further, you should ask your tax professional about ways to utilize the child-care credit and the medical deductions if you are adopting from a country, such as Guatemala, where you are the guardian of the child while the adoption is being finalized in country, and you may pay foster care and medical costs. As you can imagine, documentation of these expenses is very important. Although no one will ever say that kids are good for your finances, at least they help with taxes.

STATE BENEFITS

Some states offer tax benefits for international adoption in the form of tax credits, tax deductions, or reductions in your taxable income. The type of assistance and who qualifies vary by state. The telephone number and e-mail address for your state tax office is available at www.taxsites.com (click on State and Local Tax), or search on your favorite search engine (_____ tax office).

state name

Also, the federal government has a program administered by the states to reimburse families for the cost of adopting children with special needs. The program is primarily aimed at families who adopt children from the foster-care system, but some states also offer this reimbursement to families adopting special-needs kids internationally. Each state has its own rules about when a family must apply and who is eligible, so contact your state early in the adoption process. The North American Council on Adoptable Children has a good summary of each state's position on this reimbursement for international adoptions (www.nacac.org, click on Adoption Subsidy, click on Fact Sheets, and click on International Adoption and Subsidies). They also list the contact person for each state to call for information.

GRANTS

Both general grants and adoption-specific grants may be available to help pay for international adoptions; however, many grants are limited to families adopting special-needs children and others have income restrictions. Most foundations that make non-adoption-specific grants give only to organizations, not individuals, so your universe of potential grantors is limited. Your best bet for finding general grants is the database maintained by the Foundation Center (www.fdncenter.org). They charge a relatively modest fee to access the database for individual grants, but check first with your local library, since many have subscriptions allowing you to use the database without charge. Your library may also have a copy of the current *Annual Register of Grant Support,* which is another source of information on grants.

Additionally, there are grants specifically for adoptions. A list of grants is located at www.affordingadoption.com and at the Child Welfare Information Gateway at www.childwelfare.gov (click on adoption, for prospective adoptive parents, then on funding adoption). Other sources for finding grants are listed in the Resource Guide.

Be very wary of any grant that requires you to pay a significant application fee, or asks for a great deal of personal information (including credit card information) early in the process, or hesitates to send you written information in the mail. Review their written material to see how much they give each year and what type of adoptions they fund. Nonprofit does not necessarily equal benevolent or charitable. What our mothers told us in high school is still good advice: Don't let desire cloud your good judgment.

Before paying an application fee or providing personal information, do your research. Organizations making grants are not required to be tax-exempt, and tax-exempt status is not a guarantee of legitimacy, but at least it's an indication. Tax-exempt organizations are listed in IRS Publication 78 (www.irs.gov, type in "Publication 78" in the search form). I would be suspicious of any organization that charges a large application fee and is not listed in Publication 78.

If the nonprofit grantor is a tax-exempt organization, you can learn a great deal about their finances at GuideStar (www.guidestar.org), but much of it is available only for a fee. Ignore this information and scroll down until you reach the Form 990s that tax-exempt organizations must file with the IRS. Access through GuideStar is free and they provide a wealth of information. You can also ask the organization to send you their audited financial statement for the last year.

It's a good idea to see if the Better Business Bureau Wise Giving Alliance (www.give.org) or The American Institute of Philanthropy (www.charity-watch.org) has any information on the charitable organization you are considering; however, in my experience most organizations that make adoption grants are not large enough to warrant a report or rating from these organizations. Don't forget your best source of recommendations for all adoption-related subjects—other parents. Post a question on your favorite adoption forum. If you are thinking about applying, chances are very good someone else has already been down that road before, and you can learn from their experience.

LOANS

Loans are available from many sources, and you can use the adoption tax credit to help pay them off. Often a home equity loan or line of credit offers favorable interest rates. Depending on how much equity you have in your home, you may be able to pay for all or most of your adoption and your payments may be deductible on your income tax. But be wise: Shop around for the best terms and never forget that failure to pay may mean losing your house. The Federal Trade Commission has other words of wisdom and warnings that can be found at www.ftc.gov (search for "home equity loans").

Most people with tax-advantaged retirement savings plans, such as 401(k) and 403(b), can borrow from these plans. Restrictions may be placed on the purpose for the loan, the repayment terms, and the amount you can borrow, but in essence you are borrowing from yourself and usually at a favorable rate. As with any other loan, there are disadvantages, so talk with your employer or an investment professional.

Many of the same organizations that give grants to prospective adoptive families also make loans at good rates, but these loans will seldom cover the total cost and many are only available for special-needs adoptions. The same warnings I gave for organizations giving grants applies to organizations giving loans.

Some banks and credit unions have special adoption loans with decent rates. They are not well advertised, so you have to ask around. If you have a whole-life insurance policy, you may be able to borrow against the cash value. And of course, trusty old credit cards can always be used for travel expenses. I would only use these as a last resort because of the exorbitant interest rates, although it is worth shopping around for the low-rate introductory offers.

I'm not your mother, but I feel compelled to warn you about going too far into debt. New parenthood is stressful enough without struggling to pay off your adoption loans. Plenty of families have waited another year to build up their savings in order to avoid additional debt.

EMPLOYEE ADOPTION BENEFITS

Every year more companies are offering adoption benefits, often in the form of reimbursement for adoption expenses, with the average reimbursement being just under $4,000. See Chapter 10 for a discussion of another adoption benefit, parental leave. The Child Welfare Information Gateway reports that 39 percent of employers offered adoption benefits in a 2004 survey of 936 major employers.

Even if your company does not currently offer these benefits, you may be successful in getting them to change. Adoption benefits are good for business since they can help retain good employees and increase productivity. Since not that many employees will use these benefits, it's a fairly inexpensive way to score brownie points. The Adoption Friendly Workplace Program, sponsored by the Dave Thomas Foundation, provides a guide, complete with sample proposals, for you to use to help secure these benefits (www.adoptionfriendly-workplace.org).

The U.S. military offers adoption benefits, including reimbursement of adoption expenses. The National Military Family Association has information on these benefits and other information to help military families adopt (www.nmfa.org; search for "adoption"). Look in the Resource Guide for other resources.

Rather than ask your employer to set up a benefit package for all employees, some parents have just asked for a contribution to help fund their adoption. Your company may be willing to help an individual but not yet be ready to establish a companywide policy. You'll never know unless you ask.

FUND-RAISING TIPS FROM OTHER PARENTS

- Yard sales. You'll raise more money by using the following ideas:
  - ~ Choose a location with lots of traffic. If your house is not centrally located, consider holding it at your church or a community center.
  - ~ Ask family and friends to contribute items to sell.
  - ~ Go to other garage sales a few weeks before, explain why you are raising money, and offer to pick up any leftovers they have at the end of their sale.
  - ~ Post signs and tell people who come to your sale why you are raising money. You may get a donation, but more likely you'll hear, "Keep the change."
- Sell things on eBay. Ask friends and family to donate items for you to sell.
- Set up a side business selling products at home parties, person-to-person, or over the Internet.
- Look into credit cards that give frequent-flyer miles on an airline that you can use for adoption travel. If you plan far enough ahead and charge enough on the card, you may be able to significantly reduce your travel cost. This is particularly effective if you own a small business and can charge business costs on this card. Unfortunately, airlines limit the number of seats available for frequent-flyer miles, so you have to book your flights in advance, an option not always available with adoption travel.
- Ask family and friends to donate frequent-flyer miles.
- Ask your company to host a "Jeans Day." Employees donate $5 into a box at the door for the opportunity to wear jeans to work, with the proceeds going to a worthy cause, such as your adoption.
- Can/bottle collecting. Parents report earning a surprising amount of money this way if they live in a state that pays 5¢ per can and if they set up an organized system for collecting.
- Look at your monthly expenses. Fifty dollars per month doesn't seem like a lot, but 50×12 is $600 and that's beginning to sound like real money. Do you really need the second phone line, the premium cable package, or the DSL line?
- Put all loose change in a jar. Families tell me they were amazed at how much money they collected.
- Join the Yahoo group fundraisingforadoption and frugal_adoptions at www.groups.yahoo.com for great ideas and support.

INCREASE SAVINGS

Almost all adoptive families have found ways to save toward adoption expenses. If one parent is planning on staying at home, start right now living off just one salary. It will be good practice to see if you can succeed, and you will save a great deal of money. Another option is for one or both of you to work more hours or take on a second job. One friend worked at a local department store during the Christmas rush on the weekends. She made extra money and got a discount on her own holiday shopping—talk about a win/win situation. A second job for either of you may not be the best decision if you already have kids at home who need your time.

Another great idea is to start putting aside each week or month the amount of money you expect to spend on a child. Ask your friends with babies and toddlers how much they spend a month on their child. The figure many people use for an infant is $10 per day or $300 per month. Take this money out of each paycheck immediately and put it in your adoption savings account, but be careful that you cut back your expenses and don't make up the difference by charging more on your credit cards.

ALTER ADOPTION PLANS

If cost will prohibit you from adopting otherwise, consider changing to a less expensive country (see Country Charts appendix) or consider adopting a waiting child. Many agencies reduce their fees or provide grants for children on their waiting-child list. Do not let reduced fees sidetrack you from thoroughly checking out the agency as described in Chapter 3. Also, don't let money blind you to the reality of what child your family can best handle.

FUAQs

We want to adopt a baby from China but don't have the money. I have read about fund-raisers to raise money, but my sister says it would be tacky because it's asking for charity.

Plenty of people hold fund-raisers to help raise money to adopt, and there is nothing tacky about it. The best fund-raisers are a win/win for you and the participants. The participants should get a good product for a fair price, regardless of whether the "product" is a washed car, an ethnic meal, flower bulbs, or a well-stocked garage sale. By providing value, you are not asking for charity.

Our agency has suggested asking our parents to help finance our adoption of a baby girl from India. We want to think this through before we ask. What are the disadvantages of asking for money?

At the risk of understatement, money is an emotionally charged issue and is handled differently by each family. The primary disadvantage of asking is the emotional backlash if they say no. Your parents don't owe you the money, even if they paid for your sister's extravagant wedding or your nephew's private-school tuition. If they say no, how will that affect your relationship with them?

Have you considered asking for a loan rather than a gift? Establish a fair interest rate; depending on the market, it could turn out to be beneficial to both of you. Treat this as a real loan by putting the agreement in writing and honoring your payments as you would a loan from a bank.

If you are certain of an inheritance, you could ask for your share early. This is tricky, because you are really never certain of an inheritance, and your parents may not want to set this precedent. As mentioned, if you go this route, put the agreement in writing with signatures.

Another approach is to subtly let them know how much the adoption will cost and what you are personally doing to increase your savings by cutting back spending and working more. If they offer to help, great; if not, you won't feel the full force of a rejection. And last but not least, you can ask for money toward the adoption instead of Christmas or birthday presents.

FOR EVERY ADOPTION, A DIFFERENT STORY . . .

When we were unable to get pregnant, we felt very comfortable turning to adoption until we heard about the cost. Our combined salaries are $60,000 and adoption seemed out of our reach. We could either give up or we could find a way, and we were determined to find a way by piecing together the money from various sources. Our fund-raising efforts to date have been the following:

- Compiling and selling a cookbook of favorite recipes from friends and family. The total cost to us was about $1.00 per book and we sold it for $15.00. So far we have raised about $3,000.
- Russian dinner/silent auction. I did the planning, our church let us use the fellowship hall, friends catered, my in-laws purchased the food, friends donated items and I made items for the silent auction, friends

played instruments or sang as entertainment, and the bell choirs from our current church and previous church both performed. It was a great evening and we raised $5,000, plus we sold some cookbooks.

- A BBQ cook-off contest—$700.
- Garage sale—$800.
- Direct-sales fund-raiser party in my home. I got a percentage of the total sales from the party, but I didn't realize that in order for the company to get a charitable deduction they could only write a check to our adoption agency rather than to me directly. I made very little on the fund-raiser and it was a big hassle for our agency and me.

We never asked our family for money, but they have given us gifts to support our fund-raising efforts. I cannot find the words to directly ask anyone for the money, but I have no problem fund-raising since the people are getting something in return. We will borrow the rest of the money from our 401(k) plan and a home equity loan. I have tried everything in my power to get the money for this adoption and I will not let anything, especially money, stand between me and my child! —*LL, Washington*

We didn't let the cost affect our decision to adopt or influence which country we wanted to adopt from. I knew we would figure out a way to pay for it and, of course, the tax credit makes the whole thing doable since we can pay most of the money back after we get the credit. I tried for grants, but I found that unless you make less than $50,000 or are adopting a special-needs child, grants are just not available. I work for a smallish company and didn't think they would add adoption benefits to their employee package, but I did ask my boss if he would sponsor a specific item in our adoption, such as the airfare for our trip to China. My boss said yes! I didn't have anything to lose, so why not ask. —*WM, New York*

We didn't have luck with grants. We did not qualify for most of the grants that are out there because we were not the right religion; we were not adopting from the right country; we were not with the right agency; we were not adopting a special-needs child; our child was too young; or we made too much money. (The best rejection we got was when we didn't answer the following question with the "right" answer: "CREATION: How did it all begin and where did we come from?") In the end, we could only find five that we qualified for, and most of these required an application fee. We were rejected by all but one. Some were clearly scams, since they took our application money and did not even send us a rejection letter. —*LL, Washington*

———

When my husband and I decided we wanted to adopt, I was devastated when I learned how expensive adoption really is. We are not rich and we had absolutely no savings, but we agreed to just go for it. People adopt all the time, and there is no way that all these people have that money just lying around. The key is to take it one step at a time.

We decided to sell anything in our house we didn't need, use, or really want. We also got a huge response from an ad saying that we would pick up leftover yard-sale items. Additionally, my husband found out about auctions at storage centers where you can bid on the contents of the unit when people have not paid the rent. When we had collected enough stuff, we sold the better items on eBay and Amazon and saved the rest for a huge rummage sale. In less than two months, we raised $3,000 and we later made $640 at the rummage sale.

We sent an e-mail out to family and friends and let them know about our efforts to raise money for our adoption. Honestly, the response was minimal. My in-laws claimed it would be charity, and they "don't believe in charity" and therefore "would not contribute one cent." In the end, we received about $350, but if we were to do it all over again, I would not ask for contributions this way. The lack of response left me feeling silly and selfish.

What has helped us the most has been living on a fairly strict budget. We kept a record of our spending for a couple of months and put together a budget with a little wiggle room. Twice a month, my husband and I get an "allowance." The budget has helped us watch our spending and be aware of how much we actually spend on things that don't really matter. With my husband working as much overtime as possible and keeping to this budget, we have been able to bank all the income I receive from my part-time job. My parents have agreed to loan us $5,000 without interest if we can't raise the money in time, but we are doing everything we can to avoid taking them up on their offer. There is no doubt that it will all be worth it in the end and, who knows, we may do it all over again. —*MH, North Carolina*

I am a part-time flex employee with no benefits. I work out of my home office for a small business, so when I heard about adoption benefits, I thought I didn't have a chance. I finally got up the nerve to just ask. My relationship with my boss is somewhat playful, so instead of putting together a businesslike proposal, I sent a playful, yet serious, e-mail asking, "How much am I worth to the company?" I did my research first and included the name of another company that gave $8,000 in adoption benefits to even part-time employees. I also mentioned my need for a raise, since it had been a while since I had one. To my surprise, he not only gave me a raise but will also give me $4,000 in adoption assistance!! Yes, I did scream, dance, and jump around. —*MH, North Carolina*

My husband and I are planning to save all the money needed for the adoption. We have put off applying until we have most of the money, because the country we are interested in moves fast. We took out a home equity line of credit "just in case," but we plan on using it only if absolutely necessary. It is our goal to avoid the slippery slope of debt, especially now that we are starting a family.

We decided not to fund-raise because we don't feel entirely comfortable with the concept. Besides, it would take a lot of bake sales and garage sales to raise $20,000, and my time could be better spent working more during this time, so I can get more commissions. Also, we are relatively new to our community and don't know a lot of people, which would make fund-raising harder. —*DM, Colorado*

Coming up with the money was difficult. We ended up refinancing our house. Early on, we wrote a letter to our parents asking them to help us finance the adoption in any way they could. I was not prepared for my mother saying no, but then again, I don't really think you can prepare for this. I know it is her money and I have no right to expect her to give it to me, but I couldn't help tallying up in my head all the money she has spent on my sister's biological children. I knew I had to get past this for our child's sake, but it hasn't been easy and I wish I had thought through the risk before I asked. —*SG, Washington, D.C.*

CHAPTER 5

SURVIVING THE HOME STUDY

Do I Really Need to Sterilize the Toilet?

Kylea was born in India on March 26, 2002, and
joined her forever family in September 2003.

I f anyone should have approached the home study with confidence, it should
have been me. After all, I thought of myself as a successful parent, despite
the fact that my daughter bit her nails, my eldest son slept on the floor
under his bed most nights (don't ask), and my youngest son had been permanently kicked out of the church nursery for prolonged crying. The interviews at
the social worker's office were a breeze, almost enjoyable, but as the time for the
first home visit approached, anxiety began to creep in. I cleaned and organized in
a frenzy that would put Martha Stewart to shame. Although I didn't sterilize the
toilet, I did bleach my kitchen countertops to kill all germs. I'm not sure why I
thought it was important to have a germ-free countertop, since we are big advo-
cates of the five-second rule—if food drops on the floor, you can still eat it if you
pick it up within five seconds, counted as slowly as necessary to retrieve the food.

I was fairly sane compared to my friend, however. The day before her home visit she cleaned the house spotless, only to decide that it looked too clean to be child friendly. After selectively messing it up to a degree that showed flexibility but not filth, she was still not pleased with the overall effect. She decided that a bulletin board on the kitchen wall would solve the problem. After buying and installing the board, her husband tactfully pointed out that the blank board looked ridiculous. She stuck up the usual organizational junk of daily life, but then decided this made them look too busy and further detracted from the kid-friendly ambience she was seeking. In a moment of either desperation or brilliance, or both, she drove to her sister's house, awakened her niece and nephew, and made them draw pictures for her to stick on the board. Compared to that, bleaching the countertops was nothing.

In a nutshell, the home study is a process to educate prospective adoptive parents about adoption, help them decide on the type of child they can best parent (age and special needs), and evaluate their ability to parent an adopted child. A better name would really be *adoption study*, but although there is movement afoot to change the name, the majority of people still call it a home study. This term refers to both the process and the final report. The final report is required by the U.S. government, your state government, and the foreign government.

HOW TO SELECT A HOME-STUDY PREPARER

Home studies usually are prepared by a social worker licensed in your state. If your adoption agency does not have social workers licensed in your state, you must hire a separate agency to prepare your home study. Home-study providers vary greatly in quality, timeliness, and cost, so it pays to shop around. Home studies can be prepared by agencies or independent social workers, but most placement adoption agencies now require that you work with a nonprofit home-study agency.

Some placement agencies have an approved list of home-study agencies in your state that they require you to work with; others leave the choice up to you. When looking for a home-study agency, experience with international adoption is important. Ideally, you want them to have experience preparing home studies for both your country and your placing agency. In addition to expertise, you are looking for someone you will feel comfortable talking with. Since most agencies have more than one social worker, ask to interview the person who will be assigned to you.

INTERVIEW QUESTIONS FOR HOME-STUDY AGENCY

1. Are you licensed or authorized in my state to perform home studies?
2. Have you worked with my placing agency before?
3. Are you with a nonprofit agency? (If not, check with your placement agency to see if this is required.)
4. How many international adoption home studies have you and your agency completed in the last three years? How many for the country I will adopt from?
5. How closely do you usually work with placement adoption agencies in tailoring the home study to the specific needs of the country and placing agency? Give me an example of this working relationship.
6. Are you familiar with the USCIS regulations on home-study requirements for international adoption?
7. Are you familiar with the specific home-study requirements (number of visits, topics to address, requirements for singles) for the country we are adopting from?
8. What is your opinion on _____? (Fill in the blank if applicable.)
   a. Adopting two unrelated children at once
   b. Single mothers adopting
   c. Past or current counseling or medication for depression
   d. Combining children by birth and adoption
   e. Spanking
9. What is your caseload? How long does it usually take from the last visit until I have the completed home study?
10. How soon can we begin?
11. How quickly do you return phone calls or e-mails? Does your agency have a policy on this?
12. Do you give the family or the placement agency a draft copy of the home study to review before it becomes final?
13. What is your charge for a home study?
    a. Is there a separate application fee?
    b. Is there an extra charge for mileage and travel time?
    c. Does cost include post-adoption reports? If not, how much do you charge per report? Are mileage and travel time included in this fee?
    d. Does cost include criminal history and child-abuse checks, or do parents pay for these separately?
14. If not referred to this home-study provider by your agency, get a list of three references, preferably the names of people who adopted from the same country you are considering.

As with selecting a placement adoption agency, references for the home-study agency are very important, but they are harder to find because you need families in your geographic area. Check for local chapters of the country-specific adoption support groups listed in the Resource Guide. As always, our friends at yahoo.com can help. There is a Yahoo group for adoption for most states, and these groups are a great source for local referrals.

THE PROCESS

While home studies are supposed to educate as well as evaluate, it is obviously the evaluation part that makes parents nervous. While no one likes the idea of being judged, the home-study process seldom warrants the worry it generates. Remember, adoption agencies want you to succeed in adopting. Although they want to exclude obvious nutcases or child abusers, it is not their intent to stand like a sentry at the gates of parenthood, judging the worthy. There are no perfect parents. (Although I know a few who think they are, this smugness generally doesn't last past the diaper stage.) If you have any questions about how something in your background will be viewed, ask your placing adoption agency before the home study. They truly want to help.

I have talked to people who approach the home study as they would cross-examination at trial: the less said, the better. Undoubtedly, it is possible to outsmart your social worker or even to lie and not get caught, but it likely isn't necessary and it prevents the social worker from fully educating you and helping you decide what type of child you are best prepared to parent. And remember, if you are caught in a lie, it may very well prevent you from adopting.

Home studies must meet the requirements of three governments (state, U.S., and foreign) plus your adoption agency. Now is the time that all your hard work choosing a placement agency and home-study agency will pay off. These agencies are your team of experts to help you find your child, and it is up to them to know what needs to be included in your home study to accomplish this goal.

Your placement adoption agency is the expert on the requirements of the foreign government. For countries where the requirements differ by region, they should be thoroughly versed in the nuances (or nuisances, depending on your perspective) of the region and even the quirks of the individual foreign judges. Your home-study agency is the expert on your state requirements. And obviously, both your home-study and adoption agency should know the U.S. Citizenship and Immigration Service (USCIS) home-study requirements.

No set format or procedure must be followed and each social worker approaches the process differently; however, all home studies must address your physical, mental, and emotional abilities to parent through international adoption. In order to do this, most home-study agencies gather information on the topics listed below through various means, including an autobiographical statement, interviews, and a home visit.

AUTOBIOGRAPHICAL STATEMENT

Most agencies ask each parent to write an autobiography and submit it prior to the first interview. The social worker is looking for your history and why you want to adopt. She is not looking for grammar, writing style, or spelling. You do not have to be a good writer to be a good parent, and your social worker knows this.

Our social worker thought she was being helpful when she told us not to worry about the autobiography; it was simply the story of our life. Did she honestly think that description would alleviate anxiety? As if writing the story of my life was something that I did on a regular basis and could just whip out in a weekend! Fortunately, she also provided a list of questions to use as a guide, and I did finish in a weekend. My husband, not the most introspective of guys and prone to procrastinate on any task requiring an analysis of his emotions, took considerably longer. When he finally finished, we shared our autobiographies over a glass of wine and complimented each other on our insight and marveled at how good we looked on paper.

INTERVIEWS

Most home studies involve three to five interviews with the social worker. Agencies differ, but most will schedule a few interviews in their office and one interview in your home. If you are married, the social worker will usually interview you and your spouse jointly and individually. In the best of all worlds, the interviews are a give-and-take of information.

All adults living in the home must be interviewed. Depending on their age, your children living in the home will be interviewed, and some agencies also interview your adult children living outside the home. Some countries, such as China, specifically require that all children over the age of nine be interviewed. It is helpful to prepare your children ahead of time for this interview. The main thing the social worker is looking for is how you parent and how receptive your children are to a new sibling; however, any social worker worth his salt will understand the natural ambivalence children have to sharing their parents.

I prepped/brainwashed our kids for this visit by talking about how much love our family had to share and what great older siblings they were and would be. I also talked about how appearances didn't affect whether we could love someone. (Our son helpfully pointed out that he loved our cat and the cat didn't look anything like us.) We read books about children from all over the world and about families that didn't look alike. We read books on adoption from the older sibling's point of view. (See the Resource Guide for my favorites.) By the time the social worker arrived, our kids were convinced that they had invented the concept of adoption and they were ready to become part of our own mini United Nations.

HOME VISIT

Most of us get uptight at the thought of someone coming into our home to evaluate us. Our home is a safe haven and we therefore feel more vulnerable to the possibility of it being judged as lacking. The home visit is primarily to determine if the home meets the state's requirements for living accommodations. These requirements are usually fairly minimal, such as smoke alarms, fire extinguishers, and basic childproofing. Some states have requirements on bedroom size and well-water testing. Ask your social worker for a list of what she is looking for before the home visit.

The U.S. and state governments do not require that you own your own home to adopt. Most countries don't care either, but some are concerned that this makes the family at risk for homelessness. If you do not own your home, talk with your placement agency to make sure this will not be a problem with the country or region you want to adopt from. Most agencies I talked with said lack of home ownership could be worked around with sufficient explanations in the home study.

While you don't need to go into a cleaning frenzy, you do need to be realistic. The social worker is not going to look under your bed for dust bunnies, but if her feet stick to the floor and dirty underwear is strewn around, that may be a problem, unless it is in your teenage son's room where this degree of filth is considered normal. If your house is a pigsty, clean it, because no matter what anyone tells you, a trashed-out environment does reflect poorly on your general state of mind (to say nothing about your state of hygiene). Lived-in is fine, chaos is not. I suggest you clean up to the level you would if you were expecting an acquaintance to visit.

To prepare for the home visit, I found it helpful to practice a visualization technique I developed. Rather than visualize calm, soothing images as

CHILDPROOF YOUR HOME

Here are some easy, cheap, and logical things you can do to make your home safe for your child.

- Move harmful items (cleaners, knives, flammable liquids, and medicines of any sort) to a place that even a monkey couldn't reach. (Based on my experience with a climber, the analogy is apt and has nothing to do with Mr. Darwin.) If moving these items is not practical, put safety latches on the drawers or cabinet doors. Look for latches that are easy to install, strong enough to keep out a tugging kid, but easy enough for an adult to open without cursing. Do not trust childproof packaging, which is only designed to keep out adults.
- To keep the little Houdinis inside the house or out of rooms that could be dangerous, use baby gates, doorknob covers, or door locks.
- Reset your hot-water heater to 120 degrees Fahrenheit to help prevent burns from hot water. If you think it is necessary, anti-scald devices can also be installed.
- Install smoke detectors outside of bedrooms and on every level.
- Have an escape plan for getting everyone out of the house during a fire. Consider how you will get children out of upstairs bedrooms if the stairs are blocked by smoke. You may need to invest in a collapsible ladder.
- Put a fire extinguisher in your kitchen and learn how to use it.
- Look at your windows, balconies, decks, and landings to see if window guards or safety netting is necessary to prevent falls. Window screens will not prevent a child from falling.
- Use corner and edge bumpers on sharp-edged furniture and fireplace hearths to soften the fall of toddlers and running kids.
- Install electrical outlet covers.
- Cut miniblind cords to remove the loop and install safety tassels and inner cord stops to prevent children from becoming entangled in the cords. New window coverings should meet these safety standards. If you have older blinds, the Window Coverings Safety Council has free retrofit kits.
- Buy a cordless phone. You will need to be able to answer the phone while keeping up with your child, and a cordless phone is a must.
- Install a carbon monoxide detector near bedrooms if you use gas or oil heat, or have an attached garage.

Use your judgment on what to do now and what will only serve as a painful reminder of your absent child. Ask your social worker which ones need to be in place prior to the home study; consider postponing the others until closer to the time your little one arrives.

recommended by those with years of training, I visualized my social worker oversleeping, yelling at her kids as she ran out the door, leaving chaos in her wake. By comparison to that image, I figured my house would be a calm oasis, a virtual respite in the storm. Never underestimate the power of delusional thinking.

TOPICS TO BE COVERED

Your social worker will ask questions on the following topics to help her write the final home-study report recommending you to adopt a child.

Family history. How were you parented? What is your relationship with your parents and siblings? How did your parents discipline? What were any significant losses and how did you and your family address them? How receptive is your family to this adoption?

Education. What type of student were you? What level of education did you achieve? What are your expectations for your child? How flexible are these expectations?

Employment. What is your employment history? Are you satisfied with your work? Do you plan any significant changes after your child arrives?

Relationships. If you are married, how do you and your spouse relate? How do you solve problems and handle conflict? How do you share your life? What do you enjoy together and separately? If you are single, the social worker will ask about your relationship with the significant people in your life. How do you plan to integrate a child into your life?

For singles. The social worker will want to know about your support system. How will you provide opposite-gender role models for your child? What will happen to your child if you die when he is still a minor? Can you afford to raise a child on your salary? Some countries, including China, explicitly forbid placement with homosexuals; therefore, you will be asked questions about your sexual orientation and whether you someday hope to marry.

Guardianship. You may be asked whom you have chosen to be your child's guardian in case you and your spouse (if married) die while he is a minor. The social worker may conduct a telephone interview with this person to verify basic information such as age, health, marital status, children, and financial ability to handle another child. For some countries, single applicants are required to provide a letter from this person or couple.

Hobbies/Interests. What do you do in your spare time? What are your hobbies?

Parenting issues. What is your past experience with children (children of friends and family, coaching, volunteering)? Do you have a basic understanding of child development? How do you anticipate disciplining your child? (Some social workers have very specific ideas on corporal punishment.) What is your expectation of parenting? What are your expectations for your child?

Child care. If both parents will return to work, what are your child-care arrangements? How long will one of you stay home with your child? Some placement agencies have requirements for how long a parent must stay home before returning to work.

Neighborhood/Community. What type of neighborhood, what type of houses or apartments, how diverse? Would your community accept people of different nationalities and races?

Religion. Do you belong to a religious organization? How important is your religion in your everyday life? Do you plan on raising your child in a faith?

Alcohol/Drugs. Have you ever had a problem with alcohol or drug use? What role does alcohol play in your life now?

Counseling/Therapy. Have you ever been in therapy? What did you learn? What is your current situation? Counseling is seldom seen as a problem, depending on the resolution and your current stability; however, it needs to be addressed carefully in home studies for certain countries. Your placing adoption agency will be your best guide, so talk with them before the interview.

Adoption issues. Why do you want to adopt? Why do you want to adopt from the country you have chosen? What is your experience with adoption? Have you resolved the issues associated with infertility? What type of child can you best parent? What age child do you want? What type of special needs can you accept? Have you thought about incorporating your child's birth culture into your lives? How can you help your child feel proud about his ethnicity? Are you ready to parent a child of another race? How do you plan to talk with your child about adoption? What have you done to educate yourself about adoption? Would you support your child if she decides to search for her birth parents?

Health. You and your doctor will likely be asked to fill out a health form. Generally, agencies are simply looking for a normal life expectancy and the physical and mental capacity to parent. Some agencies and countries ask only about current health, while others also ask about your health history. If you have a physical or mental condition you are concerned about, talk with your placement adoption agency early in the process to see if it will be a problem. They should be your advocate and advisor on how to handle this issue.

Finances. You do not have to be rich to adopt internationally, but the social worker does want to see financial responsibility and stability. Some countries have specific income requirements, while others are simply looking to see if you can afford to raise a child. You will likely have to provide evidence of your income through pay stubs or income-tax returns. Agencies also want to see what you have in savings, your life and health insurance coverage, and outstanding debts. If you pay child support, most social workers will ask about your regularity and may ask for proof.

REGRETTABLE ACTIONS IN YOUR PAST

For international adoptions, the home study must address any history of child abuse, substance abuse (including alcohol), domestic violence, and criminal activity (arrests or convictions, minor or major). This information must be given for all adults over the age of eighteen living in the home. The social worker will ask you about this history even if it did not result in an arrest. In order to confirm this information, she will check police records, child-abuse registries, and sexual-perpetrator lists for all adults in the home. You will also submit your fingerprints to the USCIS for an FBI fingerprint check. Do not assume that just because there is no longer a state or local record of an arrest or conviction it will not show up on the federal check. Generally, any arrest or conviction will show up on the FBI fingerprint check. It is imperative that the home study address these violations before the USCIS finds out about them through the FBI check.

A criminal history will not automatically prohibit you from adopting. The nature of your crime, how long ago it occurred, and the extenuating circumstances are all considered. The social worker should explore what happened, what steps you have taken to rehabilitate yourself, and what you have learned from your mistakes. Those who have grown through adversity can make great parents, because when their children face problems they can advise from experience. However, major felony convictions, domestic violence, and crimes against children are definite red flags.

A history of alcoholism or drug abuse also is not an automatic bar, but the social worker must thoroughly address how long you have been sober, what you do to maintain your sobriety, what you have learned about yourself in the process, and what support systems you use to prevent a relapse. If you have specific concerns, talk with your adoption agency early in the process. They can advise you best on how it should be addressed in your home study. Not all foreign countries feel the same about these types of past problems, and your agency can advise you on the best country for you to consider.

ADOPTION EDUCATION

The home study usually summarizes the adoption education parents have received. Agencies must provide prospective adoptive parents with ten hours of adoption education to become accredited under the Hague Treaty, but all reputable agencies, even if they are not Hague accredited, should educate their applicants about adoption. If your agency does not stress parent education, find another agency. You should be educated on the international adoption process, possible delays and difficulties, expenses, the importance of post-adoption reports, and most important, on the possible issues that children adopted from abroad may face, including the health issues of post-institution-alized children. If you are adopting transracially, you should be educated on becoming a multiethnic family. Training can be in groups or individually, online or in person, by book or video. Ask your agency how many hours of credit you can receive for reading this book.

REFERENCES

Both your state and the country you are adopting from may have requirements on references. You will be required to provide your social worker with the name, address, and phone number for three to five personal references. Generally, these references must be unrelated to you, although some countries require a combination of friends and family. Choose people who have known you for a while, have been in your home, have seen you around kids, know of your desire to parent, and can attest to your great character and superior qualities. Good choices are friends, neighbors, coworkers, and ministers or rabbis. Make sure you ask your references for their permission to use them and ask if they can give you an unqualified positive reference. The home-study agency will send your references a request for a reference letter and a list of topics they should address. They will probably be asked about your personality, interests, relationship with children, and what type of parent they think you would be. Often, social workers will call your references as well, especially if they need specific information on a problem. For example, if you have had a history of substance abuse, your references will likely be asked about your rehabilitation and your current use habits.

THE FINAL REPORT

The end result of this process is a final report called the home study that will include the social worker's recommendation on whether you should adopt, as well as the number, age, and special needs of the children for which you are approved. Make sure the final report is written to include all possibilities of children you may adopt. If you are considering a range of ages or special needs or adopting more than one, make sure the final report gives a favorable rec-ommendation on these possibilities. The report should also clearly state your preference, but if you are open to any other possibility, make sure the recom-mendation is not limited to your preference.

The home study will be submitted to your agency, your state, and the U.S. government, and translated for the government in your child's birth country. Slang and colloquialisms should be avoided, because they do not translate well and can cause confusion. Documents such as your birth certificates, marriage license, divorce decrees, health exams, and letters of reference will accompany the report. Some home-study agencies send a draft copy to the adoptive family or to their placement agency for review prior to issuing a final report. This is helpful to correct any errors or misunderstandings.

FUAQs

After my third miscarriage, I was very depressed. I was treated with therapy and an antidepressant. I am doing very well now. Will this affect our ability to adopt?

Every situation is unique, but if you have been successfully treated for depression it should not prevent you from adopting. It will be covered in the home-study process and may or may not be included in the final home-study report, depending on your specific situation, the country you are adopting from, and whether the social worker thinks it is relevant. Social workers are trained professionals, and it is rare to find one who views treated depression as a reason to disapprove a family to adopt. In fact, many social workers I interviewed took the view that families that had overcome problems make the best adoptive parents. There is truth to the old adage that what doesn't break you makes you stronger. And let's face it, some-times depression is a very sane response to an insanity-provoking situation like infertility. All families run into difficulties sooner or later, and those who have had the experience of seeking help in the past will be more likely to seek help in the future if they or their kids need it. During your home-study interviews, address your depression in the context of your losses (if they are related). Focus the discussion on what you learned about yourself in the process, your strength in overcoming a problem, and your willing-ness to seek help in the future for you or your child.

However, not all countries agree. Russian and other Eastern European countries have historically looked very carefully at applicants with a history of depression. If you are adopting from one of these countries, the home study must carefully distinguish past from current depression and treated from untreated. Regardless of where you are adopting from, a history of depression should be raised with your adoption agency very early in the process and before the home study. They are the experts on how the country will view depression and they can best advise you on how it should be addressed. Not all agencies have the same approach, so you may want to call a few agencies to see how they differ.

It is one thing to take a "don't ask/don't tell" approach for something in your distant past, and some agencies recommend this for depression; it is another thing entirely to lie about a current condition. During your home study, you and your doctor will fill out medical forms that will ask for a list of current medications. You and your doctor must sign the forms attesting to the accuracy of your answers. Your social worker will also directly ask you about current medications and health during your interview, and she may ask your references. You would have to be a very accomplished liar to pull this off. Someday when your kid flirts with lying, you are going to tell her that lies are like icebergs; the first lie is only the tip. Listen to your own future wisdom.

Before we were married, my husband was arrested for driving under the influence. He tells me that his record was expunged so he sees no reason to tell the social worker about his conviction. It was a stupid mistake that was years ago. Do we need to raise the issue now?

In most home studies, you will be specifically asked about past arrests or criminal convictions. Further, it is very likely that his conviction will show up on the FBI fingerprint check. If your husband currently has a drinking problem, he must deal with it before you bring a child into the home. If he does not and this was just a stupid mistake that he learned from, then raise it with your placement agency early in the process and before the home study. They will advise you on the country's attitude toward this issue. Chances are good that if it was a long time ago and his record and life have been clean since, you will not have a problem adopting internationally. Being caught in a lie, however, may very well affect your ability to adopt.

What should I do if I suspect the social worker is going to write a negative report?

First of all, don't assume that pointed questioning will result in an unfavorable report. Every social worker has a different personality and style.

Some circle around issues, getting closer with each lap, while others march straight in with their questions cocked. Your concern may just be your defensiveness to the social worker probing a sensitive issue. If her style is not compatible with yours, ask the director of the agency to assign another social worker to work with you.

Specifically ask whether the issue you are concerned about will prevent her from recommending you as an adoptive parent. If she says yes, consider the possibility that she just might be right. Put the home study on hold while you work on the issues she has raised. Ask for her help in getting the resources you need. If she questions your preferences on the age or number of children you want to adopt, listen to her. She has experience and knowledge that you can learn from, if you let yourself.

If you are convinced that she is overreacting to something that is really not a problem and wouldn't be a problem for another home-study agency, stop the home-study process before a final report is written. Yes, you will lose the money you have already paid, but that is preferable to having an unfavorable report written. The USCIS regulations require home-study preparers to ask whether you have previously been rejected as a prospective parent or whether you have been the subject of an unfavorable home study. You want to stop the process in time to be able to honestly answer this question with the next social worker.

Now that we've finally made the decision to adopt, I am anxious to get moving. Should I start my home-study process early to get a jump start? We haven't picked out an adoption agency yet.

You can begin your home study early, but chances are that you will be spinning your wheels, wasting money, and not speeding up the process. It really is best to pick a placement adoption agency first. If you decide on an adoption agency in your state, they will likely prepare your home study, and even if they can't prepare your home study, they may specify the home-study preparer you must use.

Your adoption agency is the expert on what the country requires in the home study and on their own requirements as well. You will have to redo your report if it does not meet the country and agency requirements. Also, the USCIS has specific requirements on how old a home study can be, so once it is completed you will be under pressure to quickly select a country and agency. Your time at this stage is better spent researching and choosing a country and adoption agency and getting educated about adoption. Keep a list of all that you read to show both your home-study preparer and adoption agency—you'll impress your social worker and you may get adoption education credit from your agency.

We have scheduled our home study, which will begin soon. We have not told our two children that we are going to adopt. When and how should we do this?

Most people do not discuss whether to have another child with their children. Let's face it; they really don't have a vote. But since adoption is a different way of becoming a big brother or sister, it helps to explain your reasons so they will understand. When to tell them depends on their age. Young children have little understanding of time, so telling them too far in advance is not useful and can cause undue anxiety. However, older children should be told early enough for them to process the idea, and definitely before the home study if they will be interviewed. (Ask your social worker if she plans on talking with your older children.) See also the discussion in Chapter 7 on this topic.

In our case, the social worker wanted to talk with our older two children together with us present. We talked with them beforehand about how much we had enjoyed being their parents and how we wanted to do it again. We explained that love grew with each addition to the family. To demonstrate this concept, I gave us each a candle in a darkened room. As we lit each candle, we talked about how love was like the flame of a candle—adding more candles did not diminish the flame on any of the candles, and more candles meant more light for everyone. (I thought this was a touching demonstration, but my five-year-old appeared to be interested only in dripping wax on his younger brother.)

Over the next few weeks, we talked about what it meant to be a family and the different ways families are formed. We read books about adoption from the older child's point of view. (See the Resource Guide for suggestions.) You are never really sure what they understand, but our older two clearly thought the idea of adoption was all theirs.

Our younger son was too young for any of this, and I approached adoption just as I would the birth of a child. A couple of months before we thought she would arrive, I started preparing him for being a big brother. We read books and playacted with his stuffed animals. I didn't need to emphasize the different way she would join our family, since how he became a big brother didn't matter to him.

FOR EVERY ADOPTION, A DIFFERENT STORY . . .

I knew that I didn't need to be worried about anything, but I was a little worried that my husband, who is a "silent waters run deep" kind of guy, would come off bored, snobbish, aloof, or disinterested. He is pretty shy and prefers one-word answers to monologues, which is not very conducive to conversation. Fortunately, our social worker did a good job of bringing out his warm, loving side, and she asked open-ended questions as soon as she realized that was the only way to get him to talk. When that didn't work, she gave him multiple-choice questions. He would pause, ponder, and answer, and then she would ask why he chose that answer. This worked well with him. The social worker wants to help you adopt, and they know that none of us are perfect. —SB, Georgia

We did zero research on finding the agency to do our home study because, frankly, we thought it was just a piece of paper we needed for the dossier and that it didn't matter who did it. We got no references and asked no questions; we just walked in the door, filled out the application, wrote a check, and set up the first interview. Not surprisingly, we weren't thrilled with the agency that did our home study. If I had it to do over, I would have asked people online whom they had used and if they would use them again. —MS, Virginia

The home study was more superficial than I thought it would be. I went in thinking it would be more detailed and personalized, and was surprised when there were no probing questions or even questions that required much reflection. I'm not necessarily complaining, but I certainly worried for nothing. —MM, Maryland

It helps to ask for a list of things your state will require you to have for the home visit. Some states require an actual health-and-safety type of inspection. It's all common sense, such as smoke detectors, a way out of an upstairs window, and a first-aid kit. These were all things that I had wanted to get done anyway, but had never got around to partly because of the expense and partly because of the time. You can ask for these things the year before your adoption as gifts for birthdays and holidays. They may seem like strange gifts, but it keeps your costs down. It turns out that dads, fathers-in-law, and husbands love to give fire extinguishers and collapsible ladders. Who knew?!? —*SB, Georgia*

We have had home studies completed in two states, Georgia and New York. I have spoken with many adoptive families, and the home-study process seems to vary a great deal depending on the social worker and the state.

Both of our experiences were relaxed, supportive, and very, very positive. Our social workers presented themselves as facilitators, not judges, and that immediately put us at ease. But the first time, I didn't know it would be that way and I went into overdrive with dread. First we did a full-throttle housecleaning. Then we had endless discussions about what to say and what not to say; how best to present ourselves. Our oldest child was interviewed, so we did a little role-playing with her and laid a little groundwork.

Later, during the process, we had a totally genuine, unscripted argument in the presence of our social worker, which wasn't exactly what we had rehearsed but it ended up working to our advantage. We had an afternoon meeting planned at the social worker's office. My husband and I were coming from different locations, so we drove separate cars. I got a flat tire early on the drive but continued driving anyway on a pancake tire so I wouldn't be late or miss the appointment. When I got there, I told my husband in her office. He was noticeably miffed that I had continued to drive, and he insisted we had to go out and look at the car at that moment (the social worker came with us). The axle was bent and my husband was pretty annoyed. My response was mildly apologetic but also pretty defensive. Heated words were briefly exchanged and then we dropped it. She later remarked that it seemed to reflect a healthy, balanced relationship and decent conflict-resolution skills! —*SS, New York*

I wasn't expecting to be worried beforehand, but I was. I worried that the social worker would think we were not ready to adopt and that deep down we wanted to keep trying for a child by birth. I was also very nervous talking about my family history because of my father's depression. Things in my family were pretty bad for a few years, and although we weathered that time, I wanted to put as positive a spin on it as I could. It was particularly nerve-wracking because the social worker had to interview my parents separately since we all live together. I didn't want her judging my parents in any way, and I was worried about what my father might say simply because he can sometimes say things that come out of left field. Having my parents under the microscope was unsettling, because I couldn't be there to guide the conversation. I wanted to be in control, but I wasn't. Thankfully, none of this turned out to be a problem. My parents did great, and we actually spent very little time on family-history stuff. —*MS, Virginia*

Even though we live in a small town and there weren't many options on agencies to do our home study, it was important to us to have someone from our town. Our home study was done in the winter and we needed someone local, because the roads can get pretty iffy up here. But the main reason we wanted someone local was because we thought they would be more likely to "get us." We live in a small mountain town and we thought that someone from here would understand us better. Also, we have two large dogs (as does most of the population of our town) and we wanted someone who would be comfortable around them during the visit and would understand that kids and dogs can coexist. —*DM, Colorado*

Parts of the adoption process cause you to reflect on many things, especially the home study. Even though the social worker is on your side, you still worry. The home visit is especially tough. Is the house at the right level of cleanliness? Too clean might mean you'll have trouble dealing with the inherent disorder that goes with kids, but too dirty means you are slobs. Does the house smell funny? What does the house of a good parent smell like, anyway? Worries and concerns keep piling up.

The one thing that I was very anxious about was the cat population on our farm. Sure, we don't have any mice, but you can almost hear the herd of cats when you drive up to our house. I told her we would try to give some away if it was a problem. Not only was it not a problem, she asked if she could have one of the kittens. Then we worried that the kitten would tear up her house and she would be in a bad mood when writing our home study. So many insecurities can go through your head—it is ridiculous! Of course, it wasn't a problem, and she has promised to give us regular post-placement reports on his progress.

It is unavoidable that you will feel judged, because in fact you are being judged. This didn't bother me too much, since I'm a teacher and there have been many times that I wish some of my students' parents had been judged before they had a child. Having an egg and sperm does not make you good parents! —*KF, Iowa*

CHAPTER 6

PREPARING THE PAPERWORK

Our Version of Labor

Cassie was born in South Korea on April 2, 2001, and joined her forever family in July 2001.

When Peter and I were first starting the adoption process, being an overachiever, I immediately read everything our agency sent me from start to finish. When I came to the list of documents we would need, forms we would have to fill out, and governmental requirements both foreign and domestic, I was completely overwhelmed. I didn't even know what the word apostille *meant, and I am an attorney! I strongly recommend not skipping ahead in the process. It's like reading the chapter on labor when you're first pregnant. Some things are best not known at the beginning.*

Now, years later, when my daughter asks me to tell her how she came to be ours, her favorite part of the story is how hard we had to work to get her. Over the years, the stack of papers that Mommy and Daddy had to fill out has grown to higher than her arms can reach, and her smile grows with each additional inch.

International adoption is not for the fainthearted, and a strong constitution is needed more at the paperwork stage than at any other stage so far. Your agency is the expert on exactly what is needed, and they will guide you. Although it looks daunting, trust me, the process is more tedious than difficult, and you simply have to plod your way through. How long the process takes is mostly up to you. I've interviewed people who have completed it in less than a month and others who have taken over six months.

Before I address the specifics, allow me to preach for just a moment. Try not to view the seemingly endless paperwork as a roadblock being put in the path between you and your child. Try, as hard as it may be when you are standing in line yet again in front of your friendly (or not) neighborhood notary, to see these requirements as the governments', both domestic and foreign, honest attempt to make sure that these children go to the best possible families. For our children to have a positive self-image, it helps for them to have a positive image of their country of birth and adoption. One of our jobs as adoptive parents is to help our children understand that there were people in their birth country and in the United States who cared about them and wanted the best for them. They were not unwanted discards being rescued by noble Americans; their country of birth wanted to find good homes for them and went to great pains to do so. The paperwork that you are preparing now is tangible evidence of this concern by both countries.

Also, think of it from the standpoint of the governmental officials in your child's birth country. It has to be difficult for them to read in their newspapers about a horrible incident involving one of their children adopted abroad. This is bad for them and bad for international adoption in general. All the paper chasing, all the notarizing, all the apostilling, and all the standing on your head and holding your breath is to ensure that the good guys in your child's home country can sleep at night. It's the least we can do for the gift they are giving us. Okay, the sermon is now over; please open your hymnals and get ready to sing "Bringing in the Sheets (of paper)."

International adoption is complicated because so many governmental fingers are in the pie. Prospective adoptive parents must comply with the adoption laws of the foreign country, the immigration laws of that country, the immigration laws of the United States, and the adoption laws of their state. A little-known law of physics (or would this be mathematics?) has established that paperwork and headaches increase exponentially with the number of bureaucrats involved. Although at first glance the requirements seem complex, as an adoptive parent here's all you really need to know.

A BORING (BUT BLESSEDLY BRIEF) LEGAL OVERVIEW OF U.S. REQUIREMENTS

Your child-to-be is a citizen of another country. To enter the United States legally, all foreign citizens, including your child, must be processed as an immigrant. The keeper at the immigration gate is the U.S. Citizenship and Immigration Service (USCIS), which in the past was the INS before it was swallowed by the Department of Homeland Security. (For the trivia or acronym lovers among you, it was also known as the BCIS for a short time during the transition.) To further complicate the matter, the U.S. Department of State is also involved in international adoption, but not from the immigration and paperwork side of things, so I'll leave them out of the discussion.

The USCIS must issue a visa for immigrants to enter the United States, but fortunately they have a policy to expedite the processing of orphans. Don't get too excited about the use of the word *expedite*. When used by a governmental agency it does not necessarily mean *fast*, but in fact your child will be avoiding the usual long wait for a U.S. visa. In order to approve a visa for your child, the USCIS must do two things. First, they must make a determination that the prospective adoptive parents are capable of parenting; and second, they must decide that the child is eligible to be adopted. Both of these tasks take time, but determining your parenting capability can be done before a child has been referred to you for adoption, thus speeding up the process once you find your child.

You will submit your forms to the USCIS office with jurisdiction over your area. To find the correct office, look up field offices at www.uscis.gov. The forms are also available at this Web site. You can fill out the forms directly online and print them off for submission. There is surprising variation in exactly what each USCIS field office requires. For example, some offices require that the home study specifically name the guardians selected by the parents, but other offices require only that the home study state that guardians have been selected. Some offices require that the child-abuse check be attached to the home study, while others require only that the home study state that the check was clear. There is also a great deal of variation in how fast each office will process the forms. Your home-study preparer should know the nuances of your particular USCIS office.

The paperwork moves through the USCIS along the following path:

1st Step: Form I-600A, Application for Advance Processing of Orphan Petition

This application allows the USCIS to make the determination about your ability to parent an adopted child. By getting this part of the process out of the way, once you find a child that you want to adopt, the USCIS only has to determine the child's eligibility to be adopted. In addition to the I-600A form, you must send the following:

- Proof of citizenship. (Only one parent needs to be a citizen, but the other parent must submit proof that they are legally in the United States.)
- Proof of marriage, if applicable.
- Proof of divorces, if applicable.
- Proof of compliance with your state's pre-adoption requirement, if your child will have an IR-4 visa. (See box.) Your agency can tell you if this is necessary.
- The application fee. For the current fee, check the USCIS Web site at www.uscis.gov.
- Fingerprints for each adoptive parent. Fingerprints will not be submitted at the same time as the I-600A form. Once you submit the I-600A form, the USCIS will send you an appointment time and place for your fingerprints. After this appointment, you will submit your fingerprints.
- A home study with a favorable recommendation for adoption that meets the USCIS requirements. See Chapter 5. The home study does not have to be submitted with the I-600A application, but must be sent within one year. Your I-600A will not be approved until it has been submitted.

2nd Step: Form I-171H, Notice of Favorable Determination Concerning Application for Advance Processing of Orphan Petition

Once the USCIS has approved your I-600A application and home study, they will send you an I-171H form. Keep this safe, since in most cases it must be included with the documents you send to the birth country.

3rd Step: Form I-600, Petition to Classify Orphan as an Immediate Relative

When you have a referral of the child you are going to adopt, you will submit Form I-600. You must provide specific information on the child to prove that she meets the USCIS definition of orphan. Don't worry; any child referred to you by a reputable international agency will meet this definition, and the agency will provide you with all the proof the USCIS requires. The final processing of this document will be at the U.S. Consulate office in your child's birth country, and your agency should have personnel on hand to help. If you are adopting independently, be very careful of this step and work closely with the U.S. Embassy's Adoption Department in your child's birth country. No additional fee is charged if you file Form I-600 within a specific time frame.

It is also possible to skip the I-600A process and submit all documents with the I-600 form, but since most parents begin the adoption process without a specific child in mind, the usual method is to file the I-600A first.

VISAS 101

Children adopted from abroad are required by U.S. immigration law to have a visa to enter the country. Your child can enter on an IR-3 or IR-4 visa.

- IR-3 visas are available when the adoption is completed in the birth country. This includes most placing countries except Korea and India. However, before the United States will issue an IR-3 visa, both parents (if married) must have seen the child before the adoption was finalized.
- IR-4 visas are for all other circumstances, including those in which:
  - ~ only one parent (if there are two parents) sees the child before the adoption is finalized in country
  - ~ neither parent sees the child before the adoption is finalized in country
  - ~ the country's law requires that the child be sent to the United States under the guardianship of the agency or parent, with the adoption being finalized under the laws of the state of residence

Why should you care about visa types? You probably don't care about the intricacies of visas, but you should care how these visas affect your child's U.S. citizenship and the availability of the federal or state adoption tax credits. (See Chapters 4 and 10.) For most countries, if both parents traveled to the country and saw the child prior to finalizing the adoption, the child is issued an IR-3 visa and will automatically become a U.S. citizen when she enters the United States and you are eligible for the adoption tax credit at that time. You will receive her Certificate of Citizenship in the mail within about forty-five days. If your child was either not seen by both parents or was adopted from a country that does not complete adoptions before the child leaves, she will come into the United States on an IR-4 visa and she must be readopted according to the laws of the state where you live. Only after she has been readopted can you apply for her U.S. citizenship and are you eligible for the adoption tax credits. Keep in mind that some birth countries require that the child maintain dual citizenship up to a specified age, usually eighteen.

CALLING IN THE BIG GUNS

If you are having trouble getting documents through a federal government agency, ask your representative or senators for help. Most have a designated person on staff to help their constituents with government snafus. The easiest way to find out the names and contact information for your representative and senators is to go to www.house.gov and www.senate.gov and enter your zip code or state into the search form. You can call either their state or Washington, D.C., office. But—and this is an important but—wait a reasonable amount of time before you decide you are having problems with an agency and need to call in the big guns.

AN EQUALLY BORING (BUT BRIEF) LEGAL OVERVIEW OF THE BIRTH COUNTRY'S REQUIREMENTS

When you are in the midst of all the paperwork, it is easy to think that you are a puppet on the string of a sadistic or at least paper-crazed governmental puppeteer. Believe it or not, there is a simple and somewhat logical reason behind most of the requirements. Even I will admit that some are inane, but for the most part, the hoops the foreign government makes you jump through are logical when viewed from their perspective.

Foreign countries need to make sure that you legitimately want to adopt and parent their children and that you are capable of doing so. They set up requirements that they think will "prove" that you are mentally, physically, and legally up to the task. Each country decides what they want to see in potential adoptive parents. For example, some countries have specific financial requirements, some have marriage requirements, and some have more stringent health requirements. See the Country Charts appendix. Some countries are well-oiled machines with little change year after year, while others are in a state of flux with requirements changing frequently. If you choose a less stable country, have the good grace to roll with the punches without too much complaining.

A country obviously can't just take your word for something as important as your ability to parent, so they require you to present documentary evidence to support your qualifications. These documents will be compiled and the resulting package is called a dossier. Each country's dossier will be different, depending on what they think is necessary to prove that you are capable of parenting one of their children.

In this day of high-quality computer software, you could easily trump up official-looking documents and a foreign official may not be able to tell the difference, so they require proof of the authenticity of your documents. It's easiest to understand with an example, so let's take the employment letter most countries require from your employer stating your salary and your prospect of continued employment. Your employer writes the letter and signs it. Her signature verifies the truth of the information in the letter. But how does the foreign government know it was actually your employer and not you who signed the letter? They don't. So, depending on the foreign country and your state, the following convoluted process might be required to prove the authenticity of her signature.

Each state in the United States uses notary publics to verify the authenticity of signatures; consequently, your employer must sign in front of a notary public (see discussion on notary publics later in this chapter). But how does the foreign country know that the notary is a real notary and not your brother-in-law with a fancy-looking stamp from Office Depot? They don't. So in order to prove the authenticity of the notary, you send your employment letter with the seal and signature of a notary to the clerk of court of the county where the notary is registered. The clerk of court checks their notary registry, and if everything looks right, they attach their seal authenticating that the notary is registered in that county and is in good standing. But how does the foreign government know that the county clerk of court's seal is authentic? They don't. So you must then send the employment letter to your secretary of state (or other notary regulating office) for a seal verifying the authenticity of the county clerk of court's seal. But how does the foreign government know that the state's seal is legitimate? (Are you beginning to see a pattern here?) They don't; therefore, you must send your employment letter with the seals of the notary, county clerk of court, and secretary of state firmly affixed to the U.S. State Department for a seal attesting to the authenticity of the state seal. All together now: But how does the foreign government know that the seal of the U.S. Department of State is legitimate? They don't. (Sigh.) So the final step is to send your humble employment letter that is now weighted down with seals from the notary, county clerk of court, state, and State Department to the foreign country's embassy in the United States to authenticate the U.S. Department of State's seal. The employment letter is then returned to you for inclusion in your dossier with a trail of authentications that proves to the foreign government that you are indeed employed and have every reason to expect that you will continue to be employed. This same authentication chain must be repeated for most of the documents in your dossier, with each successive link verifying the legitimacy of the previous step.

The actual authentication process that you will follow varies depending on

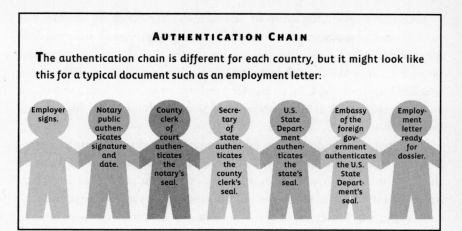

AUTHENTICATION CHAIN

The authentication chain is different for each country, but it might look like this for a typical document such as an employment letter:

Employer signs.

Notary public authenticates signature and date.

County clerk of court authenticates the notary's seal.

Secretary of state authenticates the county clerk's seal.

U.S. State Department authenticates the state's seal.

Embassy of the foreign government authenticates the U.S. State Department's seal.

Employment letter ready for dossier.

several factors, including the type of document and your state of residence. Governmental documents issued by a state government are certified by the issuing state and do not need to be notarized; hence, the notarization step can be skipped for documents such as a birth certificate, divorce decree, and marriage license. For documents that require notarizing, some states do not require that the notary's seal first be authenticated by the county clerk of court, so this step in the chain can be omitted.

Authenticating the legitimacy of documents from another country is standard practice for all sorts of business dealings between countries, and the U.S. government makes foreign nationals do the same when they present documents from their country in the United States. Our rules undoubtedly seem just as arcane to them as their rules seem to us. In order to streamline this cumbersome process, an international treaty was drafted known as The Hague Legalization Convention (convention is just another word for treaty). This treaty greatly simplifies the authentication process when both countries are parties, since parties agree to recognize a special "apostille" certificate as proof of the authenticity of the notary or the state's certification of government-issued documents. Thus, all successive steps up the chain are avoided, saving you time and money. The United States is a party to this treaty, so if the county you are adopting from is also a party, you can use the apostille method of authenticating the documents for your dossier. In the United States, the states issue the apostille certificate. To find out if your country is a party to this treaty, ask your agency or go to the U.S. State Department site: www.state.gov. (Search for the term "authentication," then scroll down the list until you find a document titled "Authentication of Documents for Use Abroad," which lists member countries to the Hague Legalization Treaty.)

Each state's apostilling authority sets its own rules. Some require that you send the document itself, while some do not. Some allow you to bring the documents in person, while others require that they be mailed. Fees per document range from free to $25. Call your state apostilling authority to find out the specifics for your state. Contact and fee information for your state's apostilling authority is included in "Authentication of Documents for Use Abroad," referenced earlier.

Keep in mind that documents must be authenticated in the state where the document originated. You very likely will have documents issued by more than one state if you were born, married, or lived in more than one state; hence, you will need to follow the procedures for each state where your documents originate. For example, if you are living in California but were born in New York, married the first time in Florida, divorced in Pennsylvania, and married the second time in Texas, you will need to get documents from California, New York, Florida, Pennsylvania, and Texas.

Some requirements for your dossier are actually your agency's suggestions based on years of experience. By choosing an experienced agency, you have someone on your team who has seen how the process works and what additional documents help things flow smoothly. You should be getting used to this refrain: This is where your agency earns its money. They are the experts;

NO-HASSLE MAILING HINTS

- Include a cover letter when sending or requesting any documents. Your name, address, telephone number, and e-mail address should be included in the letterhead or following your signature.
- When sending more than one document, list them with bullets in the text of the cover letter.
- When sending documents, print in bold letters on the envelope "Important International Adoption Documents Enclosed."
- Include a sample letter when asking others to prepare documents, such as your employment letter, financial statement, or police report. Ask your agency for an example of what the foreign country has found acceptable in the past.
- Always use a mail service that allows tracking.
- If you are looking for a fast turnaround of documents, include a self-addressed, prepaid FedEx, UPS, or DHL envelope with your original letter.
- Some state apostilling authorities will send your apostilled documents directly to your adoption agency if you include a prepaid envelope.

rely on them. Requirements change, and for some countries they change more frequently than others, and your agency should know what is current since they are in the field working with the government officials and judges. Some agencies provide a great deal of help with the authentication process as part of their fee. At the very least, your agency should provide you with a detailed list of what is needed and how to get your documents authenticated.

THE NOTARY DEVIL IS IN THE DETAILS (OR THE DEVIL IS IN THE NOTARY DETAILS)

By the end of your dossier preparation, you will have a new best friend (or worst enemy)—your notary. A notary public is a public official appointed by the state to serve the public as an impartial witness to the signing of documents and certifying copies of nongovernment documents.

State law governs the regulation of notaries and there is a great deal of variation between states. In most states, a notary can use either a stamp or a seal. Government-issued documents, such as birth certificates, do not need to be notarized before they are certified or apostilled by the state. The notary may or may not need to witness the actual signature, depending on the document, the foreign government, and your state law. Ask your agency and the notary what is required.

Finding a notary is usually not hard. When possible, try to use the same notary for all or most of your documents. This caution is most important in states that require authentication from the county clerk prior to the state authentication. If you live in such a state and use notaries registered in different counties, you will have more running or mailing around to do with each notary you use.

To find a notary, first ask around at your work, church, neighborhood, and clubs. You'll be surprised how many people are notaries. Most states do not prohibit using a notary who is related to you, but since a notary must avoid any conflict of interest, it is probably safer to use someone not related, or at least not closely related. Of course, you can also check with your adoption agency (if local) and home-study agency, since they often have notaries on staff. If you strike out with these suggestions, look at your bank, lawyer's office, or insurance agent. Some banks limit the number of documents they can notarize but may waive the limitation if they know it is for an adoption. Some city halls provide a notary service for free, and some memberships in organizations such as the American Automobile Association come with free notary services. It may be cost-effective to join or upgrade your membership.

Prices for notarizing vary, but costs will add up depending on what you pay per document.

A potential problem often arises in adoption with the notarizing of the medical evaluation. Most doctors' offices do not have a notary on site, and doctors are generally not willing to come with you to a notary to sign the medical form. Some parents have had luck finding a notary at the hospital where their doctor has privileges. Since the doctor already has reason to go to the hospital, it is less of an imposition to ask her to sign the form in front of the notary there. Others hire a traveling notary to accompany them to the doctor's office. Try looking up notaries in the yellow pages or on the Internet and ask if they travel. The price should not be exorbitant. This is where it really pays to have a notary who is a friend. In exchange for a nice meal or your undying gratitude, most friends will gladly help out.

Notarization for adoption documents is different from the notarizations that you have done in the past, because these documents will be sent to a foreign government; therefore, the notary's seal and signature must be certified, apostilled, or otherwise authenticated. Many notaries are not familiar with this process, so the burden is on you to pay attention to the details.

Each time you have a document notarized, make certain the notary completes the following steps:

- Sign exactly as he is listed on his notary commission paper.
- Print or type his name under his signature exactly the same way he signed.
- Include the expiration date of his notary commission.
- Include his county and state of residence.
- Include the date he signed.
- Seal or stamp as a notary public.

Make certain that the name and expiration date on the notary's stamp or seal is identical to the information at the secretary of state's office. Most secretary of state Web sites have a searchable directory for notaries, and you can save time and hassle by checking this directory up front to verify exactly how the notary's name is listed and the expiration date of his commission. The notary's signature must match exactly how he is registered with the secretary of state. For example, states may refuse to authenticate if the stamp or his signature includes his middle initial but the state has him listed with his middle name spelled out. Others have run into problems with minor discrepancies on the expiration dates between the seal and the registration.

Points to remember:

- Consider asking a friend or distant family member to become a notary. It is not costly, usually only involves a minimum commitment of time for training, may help them in their employment, and will save you time and inconvenience during your adoption.
- Look for a commission expiration date at least one year out when choosing a notary. Check with your agency as to what they recommend for the country you are adopting from, since countries vary as to how picky they are about the notary's commission expiring once your papers are in country.
- Make sure the stamp or seal is fully on the document and is not slightly off the paper's edge.
- Make sure the date of the notarization is the same as the date of the signature.
- Not all countries are this picky, but to be safe, make sure the notary signs on the same page as the signature.
- Redo the document if the notary makes a mistake. The legal system of other countries is no less picky than our own, and most don't like white-outs or cross-outs.
- Do not unstaple for copying any document that has been notarized.
- Check with your agency when in doubt as to what will be acceptable or how to solve a particularly sticky notary problem. That's why you pay them the big bucks!

ORGANIZATIONAL SYSTEM

I must confess that I am an absolute organizational nut. Strange, isn't it? Chalk it up to overzealous potty training in my childhood or an abnormal need for control, but whatever the cause, almost nothing brings me more pleasure than organizing a messy drawer or stack of papers. Fortunately, my inherent laziness keeps me from going overboard; indolence is a great counterbalance to obsession.

Even if you are not similarly turned on by organizational theory, there are some practical reasons to organize your adoption paperwork. Given the sheer volume of paper, without an organizational system, chaos reigns. It will take you longer to complete your dossier and increase the likelihood of making a mistake, thus adding even more time to the process. Perhaps most important, an organizational system reduces anxiety and gives you the illusion of control.

But an organizational system is only helpful if you use it, and for me to use a system, it must be simple.

Each additional step in a system reduces the likelihood of follow-through. Recently, a friend showed me her adoption paperwork binder, complete with color-coded divider tabs and plastic protective sleeves. I felt the flutter in my heart that is usually reserved for Brad Pitt and Elfa organizers. But, as much as I admired her system, I would never be willing to keep it up. Just adding the extra step of three-hole punching would guarantee that I revert to the piling method of organization. My system may not be sexy, but it is effective.

Simplicity means that you group like documents together and in order. Documents needed for the I-600A form are located together and filed before documents needed for the dossier, since you usually file the I-600A before you complete your dossier. Simplicity also means reducing wasted motions; one-step is better than multistep filing. For example, filing in an open file is faster than putting each document in a plastic sleeve. Don't overorganize by being too precise. This just kills time and doesn't really help you find anything much quicker.

Keep all necessary supplies nearby. Every time you get up to go look for the stapler provides an opportunity to not return. If you usually use something when you are working on your adoption paperwork, keep it with your filing system. For example, I kept a file folder labeled "supplies" at the back of my filing system with a mini stapler, pen, stamps, envelopes, and yellow sticky pads.

Consistency in place, method, and time is also essential for success. It helps to have all your adoption paperwork in one location rather than scattered among your office, your dining room, and your bedroom. Be consistent with how you file. Whether you file more recent documents in the front or back of a folder doesn't matter, but whichever you choose, be consistent each time so that your papers within the file are in order. If you are one of the tribe of procrastinators, choosing a set time each week or day to accomplish one adoption paperwork task is helpful. In my experience, even hard-core procrastinators are prompt about the adoption paper chase. A child is a good motivator.

My paperwork plan consists of a master checklist, a filing system, and a calendar. Many agencies send prospective parents a paperwork checklist. This list is a good starting point, but it is usually limited to documents needed for the dossier and doesn't include those needed for your home study or those documents that are specific to your situation, like divorce decrees and birth certificates for the children already in your home. I want you to be able to look at one document to see everything that needs to be done. The mounting check marks will serve as proof that you are making progress.

To compile your checklist, get the list of documents needed for the I-600A form, your home study, and the dossier for the country you will adopt from. The list for the I-600A can be found at www.uscis.gov under Forms/Fees. Your home-study agency should send you a list of required documents for your state, and your adoption agency should send you a list of documents and other items required by your child's birth country. If your agency told you something specific about the document, briefly include this on your checklist. For example, include the fact that the copy of your doctor's license must include the expiration date (if this applies).

You can create the checklist on your computer or by hand. Each document will be listed in a separate row. The number of columns you need will depend on the state you live in and the country you are adopting from. An example of a checklist for a Russian adoption in a state requiring county certification is shown.

Your checklist is a complete list of documents that are needed, not a list of documents that need to be authenticated. For example, list your autobiographies and photographs, even though neither needs to be authenticated. Just mark through the column space for certification.

Put the date in each column as that step is completed. In the column for number needed, put a check mark for each copy when it is completed so at a glance you can see what remains to be done. For example, if your country requires five reference letters, you can quickly see that you only have three checks and are waiting for two more.

Whether you keep your checklist on your computer or print it is up to you. However, I think it is important to have the checklist with the files, so unless you have a laptop or keep your files by your computer, print a copy. If you use a paper copy, leave several blank rows, since you will likely remember other items to add as you go along.

Use a hanging file system—either plastic stackable filing crate (also known as milk crates) or a metal frame—to keep the paperwork organized. Use legal-size hanging files. (I would personally avoid the baby-poop-brown ones just on principle. You might as well surround yourself with pretty colors when possible, although I suppose the color of baby poop is in keeping with the general theme of adoption.)

Each document will have its own file folder. The folders are roughly organized chronologically according to need. The documents needed for the I-600A precede the documents needed for the home study, which precede those for the dossier. Note that some documents are needed for all three. Separate the documents needed for each spouse. Some people have a separate folder for each step in the authentication chain, but that is too fussy for me. I only

Example of Master Checklist

(This is only an example. Check with your agency for the specific requirements for your country and state.)

Document	Date Requested	Notarized	County Seal	State Apostille	# Needed	Completed	Expiration Date
Birth certificate for Mom		N/A	N/A	N/A	3		N/A
Birth certificate for Dad		N/A	N/A	N/A	3		N/A
Birth certificate for children in home		N/A	N/A	N/A	3		N/A
Marriage license		N/A	N/A	N/A	2		N/A
Divorce decree for Mom		N/A	N/A	N/A	2		N/A
Divorce decree for Dad		N/A	N/A	N/A	2		N/A
Autobiographies	N/A	N/A	N/A	N/A	2		N/A
Letter from local police for Mom							
Letter from local police for Dad							
Reference letters					3		
Guardianship letter							
Contract between placement and home-study agency							
Post-placement agreement letter from home-study agency							
Copy of home-study agency license					2		
Copy of social worker's license					2		
Final home study					2		
Separate recommendation letter from home-study agency					2		
Fingerprints completed		N/A	N/A	N/A	N/A		

Document	Date Requested	Notarized	County Seal	State Apostille	# Needed	Completed	Expiration Date
I-171H approval letter		N/A	N/A	N/A	N/A		
Power of attorney for agency rep					2		
Parental power of attorney					1		
Petition to Adopt					2		
Questionnaire of the Candidate to Adoption for Mom					1		
Questionnaire of the Candidate to Adoption for Dad							
Copy of state adoption laws					1		
Photocopies of passport pages for Mom					3		
Photocopies of passport pages for Dad							
Photographs		N/A	N/A	N/A			
Medical form for Mom					2		
Medical form for Dad					2		
Copy of medical doctor's license (with expiration date shown)							
Mental health evaluation for Mom							
Mental health evaluation for Dad							
Copy of psychologist/psychiatrist's license (with expiration date shown)							
Employer's letter for Mom							
Employer's letter for Dad							
Financial statement					2		
Statement of legal residence							
Embassy registration letter from family					2		
Post-placement letter from family					2		

separate the final authenticated document by putting it in a different colored folder within the same hanging file. You can also file additional information that you might need again if the document expires. For example, the file folder for your medical evaluation might contain the following:

- Copy of the medical evaluation.
- Name of the administrative assistant who was helpful to you in getting the first evaluation notarized.
- Name and telephone number of the traveling notary. If you use her for other documents, you may want to create a separate file.
- Blue file folder with apostilled copy of your medical evaluation.

Keep a spiral-bound notebook to record your agency contacts. Divide the notebook in half with a yellow sticky pad. In the first half, record any questions you want to ask your agency. It's best to accumulate several questions before you call to avoid being perceived as high maintenance. In the second half, keep dated notes from all your phone conversations. Have a file for this notebook at the front.

The final piece to my paperwork organizational system is the calendar. Keep track of when you requested important documents and when you should receive them. Also keep track of when your documents expire. Each country decides how current the documents must be for presentation to their courts or administrative agency. Your agency should give you this information for each document. For some countries, it is probable that you will have to update certain documents during the process. The expiration dates are listed on your checklist, but the best place to keep track of them is on a calendar that you check regularly. Mark down both the actual expiration date as well as the date you need to start work on updating. These dates can be added to your regular home or business calendar if you check it often, or you can maintain an adoption-specific calendar. If you have an adoption-specific calendar, have a separate file for it at the front.

MAKE NICE

When my eldest daughter was in preschool, she went through a phase of being diplomatically challenged. The distinction between assertion and aggression was a bit fuzzy in her mind, so I dropped her off each morning at school with a reminder to use her words, not hands, and an extra reminder to use nice words,

TYPICAL ADOPTION FILE MIGHT INCLUDE THE FOLLOWING FOLDERS

Checklist

Calendar

Notebook for agency questions and telephone calls

Birth certificate for Mom

Birth certificate for Dad

Divorce decree for Mom

Divorce decree for Dad

Marriage license

Autobiographies

Letter from local police for Mom

Letter from local police for Dad

Reference letters

Guardianship letter

Contract between Homestudy (HS) agency and placement agency

Post-placement agreement/letters from HS Agency

Copy of HS agency license

Copy of social worker's license

Final HS

Recommendation letter from HS Agency

I-600A form

I-171H approval letter

Letter of petition to adopt

Letter attesting to sexual orientation for single adopters

Medical form for Mom

Medical form for Dad

Financial statement form

Employer letter for Mom

Employer letter for Dad

Power of attorney for parent not traveling (if applicable)

Photocopies of necessary pages of passport for Mom and Dad

Photographs of family and home

Referral information

Child's medical evaluation (include notes taken from consultation with pediatrician or IA doctor)

Agency information (including application)

HS agency information

FedEx, UPS, or DHL account information

Receipts for all adoption-related expenses

TIPS FROM PARENTS

- Go into the paperwork stage expecting bumps and delays along the way.
- Once you start preparing your dossier, don't drag your feet, because all the documents are time-sensitive. In an ideal world, you want to minimize the number of times you have to get them updated. For many countries, you should plan on redoing some documents at least once.
- As soon as you decide on an agency, ask when they offer the required orientation classes (not all do) so that you have your application submitted in time to enroll in the next class. Otherwise, you may "lose a month" waiting for the next class.
- Ask your agency what schedule they follow for submitting dossiers to the foreign country so that you can time your dossier to arrive before a group is scheduled to be sent. (This only applies to countries, such as China, where dossiers are submitted in batches.)
- If you live in a town where international adoptions are not common, expect to educate your notary and county clerk about the authentication process, since this may be the first time they have ever had the pleasure of authenticating documents for submittal to a foreign government. Have them read this chapter.
- State-issued documents, such as birth certificates, marriage licenses, and divorce decrees, can be ordered online at www.vitalchek.com.
- Buy a printer/fax/scanner/copier for your home. These come as all-in-one units and are reasonably priced. It will be incredibly helpful during the paper-chase stage and later on in your parenting life as well. Just this week, my home copier has been used to copy a spelling list to be put on the refrigerator for calling out, a birth certificate to register a kid for soccer, and a recipe to give to a friend. It is one gadget that is in constant use.
- Set up an account with an overnight delivery service, such as FedEx, UPS, or DHL, at the beginning to simplify mailing packages.
- Bring a small thank-you gift to those people who have gone out of their way to help you or whom you have inconvenienced more than once in collecting all the paperwork. Take the referral picture of your child to put a human face on the process and bring your child to show off once he is home.
- Make two copies of your completed dossier, including all the pages of authentications. Do not remove staples to make copies.

not mean words. She came home each day and proudly told me, "I make nice." Her response, by the way, never varied regardless of what actually happened. My experience with adoptive parents in the process of assembling their dossier compels me to drop you off at this stage with a similar reminder to make nice.

During the paperwork stage you probably are thinking about your adoption the moment you open your eyes in the morning and as you close them at night, but the rest of the world is not so similarly focused. Your friends, family, boss, coworkers, and the guy processing your fingerprints may have a few other things on their mind. Try to remember that it is unreasonable to expect others to share your obsession and sense of urgency. Be considerate of your use of office time, equipment, and supplies. Consider taking personal-leave days to focus on getting the bulk of the work done.

Be excruciatingly polite in all your written, phone, and personal contacts in preparing your dossier. Rather than make an enemy, first try very hard to make a friend by winning them over. Explain why you need the document. Admit that you are a little frenzied and that you appreciate their understanding and help in bringing your child home. Appeal to them as fellow parents.

Don't forget that you may need help from these same people again in the not-unlikely event that some documents will expire during the process and have to be redone. And even if you won't need their help in the future, other adoptive parents will follow in your footsteps. Yes, it is their job, but to poorly paraphrase the English poet Samuel Johnson, don't underestimate the benefit of spontaneous kindness. Or, if you prefer more earthy metaphors, "You catch more flies with honey than vinegar."

FUAQs

Our agency offers for an extra fee to handle all the authenticating of our paperwork. It is not cheap, but we are wondering if it is worth it for peace of mind.

Dossier-preparation services are becoming a booming business. They are offered by both adoption agencies and by independent contractors, most of whom are adoptive parents. Whether or not it is worth it depends on how busy you are, how much control you are willing to give up, and how much they cost. The actual paperwork is not difficult, but it is time-consuming and requires an organized approach. How much time it takes is largely a matter of how many states your documents are in, how many notaries you used—especially if your state requires county certification—how fast everyone can prepare the necessary documents, and how much time you have to push the process.

Dossier-preparation services handle only the authenticating, not the document preparation or notarizing. Many will not get the county certification in states where this is required. Their service is to take the notarized documents and move them up the authentication chain. For the countries that are members of the Hague Legalization Treaty, the chain ends with the state apostille. For those countries that are not parties to this treaty, the chain continues up from the state to the country embassy with maybe a stop at the U.S. Department of State. Many will also get your government-issued documents, such as birth certificates and marriage licenses.

You will have to decide if the benefit is worth the cost. The service will usually save you time, and for many people it also saves worry. They turn over the process and have no concerns about it being done right. Others don't want to turn over control. They reason that they are more motivated to quickly complete the paperwork, to quickly mail off the document to the next level for authentication, and to quickly follow through. It gives them something tangible they can do to bring their child home. Some families do their own dossier preparation but use an adoption courier service to handle the authentications in Washington, D.C.

If you decide to use a dossier-preparation service, find out exactly what is covered. Specifically ask if it covers mailing costs and overnight mailing fees. Does the price include obtaining government-issued documents or just authenticating the notarized documents? Remember, even if you hire out the actual authenticating, you still must keep track of what documents you need. Therefore, the master checklist and files are still necessary. And you absolutely must keep up with your deadlines and expiration dates. Some responsibilities you simply can't resource out.

I am anxious to begin. What can I start on right now so that I feel like I am actually doing something to become a mother?

The most important first step is to choose a country and an agency. After that, talk with your agency about what paperwork you should begin first. You can begin collecting documents for your I-600A form, your home study, and your dossier. How soon you can begin gathering these documents depends on the current expected waiting times for the country you are adopting from, since many documents will expire. It is usually safe to start the following:

- Collect documents needed for your I-600A form. Do this only if you are committed to getting started on your home study soon, since it must be submitted within one year.
- Check with your home-study preparer about the slowest steps in the process and begin those. In some locations, the child-abuse checks can take the longest. Ask whether the social worker or you will apply for these checks.

- Get copies of your birth certificates, marriage licenses, divorce decrees, or certificates of death. This can take a while if you were born, married, or divorced out of the state or country. (Not for the first time will you regret that quickie marriage to the tattooed hunk in the Vegas Elvis chapel.) Obtaining authenticated copies of these documents from another country is particularly time-consuming. Order two more copies than you think you will need.
- If you've moved around a lot, start making a list of your former addresses. For whatever reason, this step took us longer than we thought. I prefer to believe it was because I am not a pack rat, but I suppose it could also reflect the state of my record keeping.
- Begin your adoption education courses or reading. Ask if you can get credit for reading this book.
- Get a passport. If your existing passport will expire within the next couple of years, renew now.
- Call your doctor's office and schedule an appointment for a physical. Many doctors have limited appointment times for physicals, so they are scheduled far in advance.

FOR EVERY ADOPTION, A DIFFERENT STORY . . .

Everyone comes up with a mental time frame for how long the paper chase will take, and if you miss this deadline you start to get frustrated and feel that you are falling behind. I learned the hard way that you have to plan for the unexpected, such as vacations, business trips, illness, and holidays. We ran into the November holiday crunch and had not planned for it. Suddenly, there was Veterans Weekend (a government holiday), Thanksgiving, and one business trip which lasted two weeks. Between these events and our social worker having her own life (imagine that!), my initial estimate was off by about four weeks. —*SB, Georgia*

Compiling the paperwork was not that bad. We didn't waste any time and the whole dossier took one month from start to finish. We made it a priority and we received I-600A approval in less than two months.

Believe it or not, my worst experience during this process was a mean man at the post office. We had received our referral much quicker than we thought (older child/toddler adoptions go really fast) and we needed our passports ASAP. We had to fill out extra forms after we got to the post office, and when we finished, it was after the cutoff time for passports. The man told me I would have to come back the next day to hand him the form. (I had already left work early and couldn't afford to do it again the next day.) After we begged, he agreed to accept our forms and then he made a snide comment about the cost of "buying children"! My husband literally had to pull me out of the post office. Now I personally know the meaning of "going postal." I knew there would be difficulties, but I never thought it would be at the post office. Our four-year-old son is amazing, and every time we go to the post office, I always make sure I get in that nasty man's line, smile, and tell my son, "This is the man who helped Momma and Papa get you from Russia." He usually mumbles something to himself and offers my son a sucker. —*KH, North Carolina*

The paperwork—there is not much positive you can you say about having to prepare piles of documents and then have them signed by four different people, but it couldn't have been that bad, because we plan on doing it all over again in two years. Our agency was very organized and gave us a list of what paperwork to start first, which took the longest, and instructions on how to complete everything. I am a fairly organized and detail-oriented person, which is necessary to get all the paperwork together in a timely manner. The hardest part was the anxiety that somehow I would do it wrong and it would keep us from getting on the waiting list and delay us getting our child.

I think the paperwork stage was more frustrating than the waiting stage, because in the paperwork stage you are dependent on other people doing their job quickly and correctly, and you have no control over getting them to do this. You are putting forth a lot of effort, but you can't see any progress, meaning you are not on The List yet. During the waiting stage, you know you have done all you can and it is finally going to happen. Throughout it all, I just kept telling myself that as soon as our child was placed in our arms none of it would matter. I was right. —*RO, New York*

I had a funny, embarrassing, or silly (depending on how you look at it) thing happen when I mailed my I-600A form. I went to the bank to get a money order and the teller asked if I was buying something online. I blushed and said that we were adopting. She made some nice remarks and we finished up the transaction. On my way to the car, I realized that this was the first stranger I had told in person—not a family member, not an inner-circle friend, not a faceless Internet friend from an adoption forum. I know this is silly, but I was stunned and awed. It was such an emotional experience; I had to blink away the tears. It was so real—within about eight months, we are finally going to be parents. —*SB, Georgia*

So many requirements, so many forms, so many notaries—it's a bit soul-destroying. I survived by employing the same strategy that I use for my work and for housecleaning. Make a list of every piece of paper you need, do something related to an item on the list every day, and begin crossing off what you've accomplished as you work your way through the list. This systematic approach helps you feel on top of things and less overwhelmed. Plus you have tangible evidence of what you've accomplished, which makes you feel that an end is in sight. —*SS, New York*

I treated the dossier preparation like a job and just did it. I made sure I did a few easy things first to give me a sense of accomplishment and then progressed to the harder stuff. I was committed to doing two to three tasks each day. Organization was crucial since we were in a hurry, because we already had a referral. We finished the entire dossier in two weeks! —*MS, Virginia*

When you are in the middle of the paper chase and the foreign country keeps piling on new requirements, it's easy to develop a negative attitude toward your children's birth country. Don't be so quick to judge, because the United States has many of the same faults. My children have never and will never hear us say a single negative thing about their country or the hoops we had to jump through both here and abroad in order to adopt them. We have a true bond and love for their country, culture, and history, and I want them to be proud to tell whomever they please where they were born. When they are older, I am sure they will ask more pointed questions that will evoke negative, painful, or hard-to-hear facts and truths about their former lives and situations, but until then they will know every day that we are so grateful and proud of the country that not only produced them, but granted us the great privilege to be their parents and allowed them to grow up as Americans. —*KF, Alabama*

I have a silly piece of advice. When you are in the midst of compiling all the paperwork, it is hard to feel like you are preparing for a real live baby. I bought a really cute baby outfit in about the size I thought my baby would be when he came home and hung it where I could easily see it. It served as motivation to keep plugging away. —*VL, Virginia*

Expect the unexpected. When we tried to get a copy of our marriage certificate, we discovered that after almost ten years of marriage, we were not officially married! The minister did not file the certificate following the ceremony. Not to worry—we are now legal, but we had to get a "delayed" certificate of marriage issued by the state before we could proceed with our dossier. And to think, this was the one thing I had not worried about. —*KF, Iowa*

CHAPTER 7

SURVIVING THE WAIT

Pregnancy Without the Stretch Marks

YiJie was born in QuZhou, Zhejiang Province, China, on September 20, 2001, and joined her forever family in September 2002.

Emily and Bart thought they had perfected the art of waiting patiently. They had waited patiently to be pregnant each month through three years of infertility treatment, they had waited patiently through bureaucratic red tape and lost adoption paperwork, they had waited patiently for eight months for China to assign them a baby, but waiting to travel to pick up nine-month-old Sarah Lin severely tested their patience. Sarah was getting older and learning new things, and they wanted to be a part of every moment. "I thought all the waiting before she was assigned to us was hard, but once we had a picture, once we had committed to her, once she had a name, once she was ours, then it got really hard," remembers Emily.

Congratulations! Your paperwork is now signed, sealed, and delivered. The piles of documents that had taken over your dining room table and living room floor are now gone. Your house has reverted to its natural state following the spit-and-polish splendor preceding the home study. Things are back to normal. So now what do you do? You wait.

"Hurry up and wait" is the mantra for airplane travelers, soldiers, and international adopters. Most people are ready for the calm after the storm of the paper chase, but few want it to remain calm for long. They are more than ready to be caught up in the turbulence of their child.

Comparisons to pregnancy are inevitable. Like pregnancy, you have entered a period of intense excitement mixed with, at times, intense anxiety. Like pregnancy, you spend time dreaming about your child and your life as a parent. Like pregnancy, you worry.

But there are differences. Rather than a doctor looking at your private parts, you have a social worker asking private questions. Rather than a ballooning belly, you have growing piles of paper. Rather than stretch marks appearing on your body, you have them in your budget. In addition to the typical new-parent anxiety (will this child be healthy? will I be a good parent?), you very well may have your own special adoption worries (will this child bond with me? will fickle politicians shut down the program?). With pregnancy you worry about the baby coming early; with adoption you worry he'll come late.

WAITING TIMES

The typical adoption wait can be divided into the wait prior to the time a child is referred and the wait to travel to finalize the adoption. The length of the wait varies by country, and typical times are included in the Country Charts appendix and updated at www.findingyourchild.com. How the wait looks and feels depends on the referral method. See Chapter 8 for a detailed discussion, but generally there are three referral methods: standard, blind, and semi-blind.

Most placing countries use the standard referral method. Families complete the paperwork and submit it to the agency; the agency sends it to the country; the first wait (for a referral) begins. A child is referred to the family; the family reviews the medical and background information and accepts or rejects the referral; the second wait (to pick up the child) begins. A few countries in this group, most notably Russia, require parents to travel twice—the first time to meet the child and the second to finalize the adoption—so families have the additional wait between the two trips even though the total time may be no greater.

YOU KNOW YOU'RE A WAITING ADOPTIVE PARENT WHEN . . .

- You check your voice mail more than five times per hour to see if The Call came.
- You dread the weekend because you won't hear anything.
- You look forward to the weekend because you need a break from holding your breath every time the phone rings.
- You want to scream when friends and family ask if you've heard anything.
- You want to cry when friends and family don't ask if you've heard anything.
- You know the meaning of the word *apostille* and you're not afraid to use it.
- You are one of the few Americans who know that the INS is now the USCIS, with a brief stop at being the BCIS in between. Confused? You should be!

For countries that use the blind referral method, families submit their paperwork to the agency, the agency sends it to the country, and the family waits to receive an invitation to travel to the country. Once they are in the country, they meet one or several children and decide whether to accept. After acceptance, the family either waits in country to finalize the adoption or comes home to wait and then returns to finalize and bring their child home. The process for semi-blind referrals is very similar, but the family receives limited information on a specific child before they travel to meet that child and decide whether to accept or reject this referral.

No matter which way you go, waiting is a part of the process. Parents differ on whether the wait before the referral or the wait after the referral is the hardest. The wait before a referral is hard because you are still waiting to become a parent. The wait after a referral is hard because you are now a parent but you are still waiting to feel like one.

Your agency will tell you the expected range for waiting times at each step. Always expect and plan for the greater time in the range. If the agency says you can expect an assignment in six to eight months, prepare yourself for eight months. Even though I think this is great advice, I don't know of a single person who has followed it. Oh sure, we tell ourselves and the world that we are expecting an assignment in eight months, but at four months we start answering the phone on the first ring, check our phone messages the moment we walk in the door, and check e-mails every hour "just in case." At five months, we are calling our voice mail every hour we are away from the phone and checking e-mails and cell phone messages every ten minutes. The really cool among us keep up the façade to the rest of the world, but inside we are chomping at the bit. I suppose this is our equivalent of false labor.

Accepting the inevitable, my real advice is for you to tell the rest of the world the upper part of the range (plus some) to forestall the inevitable phone calls asking you if you have heard anything yet. For yourself, try your hardest to not get antsy until at least the beginning of the range. It is perfectly acceptable to call your agency midway through your wait to ask if the waiting times have changed. Agencies that place quite a few kids from the country have a good finger on the pulse of how the time frames are currently fluctuating. A good agency understands your anxiety and doesn't mind an occasional call.

EMOTIONS

The waiting period of the adoption process is often a time of surprising emotions. Up until this time, you have been busy collecting, writing, authenticating, scheduling, making lists, and checking them twice. And then it all stops. For many families this is the first time since they decided to adopt that they have time to really think and feel. Emotions can bounce from high to low depending on the week or day or hour, and both the ups and the downs are normal.

Parents are often reluctant to talk about any emotion other than joy for fear of being judged as inadequate or not ready to adopt. In many ways, this is another similarity to pregnancy. If being completely honest, most pregnant parents will admit that along with excitement, pregnancy brings anxiety. With my first pregnancy, I was unprepared for this and added to my list of worries the worry about being worried. At least with my adoption, I didn't have to worry that the anxiety would cause an unhealthy intrauterine environment for my child. Here is a piece of advice from one mom to another: Joy and anxiety are a normal part of any life-altering event, and as long as they are not overwhelming, you don't need to add being anxious to your list of things to worry about.

Elation

Most parents feel that wonderful tingly feeling of anticipation—that vague feeling when you first wake up that something good is about to happen. It's not unlike the feeling you had as a kid the week before Christmas.

In the months I was waiting for my daughter, I spent hours wondering what she would be like, what she would look like, what she would act like. I looked at every Asian face I saw and wondered if my child would look like them. I filled sheets of paper practicing her name. I worked on my capital *L*s until I had perfected what I considered to be a distinctive style—not too flashy, but with a definite flair.

One friend said she felt content for the first time since she started infertility treatments and was able to reconnect with family and friends that she had distanced herself from during that time. An acquaintance told me that during the wait for her son she had boundless energy once the burden of childlessness was gone. And still another couple told me they felt the excitement of embarking on a long-awaited adventure. Many people I have interviewed reported a peaceful feeling that God was in control.

Anxiety

Along with the sunshine of elation often comes the shadow of anxiety and doubt. Up until this time, you have been too busy to worry, but now you have the time to indulge yourself. Can you really love a child that looks different from you, that may not act like you, that didn't grow inside of you or your spouse? What type of hidden problems may this child have and can you handle them? What if some politician in his birth country overreacts to some bad news story on international adoption and shuts down the whole program? The big three sources of anxiety for international adoptions are bonding, health, and the adoption falling through.

Bonding and attachment have taken on a mystical (or maybe I should say mythical) quality in adoption literature. You can't open an adoption magazine or Google the word "adoption" without being inundated with articles and Web sites dedicated to this subject. For all its current popularity, the use of these terms is relatively new and there are no universally accepted definitions, although attachment disorders are now a specifically recognized psychiatric diagnosis. Some experts say that bonding is the process, with attachment being the end result. Others say bonding refers to the parents' tie to the child, while attachment refers to the child's connection to the parents. And many experts use the terms interchangeably. In a nutshell, both terms have to do with the feeling of connection between parent and child. See Chapter 8 for a more thorough discussion.

The questions that swirl through your head and pinch at your heart when you are stuck in the middle of attachment anxiety are usually variations of the following:

Will I love this child as much as _____?

a. a child born to me

b. my first child

c. a child who looks like me

d. all of the above

Will this child love me as much as _____?

a. a child born to me

b. my first child

c. a child who looks like me

d. all of the above

My anxiety was focused on the second question. I secretly wondered if this child would love me the same as if she had been born to me. Would she wish her birth mother had raised her? The day before I was to fly to pick her up, I started to panic that she would be autistic. The fear was so very real, even though I had no reason to think this would be a problem. It doesn't take Freud to figure out that this fear was just another version of my fear over her loving me.

No doubt bonding is crucial for child development and all adoptive parents should be informed about this issue, especially if the child they are planning to adopt is older. See Chapter 8 and the Resource Guide for suggested reading. However, the concern many pre-adoptive parents feel is exaggerated. Information is power, so here are a few facts to help quell the anxiety:

- There is no specific age at which bonding must take place between parent and child.
- A child who has attached in the past to a caregiver is likely to be able to attach to his new parents.
- The majority of adopted children (even high-risk children) do not have attachment problems.
- Parents (by birth or adoption) don't always (or even usually) bond with their child at first sight.
- Children who were abused, neglected, or adopted at an older age are more at risk.
- Attachment disorders are treatable.

Another major source of anxiety for adoptive parents is the health of their child. Actually, this is a major source of anxiety for all parents, but adoptive parents have the added worry of unknown prenatal and genetic history. On the other hand, parents by birth have to worry about birth defects that aren't apparent until the pregnancy is advanced or at birth. In some ways, I felt as if I had more information on my adopted child's health when she was referred than I did on my biological children before their birth, but her genetics and prenatal environment were a big unknown. Consider these facts:

- You will have information on your child's health to review.
- You can probably get additional medical information if needed.
- You can have an international adoption doctor review the medical information to help you assess the risks. (See Chapter 8.)

Failed infertility treatments or miscarriages may have preceded your decision to adopt, and it may be hard to shake the feeling that something will happen yet once again to thwart your efforts to become a parent. A friend described it as waiting for the other shoe to drop. There is less risk with international adoption of the adoption falling through at the last minute than with domestic adoption, but anxiety doesn't always respond to logic. Nevertheless, remember this:

- While countries do shut down their international adoption programs, agencies usually have advance notice and either stop accepting parents into that program or warn parents in advance.
- Reputable agencies screen out families that do not meet the country's criteria so no unexpected problems should crop up.
- I know of no family that met a country's criteria that was not able to adopt, even if it took longer than they wanted.

Grief

The last emotion most parents expect to feel at this stage is grief over their lost fertility, their lost biological child, their lost bloodline. Often these feelings resurface when things settle down and you relax. It does not mean that you didn't work through your grief at the beginning. Grief is a process, not an event. It would certainly be nice if you could just deal with it once, check it off your list, and move on to the next item. Unfortunately, it doesn't usually work this way.

And as weird as this may seem, you may also be identifying with the pain your child's birth parent is feeling. This is especially the case after a referral has been made and you have some, albeit limited, information. No matter how you look at it, this child can become yours only through someone else's loss. And that is sad.

Although it is normal, experiencing grief is seldom welcome and can be particularly unsettling at this stage when your long-awaited goal of becoming a parent is finally within reach. Give yourself time and read or reread *Adopting After Infertility* by Patricia Irwin Johnston. And rest assured, these feelings are normal and in no way mean that adoption in general or adoption of this specific child is not right for you.

When Emotions Peak

Some parents in the waiting stage find their negative emotions peak at the major family holidays, such as Christmas, Hanukkah, Thanksgiving, and New Year's. Other parents report that any family gathering can be a painful reminder that you are still not parents. For some, these feelings of anxiety and grief lessen once the adoption process begins; for others, they lessen once the baby is assigned; and for some, these emotions are present until they have their child. Try some of the coping techniques listed in this section to help you deal with these feelings.

WHEN THE WAIT EXCEEDS THE ESTIMATED TIME

Reputable agencies are cautious when giving time estimates because they know the anguish and frustration that result when these estimates are missed. However, some things are outside an agency's control, and as with everything else in international adoption, predictability varies by country. Countries can change their laws, resulting in delays for the families already being processed. Countries can temporarily suspend travel for public health or political reasons. And sometimes countries discontinue international adoption, although this seldom happens without advance warning.

When the wait exceeds the estimate, the lack of control is hard to handle. If a child has not been assigned, you may feel again the hopelessness of ever becoming a parent. If the child has been assigned, you will worry that your child is missing out on your love, you are missing out on these important months of her development, and you worry about the effect of these additional months in less-than-ideal circumstances. When time frames have been missed, it is particularly helpful for parents to connect either online or in person with other families in the same boat. Also, try the coping techniques suggested in this chapter.

WINNING OVER RELUCTANT FAMILY

If you haven't already told your extended family, now is the time. After deciding that adoption is the right choice for building your family, you naturally want everyone to be as excited as you. This may not happen. Your decision to

---

TECHNIQUES FOR COPING WITH ANXIETY AND GRIEF

- Accept that these feelings are normal, and since worry is inherent in parenting, this is good practice. (As the mother of four, I can truly attest to this fact.)
- These feelings do not mean that adoption in general or adoption of this specific child is not right for you.
- You can have these feelings now and still be a terrific parent.
- Give yourself time and don't gloss over your feelings or push them away.
- Arm yourself with facts about adoption included in this chapter and Chapter 1.
- If you feel stuck or the feelings are overwhelming, get help from a counselor experienced with infertility and adoption. Ask your social worker or local support group members for recommendations.
- Do something fun for yourself. Think in terms of a massage, a long bath, or a sexy new outfit. (I highly favor retail therapy.)
- Reread the stories of real families throughout this book.
- Limit time with pregnant friends or skip family gatherings if you need to.
- Get involved with a big project at work or in your community to take your mind off yourself. Try giving back by volunteering.
- Join an adoptive family support group. Spending time with families that have successfully adopted will help more than you can imagine.
- Join an online community for families in the adoption process. See the Resource Guide.

---

adopt evolved over time after much researching, soul-searching, discussing, and praying. Your family has not had the benefit of this process, so it is unfair to expect them to be at the same place as you.

How you tell your family may make a difference. If you think there may be resistance, consider writing your family a letter telling them of your decision before you talk with them in person. When you tell, choose your words carefully. One friend reported that she started the conversation with "I've got great news!" Her parents assumed she was going to tell them she was pregnant and their initial response at learning of the adoption was less than she had hoped. They recouped quickly, however, and are now doting grandparents to her two children.

You may hear some of the following from your family:

- Why are you giving up?
- It's a good idea to adopt, because then you'll get pregnant. (Adoption as a fertility elixir is a particularly stubborn myth.)

- Are you sure you can love someone else's child?
- You never know what you're going to get when you adopt.
- How much will the child cost?

There is no one right way to handle these comments and the underlying attitude they reflect. First, really listen to their concerns. So often in conversations, we are plotting our response instead of hearing what the other person is saying. Are they struggling with the basic concept of adoption and the loss of their bloodline continuing into the future? Are they grieving the loss of their biological grandchild, who would have reminded them of you when you were a baby? Are they concerned about the race or ethnicity of your child? Do they think adopted children have lots of physical and emotional problems? Are they worried about the cost and the subsequent financial burden you will carry? Don't assume you know what they are thinking; ask them to tell you.

After you understand their concerns, present them with information on adoption. Share this book with them and highlight the sections you want them to read. Stress to them that this was not a decision you made lightly. To help normalize the experience, invite them to join you at an adoption support group meeting or invite them to join you for dinner with another family who adopted kids from the same country. Just realizing that kids are kids may help.

Specifically ask for their support. Explain how important it is to you and your child. But if necessary, gently let them know that while you are open to questions, you are not open to them trying to change your mind. If they are not receptive to this, give them time and yourself space.

Once your child arrives, most extended families fall in love and their original concerns fade away. However, you need to be prepared if this doesn't happen. Be very clear in your mind and with them that once the child arrives, your allegiance is to your child. As a parent, you need to protect your child, even if it means limiting his exposure to your family.

PREPARING OLDER KIDS

The waiting period is a good time to start preparing your older children if you haven't already done so. How soon you start and how much detail depends on the ages of your children, but it is important to prepare them before they start getting questions from others. Your goal is to teach your children what adoption is, how their new sibling may react to all the changes in his life, and how they may feel as a new big brother or sister. Techniques such as playacting and reading books together are helpful. My favorite books are included in the

Resource Guide. Don't limit your reading to just those books listed for preparing an older sibling, since the general children's adoption books are great for explaining adoption and what the new child may be feeling. It helps to prepare your children for the whole range of emotions your new child might experience and how she might express her feelings. Also see the FUAQs in Chapters 1 and 5 for additional information.

SUPPORT GROUPS

I cannot stress enough how helpful you will find an adoptive parent support group. They are an invaluable source of reassurance and realistic up-to-date information (and rumors and gossip, but nothing is perfect). Only other adoptive parents can understand exactly what you are experiencing. There is so much diversity in support groups that you are bound to find one that meets your needs.

Groups generally form around the country from which the children are adopted (e.g., Families with Children from China), the agency used to adopt, the marital status of the parent (e.g., Committee for Single Adoptive Parents), or geographic location (e.g., Resolve of Orange County Adoptive Parent Support Group). They can be national, local, or online. Join more than one to see which fits you best. The larger national support groups are listed in the Resource Guide, and most agencies also have groups for families that adopt through them.

The best I can tell, there is no difference between the terms *online adoption group, discussion board, discussion list, bulletin board, newsgroup,* or *forum*—they all are places for adoptive parents to ask questions and share the ups and downs of adoption. (I think the multiple names are part of a vast conspiracy against technophobes like me.) Chat rooms have the same purpose but are in real time, while forums have a lag time like e-mail correspondence. These groups differ as to who may join, whether they are moderated, and membership rules.

Keep in mind that the anonymity of the Internet cuts both ways. Be careful about giving out your personal e-mail address. Many people create a separate e-mail address with one of the free services, such as Hotmail, Yahoo, or Gmail, to use on forums. Anonymity also brings out the worst in some folks, so shop around until you find a group that is supportive. The Internet is also ground zero for rumors, so take what you hear with a grain of salt and call your agency for the real scoop before you panic.

There is nothing like visiting with families formed through adoption to help you cope with anxiety, so join an in-person group (if possible) as well as online groups. Families living in larger cities will have no problem finding a local group. For families in smaller towns, this can be a problem. Check to see if there is a support group in a nearby larger town. If not, join national groups so that you can receive their newsletters. Join a few of the many online forums. You can also consider forming a group, although birthing a baby through adoption will leave you little time to birth a support group.

PASSING THE TIME

The old proverb is right—time does indeed move slowly for those who wait, and after a few months, *slow* takes on a whole new meaning. Keeping busy is the only way to survive. Fortunately, there is much you can do during this time to keep your mind off the creeping calendar, and it's not just busywork. You have more time now to accomplish things that need to be done, and your post-baby life will be easier if you do them now. In keeping with the pregnancy theme, I have provided nine months' worth of activities if you do one a week.

Feel free to pick and choose your way through the list. Which items we choose probably speaks volumes about us. A friend of mine favored the nesting and cleaning activities. By the time her daughter arrived, she had organized and cleaned everything in her house and had moved on to the garage. I, on the other hand, favored the pamper-yourself activities. I wanted to eat, soak, and shop my way through. In fact, we got The Call the Monday after my husband and I had returned from a romantic weekend getaway. I would recommend waiting to do the items after number 20 until after you have a referral, since the wait will be harder once the nursery is ready and baby things are scattered around the house.

1. **Get in shape.** You will soon be carrying, bending, and running more than you have since you were a kid, and you will be doing all of this carrying, bending, and running while carrying your child. You don't need to add a sore back and aching muscles to the stress of travel and new parenthood. Start exercising. Carry a five-pound sack of flour in your baby carrier throughout the day to get ready, and gradually work up to a twenty-pound sack of rice.
2. **Choose a pediatrician.** (See box for suggestions of what to look for.) Also choose an international adoption medical specialist if you plan to use one. See Chapter 8 for what to look for in an IA doctor.
3. **Get the required immunizations.** Find out if you are required or recommended to have any immunizations for your adoption trip. Some immu-

nizations, such as hepatitis B, require several shots over about six months, so get started.

4. **Prepare a will or review your existing one.** Most wills are written to cover children by birth or adoption, but make sure. Pick out guardians and Godparents.

5. **Find out your employer's policy on adoption leave.** If they do not give parents paid time off for adoption, put together a proposal to change the

---

HOW TO CHOOSE A PEDIATRICIAN

The basics for choosing a pediatrician are the same regardless of whether the patient is adopted or born into the family. You want a competent doctor that you click with and that will be available when you need her or him. However, since your child may arrive with some medical issues seldom seen by the average pediatrician and may have some developmental and behavioral issues related to his early-life experiences, you also need a doctor either experienced in international adoption or willing to learn.

You will be relying on this person more than you realize in raising your child, so spend time making sure the fit is right. Get referrals from your adoption support group or friends. Most pediatricians don't charge for an interview with prospective parents, so set one up and consider the following questions:

- Does the office accept your insurance?
- How many doctors are in the practice and how are calls handled outside of office hours?
- What are the office hours? For me, a deal breaker is hours on the weekend. My kids seem to always get sick on the weekend, so I want at least Saturday office hours.
- What is the doctor's experience with internationally adopted kids? Is he or she willing to read and follow the guidelines published in the American Academy of Pediatrics' *Red Book* or follow an international adoption doctor's recommendation on testing?
- If my child is sick, will she be able to be seen the same day?
- What hospital does she or he use? (If you have a preference, ask.)
- Will it be a problem to schedule your first visit on short notice? Your child must be seen fairly soon after arrival, but you may not have much advance notice.
- You will be spending a lot of time with your pediatrician, so consider starting your relationship with a gift of Dr. Laurie Miller's book, *The Handbook of International Adoption Medicine.*

policy. Argue the fairness factor—if the company offers leave for employees who become parents by birth, it is only fair that they offer leave for employees who become parents by adoption. Stress the long-term health benefits of firmly establishing attachment. Educate yourself about the Family and Medical Leave Act and what your employer is required to do. See FUAQs in Chapter 10 and www.adoptionfriendlyworkplace.org.

6. **Get both parents up to speed.** A typical scenario during the adoption process is for one parent to take on the role of the prepared one while the other parent remains blissfully ignorant. Now is the time to right that imbalance, at least a bit. The uninformed (read clueless) partner absolutely must read Chapters 8, 9, and 10.

7. **Have grandparents and close friends read Chapter 10.** They will better understand about parenting techniques to enhance attachment and how they can help.

8. **Singles should line up their support team.** Specifically ask if they would be willing to take over at night every once in a while to let you catch up on sleep if your child has trouble sleeping.

9. **Read adoption books and articles.** But a word of caution: In an effort to show the full picture, many adoption books and articles seem to focus on the problems of adoption. Be selective about what you read. You don't want to ignore the potential problems, but you don't need to immerse yourself in them, either. Get a subscription to *Adoptive Families* magazine.

10. **Learn as much of your child's birth language as possible.** At the very least, learn travel phrases ("Where's the bathroom?" "How much is this?") polite phrases ("please," "thank you," "hello," "good-bye"), and child phrases ("I love you," "Mama," "Daddy," "Are you hungry?").

11. **Read child-development and parenting books.** See the Resource Guide. Sometimes we become so focused on the fact that we are *adopting* this child that we forget that he is first and foremost a child and more like other children than different. Get parenting practice by volunteering to babysit for friends or for the church nursery. You will become very popular and will be banking goodwill that you can cash out when you need help in the future. Anticipate that your child may be developmentally delayed. The rule of thumb is a one-month delay for every three months in an orphanage.

12. **Choose a name.** For names with an international flavor, check out the Resource Guide for books.

13. **Pamper yourself.** Consider long soaks in a tub with candlelight and wine if money is tight, but take a vacation if you can afford to. This "babymoon" may be the last child-free vacation in a long while.

14. **Start a journal.** Save it to give to your child someday to show your feelings while you wait for her to join your family.

15. **Write your parents a thank-you letter.** Tell them how excited you are and how much you appreciate all they did and do for you.

16. **Research early-intervention programs.** Most school districts and counties have programs to help preschool kids with developmental delays. Your child may not need it, but it helps to be ready in case she does.

17. **Organize your closets, drawers, and cupboards.** If you are feeling really industrious or anxious, move on to your basement, attic, or garage. If you still have excess energy, come start on my house.

18. **Childproof your home.** See Chapter 5 for things to do and also the Resource Guide.

19. **Take a child CPR course.** In addition to CPR, it should also cover the Heimlich maneuver for babies and young children. Ask your pediatrician where a course is offered, or call the local Red Cross.

20. **Learn how to take decent pictures, especially of children.** Check out the Resource Guide for books.

21. **Prepare your pets for the baby's arrival.** Make any anticipated changes to their routine (more time outdoors or in a crate) well in advance of your child arriving so the pet does not associate the change with the new arrival. Contact your vet or local humane society for information and see the Resource Guide.

22. **Tackle your "someday" list.** Learn to knit, play tennis, dance, play the guitar, or anything that you've been meaning to do someday. Or, for the more puritanical among you, tackle your *shoulds:* catch up on that stack of paperwork, the clothes that need to be mended, or anything else that you should do.

23. **Schedule any of your regular appointments.** You won't have time for your regular dentist, doctor, optometrist, and vet appointments when you first get home, so schedule them for before you travel.

24. **Take child-care classes at the local hospital.** Ask your pediatrician or adoption agency who else offers them.

25. **Buy a cookbook from your child's country.** Learn to prepare a few simple meals.

26. **Learn a few lullabies and bouncy games.** See boxes.

27. **Shop garage sales for baby items and toys.** You will need less equipment than you think and your child may have outgrown the need for some things. Ask your pediatrician and other parents who have adopted similar-aged children for suggestions. Garage sales are a great place to find bargains,

and spring and fall are the best times for sales. See box for warnings of what not to buy.

28. **Buy a few favorite children's books.** Think back to your childhood and choose books you loved, such as a book of Mother Goose rhymes or *Good Night Moon* by Margaret Wise Brown. Also buy a few children's books on adoption. My favorites are listed in the Resource Guide.

29. **Learn baby massage techniques.** See the Resource Guide.

30. **Send a transition object or photo album to your child.** A photo album will help your child begin to recognize the VIPs in his new life, and a *transition object* (a fancy word for a blanket or stuffed animal) will make the transition easier for him since he will have grown accustomed to it in his old life and can bring it with him to his new life.

31. **Begin preparing a life book for your child.** See Chapter 10.

32. **Print your posts from the online forums.** Save these in your child's life book. Use discretion on which ones to include.

33. **Get a local or national newspaper from your child's birth date.**

34. **Arrange for the care of children if you will be leaving them at home when you travel.** Write out an authorization for the babysitter to get medical care and leave a copy of your insurance card. If they will be going to someone else's house, consider having them practice for one or two nights while you and your spouse (or friend) get away for a weekend. Buy and wrap inexpensive gifts for your child to open each day you will be gone. In addition to giving him something to look forward to each day, the dwindling stack of gifts will be a visual reminder of how soon you will return.

LULLABIES

There is almost nothing more satisfying than singing a lullaby to your child. This is the only place outside of the shower where most of us can sing without fear of ridicule. Children hear the love rather than the quality. Even on a good day I struggle with pitch, and on a bad day I struggle with tune, and yet each of my children likes me to sing to them at bedtime. Even my teens will allow me to sing while I rub their backs, and periodically (usually when sick) they'll request a favorite.

It is surprisingly hard to find resources for learning lullabies without being able to read music. CDs are the best way to learn for the musically illiterate among us, but many of them are all dolled up and not reproducible by the average mortal. My favorites for learning how to sing them yourself are included in the Resource Guide.

BOUNCY GAMES

When we first got into the parenthood business, my husband had never held a child, much less tried to entertain one on his lap. Knowing a couple of parenting/daddy tricks and games boosted his confidence. Here are a few to get you started. Vary the intensity based on the child's age and personality, and never do this until a baby can firmly support his head. Sit the baby or child facing you on your lap and bounce your knees while you chant:

1. Trot little pony, trot to town,
   Take care of _____,
   Don't fall down. (At this point, while holding the child's hands, open your legs and let the child fall a little or a lot.)
2. Ride a horse to Boston,
   Ride a horse to Lynn,
   Watch out _____,
   Don't fall in. (Same as above.)
3. Up, up, up in the sky like this. (Lift child high.)
   Down, down, down for a great big kiss!
   Up like this.
   Down for a kiss.
   Who's my very special baby?
   You, you, you. (Poke at various tickle spots.)

---

35. **Change your long-distance calling plan.** If you will be leaving children who will want to call you while you are abroad, the month before you leave change your calling plan with your long-distance provider to include international calls.

36. **Cook and freeze meals for the first weeks back home.**

37. **Get information on kid-friendly activities.** Your community likely has many inexpensive activities for you and your child to participate in, such as library story times, mother/child gym or swimming classes, and neighborhood play groups.

38. **Decorate the nursery or child's room.** Sprinkle a little baby powder around the room for that delicious baby smell. I know most pediatricians don't recommend using it on the baby, but I just love the smell.

39. **Buy baby/child announcements and address the envelopes.** For adoption-specific announcements, go to www.adoption.com or type "adoption announcement" into your favorite search engine.

GARAGE SALE WARNING

Adoption is expensive, and most adoptive parents look for ways to save money. Garage sales are great, but you have to be cautious. Safety experts and cost-conscious parents caution against buying the following items used. You can check manufacturer recalls at www.recalls.gov and www.cpsc.gov.

- Car seat of any year or make.
- Cribs older than about ten years.
- Old strollers. Stroller design has improved in recent years, so I wouldn't buy one that was more than a few years old.
- Baby walkers. Check with your pediatrician before buying, since many pediatricians recommend against using them unless they are the stationary walkers, which seems to be a contradiction in terms.
- Old playpens. Regulations on design changed in 1976, but I would avoid any playpen that is older than five years or does not seem sturdy and well maintained. Ask friends whether they used playpens before buying one. I thought they took up too much room and decided against them.
- Baby gates made before 1990 or with diamond-shaped openings with Vs at the top.
- Humidifiers. These may have mold from improper cleaning. Also, some pediatricians recommend against using them, so ask yours before you buy.

---

40. **Buy gifts for your child's caregiver and children at the orphanage.** See Chapter 9 for suggestions.
41. **Buy and read travel books on your child's birth country.**
42. **Make color copies of your child's picture.** Show it to everyone and mail a copy to family and friends who don't live nearby. Ask for their prayers and good wishes.

FUAQs

We have just been referred a twenty-six-month-old boy from Russia. We are planning to name him David, but I've recently read that you should not change the name of a toddler. His Russian name is unusual and we really don't like it.

Naming is an important part of becoming a parent—of claiming your child as your own. I spent much of my childhood imagining names for my future children. However, your child already has a name when he becomes yours, so naming gets complicated. Parents have to weigh their own desires and traditions with the needs of their child both now and as he grows. As with all decisions in adoption, I encourage you to look at it from the standpoint of what is best for the child.

There are two opposing views on changing a child's name. Some say you shouldn't change the child's name regardless of her age. Others don't think twice about changing a school-aged child's name. Both of these positions seem extreme to me.

There is no magical age cutoff, but I see no problem in parents changing the name of a baby. Yes, the baby recognizes his name at a young age, but English-speaking parents are going to pronounce his name differently anyway, so changing the name entirely is not much different. I recommend learning what the child was called (pet name or actual name) in her birth country and gradually shifting to her American name. You may also want to consider keeping part of your child's original name as his middle name. By doing this, you are preserving a part of his heritage and showing respect for his birth parents or birth culture. I would do this even if orphanage workers named him rather than his birth parents. He will have the option of using that name later in life if he thinks it fits him better.

By age four, I would be cautious about changing a child's name. At this age, the child identifies himself with his name. When he is adopted he will lose his language, his culture, and all that is familiar to him. Why add the loss of his name? A parent does have to consider, however, the advantages to having a name that is known in our culture and is easy to pronounce and spell. There are times when a child would prefer not to stand out as different. Also, some names have negative connotations in our culture. As a parent you have to weigh all these considerations, but put your child's interest before your desire to pick the name.

Regardless of the age, consider the following if you decide to change names:

- Hyphenate his name when he arrives and slowly begin to use only his English name. For example, David Vladimir eventually becomes David as his first name, Vladimir as his middle name. Or you could call him Vladimir David at first and gradually drop the Vladimir.
- If a child is old enough, he should have a voice in whether to change his name. Ask your agency to translate this discussion with him either in his birth country or when he arrives.
- Ask his caregiver to start using the new name along with his old name before you pick him up (David Vladimir or Vladimir David). This may not be possible, but it never hurts to ask.

- Consider using an English version of his Russian name.
- Consider a shortened version or nickname of his Russian name (Dimi or Mitri for Dimitri).

On a personal note: Since my husband and I have different last names, all of my children have "Davenport" as their middle name. It is a sense of family identity; even our pets have Davenport as their middle names. We felt very strongly that our youngest child also have Davenport as her middle name, but we also wanted to keep her Korean name. We decided to give her two middle names so she could have both Davenport and her Korean name. Having four names complicates filling out forms and made her work harder when learning to write her name, but it has worked out to be a good compromise. Four names have the added benefit of lending considerable weight and authority when I say them loudly and firmly when she is in trouble.

We are waiting for a referral of a baby girl from Guatemala. We expect a referral in four to six months, although the agency said the latest referrals are coming sooner. I know there are lots of things I should be doing to get ready, but I can't seem to motivate myself to do anything. My husband is getting frustrated with me. I am worried about my reaction.

Don't worry about your lack of motivation or being out of sync with your husband. Trust your instincts and just chill. While staying busy is a welcome distraction for some during the wait, for others it's simply aggravating. You may not feel the need to be distracted or you may be the type of person who likes the adrenaline rush of waiting until the last minute. Some people are afraid to tempt fate by getting everything ready. Then again, you may be just plain tired after the work of preparing your dossier. See a counselor if you think this a sign of depression or unresolved grief. If not, don't worry about it. Focus on relaxing and having fun during these last child-free months.

You may find a surge of motivation once your daughter is referred because a real baby makes impending motherhood real. Once you have a referral, reread the list and see how you feel. In the meantime, if your husband is really gung ho to do something now, consider a compromise by suggesting a project, such as painting the nursery, where he can take the lead and you can participate minimally. The added benefit is that the paint smell will be gone by the time your daughter comes home.

I am panicking about our decision to adopt. I am questioning my ability and desire to be a parent. Is this normal?

When I was about five months pregnant with my first child, I started to panic that we had made a major mistake. We weren't ready to be parents. What if something was wrong with the baby . . . so wrong that we wouldn't be able to cope? Would I be a good mother? Would this child love me? Did we really want all this responsibility? After she was born and we were ready to leave the hospital, my overwhelming thought was that they should definitely not be turning us loose with this child. We seemed so woefully incompetent. I had similar doubts when we adopted. Becoming a parent is a life-altering event. Change, even welcome change, is anxiety producing.

Will our health insurance cover an adopted child for all medical conditions as soon as she arrives?

I can answer that with a resounding "probably." If you are insured under a group health plan covered by the Employee Retirement Income Security Act (ERISA), then your adopted child will be covered as soon as you assume financial responsibility for her. The adoption does not have to be finalized, which is important for families adopting from countries such as Korea that do not finalize the adoption prior to the child being placed with the family. The coverage applies to preexisting conditions. You can enroll your child immediately and do not have to wait until a preset enrollment period. Ask your insurance provider if your plan is covered and what information they need.

If you are insured under an individual plan (not an employer-sponsored plan), then the answer depends on the laws in your state. Many states have laws requiring that individual plans follow the same rules as described above, but to be sure, check with your state insurance department. The easiest way to find contact information is at www.about.com. Search for "departments of insurance" and select your state. Also ask your insurance agent.

Before you leave to finalize the adoption, check with your health insurance company about any special directions you should follow if you or your child needs medical care while you are in your child's birth country.

What is the best way of anticipating clothing sizes for my child?

It's hard to know what size clothing to buy for a child you haven't seen. Your child may be smaller than others her age, so it's best to gauge size by weight rather than age. Size selection is further complicated because each brand differs, but all brands have a weight suggestion for their sizes.

As much as it pains me, I feel compelled to caution you against buying too many clothes before your child comes home. I know you've looked forward to it for years, but it really is hard to predict sizes. Also, your child is likely to grow rapidly once she gets home so she'll quickly outgrow the first things you buy. You will receive clothes as gifts as well. Don't go overboard. Buy just the very basics (a few terry sleepers and everyday outfits) and then splurge on at least one absolutely adorable outfit, complete with matching shoes and socks.

Is it possible to breast-feed an adopted child?

Yes, but it is labor-intensive and works best when adopting a very young infant. Even under the best of circumstances, few moms are able to produce enough milk to meet the baby's need without supplementation. But breast-feeding is a wonderful way to bond with your child even if you don't produce much milk. A lactation aid is used to supply milk to the baby while she is sucking at the breast. Talk with other moms on adoption forums or with La Leche League about which lactation aid to use. Your life will be easier if you buy two. You need to start pumping your breasts as far in advance of the baby's arrival as possible. It is best to rent a high-quality electric pump that allows you to pump both breasts at the same time.

The older the baby when you start trying to breast-feed, the more difficult the process. I can only imagine what a baby accustomed to a bottle must think when you try to get her to latch on to your breast. "Why in the world do you want me to suck on that?!?" For support, contact your local La Leche League or introduce a thread in your favorite adoption forum. And if you decide against trying to breast-feed, remember that despite all the hype about the importance of breast milk, plenty of people have been fed formula and have thrived. My own formula-fed daughter has no allergies, is almost never sick, and is smart as a whip.

FOR EVERY ADOPTION, A DIFFERENT STORY . . .

I thought I would start to feel excited once we got all the paperwork finished, but I don't. We had a very disappointing experience with a couple of domestic adoption attempts, and I don't want to get my hopes up or get too excited until I know for sure that I will actually have a baby. I am still waiting for something bad to happen that will prevent us from adopting. Our dossier has been submitted to China, but we have not heard that it has been logged in yet. My agency says not to worry, but

I do. I worry that the adoption will fall through, that China will not approve us, or that something will happen to prevent us from getting our child. I will celebrate when we have a referral. My husband is excited now and feels certain that it will happen this time, but I have to protect myself until I know for sure. —*RH, Delaware*

———

Last month I was at our ladies' breakfast and all my friends were jabbering on about home decor and clothes. I felt so far removed and withdrawn. I mean, I just had read about starving children in Africa and was trying to come to grips with the fact that my child was one of them. It didn't help that every time my pregnant friend came, all attention went to her. They can all relate since they have all experienced pregnancy. I felt left out. I wanted to shout, "I'm expecting too!"

I know people don't understand about adoption and that I have to open up so they will understand, but that is hard. I did tell one person how I was feeling, and since that moment she has been my biggest supporter. She gushes over my one sad-looking referral picture and she is genuinely excited for us. You have to trust people with your feelings. —*KB, Arizona*

———

One of the real advantages to me for adopting from Guatemala is that we can visit with our child during the wait. We have visited with her twice for five days each and it has definitely made the wait easier and has allowed us to start the bonding process. It took about three days the first visit for her to "come out of her shell" and relax with us. By Sunday night, she was being playful with big sis and Dad.

It was very hard to give her back to the foster family, but it was also wonderful to see the love the foster family had for her. We are very grateful to this wonderful family who are so loving to our precious baby girl, but it was still difficult to actually hand her over and walk away. —*DF, Florida*

———

The wait before we got a picture was not so bad, but once we had a picture I was always thinking about him. We have cherished like gold the referral picture we have of him. I have stayed up studying him, dreaming of him, waiting for him. One night I woke up in a panic and couldn't remember where I put him. It was a horrible feeling because I dreamed I left him in his car seat. I couldn't remember putting him to bed. I thought I would literally pass out from the fear until I gathered my senses and remembered that he isn't here yet. —*KB, Arizona*

———

We used the waiting time to prepare our three bio kids (ages seven, six, and three). We believe that preparation and expectations are key to the success of any endeavor. Our children prayed for their new brother every night, and I believe that made them more aware of his circumstances and gave them a connection to him. They would wake up and say, "I guess he's going to bed now" or they would lie in bed and say, "I guess he's waking up now." He was a part of the family conversation long before we got him. We also constantly told them how sad he may be because he was losing all his friends and how scared he would be because he didn't know us. We tried to explain it as if was happening to them. We would play out the scenario with them as the child getting adopted. We have been home now five weeks and we have had a smooth transition, in part because we were all prepared. —*AR, Colorado*

———

With China the waiting times for referrals have fluctuated in the past and will in the future, but they have never closed down. Once you have your child, you can look back and see that in the long run the extra time was not such a big deal. We completed our adoption last year. The group before us waited only five and a half months for referrals, but for some reason our group was told that it would be about four weeks longer. Four turned into seven with no explanation and no referral. I'll admit it was hard at the time, but I can honestly say that now I am glad we were delayed. If we had not been, we would have referred another child, not our child. She was worth the wait—I would have waited another year for her. —*AY, Georgia*

———

Although I post on them all the time, Internet adoption support groups are both a blessing and a curse. I get buoyed up when I hear someone's good news or rumors of things speeding up, but then I get down when I hear rumors of another slowdown. It's hard to keep on an even keel when you are glued to these forums. —*DF, Florida*

———

So many people make themselves frantic with worry and impatience during the waiting period. You can choose what level of frustration you wish to endure, because it comes from within. My wife and I decided up front that we would not worry about things we could not control. We refused to plan ahead for having our child for certain special events, and we focused instead on enjoying the remains of our child-free life. Sure, we worried about it now and then, but neither of us obsessed about it, and we didn't make ourselves and those around us frantic like we have seen so many do during the wait. This attitude is coined "the un-wait" because you choose not to wait. Just put it out of your mind as best you can. Expect delays and know that you can't control them. The only thing we could control was how frustrated we became. We took the approach that sooner or later it would happen whether or not we worried. And it did . . . two times. —*TG, Georgia*

———

The hardest part of the wait is just getting ready to begin for me. My husband leaves tomorrow to go pick up our son. I am so envious of him that I almost got mad at him tonight while I was helping him pack. This is my lifelong dream and he's getting to go. I know that he was the logical one to go since I am a stay-at-home mom and it would not be fair to our two- and three-year-olds for me to leave them to pick up our new child. But even though it is logical, I'm still jealous and also a little afraid that our new son will become more attached to my husband than to me. I guess I'll just deal with it, but how am I going to get through these next two weeks? How am I ever going to sleep? —*KB, Arizona*

———

The wait has been excruciating. First there was the wait for referral. Our wait was much longer than expected because the orphanage had to be relicensed by the Indian government before they could make any more referrals. We understood, but it still took ten months, which we were not mentally prepared for. After the orphanage received their license, things moved smoothly until we reached the final step—getting our child's passport. I don't know what is happening, but it is taking forever. This has been the most difficult part of the wait. We are so close and yet so far. We can't book our flight, hotel, or anything until we get the passport. So we're still waiting.

The emotions have been all over the spectrum. During the long wait for a referral, I questioned if it was ever going to happen. With all of the delays we thought about changing countries, but we really felt like our son was in India, so we stayed the course. I've been angry, joyous beyond explanation, frustrated . . . you name it and I've probably felt it. During those moments when I've been really, really sad or discouraged, not much helped. The only thing that helped somewhat was relying on my faith to get me through. I know that God has been in the middle of this from the very beginning.

The most trying aspect of this is the total lack of control over anything. I'm pretty much a control freak, so this has been difficult for me to manage. I'm learning to control the things I can, like paperwork deadlines, and turn over the things I can't, which is almost everything during the wait. Accepting this has been an ongoing struggle. —*NC, Oklahoma*

My level of commitment to these children whom I had never even met surprised me during the waiting period. From the moment we accepted their referrals, I became a parent. I, who had to be dragged into the whole adoption process, was now totally and completely the mother to these two children and I had all the worries that all mothers feel: Are they healthy? Are they eating well? In addition to these regular mother worries, I also had the adoptive mom worries: Is the country going to close down? Is a local family going to come in and adopt them out from under us? It was as if I was always waiting for something to fall through. Our wait was very short—thank goodness—but it seemed like an eternity. —*MS, Virginia*

The whole adoption process is about waiting—as if we haven't waited long enough through the childless period of our life. We just submitted our dossier to our agency and have started on the longest part of our wait. These are the things you think about while you wait: Is a woman pregnant with our daughter at this moment? Has she already been born, or been left to be found somewhere? Will bird flu delay the process? Will some politician say something stupid and foul everything up? Will our dossier get lost? These and a host of other questions come to mind every day. It's not all that different from the thoughts and feelings experienced in the infertility process . . . always wondering if there was anything that could have been done differently to have sped up the process, or to have ensured a more favorable result. At least the odds of a successful outcome are much higher with adoption.

The Red Thread is a theme in many China adoption stories, following the idea that the new parents are already connected to the child they will receive, and that it is only a matter of time until they meet. The referral times for China have recently lengthened, and I know some parents feel that they will be getting a "different" child than the one they "should" have gotten had the referral time stayed the same. This is where we feel the connection of the Red Thread. Our daughter is there waiting for us; she doesn't have a specific face, or a certain Chinese name, and she may not have been born yet, but she is still there waiting for us and when the time is right we'll be united.

While we wait, we are starting to let ourselves get excited and think about buying baby things. (Wow, that sure seems strange to say! After nearly ten years of marriage and almost that long hoping in vain for something to happen, it's really getting closer.) There's nothing we've done that has made us feel so inadequate and lost as looking at baby things. How can someone so small need so many things, and so many of them large and expensive? —*KF, Iowa*

———

When we started the adoption process, I checked my company's adoption leave policy and found they had none. Through networking with other adoptive parents at work, I discovered there was usually an "unwritten agreement" at the manager's discretion between the employee, manager, and human resources to allow the employee four weeks' paid leave (essentially, the manager agreeing to not submit paperwork that the employee was taking a leave of absence). While my manager told me that they would likely apply the "unwritten agreement" in my situation, I was not comfortable about being given a "privilege" that may not apply to other employees in my same situation. Also, I was worried that others would assume I was simply working from home, since no one could technically know that I was on a paid leave, and they would feel free to send me work.

I wanted to change my company's benefit package. I first made my pitch to the head of our benefits department. I stressed the importance of our company core values to provide support and hope to those in need, and also highlighted a recent corporate policy allowing employees up to two weeks' paid leave (with benefits) to help with natural disaster relief. I provided information on what five companies within the state of NJ (similar product and size) were offering employees who adopt a child. (I learned through friends employed at these companies that adoption policies differed from as little as three days' to a maximum of six weeks' paid leave with benefits.) I stressed that time out of the office was needed not only to allow for the formal adoption process but, more important, to provide quality time for these children who are often abandoned and living in orphanages to adjust and bond to their new surroundings and permanent family. To adopt a child and immediately put them in a day-care setting would only further delay or even prevent the bonding process.

For the next three months, I continued to contact human resources (via e-mail, phone, and even during a retirement benefits meeting in the employee cafeteria) as to when a policy would be in place supporting families who adopt a child. A few days ago, I learned that adoption benefits have now been included in our benefits package—six weeks' paid leave with benefits, an additional six weeks' unpaid leave with benefits, for a total of twelve weeks' consecutive leave. I am ecstatic with this outcome and feel it's proof positive that people really do care and appreciate that we are new parents in every sense of the word! While they may not be our biological children, they are human beings and are definitely OUR children. —PA, New Jersey

Seeing our little girl grow up is so rewarding, but also tugs at my heart, since the proverbial bud is blooming and the little baby we picked up fourteen months ago is turning into a little girl. Where did the time go?

I remember so well the anxiety, frustrations, and excitement of waiting for the referral to come and waiting for our travel dates. Now that is a distant memory. How awesome these kids are, how they impact our lives and create a sense of completeness that we did not know was absent before they arrived.

Being a parent (that still sounds awesome) is a gift beyond words, and hearing your little one call you "Daddy" is just mind-blowing. I wish all the people in the waiting stage could understand how worthwhile it will be when it is finally over and you have your child. These kids are truly a blessing beyond imagination. —*AW, Texas*

CHAPTER 8

THE REFERRAL AND MEDICAL EVALUATION

We Have a Child for You!

Jacob Ivan was born in Tyumen, Russia, on August 9, 2004, and joined his forever family in June 2005.

*A*fter all our paperwork was finally signed, sealed, and delivered, our agency told us we could expect a referral in about four months. After about two months, I found myself running to answer the phone, checking for voice messages the second I walked in the house, and listening for our caseworker's voice when I picked up the phone. I insulted more that one friend by starting my side of the conversation with "Oh, it's just you." It was magic when we finally heard, "I have a baby for you to consider."

Although we had been open to some special needs, the first baby that was referred to us had more problems than we thought we could handle with three young children. It was a heartbreaking decision. In my mind, I knew we had to make the decision that was best for us as a family, but in my heart I worried that we were giving into fear and that with enough love we could make it work. Our *agency stood by our decision and never pushed or even encouraged us to stretch to accept this child. The decision haunted me long after we were told that the baby had found a family that was up to the challenge.*

The following month, we were referred our daughter. She was classified as a "failure to thrive" baby and there were a few medical concerns. I would be lying if I told you we weren't scared and worried. It felt like we were stepping into the unknown, which I now realize is exactly how you should feel every time you open your life to a child regardless of whether that child is yours through birth or adoption. We consulted our pediatrician and an international adoption medical specialist and within days we said yes. Although this is not always the case, our "failure to thrive" baby has thrived spectacularly, and even if she hadn't, I now firmly believe that she is the child God always wanted us to have.

The process of offering information on a child to a family for consideration is known as a *referral*. The referral is more than just a phone call followed by a picture or video with a medical report attached—it is the potential beginning of a lifetime commitment to love and raise not just any child, but this particular child. Most parents, when pressed, will admit they experienced a mixture of excitement and fear regardless of what the referral "looked like on paper." Prospective parents must use their head and heart in making the decision to accept a referral.

When discussing the idea of evaluating a referral, it's impossible to avoid the feeling that you are discussing a commodity. Even the word *referral* seems to dehumanize the child, and never should we forget that it is a child we are talking about. Nothing in this world is more precious to me, and every parent I know, than a child, and every child deserves a family to love them, protect them, and advocate for them in this world. But not every family is the right one for every child. Rescuing is not the same thing as parenting.

How much information you have to evaluate will depend on the country, the age of the child, how the child entered government care, and your agency. Often the response on whether to accept is a ready and joyous "yes" accompanied by much dancing, arm waving, and phone calling. Sometimes, however, the initial response is "I'm not sure." Be prepared for either.

METHOD OF REFERRAL

The way your child will be referred will depend on the country, and with some countries it also depends on the region within the country. Although there are many variations, referral methods can be divided into three general groups:

standard (prospective parents receive a picture and information on the child and decide before travel or escort), blind (prospective parents travel to meet the child or children with no information beforehand), and semi-blind (prospective parents receive limited information on a child but decide only after meeting this child).

Standard Referral

Standard referral is the oldest and most common method. You send your completed dossier to the country; the country or orphanage matches a child that meets, or comes close to meeting, your preferences on age, gender, and health; the country sends a picture (or video) and medical evaluation to your agency; your agency forwards the information to you. With some countries, the agency does the *matching:* The country sends information on the child to the agency and the agency matches this referral to a family on its waiting list.

You decide to accept or reject the referral based on the information you are given. Your agency should make every attempt to get additional information if you need it to make a decision, although parents report that agencies and countries vary on their willingness and ability to do this. After you accept, you travel to pick up this child. You always have the option to decide against finalizing the adoption once you actually meet the child in country and have more information, but this is especially difficult since you've already started to bond with that child and you run the risk of not getting another referral on that trip.

The advantage of this standard referral method is time. You have time to ponder and make your decision. You have time to get an evaluation by an international adoption doctor (IA doctor) before you travel. You have time to let both the emotional and rational thought processes play out.

The disadvantage is that you are emotionally vested in the child before you actually meet the child, and for some parents this makes it hard to clearly evaluate the child once you see her in person. Also, many parents report that once they accept the referral the wait to travel is excruciating. I found that once we accepted our referral, my maternal worries began: Was she sick, were her needs being met, were her caregivers kind? Every part of me was convinced that no one could care for her like me. As it turned out, I was wrong. She was very well cared for, but no one could have convinced me of that at the time.

A variation to this method is a standard referral with escort rather than travel. You receive a standard referral and accept or reject while at home, but the child is brought to you rather than you traveling to pick up the child. The advantage of this variation is less disruption to the children already in the family, since parents do not have to leave them at home or take them on the adoption trip. Without travel, parents can save their time off work for when the child is at home. Another advantage is that the child is the only jet-lagged member of the family, which may make the first weeks easier. The disadvantage to this method is that parents miss out on a glimpse of their child's birth country and culture and won't have this information to share with their child as he matures. Parents will not have the opportunity to gather information from the caregiver or orphanage director. And arguably it is a rougher transition for the child to be removed from his familiar environment, placed into the arms of strangers for the plane ride home, and then be removed and placed once again with strangers when he arrives.

Blind Referral

The blind referral method, also known as traveling blind, is standard in some Eastern European and Central Asian countries. Your dossier is sent to the country and the country issues you an invitation to travel. Once you are in country, you will be given information on one child or several children. Based on this information, you decide whether to meet this child or these children. You will be given more detailed medical and background information once you meet the child. In some countries, you will be encouraged to meet several children before you decide.

The advantage of this method is that you are able to choose your child; the disadvantage is that you have to choose your child. You will be making a life-altering decision in a short period of time, but potentially you will have more information with which to make this decision. When faced with a real child or children, some parents find it very difficult to maintain the objectivity necessary to decide. Agencies and parents report that the adoption process is faster if you travel with no referral, since you do not have to wait for a match to be made and sent to you in the United States. The children are potentially younger at placement for this same reason. Unfortunately, you risk not finding a child that is the best fit for your family and returning home without a child. Most agencies try hard to prevent this from happening, but before you travel, specifically ask your agency what happens if you do not accept the first child that is presented to you, or the second.

Semi-Blind Referral

Some countries or regions use a modified version of blind travel: Before you travel, you receive very basic information on a specific child, such as age, gender, and maybe limited health information. Once you are in the country, you will be given more detailed medical and background information on that child and you can choose to meet that child or ask to be matched with another child. As with the blind referral method, you will accept the referral only after you meet the child. The advantages and disadvantages of this method are similar to those of the blind referral method, but some parents report that they rest easier knowing that there is a specific child they are traveling to meet.

Which Is Best?

When I first heard about traveling blind, I thought it would be emotionally wrenching. In our adoption, we had a specific referral and accepted that referral without ever having laid eyes on our child. That seemed to me like the logical way to go about it, since that is what we did. Since that time, I have talked with many families who have traveled without a referral. To them, that is the logical way to go about it, since that is what they did. There are advantages and disadvantages to all the referral methods, and one is not necessarily better than the other. Based on my interviews, I have concluded that if you are satisfied with the results you will be satisfied with the referral method, and vice versa.

EVALUATING HEALTH

The desire for a healthy baby is perfectly normal and is shared by most parents regardless of whether they are expecting a baby through birth or adoption. However, some parents who turned to adoption due to infertility have a fantasy that a child born to them would be flawless. Unfortunately, no child is perfect and none comes with a guarantee (or a return policy, although there are days when every parent wishes for one).

In Chapter 2, I defined health broadly to include physical, cognitive, and emotional dimensions. Most children adopted from orphanages will have some health issues when they first arrive home; most will improve significantly with love and nourishment, but some problems are for life and may be too big for you to handle.

When evaluating a referral, you owe it to yourself and to the child to ruthlessly decide what you are willing and able to live with. What is a problem for one family will just be a variation on normal for another, but you must give yourself permission when you start this journey to say no. It is my fervent wish that all children find a forever home, but I pray equally hard that no family adopts a child they are not equipped to parent. Information is power, so get as much as possible. The information you gain is useful not just for deciding whether to accept a referral but also for parenting that special person who will be your child if you accept.

The Medical Report

Regardless of which referral method is used, you will receive some medical and background information on the child before you decide whether this is the child you want to make your own. Although a child is more than how she looks on paper, paper is all you have right now; so you want the paper to provide as much information as possible. A child's health (physical, cognitive, and emotional) is influenced by many factors, including prenatal care (nutrition and habits of the mother), birth history (length of pregnancy, birth weight, and head circumference), early environment (presence of a consistent and loving caregiver; adequate nutrition; and physical, emotional, and language stimulation) and intangibles (resiliency, temperament, and genetics). Your job during the referral evaluation stage is to get as much information as possible on these factors to help you assess your child's current health and prognosis for future health. The Hague Treaty regulations require agencies to make a reasonable effort to obtain this information, and to provide a translated and original copy of all medical records. This is what you should expect of your agency regardless of whether or not they are accredited under the Hague regulations. You will never have all the information you want, but additional information is sometimes available if you ask for it.

The medical reports reflect the philosophy and training of the medical professionals in the birth country, and thus may contain diagnoses that are difficult to understand for Western-trained doctors. For example, almost all referrals from Russia diagnose the child with the scary-sounding "perinatal encephalopathy." Russian physicians apparently use this term to imply a *risk* for neurological injury that would accompany most births, especially if the child has a low birth weight. Western-trained doctors use this term to mean the *existence* of brain damage, not the risk, and presence of this diagnosis does little to help assess the risk. Although some diagnoses should be taken with a grain of salt, don't offhandedly disregard all foreign-sounding diagnoses.

In an ideal world, you would get the following types of information to judge the current and long-term health of the child. The world of adoption exists in the real world of poverty, social instability, and political unrest, so you will likely not find it all.

- **Date of birth.** (May be approximate.)
- **Current weight and height.** It is helpful to have a history of these measurements over time to see a pattern of growth.
- **Head circumference.** A pattern of growth over time is more important than a single measurement; therefore, ask your agency if there are records of circumference measurements taken over the child's life. The measurement should be taken around the largest part of the head; incorrectly placing the measuring tape can result in inaccurate results. If you will be visiting with the child in country and sending information back to your IA doctor, learn how to take the measurement before you go.
- **Medical reports.** The original and translated copy of all medical evaluations performed on the child and the results of all medical tests. It is wise to get an independent translation of all medical reports.
- **Immunization record.** Your pediatrician or IA doctor may suggest re-immunizing once you get home, depending on the country.
- **History of hospitalizations or significant illnesses.**
- **Developmental information.** This should include information on gross motor, fine motor, and language. Notes from caregivers and teachers are very helpful. Keep in mind that the age of your child will affect how much developmental information is available; young babies have simply not reached many developmental milestones.
- **General personality characteristics.** (Easygoing, active, shy, etc.)
- **Prenatal and birth history (if available).** Length of pregnancy, information on the birth, and did mother drink alcohol, smoke, or use drugs during pregnancy.
- **Birth family history.** Occupations, age, living conditions, and health. Why is child in state care?
- **Social history of child.** Varies by age. Placement history. Relationship with caregivers, other children, and teachers. School history. Feelings about adoption.
- **Picture and videotape of child.** Pictures are standard for all countries where you receive a referral. A few countries will send a video. Ideally, you would like to see a picture of the child's face close up and, for babies and young children, a picture of her with only a diaper or underclothes. Your agency can tell you whether this is routinely available in the country you are adopting from. If you will be traveling to the country to see the child before accepting the referral, see the box for suggestions on how to take useful pictures and videos.

The adequacy of medical records varies greatly by country. See the Country Charts appendix. If this information is incomplete or not included, ask your adoption agency to try to get more information and to provide the name and contact information of the physician who examined the child if it is available. This is easier in some countries than in others, but parents have also

HOW TO TAKE USEFUL VIDEOS AND PICTURES

In some countries, you may be in a position to take pictures or a video of the child and have them reviewed by your IA doctor to help you assess the potential health risks of this child. Although a video or pictures are never as good as a physical exam, they can provide a great deal of information for trained eyes. Typical kid pictures may not provide the information your doctor is looking for, so follow these suggestions by IA doctors:

- The environment should be familiar to the child and well lit. Some IA doctors want no other children in the video and others like to see some interaction. Ask your IA doctor which she prefers.
- IA doctors I spoke with are split on how long the video should be. Some prefer no more than five minutes of filming, while others recommend "long and boring," reasoning that you are more likely to capture useful information if the child has a chance to become familiar with you and the video-taping experience. If you are sending the video back to your IA doctor when you are in country, consider how much can be sent with the available technology.
- Spread filming out over several days in case you catch the child on a bad day. (We are all entitled to a few of those.)
- Get a close-up shot of the face from different angles, at different times and in different moods, including some pictures of the child when her face is relaxed and not smiling. Your IA doctor may have specific requirements for taking these close-ups. The rest of the filming should be no farther than about three or four feet away.
- Show the child dressed and partially undressed. It's best not to ask to film the child completely undressed.
- Some doctors want to see a tape of you administering a developmental test they give you, while others recommend just playing with the child. In either case, the doctor is looking for evidence of development, such as whether the child can sit by himself, feed himself, throw a ball, hop, run, and answer simple questions when asked in his language.

reported a great deal of variation among agencies in their willingness to gather additional information. Unfortunately, information on prenatal and birth history is seldom complete.

International Adoption Doctors

The decision of whether to accept a referral is an awesome responsibility, but help is available. Doctors that specialize in international adoption medicine (IA doctors) can review the medical data in your referral and help you assess the health risks for this child. Your regular pediatrician may be able to help as well, but depending on the details in the medical report, you may need a doctor that has reviewed many adoption referrals from this country and is up on the current literature in this field. The doctor will not and should not tell you whether to accept or reject the referral. Their only job is to help you assess the risks; you and only you (and your partner) can decide if you should accept these risks. If the medical report is complex and the potential medical issues unclear, consider consulting more than one IA doctor.

Long-term studies evaluating the effectiveness or accuracy of pre-adoption evaluations by IA doctors have not been conducted. However, since many families bring their children to the same IA doctor post-adoption, the doctors are in a good position to determine the accuracy of the medical report and their assessment. The IA doctors I interviewed thought their evaluations of the health risks were fairly accurate, but readily acknowledged that they were not perfect.

If you are adopting from a country that requires you to meet the child before medical information is released, you can still use an IA doctor. Before you travel, select one or two and ask how they prefer to receive information when you are abroad. You may also be able to hire a doctor in the birth country to examine the child at the orphanage. This is becoming increasingly common in some countries. I have even heard of people hiring an in-country doctor to evaluate the child before they traveled to meet her for the first trip. If you are interested, ask your agency if this is possible and if they can arrange it for you. This doctor may speak directly with your IA doctor in the United States or may give you a separate evaluation.

When the medical and developmental information is easy to understand and appears normal, parents may decide that a medical assessment by an IA doctor is unnecessary. This is a valid choice, especially if there is little information in the medical report. Additionally, some families prefer to rely on their instincts for making this decision. If you feel this way, make sure your instincts

---

HOW TO FIND AN INTERNATIONAL ADOPTION DOCTOR

Many families choose to have their referral information evaluated by a doctor to help them assess the health risks of this child. Although general pediatricians may be able to help, increasingly families are turning to doctors specializing in international adoption medicine (IA doctors). The American Academy of Pediatrics has a directory of members of their Section on Adoption and Foster Care (www.aap.org/sections/adoption). Members of this section specialize in health issues for children adopted from abroad and keep up with new developments. Another list of IA doctors, although they are not necessarily members of the AAP Adoption Section, can be found at the University of Minnesota International Adoption Clinic Web site (www.med.umn.edu/peds/iac; click on Other Adoption Medicine Professionals). It is not necessary for the doctor to be located nearby, but some families want to be able to talk with someone in person or be able to take their child for a post-adoption evaluation to the same doctor who reviewed the referral. Different doctors have different personalities, so talk with them first to see if your personalities mesh. When interviewing an IA doctor, consider the following questions:

- How many adoption referrals have you evaluated? In the last year?
- How many adoption referrals have you evaluated from my country?
- How long does it usually take to have a referral evaluated if we have medical information before we travel?
- How do you arrange to review data if we receive medical information when we are in country?
- How comfortable do you feel with diagnosing fetal alcohol syndrome in a child ____ of age and of _____ethnicity?
- How much do you charge and what is included? Are phone calls after the initial review included, or are they an extra charge?

---

are well educated by reading as much as you can on the possible medical issues, and remain open to asking for outside help to guide you if you later decide it is necessary.

POTENTIAL PROBLEMS

Developmental and Growth Delays

As discussed in Chapter 2, growth and developmental delays are common in children who have spent much time in orphanages and can be caused by many factors including pre- and postnatal malnutrition, neglect, lack of stimulation, and genetic factors. Most parents are less worried about the presence of delays upon arrival than they are with the chances that the child will make up these delays. Research indicates that once adopted into loving homes children can make remarkable growth and developmental progress (Rutter et al., 1998; O'Connor et al., 2000; Bledsoe and Johnston, 2004). The following factors impact a child's ability to catch up from developmental delays:

- **Age at adoption.** Research results are not consistent regarding the importance of adoption age on predicting a child's ability to make up developmental and growth delays, but it is certainly a factor to consider (O'Connor et al., 2000; Tan and Marfo, 2006). No magical cutoff time exists for how long a child can be in an orphanage and still escape unharmed, but children who reside in an orphanage for fewer than six months usually show little long-term effects of institutional life, with risk increasing linearly after that time (International Adoption Project, 2002). Children raised in an orphanage are not doomed for life, but they are at higher risk for the long-term effects of institutionalization.
- **Birth weight.** Doctors are more concerned with low birth weight in a full-term pregnancy than with low birth weight associated with premature birth. A significantly smaller full-term baby indicates stunted prenatal growth during a time when multiple organ systems, including the brain, were developing and might indicate prenatal alcohol exposure or poor maternal health or nutrition.
- **Prenatal exposure to alcohol or drugs.**
- **Head circumference at birth and growth over time.** See discussion later.
- **Quality of postnatal care.** The presence of a consistent caregiver, adequate nutrition, a high staff-to-child ratio, and lack of abuse in the institution or home.

Some, but not all, of this information will be available in the medical records. Researchers in this field speculate that all of these factors interact to create a cumulative impact; each additional factor increases the odds that the child will suffer from long-term effects of institutionalization (International Adoption Project Newsletter, 2002).

Parents should plan on providing developmental therapy for institutionalized children, especially for those kids who were in an orphanage for more than two years, to help correct delays caused by orphanage life. Most counties and public school systems have free early-intervention programs for addressing these types of delays, but many parents find they need to use private services as well. Check with your insurance to see if it covers physical, occupational, and speech therapies.

While the likelihood of developmental delays for children who have spent much time in an institution is great, the likelihood of severe problems is small. You can reduce the chance of adopting a child with severe problems even more by having your referral information reviewed by an IA doctor. But the truth is you will never have all the information you need to eliminate all risks. Parenting is risky, and adopting an institutionalized child makes it even riskier. The good news is that most parents who adopt institutionalized children are very satisfied with their decision (Ryan and Groza, 2004).

Small Head Circumference

Head circumference has been singled out from among the typical growth delays because it is an indicator of brain growth. The most rapid period of brain development occurs during gestation and up to about two years of age. Poor prenatal conditions, including malnutrition, alcohol abuse, smoking, and environmental toxins, combined with lack of stimulation and care after birth can affect brain development and may be reflected in reduced head circumference.

Although head circumference has long been used as one measure of brain health in Western medicine, it is seldom used in isolation. Unfortunately, in international adoption it may be the only objective measurement you have available. If the head circumference is smaller than average for that country, your IA doctor will help you assess the risk. Doctors prefer to see a series of head-circumference measurements over time and information on birth and prenatal history to help determine current and future brain health and development.

The long-term impact of small head circumference is unknown. Doctors know that small head circumference can indicate prenatal exposure to alcohol, poor nutrition before and after birth, and lack of postnatal stimulation, all factors that can affect future cognitive and emotional health. However, research also shows that children's heads will grow substantially after adoption, and in one study of Romanian children, head circumference at adoption had no appreciable effect on cognitive development four years later (Rutter et al., 1998; Bledsoe and Johnston, 2004). Head circumference must be looked at in context with other medical and background information and what is typical for children from this country to draw any reasonable conclusions on long-term health risks.

Attachment Issues

Children raised in an institution are at a higher risk for failing to develop a sense of attachment and trust that is a major foundation for mental health. Imagine the life of a typical infant: the child cries; his parent arrives to feed, diaper, or hold him; his need is met. Over time the parent becomes proficient at meeting his needs quickly and consistently, and the baby comes to trust that this person is reliable and worthy of his trust. This is called the attachment cycle. In a poorly staffed orphanage, the attachment cycle may be broken. The baby cries and waits; the caregiver eventually arrives and has a limited amount of time to figure out what he wants; his need may or may not be met before she moves on to another child. Each day or week there is a different caregiver, so no one ever learns how to quickly and consistently satisfy him. Over time his unmet cries train him that crying is useless and the adults in his life cannot be trusted to meet his needs.

All children from orphanages (as well as neglectful homes) are at risk for attachment issues, but the quality of orphanage care makes a difference. The following are present in the better orphanages:

- Low turnover among caregivers
- Caregiver assigned to care for the same children each day
- Fewer children assigned to each caregiver
- Consistency of placement within an institution
- Absence of abuse from staff or other children
- Adequate nutrition

Attachment is not all or none, and the problems caused by poor attachment can be mild or severe, or anywhere in between. Symptoms can range from fear of being out of sight of the parent to resisting intimacy with parents to excessive desire for control and unrestrained anger. Attachment disorders can be treated and parents can learn specific parenting techniques, discussed in Chapter 10, to help a child who is struggling with attachment. Children with multiple risk factors are more likely to have long-term problems attaching in their new families (Edelsward, 2005; Judge, 2004). Research on internationally adopted children clearly shows that "the vast majority of traumatized children recover from much of their early trauma once they enter safe, stable and nourishing families" (Ryan and Groza, 2004). Sadly, a few carry scars for life. See the Resource Guide for books on attachment.

Fetal Alcohol Syndrome

The term *fetal alcohol syndrome* (FAS) refers to the physical, cognitive, and behavioral impairments caused by prenatal exposure to alcohol. Maternal alcohol use can cause different degrees of impairment, with the severity tied to the quantity of alcohol consumed, the pattern of consumption (binge drinking versus daily consumption), timing during the pregnancy, and genetic susceptibility of the child (Davies and Bledsoe, 2005). In the past, the term *fetal alcohol effect* (FAE) was used to describe the alcohol-related birth defects that weren't quite as bad as FAS—FAS lite, so to speak. This term has fallen out of favor and has been replaced by *fetal alcohol spectrum disorder* (FASD). FASD encompasses all degrees of impairment—from subtle developmental and behavioral defects to full-blown FAS—caused by prenatal alcohol exposure. Under the FASD umbrella a child can be diagnosed with FAS, partial FAS, alcohol-related neurodevelopmental disorder (ARND), or alcohol-related birth defects (ARBD). Researchers estimate that the incidence of the full range of alcohol-related disorders is three to five times the incidence of FAS alone (Kyskan and Moore, 2005).

FAS is difficult to diagnose. No test is available to determine prenatal alcohol exposure or the degree, if any, of impairment. A definitive diagnosis of FAS requires the following: history of maternal alcohol use during pregnancy, growth deficiencies, central nervous system damage, and a cluster of minor facial anomalies, known as the face of FAS (Davies and Bledsoe, 2005).

In any type of adoption, detailed information on maternal alcohol use is seldom available, and even when it is mentioned in the medical reports, important details on the amount and timing during the pregnancy are usually missing. (The exception is Korea, which often provides specific information.) Risk factors that may indicate a higher risk for maternal alcohol use include a history of alcoholism, multiple pregnancies, older age at the time of this pregnancy, and a history of mental illness (Davies and Bledsoe, 2005; Miller et al., 2006). Information on these risk factors may be found in the medical evaluation. Even when there is evidence of drinking, not all children who are exposed to alcohol in utero will be impaired. Research suggests that only a little over 4 percent of heavy drinkers will give birth to a child with FAS (Abel, 1995); however, this statistic does not address the risk of other, less obvious impairments along the FASD spectrum.

Growth deficiencies are common in children whose birth mothers drank, but are also common to all children raised in institutions regardless of whether they were exposed to alcohol prenatally. As a result, growth deficiencies are not very helpful in predicting whether a child has FAS pre-adoption. After adoption, children who are growth-delayed due to malnourishment or institution-alized care usually catch up within the first couple of years, while children with FAS usually do not.

Alcohol exposure can damage the central nervous system of a developing fetus, depending on the amount of alcohol and timing during the pregnancy. Deficits can be found in intelligence, information processing, higher-level thinking, focus, and memory. Children with FAS are often uncoordinated, with poor muscle tone. Behavioral issues may be present, including difficulty reading nonverbal cues, poor impulse control, and poor social skills. Hyperactivity, hypersensitivity to sensory stimulation, and poorly defined sleep/wake cycles also are common with FAS.

Unfortunately, evidence of central nervous system damage is also not very useful by itself in diagnosing FAS pre-adoption, since many of these symptoms do not manifest themselves until the child is older and because these delays can also be caused by lack of stimulation and care in early life. As with growth deficiencies, a child is more likely to make up these cognitive and emotional delays if caused by general orphanage life rather than FAS.

Currently, the most accurate way of diagnosing FAS is to look for the classic facial features—what Drs. Bledsoe and Johnston have called the stigmata of FAS—that are often seen in children with FAS. These features include a thin upper lip with an undeveloped Cupid's bow, a flat area between the nose and upper lip without the usual two ridges, and tiny folds at the inner corners of the eyes (called epicanthal folds), which result in smaller eyes when measured from side to side.

I know it is human nature to read the above description while looking at your referral picture, trying to decide if that lip is flat and those eyes small. I must admit that when I was researching FAS I scrutinized every face I saw. (Peter took offense when I pointed out the possible implications of his undefined upper lip and under-nose ridges.) Don't try to diagnose a disorder as complicated as FAS by yourself. Don't turn down a referral because you think you see some of these characteristics. Get help from a qualified IA doctor with lots of experience evaluating adoption referrals.

FAS is difficult even for IA doctors to diagnose. The causes for growth and developmental delays are hard to untangle, and the classic facial features of FAS can be easily confused with racial features, especially in Asians. Also, a picture meeting very specific criteria is required for an accurate assessment of risk.

This disorder is especially hard to diagnosis in infants, since the facial characteristics are not readily apparent until the child's facial growth slows down around age two or three. The developmental delays are more apparent after age two as well. It is a difficult irony that parents face: Adopting a toddler reduces the possibility of unknowingly adopting a child with FAS, but increases the possibility of adopting a child more affected by institutional life.

To further complicate the diagnosis, not all children who are impaired by alcohol will have the facial anomalies, especially those children at the lesser end of the impairment spectrum. Although evidence suggests that the more pronounced the facial features, the higher the risk of brain damage, it is still possible for a child to have the learning and behavior problems caused by maternal drinking without having the FAS stigmata (Davies and Bledsoe, 2005).

One of the biggest unknowns for parents considering adopting a child with possible FAS is predicting the future for that particular child. The truth is you can't. Much of the research on outcomes for adolescents and adults with FAS is not able to distinguish the effect of FAS from the effect of being raised in an alcoholic environment. Those studies of children raised in adoptive or foster homes did not show an improvement in the cognitive outcomes, but did show an improvement in behavior if the child was removed from the alcoholic home before the age of six months (Aronson, 2003a). The factors that protect children with FAS from the worst outcomes are a stable, loving home and early diagnosis. Parents must be prepared to provide a structured, loving environment with ongoing developmental therapy and educational support.

Prenatal Exposure to Tobacco and Drugs

Smoking is common throughout the world, and tobacco exposure during pregnancy can cause low birth weight and developmental delays. You will likely have little information on the birth mother's smoking habits, but smoking is common in many of the sending countries.

Drug use during pregnancy in most of the sending countries is thought to be less than alcohol use. Information on the birth mother's use of drugs is seldom in the medical report, but you may be able to assess the risk based on information on her lifestyle. The impact of prenatal exposure to drugs depends on the drugs, the frequency, and the timing, but with many recreational drugs the effect is less severe than the impact of alcohol exposure. If the birth mother was in a high-risk group for drug use, discuss the possible impacts with your IA doctor.

Lead Poisoning

Children from some countries are at a higher risk for lead poisoning. Testing on adoptees from China, Russia, and other Eastern European countries has shown a higher incidence of lead poisoning, although the percentage of children with elevated levels was still low (1 to 13 percent for China, 1 to 5 percent for Russia, and 3 to 7 percent for Eastern Europe) (Miller, 2005). Lead poisoning can cause growth delays, learning disabilities, and other neurological problems; therefore, the American Academy of Pediatrics recommends that children who have been adopted from countries where there is an increased risk of exposure to lead be screened upon arrival home and treated if necessary.

Parasites, Mites, and Lice

Intestinal parasites, such as roundworms, hookworms, and *Giardia*, are common in institutional living. The Centers for Disease Control estimate that up to 35 percent of children adopted internationally have intestinal parasites, with international adoption doctors finding a range of 7 to 50 percent, depending on the country. Intestinal parasites are more common in older children and children adopted from Russia, Eastern Europe, India, and Africa. Infected children may have no symptoms, but many are malnourished with chronic diarrhea.

Fortunately, intestinal infestations are usually easy to treat, although repeated testing may be required. Some are easily transmitted to other family members, so the whole family may need to be tested. If treated, they are not likely to cause long-term health problems.

Scabies, microscopic mites that burrow under the skin and cause intense itching and tiny red spots, are common in orphanages and pass easily between children. They are easily treated but sometimes hard to diagnose, since children can grow accustomed to the itching, and secondary bacterial infections can mask the typical look of scabies. The mites can easily be transmitted to family members, so care must be taken to wash all clothing and bedding. Check with an IA doctor about bringing the prescription treatment with you when you travel to pick up your child. Some doctors recommend that you wait to start treatment until the child is home, since scabies can be difficult to diagnose and the medication has potential side effects. Other doctors don't object if parents are trained to identify scabies.

Lice are the lousy little buggers (pun intended) that love to hide out on your head and cause you to want to pull your hair out or at least shave it off. They are common everywhere, including most elementary schools in the United States. They are easily treated, although it may take more than one treatment. Just like parasites and mites, the entire family may need to be treated. Although it sounds gross, few families anywhere have escaped life with children without at least one run-in with lice. When we had an infestation crawling through our home, I thought it was quite romantic when Peter offered to pick the nits out of my hair, which is proof that parenting can warp your sense of romance.

Anemia

Children adopted internationally should always be tested for anemia once they arrive home. In a study of children adopted from China, 35 percent of the children were anemic, whereas a study of Guatemalan adopted children showed 30 percent to be anemic (Miller and Hendrie, 2000; Miller et al., 2005). The anemia is usually due to iron deficiency caused by an inadequate diet. Depending on the degree of anemia, your pediatrician may recommend supplementing your child's diet with iron.

Tuberculosis

Tuberculosis is common in most of the countries placing children for international adoption. IA doctors estimate that the rate of latent tuberculosis infection upon arrival is from 3 to 19 percent, while the rate of active infection is very low. You will likely have test results for tuberculosis in your referral package. Tuberculosis is treatable and should not cause you to reject a referral, but discuss the implications with your pediatrician or IA doctor.

All children being adopted from abroad should be tested once they arrive home, since the testing done pre-adoption may not be accurate and the incubation period can be years. Some U.S. pediatricians resist testing internationally born children because they assume that the BCG vaccine, standard in other countries, renders testing in the United States unnecessary or inaccurate. Both assumptions are wrong. Have your pediatrician check out the American Academy of Pediatrics' *Red Book* for a complete discussion on the recommended testing and interpretation of the results.

Hepatitis B

Hepatitis B, a viral infection affecting the liver, is common in many of the countries placing children for international adoption. Virtually all children referred for adoption will have been tested for hepatitis B, and if they have the virus they will usually be placed as a special-needs child. Approximately 5 to 7 percent of children adopted internationally are carriers of this disease, and family members should be vaccinated prior to adoption. Young children who are carriers most commonly have no symptoms, but will have a higher risk of developing cirrhosis and liver cancer in the future. Many orphanages now give the hepatitis B vaccine to all children in their care, and although it comes too late to prevent an infection in a child exposed at birth, it does reduce the chances of spreading the disease within the orphanage. Great strides are being made in the treatment of this disease. If your referred child has hepatitis B, talk with your pediatrician or IA doctor before you automatically turn down the referral.

Syphilis

Syphilis is a common sexually transmitted disease that is easily passed from mother to child during pregnancy or birth. Although it is present throughout the world, it is more common in Russia, Kazakhstan, and other Eastern European countries, with about 15 percent of the medical reports indicating a history of maternal syphilis (Miller, 2005). Testing and treatment are routine and adequate in most placing countries, and it is rare for a child to arrive in the United States with undiagnosed syphilis. As a precaution, however, all children should be retested once home. Make sure your pediatrician knows if your child was previously treated for syphilis.

HIV

The incidence of HIV infection in internationally adopted children is very low (less than 0.16 percent in one large study), but it is likely to increase as the worldwide rate of infection increases (Miller, 2005). HIV testing is common in most countries, and the results will be included in your medical evaluation. Even if your child has been tested for HIV, you should repeat the test once home.

Rickets

Rickets is a disorder of bone formation caused primarily by a diet lacking in vitamin D and calcium. It is more common in children coming from northern countries, since the number of hours of sunshine is greatly reduced in the winter and sunlight is essential for vitamin D formation and absorption in humans. The classic feature of rickets, the bowing of the legs, is apparent only after a child is walking. Your pediatrician will want to follow your child closely, but rickets usually resolves with a good diet.

Dental Problems

Malnutrition during the time that teeth are forming can cause dental problems in both baby teeth and permanent teeth. One report found that up to 20 percent of children adopted internationally had dental problems, including cavities and defects in tooth enamel (Mitchell and Jenista, 1997). These problems may present themselves later in childhood, even with children who were adopted before six months of age.

Mongolian Spots

Although not a medical issue or a risk factor for future medical issues, I include this discussion because your child's medical evaluation may indicate that she has Mongolian spots. Mongolian spots are harmless skin discolorations commonly found on the lower back or bottom in Asians, Africans, and Latin American children that usually fade as the child ages. Since they can look like bruising, it is advisable to let others who care for your child know about them in advance. After we had accepted the referral of our daughter, our agency required us to sign a statement acknowledging that we had accepted the referral with the knowledge that she had Mongolian spots. Of course, we readily signed the statement, but my curiosity was piqued. I assumed they must be really bad to require a signed statement. The first thing I did when I was first alone with her was undress her to see how bad they really were. I laughed out loud. In her case, they were nothing more than minor birthmarks that were gone by the time she was six.

POTENTIAL SUCCESSES

Most international adoption research is designed to uncover the problems and pathologies of these kids, and perhaps as a result, most of the literature on adoption is similarly focused. This concentration on the negative is a legitimate attempt to paint a clear picture for parents, many of whom view the process at the beginning through rose-colored glasses. And yet I think we have an obligation to show the full picture, which includes the many successes as well as problems. The fact is that most children adopted internationally are doing well. In a large study of 2,300 children adopted internationally (the majority over the age of five at the time of the survey), researchers found that 33 percent of the school-aged children were excelling in school, 16 percent were in programs for the talented and gifted (24 percent of those children whose parents said that prior to adoption they had been cared for "extremely well" were in these programs), and 44 percent had received academic, artistic, or athletic awards (International Adoption Project, 2002). Another large study of 695 adopted Chinese girls found that the Chinese girls had "significantly better behavioral adjustment" than the U.S. norm and warned against adoption professionals automatically assuming the presence of problems (Tan and Marfo, 2006).

Not only are the children thriving, so are the families. Ninety-eight percent of the parents in the first study mentioned would recommend international adoption (International Adoption Project, 2002). In another study of children adopted from Romania, researchers found that even though these children came from extreme deprivation and arrived with very significant delays, almost 92 percent of the parents had a positive view of the adoption; almost 98 percent said they got along well with the child; and about 96 percent said they felt close to the child (Ryan and Groza, 2004). Post the question of satisfaction on any adoption forum and see what response you get. In my experience, adoptive parents have the same ups and downs as most parents and on the whole find the experience just as satisfying.

MAKING THE DECISION

Getting More Information

You or your IA doctor may want additional information either to help you decide whether to accept the referral or to help better prepare you to parent this child, and your agency should be your advocate in getting this information. It may be possible for the IA doctor to e-mail or telephone your child's doctor directly, with your agency acting as translator if necessary. Some information that you would love to have, such as prenatal habits and care, may simply be unavailable, but if the birth mother is known, your agency should make every effort to obtain this information and should not readily accept the claim that no information is available. If they are unable to obtain the requested information, they should at least document their efforts.

To get more information on the quality of the orphanage, you may be able to talk with other parents who have adopted from the same region and even the same orphanage. Ask your agency for the names of families with whom they have placed children from this region or orphanage. Yahoo groups have formed for some regions and even specific orphanages, or you can post the name of the orphanage on a country-specific Internet forum. Ask about the quality of care and how the children have fared once home. Keep in mind that the actual care your child received may vary even if they were in the same orphanage.

If you are adopting from a country that requires you to meet the child before you accept a referral, visit with the child as much as possible before you decide. The child's behavior and mood will change as he becomes more comfortable with you. Notice how he reacts with his caregivers: Is he affectionate, does he look them in the eye, does he go to them for comfort? Do the caregivers seem to know him and how to comfort him?

While at the orphanage, ask for a copy of all records on the child and have them translated. Ask caregivers about developmental milestones, such as rolling over, sitting, and crawling, and how the child compares developmentally with the other children in their care. You may not meet the caregivers in all countries, and even if you do, the caregiver may not know or remember, but it doesn't hurt to ask. Speak with the orphanage doctor or any doctor who evaluated the child.

But—and this is a big but—don't drive yourself crazy searching for that one piece of information that will eliminate all doubt about whether to accept this referral. It doesn't exist. All deliberate decisions to have a child will involve some degree of uncertainty, whether the decision is to try a higher level of infertility treatment, or to use donor eggs, or to have another biological child, or to adopt. Listen to your IA doctor; listen to your adoption agency; and most of all, listen to yourself.

Be suspicious of anyone, especially your agency, guaranteeing that your child is healthy or that all the information is 100 percent correct. The most an agency should promise is that they have done everything in their power to obtain relevant information, and that they have turned it all over to you. Unknowns are simply a part of international adoption, and false assurances help no one.

How Long to Decide

The reasonableness test should apply when deciding how long you have to decide whether to accept or reject a referral. The Hague regulations require that agencies give you two weeks to decide, and this is a good rule of thumb for what is reasonable even if your agency is not required to be accredited under the Hague regulations. You need time to have an IA doctor review the referral information, and fortunately, most IA doctors are very prompt. You should have additional time to obtain and evaluate new information. But once you have all the information that you are going to get, it is your turn to be reasonable. If you are not the family for this child, reject the referral and let the child have the chance to be referred to another family. If you are the family for this child, then it's time to get moving and bring her home.

If you decide against the referral while you are in the placing country, immediately ask for another child to be referred to you. Countries and regions vary in their willingness to refer another child right away, and agencies differ in their willingness to advocate for this. Your agency's and the country's perception of the reasonableness of your decision to reject the first referral will influence their willingness. It is reasonable to turn down a referral because of health concerns; it is not considered reasonable to turn down a referral because of skin coloring or minor differences from your requested age.

Know Yourself

When making this decision, be honest with yourself about the child you want to parent. This is not a charity, this is your family. No reputable agency should push you to accept a child with problems or potential problems that you are not equipped to handle. However, don't automatically reject a referral with a medical issue without being informed. I know I sound like a broken record, but knowledge is power. If you are considering a child with a potential health problem, get as much information as possible from your doctor, other parents who have children with this issue, and online support groups for this specific disability. As the mom of children who have had their share of medical and learning issues, I can tell you that for me, the ride has been well worth the price of admission, but you will have to decide what is best for you.

If you decide against a referral, no matter how reasonable your decision, be prepared to feel awful. You will worry about what will happen to that child, you will feel guilty, you will question your decision, you will grieve. Don't expect the rest of the world to understand, but know that I do and so do the thousands of other adoptive parents who have either been there or, but for the grace of God, would have been there.

HOW MUCH INFORMATION TO SHARE AT THIS STAGE

When your long-awaited referral finally comes, you may want to shout it from the rooftops so all can hear. But unless you are absolutely sure you will accept, I urge you to think carefully about whom you tell when you are deciding. Do you really want advice on this life-altering decision, especially from people who have little knowledge of the issues? If you decide to turn down the referral, you may get the "Oh, how could you" response or your expressions of sadness may be dismissed with the "You never even met the kid" response. Consider letting only those in your inner circle know during the consideration stage.

Once you have accepted a referral, go ahead and shout. Make copies of your referral picture to hand out. I kept a copy in my purse and showed everyone, including complete strangers who were unlucky enough to be stuck in the grocery line with me. Although you should share your good news with the world, be careful what information you share along with the good news. I will address the issue more fully in Chapter 10, but I want to particularly caution you at this stage about being a blabbermouth.

Since your child is not here, it is easy to forget that a real person is attached to the background and medical information. A real person who will grow up around the people you may be tempted to share very personal information with; a real person who will be old enough to understand the implication of this information someday. Imagine little Johnny playing with his eavesdropping cousin and hearing, "How come your mom had syphilis?" Or little Emily overhearing some sweet lady at church saying, "Can you imagine—her real mother just dumped her on the side of the road!"

It may seem innocent enough talking about this information when she is a baby, but she will not always be a baby, and the people you are telling will not forget the details, and will probably share the information with a few of their closest friends, who will share with a few of their closest friends, and on and on. A friend reported that when her preteen son went through the typical sticky-finger stage and snitched a candy bar at the store, her grandmother's neighbor remarked, "Well, his mother was in prison, so what can you expect."

This information belongs to your child, not to the world or even to members of your extended family. Privacy is not the same as secrecy. As your child grows, you will honestly and compassionately share all of her information in a manner that she can understand. You will answer her questions and assure her that she is more than a reflection of her birth parents' history. You will place her birth parents' action in the context of their society and culture. This is what parents do, but you will not have the opportunity to shape what your child hears if your child is getting this information from others. It is for you and your child to decide who else should know this information, and now is not the time to make that decision.

There is no one right way to deflect questions. Some people suggest the "It's private information and not to be shared" approach. Others take the "We know nothing" approach. I have used these at times, but my favorite is the "assume good intent and respond generally" approach followed by the "change the subject" approach. For example:

Q: *Why did his real mother not want him?*

A: There are lots of reasons birth parents place their child for adoption, like extreme poverty or not being ready to parent. By the way, I love those shoes—where did you get them?

Q: *How much do you know about his parents?*

A: Why do you ask? (This is my fallback response, because it flushes out those who are asking out of idle curiosity and usually embarrasses them, at least a little. I can then respond with something very general, like "That depends on the country and the specific circumstances of the child. Can you believe the weather we've been having?"

Q: *How much did you pay for her?*

A: Are you asking about the cost of international adoption? Why do you ask? (If they are thinking about international adoption, I will give them a range of adoption costs using more appropriate language. If they are not interested in adoption, I will say something like "Children aren't for sale, of course, but we did pay for services. The cost varies by country. Would you like some onion dip?"

You may choose to share more with family members, but I still urge some restraint. You have to assume that whatever you say may be repeated to your child someday, so tell only what you want her to hear from others. For example, you might say that her birth mother was young, estranged from her family, and struggling as many young Russians are right now, but leave out the part about supporting herself through prostitution. You can always share more information in the future if you think they need to know or if your child wants to, but you can never take back information once it's told. The good news is that in my experience the nosy background-type questions diminish once your child has been home for a while.

FUAQs

My agency has an IA doctor under contract to review the referrals. Do I need to hire an independent IA doctor?

I would certainly welcome the agency's doctor's review, but I would be concerned about an agency that prohibited or discouraged a parent from seeking an independent medical evaluation. Good agencies want parents to have all the information they need before they decide to parent a child. Personally, I would want an independent evaluation if there were any issues of concern in the medical report.

How much can an IA doctor really tell from looking at the medical report and pictures?

Doctors are not seers and can't predict the future for the child you are considering; however, they can apply their education and experience to help you assess the health risks of this child. The factors that affect the accuracy of the assessment are:

- Quality of medical report
- Age of the child
- Experience of the doctor

If I turn down a referral, will I go back to the bottom of the list?

No responsible agency wants a family to accept a child they are not prepared to parent. If your reasons for turning down the referral are reasonable, you should not have any problem getting another referral soon. If, however, you have turned down several referrals or if your reasons seem trivial, your caseworker will probably talk to you about what you can realistically expect from adoption before they offer you another referral. Consider going back through the parental preference worksheet in Chapter 2 and rethink your choice of country or your readiness to adopt.

FOR EVERY ADOPTION, A DIFFERENT STORY . . .

Depending on the type of referral, there may not be a clear distinction between referral and meeting stories; therefore, read the stories at the end of Chapter 9 as well. Keep in mind that the exact process may have changed since these adoptions were completed.

We received a referral of a beautiful nine-month-old from China. Our case manager called to tell us that a baby had been referred to us. All she knew at the time was her age. The next day, she received the referral package and we immediately drove to her office. The packet contained basic information: her name, what province she was from, and her height and weight measurements, which were a couple of months old. The medical report contained very little detail, but said she was healthy. There was a basic developmental checklist, with all the boxes checked as normal. We had our pediatrician look over the medical and developmental information, but we weren't worried because there was little information other than she was developing normally. We also received three pictures: one head shot and two body shots. The narrative said she was in foster care, but there was also a mention of being at an orphanage, so we really don't know where she lived or for how long. There was very little other information except for a comment that she liked to watch TV! I wasn't sure how I felt about my baby being a couch potato at nine months. We immediately accepted the referral without reservations. —*CH, North Carolina*

———

We got fairly detailed information in our referral from Guatemala. Of course, our son was very young, so they didn't have a lot of developmental milestones to report in the referral, but we got regular updates of how he was developing. We went to visit him for two weeks after we accepted the referral, so we were able to see for ourselves how he was doing. There was some information on the birth mother's background and medical history. It was an easy decision to accept this referral, because it was exactly what we were hoping for. —*VL, Virginia*

———

Our referral from China was confusing. The weight listed was very low, but the narrative described her as chunky and chubby. In the picture she had on lots of clothes, but from what we could tell, she did not look scrawny. The IA doctor we consulted thought that since the narrative and the photos were consistent, it was possible that the numbers of the weight were transposed or recorded incorrectly. We asked our agency for more information, but they were not able to get an update. We accepted the referral, but the wait to travel was an anxiety-filled time. We assume now that the IA doctor was right, since the adjective "robust" is the most accurate description of our beautiful girl. —*JF, New York*

———

We wanted to adopt two children at once and were open to either two unrelated children or siblings. Our region in Russia used the standard referral method and we received pictures and medical information, which we had reviewed by two separate international adoption specialists. We turned down the referral of two sibling groups before we accepted the third referral of two unrelated boys. We received no pressure from our agency to accept the first two referrals. As hard as it is, you need to view the referrals without emotion in order to make the best decision for your family. It's like rewiring your emotions, although to this day I think of the pictures of our first two referrals.

While we were gathering information and trying to decide whether to accept the referrals, we did not share information or discuss it with anyone, since we did not want advice. After we accepted the referrals, we shared very little background information on our sons, since I didn't want people to have preconceived ideas about them. We didn't even show their referral pictures, since the picture of one boy was not good and we thought it would engrave a negative image of "the poor orphan" in the minds of our family and friends, which might affect how they treated him. I probably would have taken a different approach if both pictures had been really cute. —*MG, Virginia*

We were pleasantly surprised by how detailed our daughter's medical report from Colombia was. It included a detailed account of her health from entering the orphanage at three days old to a week before we reviewed it. They recorded her weight, height, and head size regularly and we were able to chart her on the growth charts and see that she was making good growth progress. Our daughter had some minor health episodes, and the doctor's account of what they did to correct and monitor them was impressive to my husband (an ER nurse and physician's assistant student), as well as several doctors who saw the report. We spoke with some doctors we knew and had our pediatrician review her information to help determine whether we would be dealing with other health issues due to some behaviors that were documented during the pregnancy. We didn't know how to find an international adoption doctor, so we did not use one. Her medical report also had good developmental information and she was on target for all areas. We did ask for more information on a few things, and we got our answers within a few days. Now that she is home, I can say that the medical and developmental information was completely accurate. —*RO, New York*

Exactly eight weeks after we submitted our dossier to Ethiopia, I got an e-mail from our agency asking me to call. I tried to call but got voice mail, so resigned myself to not knowing what they wanted until the afternoon when I was finished teaching. As I was walking into my classroom, my cell phone rang and I couldn't resist answering it. My husband said, "His name is _____ and he was born three months ago." I started crying, much to the concern of my students. When I pulled it together, I announced, "It's a boy; I have a son," and my tenth-graders all cheered. The next day, we got our official referral packet with medical information, family history, and two pictures of our little guy. The information was relatively minimal, but enough to make me cry for the heartache my son had already endured. I had expected to be ecstatic when we got our referral, and I was, but I also was devastated. My heart just broke for the tragedies that he had already lived through at three months old. My heart hurt for him and for the surviving members of his birth family who were no longer able to care for him. —*HMJ, California*

———

When we received our referral from Korea for the twins, we got some information on their health, medical test results, medical history, background information on their birth parents, and more. I didn't think it was a lot of information, but compared to other countries it probably was. There was nothing in their report that indicated any reason for concern, but we had our pediatrician look over it. For our next adoption, we chose a waiting child in Korea and we got thorough information on his medical condition, how it was treated, and background information on his birth parents. We had our pediatrician look over his medical information and he was not concerned, but at that point, nothing he would have said would have made us change our minds. We were already committed to him and we were already aware of his health issue before we received the referral, since we had chosen him. —*RM, Pennsylvania*

———

Our referral took me a little by surprise. We had been expecting a young baby. In all our paperwork I stated our preference for a young baby. Even in my letter to the government, I was very clear. But in my home study the social worker approved us for a child up to two years. Our facilitator didn't look at anything else and chose our son based on that one check in one little box. That's all it took to determine who our son was going to be. We got a referral for a sixteen-month-old little boy. Two weeks prior to the referral, I had read a book about older child

adoption, so my heart was ready. Now that he's home, I can't imagine anything different. It was meant to be, despite what I thought I wanted.
—*KB, Arizona*

———

I was hesitant to accept the referral for my daughter because she was on a respirator when she was referred. I felt my agency was pushing me by telling me that she would be fine. The attitude of the Guatemalan attorney seemed to be that I should be happy with whatever I was referred since I was a single woman. I used a medical specialist here, but he recommended that I wait a few months to see how she developed. That was not an option with my agency or the Guatemalan attorney. Fortunately, the Guatemalan doctor who was treating her spoke English, so I was able to talk directly with him, but I still waited ten days before I felt comfortable enough to say yes. I am, of course, immensely happy that I accepted, but I had to pay all the medical costs for her hospital stay in Guatemala, which made my adoption more expensive. I was able to get my health insurance to cover some of the cost, but I had to fight them every step of the way. Documenting the expenses was a major hassle, because I needed to submit the original bills for reimbursement. Once the Guatemalan attorneys were paid, they weren't very helpful in tracking these down.
—*MM, Maryland*

———

Referral day was not exactly as I had anticipated. We got a call from our social worker telling us that they had a referral of a little boy with "hydrocephalus" (basically, water on the brain). We had indicated in our paperwork that we were open to hydrocephalus, but when it was staring us in the face it was more than a little frightening. They faxed over the referral and sixteen pages of medical information for us to take a look at. India is known for providing thorough medical data, and our agency was helpful in getting additional information. We dropped off this information at our pediatrician and I started researching this condition on the Internet. While it was information that we needed to know, I think it became information overload for me for a while. Fortunately, we had time to process all the information and our research, and by the time we finally met with the pediatrician to get his input, we already knew that this was our son. When trying to decide, we looked at the best- and worst-case scenarios and became comfortable with either of them. Once we knew we could handle the likely best or worse, we knew that this little boy was meant to be ours. Still, the decision was difficult, mostly because of the "what if"s that kept creeping in. But, once we accepted the referral, I felt a "peace" come over me. That feeling was indescribable. We knew that we had made the right decision. By the way, our son is doing great now except for a few minor developmental delays. —*NC, Oklahoma*

———

We traveled blind for our adoption. We turned down two referrals before accepting the third. The two children we turned down had medical issues (suspected FAS and severe prematurity) that we had specifically stated we could not accept prior to leaving the United States. The third child that we did accept was much older than we had hoped and asked for. We were told if we did not accept the third we would be asked to leave the region. The whole trip was a nightmare and extremely traumatic for us. We were treated very poorly after declining the first two children. Things improved slightly after accepting the third referral.

I know I sound so cynical, but it has been a difficult journey that we hope will brighten soon. It has been five months since our first trip, with no court date yet. As a mental health professional, I am well aware of the potential problems of adopting "older" children. I struggle daily with these fears, and as the days go by and she is not home, the fears become larger. But of course the little face and being that we met haunts us as well. We have debated walking away; drawing a line in the sand—if she is not home by this date we will stop everything. But, of course, the line moves as our emotions influence our intellect.

I have much to say about this process when looking in the rearview mirror, so to speak, and have many ideas about what we "should" have done. We talk about this daily in our house and grieve daily the way in which we approached this. I think our biggest mistake was approaching adoption with such a trusting attitude (trusting the agency, trusting that we would be prepared for every piece of the process, trusting that all involved would be working in our best interest). This may be a reflection on our agency rather than on the entire process of international adoption. I know my perspective will continue to shift as our journey continues. I hope that someday we will look back and feel the process went exactly as it should have to bring our daughter to our family. —*VC, Oregon*

———

My daughter was referred at ten months from Vietnam. They gave me basic information such as her name, age, weight, height, and how she came to live at the orphanage. The referral stated that she was healthy, but there was little other medical information. Since I had asked for a healthy child and her report indicated that she was healthy, I saw no need to get a review by a doctor. Also, there wasn't much information for a doctor to review. I trusted God to give me the child that belonged to me and I figured that I would deal with any problems if they happened. There is always the possibility of something unexpected turning up after you get your child, but that can happen with any adoption or birth.

As silly as it sounds, I remember mostly being worried about whether I would think she was beautiful. I knew referrals were coming quickly, but I was thinking in terms of weeks, not days. I was sleeping in one morning when the phone rang. I was totally shocked to hear my case manager's voice. I stumbled around to find pen and paper. She told me she was sending me pictures right then by e-mail, and I couldn't get my laptop on fast enough. I was so scared that I would think she was ugly, but then her picture came up and all I could see was her beautiful eyes and heart-shaped lips. I would have accepted her referral regardless of her looks, but she was truly beautiful.

She had a constant cough after I brought her home, so we tested for TB several times, but it ended up being asthma. I never thought that they should have told me about this or that I was tricked; I just knew that this was part of the unknown with international adoption. —*SR, North Carolina*

———

We traveled to Ukraine with only an appointment date with the National Adoption Center; we knew absolutely nothing about the possible child we would see other than that we had requested a toddler. We showed up at the appointed time and were presented with the "books"— three-ring binders filled with pictures of children. The children we looked at in the binders were mainly children who were very sick or out of our preferred age range. The NAC official then handed our translator a loose referral of two children—a fourteen-year-old girl and a three-year-old boy. The facilitator called the directors of the orphanages where the two children lived. She was told that they were half-siblings and that although the fourteen-year-old girl did not want to be adopted, she gave verbal consent to her brother being adopted during the call. The orphanage of the three-year-old boy stated he was in good health, but there was some kind of issue with his testicles—not a big deal, they said, and he was healthy otherwise. (We now know that she was referring to phimosis, which is where the foreskin does not retract, and they were correct that it has not been a problem.) We had no other health information, no picture, and no information on how or when he entered the orphanage.

We had some concern about meeting this child, because he was only two and a half months younger than our birth daughter, and we thought a bigger age difference might be better for them both. We were strongly encouraged to visit this child and then make the decision. Our facilitator told us that the NAC would disapprove of us refusing to meet this basically healthy referral, but if the referral did not work out for some reason because of health or personality issues, we could request an appointment for another referral and this request would be looked on more favorably. We were hearing from others that some families had been waiting weeks for a second referral. We chose to meet him and accepted his referral at the end of that meeting. —*AC, Ohio*

W̲e had a referral that included the child's age, name, picture, and a statement that he met our request of a healthy boy between the ages of twelve and eighteen months. When we arrived at the orphanage, we met with the doctor first to get more medical and background information on this child. There was nothing in the report unexpected or particularly worrisome. When we met the child we felt no instant connection, but we knew we needed to give it some time. As we played with him, we began to be concerned. We noticed that he would not make eye contact with us or his caregivers, and he was also holding one of his hands in a very odd way. He seemed fairly out of it. The therapist at the orphanage gave him a good review for his overall development, but he just didn't seem "all there" to us. (We have a biological son, so we have experience with babies.) We took a lot of pictures, which we intended to e-mail to our IA doctor in the United States, but we were getting pretty bad vibes about this little boy. At one point, he got upset and started repeatedly banging his head against the floor. That totally freaked my husband out.

While we were playing with the child we had been referred, another little boy in the playroom really caught our eye. He looked very similar to our bio son. My husband was checking him out while I was playing with our referral. After the head-banging incident, even our facilitator was beginning to realize that this child had some serious issues.

My husband asked about the other little boy, and our facilitator made some discreet inquiries and found out he was available. The therapist told her, however, that she really thought that our referral was a "better boy, more advanced." Our facilitator told us that if we rejected our referral, he could get us a formal referral for the other boy. We rejected him in writing (without hesitation, really), and the next day we went back to the minister of education. We asked to see the other boy in the group and she gave us a formal referral. The second I held this child, I knew he was mine. He cuddled up to me and never let go. The caregivers were amazed. That child has been our son for almost two years and he is perfect. At sixteen months he weighed seventeen pounds and could not walk. He caught up in no time and attached immediately. Every time I think that this jubilant little boy almost languished forever in an orphanage, I shudder.

I was not particularly impressed with our agency during this process. On the other hand, I felt like our facilitator in country would help us in any way he could. It was the first time I felt like someone from my agency was working for us instead of the other way around. —JS, Pennsylvania

———

We decided at the beginning against any country that used a blind referral, because it felt too much like baby shopping to us—picking out the perfect child and rejecting others. We didn't want any part of that. We chose Russia and were referred a six-month-old boy. The referral had his name and age but little else other than a statement that he was healthy. We received no medical information on him until I arrived in Russia. The medical report on this little boy was alarming, and the minute I saw him I knew that he was not the "right" child for us. The potential problems were just too great. I felt like such a mean, hateful person, but my gut was telling me this was all wrong. When I asked in the car on the drive back to the hotel if I could see another baby, the facilitator kept asking me why I didn't like the baby and why was I rejecting the baby. His choice of words made me feel even worse. Finally, I said that I was hoping for a baby that looked more like my husband. Although it wasn't exactly true, it seemed to satisfy the facilitator as to my reasons.

I had no idea what would happen next. I realized that I had spent all this money to get to Russia and there was no guarantee of getting another referral while I was there. Also, this was getting uncomfortably close to feeling like baby shopping.

Fortunately, I was given the referral of a seven-month-old boy the next day. His medical report showed that there was some concern about a hearing impairment due to chronic ear infections, he had been hospitalized for pneumonia three times, his mother had unsuccessfully tried to abort the pregnancy, he had a low birth weight, and there was something mentioned about possible brain damage. On the bright side, the social worker at the orphanage had met his birth mother and told us she was not an alcoholic.

I was scared to death on the drive to the orphanage, but when they handed him to me, I became unglued. I knew absolutely that he was my son. I had to really struggle to be objective after that. I hired a doctor in Russia to come to the orphanage and evaluate him. It wasn't cheap, since the doctor had to be flown in from Moscow, but it was worth it. The doctor saw no signs of fetal alcohol syndrome or other problems, but couldn't be sure about his hearing. I called my husband and we decided we could handle a hearing problem, and we accepted the referral the next day. He's been home a year now and is remarkably healthy and his hearing is fine. He is everything we could have possibly wanted in a son.
—RM, Virginia

———

Ours is not the typical referral story from Guatemala, since most people adopt infants through private attorneys and we wanted to adopt a sibling group. We had already submitted our dossier to Russia with another agency when I found two sisters from Guatemala on a photolisting Web site and spoke with their agency on the phone. The next day we signed with that agency, but lost the two sisters to another family that week. The agency then gave us information on a brother and sister, but before we could accept, they realized there was a problem with the relinquishment papers. They then gave us a referral on a one-year-old who was born premature and had required surgery to correct a congenital eye problem.

During this referral process, we specifically did not want to see a picture at first because we felt very strongly that we were not "shopping" for the right-looking kid. My husband said he didn't care if the child was purple; if God meant for her to be ours, she would be ours.

We consulted an ophthalmologist and our pediatrician about the medical information on this little girl. At our agency's suggestions, our ophthalmologist called the Guatemalan eye surgeon for additional information. It really helped that our doctor could talk with the Guatemalan doctor to ask questions. With this information we readily accepted this referral.

The agency then gave us another referral for a five-year-old girl. After checking her medical report, we decided we would adopt these two unrelated girls and our family would be complete. Our process of review and acceptance was hurried because our agency was concerned that Guatemala would change their adoption laws and they wanted us to have our adoption in process in case that happened. We hurriedly accepted this last referral and flew to Guatemala one week later to meet our new daughters. —DF, Florida

———

We traveled without a referral to Kazakhstan to adopt. We were planning on adopting a baby girl, but we were open to the idea of adopting two children at once. We hadn't given it much thought other than making sure that it was an option in our home study. At the orphanage we were shown eight baby and toddler girls. We narrowed our choices down to four after the first two-hour visit. The director gave us the medical reports on these four. We were told to take as much time as needed to decide which child, because it is a life-altering decision. We couldn't decide between two little girls—an eight-month-old and a twenty-two-month-old—so we accepted both.

The medical reports indicated that both were born healthy and were currently healthy. The eight-month-old had been relinquished at birth and her report said that the birth mom had not used drugs or alcohol during the pregnancy. We were told the birth mom of the twenty-two-month-old had died but they didn't know the cause. The maternal grandmother was a registered alcoholic and was unable to care for the child after her mother's death. She lived with other family members but was brought to the orphanage due to financial strain, according to the orphanage's information. We did not have an IA doctor review the medical records since they said the girls were healthy, but we read about developmental stages in a baby book we brought from home and both girls seemed to be pretty much on target or just slightly behind.

After we visited with the girls for fourteen days in the morning and afternoon, we went to court and were given custody of the girls until the rest of the paperwork was complete. We brought the girls back to our hotel, and within twenty-four hours we realized we had made a huge mistake. Although our eight-month-old was perfect in every way, the twenty-two-month-old was exhibiting very worrisome behavior. We had not seen these behaviors in the orphanage, but this was a new environment and a very different child. Also, we realized that we were not ready to adopt two children, and we had never really intended to adopt a child over the age of one.

It was at this point that we started to feel pressure from our agency. After the first twenty-four hours, we called our facilitator and told her we were sure we had made a mistake and asked if we could send the twenty-two-month-old back to the orphanage. She told us that it was too late to change our minds, and if we sent her back we would also lose the eight-month-old. Our agency in the United States confirmed this the next day and added that if we sent her back it would cause big problems for them. They encouraged us to give it more time, but each day only got worse. We felt very alone and scared. Our agency encouraged us to come home while the adoption was being finalized instead of staying in Kazakhstan for the entire time, as we had originally planned.

We have been home now for two weeks. At this point, we are trying to clear our heads and make the right decision. My husband is an emotional wreck and totally beside himself. I'm trying to be levelheaded and logical, but I'm scared. If we bring her home, she is our total responsibility and we may not be able to meet her needs. If we don't bring her home, we lose the eight-month-old and will have trouble adopting from Kazakhstan again.

Looking back, there was one warning sign we should have paid more attention to. The day before court, we had a required meeting with a Kazakh social worker. The social worker told us that both of the birth parents of our twenty-two-month-old were alcoholics, but the orphanage didn't have that information. She said her bio mom died from TB, and that the aunt she was living with could not control her. The social worker was very emotional about what we were about to do, but had nothing to back up her argument. After we left her office, our facilitator told us she had never trusted that social worker and that she thought the social worker was lying. We realize now that our facilitator betrayed us. We thought she was the one to trust, but now I realize we had no one to trust. If we could only go back in time to that day and make a different decision—but, of course, we can't.

Too late, but I now realize that we were blinded by our dreams when we were presented with all those children. We should have stuck with our original intention of adopting one healthy girl under the age of one. Unfortunately, we had stars in our eyes. —*RH, New York*

CHAPTER 9

MEETING YOUR CHILD

How to Maneuver Through Airports with Luggage and Child While Maintaining Your Sanity and Sense of Humor

Aislin Suzanne Paulina was born in Kursk, Russia, on October 16, 2002, and joined her forever family in July 2003.

When Sara and Ben arrived at the orphanage to meet their new son, Luke, they were both terrified. "I had no idea what to expect and was still trying to adjust to the new time zone and culture," remembers Ben. "Truthfully, I felt like I was in shock and was processing things slowly." Within thirty minutes of arriving at the orphanage, twelve-month-old Luke was brought to them. "He also looked kind of shocked and sleepy, so I felt like we had something in common," says Ben. Sara was prepared to not feel an overwhelming bond and was content to just sit on the floor and play with Luke. They had agreed ahead of time to spend three days with him before they decided anything. "Giving ourselves this time took the pressure off of us and allowed us to relax," notes Sara. They sent pictures and information to their international adoption doctor back home and talked with her twice during those three days. At *the end of that time, they had no reservations accepting the referral and starting the process to adopt Luke. "Everything went just as we had planned, except that I didn't realize how hard it would be to leave him when our first trip was over."*

Ask any parent and they will talk for hours about the first time they met their child. If they are parents by birth, they will tell you birthing stories; if they are parents by adoption, they will tell you meeting stories (wonderfully known as "gotcha stories"). No other aspect of the adoption journey is more fun for parents to tell and prospective parents to hear. The fun begins with an invitation to travel to meet or pick up your child.

For most countries, parents are responsible for arranging their flight to the country. Depending on the agency and the country, either the agency or the parents will make the hotel arrangements. In some countries, parents usually stay in apartments rather than hotels, and in a few countries parents can stay in "guest houses" associated with the orphanages. They are usually met in the country by agency representatives consisting of some combination of facilitator, translator, and driver.

There are variations, of course—traveling in groups or alone, length of stay, and number of trips—but the following events must happen in all countries.

1. Meeting the child
2. Finalizing the adoption (in most countries)
3. Obtaining child's passport from birth country
4. Obtaining child's immigration visa from the U.S. Embassy

Meeting your child is the fun part, so like dessert, I'll save it for last. We'll start with the meat and potatoes of your trip, the boring but necessary legal stuff.

Finalizing the Adoption

In most countries, the adoption is finalized in the country according to the laws of that country. (The exceptions are countries, such as Korea and India, where the adoption is finalized in the United States according to the adoption law of your state of residence.) Therefore, at some point in their travel, parents or an agency representative must appear in court or before a notary to finalize the adoption. What you can expect in court varies from a cursory stamping of documents to an in-depth review including questions aimed at you. Your agency, as always, should fill you in on the details for your country, region, and, in some cases, judge. Usually parents will receive the final adoption decree and birth certificate for the child at that time.

Obtaining Child's Passport

Once parents have the final adoption decree and birth certificate, they can apply for a passport from the country that will allow the child to travel to the United States. The process for obtaining the passport and the time required varies by country, and usually your agency will handle the details.

Obtaining U.S. Immigration Visa

You got the immigration ball rolling with the I-600A form you filled out for the USCIS when preparing your dossier. (Refer back to the discussion in Chapter 6.) The final step (the I-600) must be completed in your child's birth country. Depending on where the orphanage is located, you will probably have to travel within the country to the U.S. Embassy or the consulate that processes these visas. Your child must be examined by an embassy-approved doctor and you will be interviewed by embassy personnel.

The medical exam is brief and is intended only to rule out any obvious infectious diseases that might impact U.S. public health. You will usually have medical records from the orphanage to give to the embassy-approved doctor. Be prepared to wait, because invariably there is a line. The interview is also cursory, and your agency will tell you what documents you need to bring with you. If only one parent travels, ask your agency the exact procedure the U.S. Embassy in this country requires for one parent to fill out the I-600 form. The wait for the paperwork can take a day or two, but at the end you will be handed the Holy Grail—a sealed envelope containing the immigration documents that will allow your child to come home. U.S. Immigration is very touchy about these papers, so do not open the envelope or in any way disturb the original seal. Make a copy of the front of the envelope while you are in country. Keep the envelope readily available in the travel folder (described later in this chapter), because you'll be flashing this envelope to all sorts of officials on your trip home.

MEETING THE CHILD

The way your child was referred will obviously influence the meeting process. With blind or semi-blind referrals, the parents meet the child at about the same time they receive detailed medical information. In standard referral countries, no additional medical information is given when the parents meet their child unless there has been a change in the child's medical status. In essence, in standard referral countries the first time parents see the child they know that he is theirs. With blind and semi-blind referral countries, the first time parents meet the child they are still deciding if he will be their child. This distinction obviously affects how parents approach the first meeting.

The typical meeting process for the following countries will give you a feel for the variety out there. The process in other countries varies along these general themes.

China Families travel in groups of adoptive families to China after having accepted a specific referral. An English-speaking guide is almost always with the group at all times. Usually, parents will spend a day or two in Beijing before going to the capital city of the province where the orphanage is located. Parents will receive custody of the child either that day or the next at either the civil affairs office or the hotel. Every so often, families will be allowed to go to the orphanage or foster home to pick up their child, but this is unlikely. Usually, the orphanage director and a caregiver will be present when the children are given to their parents and are available at that time to answer questions. Unfortunately, the caregiver who brings the child may not have been the primary caregiver at the orphanage and so may not know many specifics on your child. Parents will sign the Chinese adoption papers finalizing the adoption that day or within a few days, depending on the region. The adoption is final at that point, but it is possible to ask for more time if a parent is uncertain. The family will stay in the child's province until the adoption paperwork is processed and then fly to Guangzhou to complete the immigration paperwork with the U.S. Consulate.

Russia The only thing consistent about Russia is its inconsistency, and a great deal of variation exists between regions and agencies. Referrals from Russia can be blind, semi-blind, or standard, but the meeting process is similar with each referral method. Parents usually do not travel in groups, but most agencies provide an English-speaking representative to accompany parents to all important meetings. Parents first meet with the regional minister of education to be given basic information on a child, then travel to the orphanage to meet the child and receive more detailed medical information from the director of the orphanage and orphanage doctor. It is common to have a couple of meetings with the child at the orphanage before the parent decides whether to accept this referral, but it is expected that the decision will be made within a few days. Parents can ask questions of the primary caregiver and observe her caring for the child. Although agencies report that most families accept the first referral, unlike China, it is not uncommon for families to see one or two other children before they find their child. Parents return home and await a court date. This waiting time can vary significantly by year and region, so ask your agency about the current wait. The adoption is finalized on the second trip and parents are given custody after the court hearing. Once the parents have the adoption and passport paperwork, they return to Moscow with their child to get the child's U.S. visa.

Guatemala Guatemala uses the standard referral method, and although most families go to Guatemala to pick up their child, it is possible to have her escorted. Most families travel alone and stay in country three to five days. Most agencies have an English-speaking representative accompany parents to official meetings, but they are not with parents otherwise. Children are usually referred soon after birth and live in foster homes. Parents can travel to visit with their child during the wait for the adoption to be finalized, although many agencies recommend waiting until the relinquishment papers are finalized. On the trip to bring the child home, the foster mother and agency representative will turn over custody to you at your hotel on the first or second day and the foster mother is available to answer your questions. It may be possible to meet the birth mother on this trip. The adoption is usually finalized before you arrive in Guatemala, so most families have no court proceedings to attend. The immigration paperwork is completed at the U.S. Embassy in Guatemala City.

South Korea Korea uses a standard referral method and parents have a choice of whether to travel to Korea to pick up their child or have her escorted to them in the United States. Agencies report that parents are divided evenly between travel and escort. When parents travel, they travel alone and stay in Korea three to five days. Most agencies have an English-speaking representative accompany parents to official meetings, but they are not with parents otherwise. Parents will meet with the child and foster mother, usually at the Korean placement agency's office for about an hour, and can ask the foster mother and agency personnel questions. Sometimes parents are able to go to the foster mother's house for another meeting. Usually parents do not receive custody of the child until the day of their return to the United States, or the night before if they have a morning flight. If the child is escorted, parents meet their child for the first time at either the airport of entry to the United States or an airport near their home.

Kazakhstan There is a great deal of variation between how agencies refer children from Kazakhstan. Both the blind and semi-blind referral methods are used, but the trend is now toward blind referrals. Parents do not travel in groups with an assigned guide, but most agencies have an English-speaking representative accompany the parents to all important meetings.

The process for meeting the children also varies considerably, depending on region, agency, referral method, orphanage, and age of children. If parents have a referral of a specific child, they go to the orphanage and visit with only that child. If they travel blind they will usually be shown more than one child, sometimes one at a time, sometimes in groups. Medical information is available from the orphanage director and doctor. Parents are encouraged to decide within about three days if this is the child they want to adopt. If they decide that this child is not a good match for their family, they can ask to see additional children.

Kazakhs law requires parents to spend fourteen days bonding with the child before they can petition the court to adopt. During these two weeks, parents visit with the child daily and have ample opportunity to ask questions of the primary caregivers and to observe how the child is cared for. After the court proceedings, parents can either take custody of their child and remain in Kazakhstan for the next several weeks while the paperwork is completed, or they can return home and only one parent needs to return to pick up the child.

CULTURE SHOCK

Culture shock—that unpleasant feeling of disorientation—is extremely common with families traveling to meet their child. Your senses will be bombarded with new sights, sounds, smells, and tastes. Often you will not be in tourist spots, since orphanages may be in out-of-the-way places with few Western amenities. Communication will be difficult and you will look, dress, and act different from the majority. It can be overwhelming. Be kind to yourself and

---

REGISTER WITH THE U.S. EMBASSY

When traveling abroad, it is a good idea to register with the U.S. Embassy so they can notify you in the event of a disaster, emergency, or other crisis. Registration is voluntary and free. The information you give is protected by the Privacy Act of 1974. You can register before you leave online at https://travelregistration.state.gov.

to your travel partner: Hibernate for a day or two if you can, spend quiet time with your child, and take long soaks in the tub.

Note the irony of what is happening. You are getting a hint of what your child will soon experience. The only difference is that you understand what is happening and she won't have a clue. Consider culture shock a gift of empathy.

EMOTIONS

You have waited for many months and often many years for this moment—the moment you finally meet your child. The myth of love at first sight is a stock theme in most chick flicks and romance novels, with or without the bodice-ripping covers. When the lover first lays eyes on the adored, the soundtrack reaches a harmonious crescendo. Unfortunately, in real life, or at least in the emotionally charged environment of meeting your child, the soundtrack and your emotions may be more discordant.

If you are traveling blind, at the first meeting you don't even know yet if this will be your child. You are trying to remain objective, which is not conducive to falling in love. Even when you are meeting a child whose referral you have already accepted, most parents don't fall in love immediately. Oh sure, they will regale you with every detail and often report a sense of awe, but if pressed, most will also admit to feelings of fear and confusion.

Parents are usually stressed from jet lag, culture shock, and emotional overload. The child is stressed by being separated from her caregiver and the change in her routine and environment. A stressed-out parent meeting a stressed-out kid does not inspire the usual soundtrack for love.

Most often these meetings are planned around the adults' schedule, not the child's. The child may have been in a car for hours driving to meet you; he may be hungry and tired. He is brought into a room and handed to complete strangers, who probably look different and most assuredly sound, smell, and act different. Parents also report being surprised by how different the child looks from the picture they bonded with. He is older and bigger, and even though obviously known beforehand, racial differences become very real.

Go into the meeting with your expectations firmly in check. Don't expect to feel an immediate connection with your child or expect your child to react positively to you. If you get lucky and your child is indifferent or maybe even slightly interested, then count your blessings. If you are not so lucky and your child wants nothing to do with you, at least know you are in good company. Remember—you have a lifetime to grow in love.

GATHERING INFORMATION

Make the most of this meeting with your child and her caregiver to gather information. You want information on your child's early environment to give to your pediatrician, to share with her later in life, and to help ease her transition in the next few months. In the excitement and stress of the moment it's easy to forget to ask all your questions, so I've included a list. Before you meet your child and her caregiver, ask your guide to translate the questions for you. If you will be meeting with your child and her caregivers on several occasions, spread the questions out so you don't overwhelm them. If you have only one opportunity, pick and choose the most important questions if time is limited.

Unfortunately, sometimes the person who brings the child to you will not be the person who cared for him, so little information is available. If this is the case, check this off your list of things to do and don't worry about it. Plenty of adoptive parents, including me, have been in this same boat and we have lived to tell the tale.

EASING THE TRANSITION

The fewer things you change in your child's life, the smoother her transition into your family. You have no control over the biggies—environment and caregiver—so do your best to minimize all other changes. Let your child be your guide in what you do. Your job is to go with the flow. The following will become your mantras:

- I will not worry during this time about forming bad habits or correcting existing ones.
- I will not worry during this time about every little thing being an indication of attachment issues or other major problems.
- I will not worry during this time if my child does not respond the way I had dreamed.
- I will be flexible and patient, flexible and patient, flexible and patient.

In countries where this is possible, spend as much time as you can with your child before you actually get custody so you become more familiar to him. To encourage interaction, bring a small toy or treat each time you visit (Matchbox car, lollipop, stickers, rattle, fruit, Cheerios). Kids love Santa Claus for a reason, and it's not the round belly and beard. Be sensitive to whether you should bring some for all the kids in his group. It's also a nice gesture to

QUESTIONS TO ASK YOUR CHILD'S CAREGIVER

Don't make yourself crazy trying to get all this information, but this list gives you an idea of the type of questions to ask. Videotape this interview for your child to have later if the caregiver is agreeable. If there is no one to ask, don't worry about it. Plenty of kids and parents have done just fine without this knowledge.

1. What kind of formula has she been fed? How much, what ratio of formula to water, and what temperature?
2. Does she drink from a bottle? If so, what type bottle and what type nipple? Ask to see what she uses.
3. Does she use a pacifier?
4. What food does she eat?
5. Are there any staff at the orphanage whom she is close to? Ask to take a picture of them.
6. How do you pronounce the name she has been called? Was she called by a pet name? Practice the pronunciation until you get it right.
7. What is her daily schedule for eating, sleeping, and playing?
8. What are her sleep habits? When, how long, and what position (tummy, back, or side)? Does she sleep through the night?
9. Get a complete copy of all her medical records, including the untranslated version.
10. Is her birth date real or approximate?
11. Is she frightened of anything?
12. What upsets her?
13. How do you soothe her? How does she soothe herself?
14. What makes her happy?
15. What toys does she like?
16. How has she been bathed, and does she like it?
17. What are the specifics of how she came to be in the orphanage? Did you know her birth parents?
18. Has she always lived at the orphanage, or did she live elsewhere for a time?
19. How did she get her name? Birth parent or orphanage? Does it have any special meaning?
20. Is there anything you would like us to tell her as she grows up?
21. Was there a note or memento left with her when she was found? May we have it, or at least a copy?
22. Are there any pictures or videos that have been taken of her, and can we make a copy?

---

23. Would the caregiver like to write a note to your child? Ask your translator to translate it for you later.
24. Is there a personal object or blanket or sheet that you can take in exchange for a new one? Try to get something that has the smell of her primary caregiver.
25. Is there a baptism certificate? (It's a long shot but worth the question, depending on the country and the likelihood of having one.)
26. Is there anything else you want to tell me about her?

---

take a small token of appreciation for the caregivers, such as cut flowers or fresh fruit, on each visit.

If you are adopting from a two-trip country, bring a small durable photo album with lots of pictures of you and his new house and pets, to leave on the first trip. Take some pictures of you holding him at the orphanage and include these in the album if you can get them printed before you leave. If you are adopting from a one-trip country, ask if you can send the album to him before you go.

Bring or send a transition object for your child, such as a stuffed animal or blanket. Buy good quality that will hold up to repeated washings and dryings. (Although one of Murphy's Parenting Laws states: The cheaper the object, the greater the chance that your kid will become attached. Since it will fall apart at the first washing, you will be stuck with a grubby, well-loved object as a part of your family for the foreseeable future.) To familiarize him with his new environment, bring pictures that you took of the toy in his crib or with his grandparents.

When you leave with your child, ask for a bottle and nipple that he has used. You will thank your lucky stars for these if your child is a finicky little sucker. (Yes, that pun was intended.) If practical, ask for something that the caregiver has used that will have her smell—for example, the blanket or sheets from the crib. Leave new ones as a trade. The feel and smell of these objects will be reassuring when your child is first with you. Don't wash any of these objects for a long time so they maintain their familiar smell. Your particular smell and the smells of your environment will gradually intermingle and permeate these objects, which is a good metaphor for a smooth transition.

Make sure someone explains to her what is happening in her language. Don't assume she is too young to understand. Pictures and toys can also be used to explain about airplanes, cars, car seats, strollers, and anything else that may be new. Have someone explain that you will take care of her and help her. Use some of the phrases in her language that you have learned.

GIFT IDEAS

Ask your agency whether they suggest that you bring gifts and if so, for whom. Some agencies and countries encourage only gifts for the orphanage, others encourage gifts to specific individuals, while others discourage the practice entirely. It's always a good idea to bring a few small gifts to give as a thank-you for people who go out of their way to help you in your travels. Do not wrap the gifts, since airport security may want to see inside. The best gift ideas are those that have some personal connection to you.

- Souvenirs from your hometown or region
- Hometown sports team memorabilia
- Framed pictures of your other children, if they were adopted from the same country, to give to government officials. Parents report that officials seem to relish these smiling faces.
- Wallet or money clips
- Perfume
- Lipstick
- Fancy soaps and lotions. Do NOT give as a gift the free toiletries supplied by hotels.
- Multipurpose tool such as a Leatherman
- Nonbreakable crafts from your state or region, such as scarves
- Nice-quality candy (beware of melting)

Many parents like to have a simple good-bye ceremony for the caregivers and child. Ask at the orphanage what has been done in the past or what they recommend. This ceremony gives the caregiver an opportunity to say good-bye and your child permission to leave.

Don't immediately change him into that adorable outfit you splurged on. The familiarity of his old clothes may offer some support during that first day when all else is new. Do your best to follow his schedule and habits. This won't be entirely possible, since you will be going to appointments and traveling, but make an attempt.

Keep things calm and low-key. Your child will probably not be accustomed to crowds, so sightsee before you have her. Spend time in your room sitting on the floor and playing. Don't overwhelm her with toys. Kids need very little to entertain them, and kids from orphanages usually need even less. Don't push yourself or your attention on her. Just be near her and interact to the degree she is comfortable with. Some kids love the attention, but others find it disconcerting. You will not worry that this means anything other than that she is not used to this much attention.

Don't push if your child resists something. For example, if your child screams through your attempt at a bath, forget about bathing him. All the vital areas that get dirty (bottom, face, and hands) get wiped frequently anyway, so forgo baths until he is more secure with you. Trust me; no one will be checking for navel lint or toe jam at the border, and in later years you'll be amazed at what you'll accept in the way of hygiene. You will not worry at this time about forming bad habits.

If your child refuses to eat, don't force her, but try the following: Use local formula and nipples, enlarge the holes in the nipple, make the formula hotter, mix the formula weaker, or avoid making eye contact while feeding her. If you have the opposite problem of a child who wants to eat excessively, let her, unless it starts coming out either end in copious quantities. Remember, you are not worrying about forming bad habits.

Buy enough local formula (preferably that which was used in the orphanage) to last for at least a few weeks at home. You can gradually mix American formula with this formula when you get home and your child will never notice the transition. If your child eats solid food, find out what he likes and buy a supply to bring home. In addition to easing the transition, keeping the same diet will reduce the likelihood of stomach upsets. Diaper blowouts and a cranky kid are no fun anytime but are especially bad when traveling.

PAPERWORK ON THE ROAD

Unfortunately, your adoption paperwork hassles are not quite over. You must bring various documents with you from the United States, and you'll be receiving more once you are in country. What is required varies by country, and as always, your agency is your guide, but I can help you stay organized.

You will need a twenty-one-pocket expandable file folder with an elastic cord closure. In the back pocket keep some extra labels, a pen, and a mini stapler. Label a pocket for each document your agency tells you to bring with you when you travel. When you are given additional documents in country—for example, your child's immunization records—label a pocket and drop it in. You can store non-adoption-related information in this folder as well, such as a copy of your passport and visa, travel itinerary, telephone numbers and e-mail addresses, and instructions for how to use the camera. You will carry this folder with you in your backpack so it will always be close at hand.

A typical expandable folder might be labeled as follows:

- Hotel information
- Travel itinerary and plane tickets
- Copy of passports and visas (labeled to fool would-be thieves)
- Parental power of attorney
- I-600
- Tax returns
- Employment verification
- Original I-171H
- Pediatrician's letter
- Updated documents for dossier
- Updated medicals for parents
- Copy of home study with addendum
- Child's birth certificate and adoption decree
- Copy of child's passport
- U.S. immigration papers for child
- Medical records for child
- Immunization records for child
- Instructions for video camera

DON'T SHOW ME THE MONEY, HONEY

For many countries, a fact of adoption life is carrying large amounts of cash. The money exchanges and banks in other countries require you to have the new-style bills, and although they do not actually have to be brand-new bills, they should be crisp with no creases, stains, or marks. Your bank may require some advance notice to get you the nice crisp bills you need. Another trick is to frequent ATM machines in the weeks prior to traveling, since they usually distribute only crisp bills. Ask your agency, but usually parents take the bulk of the money in $100 bills, with the remaining split between $50 and $20 bills. The good news is that usually you pay the big fees at the beginning of the trip so you don't have to carry the wad of money around for long.

Obviously, you need to keep the money tucked away and out of sight. I prefer the document/money pouches worn around the neck under a shirt. Your passport and the money should both be able to fit. Never carry either passport or major bucks in a pocket, backpack, fanny pack, or purse. Both travel partners should have a pouch and the money should be split between the two. To prevent the bills from getting damp, put them in a Ziploc bag. Keep small change needed for daily spending in your pocket so you do not have to go into the pouch in public.

- Receipts for tax credit
- Phone card
- Extra labels and miscellaneous supplies

You must be extraordinarily careful with your passport and visa at all times, since U.S. passports have a very high value on the black market. I will warn you that hotels commonly take your passport and visa to register you in the region. Some hold them the entire time you are at the hotel and others return it the same or next day—ask your agency what you should expect. It is usually safe to walk around without your passport, but when it's returned, keep it with you at all times or put it in the hotel safe. When carrying it with you, it is best to put it in a money/document pouch that you wear under your shirt. Make three color photocopies of your passport before you leave home. Put one copy in your luggage, one copy in a labeled pocket of the expandable folder, and leave one copy with an emergency contact at home.

PACKING

At the risk of overgeneralizing, I think there are two types of travelers: those who pack to avoid needing anything and those who pack to avoid being burdened. You should know up front that I am firmly in the latter camp. I am famous in my family for my four-underwear theory on packing: As long as there is a sink where you are going, you need no more than four pairs of underwear. Apparently, I was a wee bit overzealous on this point once and have never been able to live it down. I usually hear "Remember, only four pairs of underwear" repeated over and over in a fake falsetto while we are packing, reminiscent of Joan Crawford's lament against wire clothes hangers. Undeterred, I stand by my theory, if not quite so zealously, and extrapolate it outward to all other clothes.

We have traveled all over the world with our kids for long trips, carrying only what can be stored in the overhead compartment of an airplane. Each child has a backpack or school book bag, and Peter and I each pull a small suitcase on wheels and a small backpack. I'm not suggesting that you have to go this far, and the truth is that we didn't travel this light when one of ours was a baby or toddler, but having to bring all the extra baby paraphernalia makes it even more important to reduce the rest of your luggage.

The reason for controlling your luggage is simple: mobility. Unless you bring your own porter, you and only you will be carrying your luggage. You will be stuffing it into the small trunks of taxis and cars, lugging it as you run

---

THE GOLDEN RULES OF TRAVEL

- You are a guest in this country.
- You are an ambassador for international adoption. People are watching you and your attitude. Be gracious and patient.
- Different does not mean worse. No one likes to hear criticisms of their country or how things are done better back in the good ole US of A. (The truth of your observation does not change this rule.)
- Be flexible. Expect that you will be tired, bureaucrats will be inefficient, papers will be lost, and appointments will be missed. Murphy's Law applies throughout the world. Expect it and you won't be as frustrated when it surely happens.
- Learn the polite words in the language ("thank you," "hello," "good-bye," "excuse me," "I'm sorry," "you're welcome") and use them often.
- Avoid discussing politics, religion, money, and sex, just as you should at family gatherings.

---

to catch planes, and cursing it as you climb stairs to your room. On the return trip, you will be doing all this stuffing, lugging, and cursing while you are carrying, pushing, or chasing a child. I have never, and I mean never, heard of someone who was sorry that they packed light, but I hear all the time from people who were sorry they didn't.

To add further insult to your back, most adoptive families return home with more stuff than they brought (I mean in addition to their child). Since you may not be in your child's birth country again, you will want to stock up on things you can show and share with her later in life. This may surprise you given my earlier stated theories on packing, but I think you should do just that. You will want to add souvenirs, cans of local baby formula, toys and books popular with kids in the birth country, keepsakes from the orphanage, and items for which the birth country is famous.

If you pack light enough before you leave, you should have room in your suitcases for these added purchases. If not, adding one more suitcase to your load will be less burdensome at the end of your journey, since your hauling days are numbered at that point. Consider stuffing an expandable duffel bag–style suitcase (like an athletic gear bag) in your luggage on the trip over. You can use it as an extra suitcase on the return trip. If you don't have room, buy one abroad. It will offer no protection from baggage handlers, so you'll use it for clothes and put anything that needs protection in your sturdier suitcase.

> ### MAKE SURE YOU BUY
>
> While in your child's birth country, buy items to share with your child as he ages. Also look for items that you can share with his preschool and elementary school class when you do your annual presentation on his birth country. Another idea is to buy special items to give your child on special occasions, such as birthdays and anniversaries of her "Gotcha Day."
>
> - Toys/puzzles
> - Money
> - Traditional clothing
> - Children's books
> - Craft items
> - Country flag
> - Map
> - Children's clothing

If I am able to convince you to scale down your luggage, I can't promise that you will never wish for something you don't have. In fact, I can promise you that at least once on the trip you will want something and probably want it badly. The problem is that you don't know ahead of time what that something will be. If you try to pack in anticipation of all the possible somethings that it could be, you will be hauling around way too much stuff. Besides, most things you need can be bought in your child's birth country. I absolutely love to go into grocery stores and household goods–type stores in other countries—it's like a window to another culture. My kids think it's bizarre that I have to be dragged into a Wal-Mart at home, but I readily spend hours in the foreign equivalent.

Your goal is for each person to take one medium-to-small lightweight suitcase on wheels. Two smaller suitcases are better for a couple than one larger suitcase because of airline weight limits and in case one suitcase is lost by the airlines for a few days. Divide the clothes for each person between the two suitcases, just in case. That way if one suitcase is lost, everyone shares the pain, and shared pain makes for marital and travel harmony. Don't let the wheels trick you into packing more since you figure you'll be pulling rather than carrying most of the weight. Although wheels are definitely handy, they have limited usefulness outside of airports because of stairs, curbs, and crowds.

Each of you will also carry a backpack. One of these backpacks will serve as your diaper bag/toy carrier on the return trip, so don't stuff it at the beginning. Take anything you can't afford to be without in your carry-on backpack, such as your expandable folder of paperwork, camera equipment, medicine, and contact lens case and solution. Take one change of clothes for each adult and two changes of clothes for your child on the return trip.

ETIQUETTE FOR TRAVELING LIGHT

Don't notice, or at least refrain from mentioning, that your travel partner has worn the same outfit a few times between washings. Some people suggest taking a bottle of Febreze; I've never found it necessary, but perhaps my travel partners would disagree.

Packing light is a travel philosophy that must be adapted to the specifics of your situation. Your guiding principles should be:

- Comfort over fashion
- Appropriate for the occasion and culture
- Sink washable and hotel room dryable
- Wear pants a few times between washings
- Do laundry once a week
- Buy what you need

Unfortunately, philosophy alone seldom gets the job done, so here are the specifics.

Adult

- **Two everyday pants or skirts.** One of the pants should be comfortable enough for long travel days and airplane sleeping. All pants should be of a dirt-hiding color: black and light khaki is out; blue jean and medium brown is in. (Blue jeans have amazing dirt-hiding capacity and can be worn three to five times before washing.) Shorts are considered inappropriate for both men and women in many countries.
- **Three or four shirts that coordinate with your pants.** At least two should be sink washable/room dryable.
- **One nice outfit.** Each parent should have one nicer outfit to be worn when you need to show respect (at meetings with officials or for court), for church (even if going in just as a tourist), and for nicer restaurants. Knit dresses and shirts are virtually wrinkle-proof and take up little room in the suitcase. To lessen wrinkles in cotton shirts, pack them in a gallon-size Ziploc bag. Ask your agency if a coat and tie are needed for the adoption proceedings.
- **Two pairs of shoes.** You will wear your bulkiest pair on travel days to avoid taking up room in your suitcase. Usually people bring one pair of

running/walking-type shoes and one pair that will work with their nicer outfit as well as with their everyday clothes. If you are traveling to a country where you expect snow, consider taking a waterproof pair of walking shoes instead of the sneakers. Before you go to the expense, talk with your agency and other parents who have gone to this region to see if they really did much marching through slush. All shoes should be well broken in and comfortable.

- **Socks and underwear**. You already know my theory on underwear. If your socks are too thick to dry quickly, bring enough to last you between trips to the laundry. Wet socks draped around a hotel room for days on end are particularly unappealing.
- **Jacket.** Always take some sort of jacket unless you are going to a very warm country in the summer with no air-conditioning. Even then, I bring something light for the airplane. It should be waterproof with a hood so it can double as a raincoat. Tie the jacket around your waist or neck on travel days to save room in your suitcase. Tuck gloves, stocking cap, and ChapStick in a zippered or deep pocket. All your cold-weather outerwear is in one place and not taking up room in your suitcase.
- **Cold-weather clothing**. For cold-weather travel, think layers. Start with two pairs of washable silk or nylon long underwear tops and bottoms. Wear one pair and wash one pair every night. Splurge for one or two shirts that are designed for hikers and are lightweight, warm, and washable. You can add another shirt on top if it's really cold, but avoid sweatshirts, because they take up too much space in your suitcase. With your coat you have four layers, which is enough for any climate. If the orphanage is hot, you can shed layers.
- **Toiletries**. The key is to find small sizes of everything. Prescription medicines should be kept in their original containers. In countries where there is a possibility of delay, assume the worst and bring enough medicine to last. Bring any over-the-counter medicines that you take frequently or when sick. I dump all my vitamins together in the same small Ziploc bag. Vitamin C is easily distinguished from my multi and calcium. Take an extra pair of contact lenses or glasses.

Child

What to bring for your child varies by age, how long you will have custody, and how long the trip. The basic principles of comfortable and sink washable/room dryable still apply. You should plan on buying some clothes locally, both for keepsakes and because size is easier to judge once you see your child.

- **Clothes.** Approximately four outfits for your child. Sizes are difficult to gauge, so bring loose-style clothes that can cover a few sizes. Children are often dressed more warmly in other countries, and you should respect this custom.
- **Winter outerwear.** Your child will probably be in a baby sling or carrier when outside, so extra layers other than a jacket and warm pants may not be needed. If more is necessary, plan on buying locally.
- **Diapers.** Eight ultrathin diapers should last until you can buy some locally. Even for potty-trained toddlers and preschoolers, consider bringing some pull-up–style diapers, since disrupted schedules make accidents more likely. Be sensitive to your child's feelings on whether to use these; some kids couldn't care less, while others are deeply offended by the thought.
- **Wipes.** The refill packs are easier to pack than the plastic tub. Even if you don't have a child in diapers, bring some for general cleanup.
- **Diaper rash cream.** Bring regular cream and an antiyeast cream, such as Lotrimin, for a yeast rash (red, blistered, open sores).
- **Bottles and nipples.** It really doesn't matter whether you take disposable or regular bottles, but disposable are more compact and you don't have to worry about cleaning. Take a variety of nipples. The uninitiated are surprised by how picky some babies are about nipples and by the variety of nipple styles available. They come in different shapes (regular, Nuk, or the original disposable style), materials (silicone or latex), and openings (regular, crosscut, or enlarged). I recommend you buy locally to approximate what your child is used to, but you have to carry some, just in case. Bring a bottle/nipple brush. For toddlers, bring a sippy cup to minimize spills.
- **Formula.** I recommend buying formula locally once you find out what your child drinks, but you should take some U.S. formula in case there is no time to shop before you get your child. Ask your pediatrician or IA doctor what they recommend, but generally most say that soy-based formulas are unnecessary and can cause constipation. Powdered formula is a must for traveling. Buy single-serving tubes if you can find them. For mixing formula, take a stainless-steel thermos for holding hot water and a plastic cup with a tight-fitting lid for mixing.
- **Food.** Talk with your pediatrician about what foods a typical child at this age would eat, but what really matters is what your child is accustomed to eating. Ask and then replicate it until you've been home awhile. Take some finger foods (Cheerios, raisins, Kix) in a Ziploc and maybe a nonbreakable container or two of baby food. Plan on buying locally what your child has enjoyed eating in the past. Also, talk with your pediatrician about feeding your child small pieces of table food.

- **Pacifier**. Most orphanage babies aren't attached to a pacifier. Babies who have not attached to a pacifier are not likely to start using one. If you do have a pacifier baby, find out the style and brand and buy as many in country as you have room to take home, since kids can be amazingly brand conscious.
- **Toys.** You will primarily bring toys to entertain your child during traveling. See box on traveling with kids. If you spend much time with your child in your hotel room, you can always buy a few toys for floor play and donate them to someone before you leave.
- **Baby equipment.** In general, new parents think they need more than they really do. You don't need baby bathtubs, nose syringes, or a large blanket for the floor. For traveling, the only two things that you really need are a baby carrier and stroller.
  - ~ Baby carriers are wonderful for bonding with your child and for hands-free carrying. Bring two styles of baby carriers with you (front pack and hip sling), since you don't know which style your child will prefer and which style will be easier on your back. They should fit both parents. You probably won't be able to find much variety locally, so bring these with you.
  - ~ Cheap umbrella strollers are the best for traveling and are available in almost every country, so buy locally to save you the hassle on the trip over. Being pushed ahead into a new environment can be frightening to some children, so use a child carrier if possible.
- **Miscellaneous kid stuff.**
  - ~ Baby shampoo (need just a small amount, but it really does sting the eyes less than regular shampoo).
  - ~ Benadryl (generic name is diphenhydramine). Can be used as a sleep aid just in case your child is inconsolable on the airplane. Some parents swear by it and it usually does cause drowsiness; but beware—it can cause the reverse. Before you try it at 30,000 feet, try it on the ground. It also will dry your child up and this effect will be compounded by the dryness of the air on the plane. Talk with your pediatrician about this option.
  - ~ Digital baby thermometer. Ask your pediatrician whether to use rectal, underarm, or ear.

Miscellaneous

- **Reading material**. This is the hardest area for me to pack light, and to be truthful, unless space is at a premium, I don't even try. I don't mind not being fashionable, but I hate to be without something interesting to read, and what I find interesting changes frequently. However, space is tight on adoption travel, so take one paperback and several magazines to last you for the trip over, and then plan on buying something to read abroad. English-language books and magazines are available in almost all larger cities and airports, but I can't promise that they'll suit your mood. This and bad coffee are the only real hardships of traveling. Alas, this is but the first of many sacrifices you'll make as a parent.

- **Video equipment and cameras**.
- **Different-size Ziploc bags.** You won't believe how many uses you can find, such as containing food, the dirty pants from a diaper blowout (although I've been known to throw these away when traveling), the shampoo that doesn't quite close perfectly, the clothes that are still damp but have to be put in your suitcase for the next leg of the trip, dirty shoes, and on and on. The quart size is perfect for containing stinky diapers so you don't have to smell them all night.
- **International cell phone.** These can be rented in the United States and brought with you. Whether it is worth the cost depends on where you are going and the availability of phones. If phones are readily available, international calling cards purchased in the region are the way to go.
- **Travel guide books** for the country and region.
- **Foreign/English dictionary or phrase book**.
- **This book**. (Like American Express, don't leave home without it.)
- **High-protein snacks (nuts, protein bars, etc.).** These can hold off a meltdown in case you have to miss a meal. You don't need a lot and you can replenish your stash locally.
- **Quick foods**. If you are a picky eater or a vegetarian and are anxious about finding food that you can eat, bring something easy, such as peanut butter, to lessen your anxiety.
- **Powdered clothes-washing detergent**. Put some powdered detergent in a Ziploc bag for sink washings or bring a small container of liquid detergent.
- **Travel clothesline**.
- **Dish soap** in small container.
- **Travel alarm clock**.
- **Small pad and pen** for backpack.
- **Hand sanitizer** for backpack.
- **Journal** if you are keeping one.
- **Portable music player**.
- **Relaxing ritual supplies** (Bath oil, lotion, corkscrew, etc.).
- **First-aid kit**. See box.

- **Electrical adapter** if you bring any electrical appliance.
- **Bug repellant**. Ask your agency if this is necessary where and when you are going. You can buy locally, but I am paranoid about any form of insecticide on skin, so I bring my own.
- **Sunscreen** if necessary.
- **Playing cards**.
- **Travel-size roll of toilet paper** or a couple of travel packs of tissues.
- **Multipurpose tool** (such as a Leatherman).
- **Earplugs and eye mask for sleeping**.
- **Small, inexpensive calculator** for converting money.

TRAVELING WITH KIDS

Traveling with newly adopted kids can be challenging. Your child is adjusting to tremendous changes, and international airplane travel is just one more. The key to successful adoption travel is the attitude of the adults. No matter how your child behaves, she is not being bad. She is coping the best way she knows how, and it's your job as the adult to help her. Sometimes all you can do to help is control your frustration.

The one major mistake I see parents make when traveling with children is expecting them to entertain themselves while the parent reads or sleeps or zones out. Fellow travelers have always complimented my kids on how well they behave on planes and in airports. Yes, my kids are usually well behaved when we travel (notice that I had to put in that qualifier), but having my undivided attention certainly helps.

I try to anticipate their mood. When I see them starting to tire of the markers, I whip out the Play-Doh before they have a chance to chuck the marker across the aisle. When killing time and using up energy at the airport, I stand, balance, and jump right along with them. Having the time when my only focus is on my kids and not on the thousands of other things that demand my attention is one of the pleasures of family travel. You can trade off with your partner, unless of course the child has decided that you are the preferred flavor of the week—a common occurrence with newly adopted kids.

Traveling with a child you don't know and who doesn't know you is considerably harder, because neither of you knows how to read the other. There are, however, some tricks of the parenting trade that might ease the way. Bring a backpack or diaper bag well stocked with snacks and toys. It is surprisingly simple to entertain a baby or young child. Talk with friends with children several months younger than your child to see what entertains them. (See box for ideas.) And if worse comes to worst, apologize to the people around you and don't worry about the inconvenience. An upset child is, after all, just part of life.

Here's a word of warning to parents adopting kids from one to three. I have traveled the world with my children from newborns to teens, and by far, tod-

---

FIRST-AID KIT

It's an unfortunate fact of life that kids get sick. Communal living and all the changes and stress from the adoption make illness more likely. Your child will see a doctor for a medical exam before he will be given a visa to leave the country, and although these exams are not extensive, you should be able to get help with minor problems such as ear infections and colds.

Pediatricians generally do not recommend treating every symptom of the typical kid illnesses (colds, coughs, runny noses) with medicine. Most new parents tend to overuse over-the-counter medicine for their child if only because it makes them feel like they are doing something to help. Talk with your pediatrician about what she recommends for these illnesses. It is a good idea to bring the following basic supplies:

- Children's acetaminophen (brand name is Tylenol) and dosage cup or syringe (for babies)
- Band-Aids (you need just a few)
- Antibiotic ointment, hydrocortisone cream, and scabies prescription cream. (Doctors are divided about the wisdom of bringing scabies medicine, since diagnosis is difficult and the medicine has side effects. Ask your pediatrician what she recommends.)
- Lice shampoo
- Broad-spectrum antibiotic. Many pediatricians are reluctant to prescribe in advance, and since most childhood illnesses are viral, an antibiotic is seldom needed. But when it is needed, it is handy to have with you. Before you leave, discuss with your doctor what symptoms require treatment with an antibiotic. If you decide to bring some with you, request one that comes in powdered form (with the sterilized water in a separate bottle) and doesn't require refrigeration once mixed.
- Oral rehydration product, such as Pedialyte or Kaolectrolyte, in case of prolonged fever or diarrhea. Bring the powdered variety. If you can't find it on the shelf, ask your pharmacist to order it for you.
- Glycerin suppositories, but your pediatrician may first suggest trying apple juice or prune juice for constipation.
- Gum-numbing gel in case your child is teething.

dlers present the biggest challenge. Once the little buggers can move around, that becomes their mission in life. Illuminated seat-belt signs and the captain's wishes have little meaning even if your kid understands the language—this age is not known for reasonableness. The key to survival is movement. Find opportunities for your toddler to walk, run, and jump. Walk up and down the aisle of the airplane with her when it's allowed. Do your best to divert your child when she has to remain seated. Use airport time to wear her out with all the walking, jumping, and running she (and you) can handle.

TOP TEN TRAVEL TIPS FROM OTHER PARENTS

- Notify your credit-card companies of when and where you will be traveling so they don't assume your card is stolen when they see charges from abroad coming through. The last thing you need is to have your card put on hold when traveling.
- You and your travel partner should carry different-brand credit cards in case one is not accepted or one is stolen.
- Don't wrap gifts for orphanage workers and children, because immigration and airport security may want to see inside. Bring nice gift bags and tissue from home for wrapping gifts after you arrive in the country, since you will not have time to shop for these items once you arrive.
- Find out the limit on the number of bags and the weight limit per bag for both travel to the country and travel within the country. Flights within a country may have more restrictive weight limits than international flights. Also, ask what the international and in-country fine is for luggage that exceeds the limit.
- Bring minimal jewelry to avoid attracting attention.
- In two-trip countries, bring blank paper for tracing your child's foot for buying shoes back home and a tape measure for measuring the child for clothing size.
- Whenever possible, use a baby carrier instead of a stroller to accelerate the bonding process.
- Before you leave home, make a list of people you want to buy souvenirs for so you don't forget someone.
- Keep family and friends informed via the Internet. Use a password-protected blog site or create an e-mail distribution list for updates. Internet cafés are common in most countries. Print off the updates for your child's lifebook (see Chapter 10).
- Don't wear perfume or heavily scented lotions. The sense of smell is very important for the bonding process, and these smells may be too strong or unpleasant to your child.

TIPS FOR ENTERTAINING KIDS WHILE TRAVELING

- Toys lose their WOW value (otherwise known as their diversion power) once they are played with; therefore, save most of your toys until you are on the plane. Toys should also be put away when you are in the airport so that the child will have less opportunity to become bored with them.
- This is one place where I don't recommend packing light. The toys can be small, but you should bring more than you think you'll need.
- Always carry protein-rich food, water, and juice boxes in your backpack or diaper bag. You never know when you will get stuck without a meal or need a distraction to prevent a meltdown—child or parental. I carry raw almonds and protein bars for older kids and adults. With babies, I carry formula and a bottle. It's a bit tricky to find something that works for toddlers who can't eat nuts. The packets of peanut butter crackers usually get crushed in transit. Raisins are good, and I usually take some, but they are not filling. Protein bars are good if your child can chew them. Find out what your child likes that is relatively small and filling. In addition, take some non-nutritious snacks. The hard gingersnap cookies stand up well to the rigors of travel and take a long time to suck/eat.
- Pack lollipops to help clear ears during takeoffs and landings and to use as a bribe at other times. It's hard, although not impossible, to cry while licking. If they are going to be given to a toddler, bring the ones with the soft loop rather than the rigid stick.
- A portable DVD player and child-friendly DVDs can be a lifesaver, depending on the age of your child. They are expensive, but you will use them on long car trips and plane rides in the future, so they are worth the price. Kids thrive on repetition, so you won't need many DVDs. Bring a kid DVD and buy one in country as well. Hearing his own language could soothe a frightened child.
- Bring handheld games such as GameBoy for older kids. Ask your friends with children a little younger if their children are playing with these.
- Portable CD players. Especially good for preschool and older kids. Try to buy a kid-music CD in country and also bring one from home.
- The most entertaining toys are those your child can manipulate, such as:
  - ~ Colored pencils, waterproof markers, or crayons and paper for scribbling. (Crayons tend to break easier and melt in the sun, and are usually found to be tastier than colored pencils.)
  - ~ Magna Doodle (comes in regular and travel size)
  - ~ Stickers

- ~ Play-Doh
- ~ Stacking cups
- Simple games that you can play with babies and young children on the airplane:
  - ~ Stacking anything you can find, like toy cups, jelly tubs, and raisins.
  - ~ Dropping Cheerios into a cup or your mouth.
  - ~ Keys usually work for a while, but it's best to save these for when you are stranded without other options.
  - ~ Interactive books. Buy those that are for an age younger than your child, since he may be delayed.
  - ~ For older babies and toddlers, a roll of Scotch tape can provide more entertainment than, well, a barrel of monkeys. Use your imagination and you'll be surprised what you can come up with. Stick some on the back of his hand and let him pull it off. Stick some over your mouth and let him rip. The parental pantomime of agony is the best part. (Eye contact is an ulterior motive!) Tape a spoon on the tray and let him pull it off. Make a ball out of wadded-up tape and roll it around or throw into a cup. When traveling with a toddler, I carry a roll in my pocket to use in an emergency or when I've run out of ideas.
- Simple ways to entertain a baby or a young child in an airport:
  - ~ Use the airport time to give your child a change of position. Give babies some floor time to stretch and not be held. You can spread a blanket— or just don't worry about the germs.
  - ~ Bubbles
  - ~ Chinese paper balls. These are absolutely magical. I have been known to entertain my kids and all the other kids nearby for hours at airports with these wonderful paper balls. You puff air into them to make a ball. The game possibilities are endless, and nothing can be hurt by the ball since it is only paper. When you are finished, gently squeeze the air out and you have a flat piece of paper to tuck in a backpack or pocket and reuse next time you need to keep your child occupied. They weigh nothing, are inexpensive, and will give you literally hours of fun. They are hard to find, but check out www.magiccabin.com.
  - ~ Walk, jump, run.

BRINGING OLDER KIDS

Most agencies I have talked with discourage families from bringing older children on the adoption trip, but I don't think it's so cut-and-dried. Whether to take an older child with you depends on the age and personality of the older child, the age of the new child, your agency's attitude, the referral method, the parents' travel experience, the parents' adoption experience, and the adoption process in the country. See the box for the advantages and disadvantages.

If you want to take an older child, talk with your agency at the beginning to gauge their attitude. Some families recommend bringing a grandparent or friend along to stay with the older child while the parents are tied up elsewhere; otherwise, one parent can stay with the older child while the other parent runs around. If you decide to leave the older child at home, consider whether one parent should stay home with her to minimize the disruption in her life. If this is not possible or desirable, it is usually less disruptive if someone familiar to the older child moves into your house and stays with her there.

Reasons to take older kids	*Reasons to leave older kids at home*
No one able to stay with older child at home and both parents need or want to travel.	Want to focus undivided attention on new child without having to meet the needs of older child.
Adoption trip is too long to leave older child.	Older child is not flexible, doesn't handle change well, or is extremely shy.
Belief that adoption is a family affair; the whole family is adopting, not just the parents.	Older child is a picky eater.
The trip is a time for the family to bond without the pressures of work and everyday life.	Older child does not play well by himself and needs TV, video games, and toys for entertainment.
Older child may feel resentful of new child for being the reason his parents went away.	Better to postpone dealing with sibling rivalry until you aren't under the stress of traveling.
Helps older child understand new child better if he sees where he came from.	Expense of airfare and in-country travel costs.
New child often bonds first with a sibling and can learn how to relate to parents by watching and emulating older child.	Want to avoid the possibility of older child getting sick in a foreign country.

Reasons to take older kids	Reasons to leave older kids at home
Educational experience if child is old enough. Can study the country as a family before the trip by reading books, watching videos, and preparing food.	Older child may get behind on school work.
Lessens anxiety of parents if the adoption process is delayed in country. Puts less pressure on getting home soon.	Older child too young to remember the trip, so why spend the money.
Children open up your experience of a new culture. People in many countries love to interact with your children.	No one to take care of older child while parents attend to the business of adoption, such as court hearings and trips to passport office.
Consider this to be a family trip of a lifetime and want all family members to be a part of it.	Not all orphanages will allow the older child in the orphanage with you when you are visiting with your new child.
Parents are comfortable travelers who embrace new experiences and cultures.	Additional luggage and laundry.
Parents are fairly relaxed about the adoption experience, so stress won't be too high.	Don't want older child to have to get immunization shots if required.
Depending on ages and personalities, older child can be a help to parents by entertaining new child.	If traveling in a group, older children may not be welcomed.

PARTING WORDS

I love to travel, so it's easy for me to advise you to relax and relish every moment to savor and relive with your child in the future, but I realize that not everyone feels as I do. Even if you are dreading the trip and living for the moment when you are back home with your child, remember that this trip will become a part of your child's story of how she came to be yours. She will ask for every detail over and over.

Once I witnessed a father telling others in front of his son about the filth and corruption of the boy's birth country. The dad regaled us at length about the awful food and the ineptitude of every person he met. My reaction was probably not what was intended. I felt immeasurable sadness for this child not because of his past, but because of his present. How can his view of himself not be altered by this story of rescue and his father's contempt for his birth culture? I doubt not the accuracy of the tale, but the completeness.

Every child deserves to know the good in their birth culture, and the adoption trip is an opportunity to find it. You can certainly share the negative as she ages, but balance it by the positive. As you travel, make it your goal to look for the positive. We usually find what we seek.

FUAQs

Should I bring a car seat?

Unlike in the United States, car seats are not required for traveling with kids in most birth countries or on planes, but check with your agency and airline to make sure that is the case. But even if not required, car seats protect children. The problem with bringing a car seat for international adoption travel is that in many countries, the cars and taxis do not have backseat seat belts. Ask your agency about the situation in your country. A car seat would still be useful on the airplane, but some kids who have never been constrained in a car seat reject the idea out of hand. While this is a habit that must be formed, I would personally not fight this battle on the plane ride home. You will have to decide if the hassle of lugging a car seat around is worth the safety and peace of mind it gives. If you decide to bring one, look for the type that converts to a stroller.

At home I am an absolute car seat fanatic, but when traveling, I decide whether to take a car seat by balancing the hassle with how much use it will get. If we'll be renting a car or if I have a place I can store it, I bring it; if not, I usually leave it at home and pray like crazy.

I am single and adopting. Is it necessary for me to have a travel companion?

It depends on the country and agency whether it is required, but even if it is not required, there are some very good reasons to consider asking someone to come along. It helps to have someone to bounce ideas off of, and this is especially true for a first-time parent. You may prefer to have someone to help figure out why she won't take a bottle or whether that rash is something to worry about. Also, if you travel solo, you will never get a break from your child—she'll accompany you everywhere (meetings, dinner, and the bathroom), and showering will be squeezed in around her naps. You should also consider what would happen if you get sick.

On the other hand, you may not have someone that you are comfortable traveling with or the person you want is unavailable. Also, sometimes a travel date comes sooner than expected and your planned partner can't get off work. Traveling by yourself is definitely preferable to traveling with someone who is inflexible, judgmental, or a general pain in the neck. Your travel partner must be in good health and up to the rigors of international travel to places off the beaten path. The person you choose must come with the attitude that this is not a vacation or a sightseeing trip. Have them read Chapters 9 and 10 in this book so they will understand what the challenges might be and how they can best help. Parents who have traveled alone usually appreciate the time for bonding one-on-one with the child. Note also that some of the disadvantages to traveling without a partner can be alleviated if you adopt from a country where families travel in groups. If you decide to go alone, it is even more important that you travel light.

FOR EVERY ADOPTION, A DIFFERENT STORY . . .

With blind and semi-blind referrals, there is little distinction between meeting stories and referral stories, so refer also to the stories in Chapter 8.

Our son was living in a hospital in Russia and had literally never been outside. He was the palest and baldest baby I had ever seen. He was also beautiful in a Cabbage Patch doll sort of way. After seventeen hours of flying and five hours of driving, we only got to see him for one hour before we had to leave, but we felt an instant connection and both knew that he was meant to be ours. —*SH, Virginia*

The trip to pick up our son from Guatemala was incredibly easy. We loved the country and couldn't get enough of seeing and experiencing the culture, the food, the people. I think most adoption agencies discourage adoptive parents from really experiencing Guatemala, and that's a shame because it is such an interesting country to visit.

Our son adjusted to us almost immediately. He was very young, had been in foster care, and was healthy with no developmental delays. And we had already spent two weeks with him while we were waiting for the adoption to be finalized, so he knew us—at least a little. For all these reasons, his transition and our transition were very smooth. —*IL, Virginia*

Our first daughter was escorted to us from South Korea. A representative from our agency was at the airport to oversee the exchange, and it was especially nice because she had been adopted from Korea as an infant. As people started coming off the plane, they saw us with our cameras and diaper bag and asked us if we were the new parents. Many of them waited to see us get our daughter. We had expected a cranky baby after twenty-plus hours of travel, but she just looked up at me and laughed. It was love at first sight.

Meeting our second daughter was a much different experience—not bad, just different. We had to fly to China, since China doesn't do escorts. We traveled with two other families. On the morning we got our daughter, we went to the Office of Civil Affairs, where we were to meet the babies. When we walked into the room, the babies were already there. Our daughter had been in foster care, but a worker from the orphanage, not her foster mother, had brought her five hours on a bus that morning to get there. She looked anxious and tired and was already crying when we walked in. We wanted to go to comfort her, but weren't allowed to hold her until the director of civil affairs reviewed our paperwork to make sure this was our baby. When she was finally handed to me, she cried for about fifteen minutes while rubbing her eyes. She was so tired and skinny.

I was excited to finally have her but also nervous about whether she would accept me. I needn't have worried. She was happy and content from that moment on and seemed to soak up the love and attention I gave her. Unfortunately, she didn't respond as well to her father; she clung to me but didn't want anything to do with him. Her clinginess was endearing at first but exhausting after a while, especially combined with the stress of being away from home, unfamiliar food, lack of sleep, and jet lag. But other than being clingy, she didn't give us any trouble. The two other babies in our group weren't so easy. One baby was older and had apparently not had much attention. She didn't want anything to do with either of her new parents, but after about five days of screaming she settled in and warmed up to them. The other baby had been sick right before we got there and took several days to feel better. We gladly took clingy over the other two options. —*CH, North Carolina*

Meeting our son for the first time was unbelievable. We went to the orphanage with three other families and waited in the music room for the caregivers to bring in the children. I couldn't get over how beautiful he was. I was totally and completely in love. He was much smaller and frailer than we were expecting, but other than that he seemed perfect. We saw him only a few times and then we had to return home to await a court date to finalize the adoption. Leaving him there was the hardest thing I have ever had to do. To this day, I can't watch the video from that day. —JL, Virginia

We had been told that we would have our daughter with us at our hotel shortly after we arrived in Colombia while we finalized the adoption. About an hour before we were to go to the orphanage to get her, our representative called to tell us that our daughter had developed a rash and the orphanage would not release her to us until it cleared up. This news was extremely upsetting, since it was a little too familiar to a failed domestic adoption attempt when a birth mother changed her mind about an hour before we were to bring our daughter home from the hospital. They gave us permission to go to the orphanage but told us that we would not be allowed to hold her. Once we were at the orphanage, the director had no problem with us holding her and visiting as often as we liked until we could take her back to the hotel.

The orphanage was an old building obviously in need of repair, but the area where the children were was neat and clean. Since our daughter's rash didn't clear up for three days, we spent that time observing and were impressed. The orphanage workers were kind and loving. When her rash cleared up, we were given custody and almost immediately we couldn't imagine life without her. All the waiting and paperwork hassles disappeared. She is such a perfect fit for us, and we know that God handpicked her for our family. —RO, New York

After looking at many countries, we chose Kazakhstan because we wanted to meet our child face-to-face before committing to adopt her. We were met at the airport in Kazakhstan by our translator, and as he dropped us at the hotel he said to be ready in an hour to go find our new daughter. We first met with the orphanage director, who wrote down the names of three babies for us to meet. We were then taken to the baby house and brought upstairs to the play room, where a representative from the Ministry of Education was waiting for us. She opened a large binder and pulled out three pictures, describing each child as she slowly placed their picture in front of us. The first was a child with a cleft lip. We immediately said that we were looking for a baby girl as healthy as possible.

The next two were healthy. I looked at their pictures forever, trying to find something that would say, "Pick me! I'm your daughter!" They asked me which baby we wanted to meet first. I couldn't decide. I asked if there were any other girls. The representative hemmed and hawed and flipped through the pages. She asked, "Are you sure you don't want a boy? We have many boys." I thought of the lavender nursery and the pink clothes hanging in the closet, plus the name we had been saying over and over in our hearts for the nine months we had been waiting to meet her. "No," I insisted. "We are looking for a girl." After a few more silent minutes, she pulled out a fourth picture and placed it in front of me. "There is one more," she said. As soon as I looked into her eyes, it was like something in my soul touched hers and I recognized her as my child. "This one," I said. They brought her in to me and placed her on my lap. She was so small. They started telling me about her history, but I barely heard them. They could have been saying any sort of horrible things and it would not have mattered. "Do you want her?" the representative asked. We both smiled and said, "Oh, yes!" Our forty-three days in Kazakhstan were filled with the expected and the unexpected, but in the end we came home with a beautiful eight-month-old daughter. We chose her name because it means "precious child." —AG, Texas

We traveled without a referral to Ukraine and met our three-year-old son at the orphanage. Although it may be good advice to remain objective, I'm not sure it is possible when meeting a child that may or may not be your son, depending on your decision after this meeting. We had already heard his medical and background information before we met him, and we had decided before we left home that as long as there were no big red flags we would accept the referral. I think this decision made the first meeting easier. I did not feel love when I first saw him, but I did feel a connection—a parental-type concern.

He was shy, but interested in us, and his nurse encouraged his interactions. At first, he was more interested in our daughter, who is the same age, and then he began to warm up to my husband. The meeting lasted only about twenty minutes, but when he left, he told my daughter she was "pretty," and gave me a hug and my husband a kiss. At that point, I turned to my husband and said simply, "Yes." —AC, Ohio

We flew to Guatemala to meet the two girls we had just accepted referrals on. The girls were one and five and were not biological sisters. We didn't know what to expect other than we were supposed to meet the executive director of our agency in our hotel lobby and she would have the girls with her. As we were waiting, I saw two women walk by carrying a baby and I just knew it was our baby . . . and it was. We sat in the lobby and fell in love with her right then and there. The executive director showed up a little later and told us the birth mom of the five-year-old had changed her mind, but she had brought a two-year-old with her for us to consider. We were a bit taken aback, since we had just found out that the five-year-old whom we had accepted a referral on would not be our child and we had no information on this new child at all.

We all moved to the adoption lounge of the Marriott and visited with both girls. It was overwhelming to have to make a lifelong decision right there, but my husband and I prayed and God answered right away. Within minutes, we knew that the one-year-old was the only child we would be adopting. Saying "no" to the two-year-old was incredibly hard, but we were at peace with the decision. —DF, Florida

Our meeting experience was not at all what I thought it would be. We were adopting two boys under eighteen months from Russia. We took a thirteen-hour overnight train ride to the orphanage and were not able to sleep on the train. We arrived exhausted at the orphanage at 8:30 in the morning with three other couples. The orphanage looked like an old school and we were all taken into a classroom and told to wait. I had hoped for a little more privacy for this first meeting. Things were OK when they handed us our first son, but when they brought in the second, my husband had an anxiety attack. The reality of what we were undertaking overwhelmed him. I tried to remain calm for him and the boys, and he was able to eventually get it together. The remainder of the day was a whirlwind: After forty minutes with them we went to court to finalize the adoptions; we went back to the orphanage to pick up the boys; then we boarded the train for the thirteen-hour trip back to Moscow. It was quite an experience, but the boys are great and we have all bonded well. Now, two years later, we are in the process of doing it all again for a little girl. —*MG, Virginia*

———

I thought I had prepared myself thoroughly on what to expect when we went to China to pick up our fifteen-month-old daughter. I thought I was prepared for her to be reluctant and scared of us since we were unfamiliar to her, but I wasn't prepared for her to grieve so intensely from the moment she was placed in our arms. She cried and cried for the first few days, then clung to my husband and cried whenever I tried to touch her. She was terrified and MAD and pushed me away day after day. I cried in the bathroom in our hotel room so that she wouldn't see me upset (which I thought would upset her further). The second day I tried to force her to allow me to hold her, but it was awful for both of us, and I think it set us back in the process. On one level, I was glad she was bonding with one of us at least, but I was still hurt and sad. I had waited so long to hold her in my arms and mother her. I couldn't help but wonder why the other babies (or most of them) were at least tolerating their new mothers, and I felt strangely embarrassed and started to think maybe I wasn't cut out for motherhood after all. The whole time in China and the whole way home, she would barely let me touch her without crying as she clung to my husband. It stayed this way for a week after we got home, but then my husband left on a four-day business trip. I was very worried how she would react, but she soon realized that I wasn't so bad after all and the bonding began. We've been as close as can be since then, and she now goes to my husband and me equally for reassurance and cuddling. When she asks for Mommy a hundred times a day, it is music to my ears. —*SM, Maryland*

———

We have adopted twice and both times we were very nervous when we first met our daughters, but both times we were lucky. Neither of our daughters cried when we received them. It was so wonderful to have all the waiting and uncertainties be over and to be able to live in this moment of holding a real, live beautiful child—my child—in my arms. It was truly a joyful occasion.

When we first met, our eldest daughter reached out and touched my face and we both smiled. I rocked her back and forth and held her in my arms while we talked to her caretakers. Our second daughter was holding a small photo album that we had sent ahead of us. She also came right to us, but we could tell that she was sad at losing her familiar caretakers. It was two days before she started to smile at us.

Yet even our "easy" experiences were not without problems. Our first daughter resisted taking a bottle for several days. It was very frustrating for me to feel such a strong bond with this child but have her refuse to eat. This problem did not resolve quickly. She also had several ugly-looking skin infections that were hard to diagnose. Our second daughter never had any difficulties eating or sleeping, but was extremely clingy. This, too, did not resolve quickly.

During the transition, I would recommend trying to talk to their caretakers as much as possible and even pass the child back and forth between you and the caretakers to help establish a sense of transition. This gives you time to ask practical questions about sleeping and feeding. Right away, try to find something the child really likes, maybe a food or a toy, so that you can engage them with this favorite activity as a diversion from the trauma of separation. Make sure that you carry them as much as you can, because it really does speed bonding. Also, go in expecting them to act a few months younger than their chronological ages. —*JF, New York*

———

Our first meeting with our son came after a miserable seventy-two-hour ordeal that included being stranded in Newark, New Jersey, for thirty hours and an unexpected detour to Frankfurt, Germany. We were beyond exhausted when we finally arrived in Ethiopia on our son's five-month birthday. We drove through Addis with the driver from our agency and then drove down an alley at the end of which was a huge gate. The van honked, and when the gates opened we pulled into a courtyard. Our bags were immediately whisked out of our car and brought to our room at the guesthouse. We assumed we would follow, but our facilitator had other plans and immediately brought us to the baby room. The nanny pointed out our son's crib, and we stood next to it crying and watching him sleep. I didn't want to wake him up, but the nanny didn't have the same concerns. She gently picked him up and rocked him back and forth, saying "Ashoo, Ashoo" (Mommy). I cried even harder! When she handed him to me, I was instantly in love with our little son. It all happened so fast—arriving after what seemed like endless travel and being brought immediately into the baby room—we didn't even have time to locate our cameras, so our first moments together aren't captured on film.

We brought him to our room that afternoon and he was clearly agitated. He didn't make eye contact, fussed, and refused the bottle. We decided he might respond better to us in a familiar environment, so we brought him back to the infant room, where he visibly relaxed and began to interact with us.

I am a firm believer in baby wearing to aid bonding, and between my husband and me our son was held pretty much constantly except at night. This was clearly new for our little guy, but he adjusted really well and seemed to be quite interested in seeing the world. He was easily overstimulated, and would turn his head into my chest and just go to sleep when things were too much for him. —*HMJ, California*

W e just returned five weeks ago from picking up our four-year-old son from China. We took our three bio children, ages seven, six, and three, with us. We had an absolute blast, and so did the kids. Our new son is doing well, and we attribute much of it to having our children with us to help with his transition. I think our children understood their new brother better having seen his culture and where he came from. It also really helped my sanity to not have to live in two worlds. Things were so stressful at times that I was really glad to not have to worry about my kids at home.

We included our kids from the beginning in this adoption, and that helped with preparing them for the trip. We told them this trip was not for them and that their new brother would get a lot of Mommy and Daddy's attention. Since they had been talking and thinking about him all year, they were better able to understand.

We talked about how the food might be really disgusting and that they might have to eat rice for two weeks. They were pleasantly surprised when the food was not as bad as we had told them. We discussed the strange "hole in the ground" potties. They couldn't wait to finally see and use them. My daughters would have to go potty everywhere and would choose the Chinese style over the Western one every time.

One thing I must mention is that both sets of grandparents traveled with us. That was really wonderful, but I would still recommend bringing your children even without the grandparents. We had in mind prior to traveling that some of the kids would stay in hotel rooms with the grandparents, but we never did that. Our kids ended up alternating sleeping on blankets on the floor. We decided that with all the extra people with us it was important for our new son to understand who belongs in the immediate family unit. I would recommend taking one extra person to help out if possible. —*AR, Colorado*

We left our fifteen-year-old at home when we adopted our four-and-a-half-year-old and this was definitely the right decision for us. We decided not to bring him for several reasons. We did not want him to have to get the vaccinations that were required and we didn't want to worry about him getting sick from the food and water. Mostly, we wanted our entire attention to be focused on what was best for our new child during this transition time without having to worry about balancing the needs of our older child. In a way, he would have been a distraction from the real purpose of the trip. He would also have had to miss school and would have had a lot of makeup work when he returned. He was quite content to be left in the very capable hands of his grandmother, and we talked frequently by phone. —*LM, New York*

We have two older birth children and we have adopted twice. The first time, we did not take our older children. We were new to adoption and to international travel, and there were just too many unknowns. Financially, we also did not have the money to take them. We had such a good experience on that trip, however, that we wanted to share the experience with the older two kids the next time. Our kids were eight and a half and ten years old, and that has to be the perfect age to bring children along. They had a wonderful time, but they also learned a lot about adoption, which has helped them understand their brother's reactions when we got home. I'm convinced that their presence on the trip helped with our son's smooth adjustment, since he bonded so quickly to them. —*RM, Pennsylvania*

———

Another single mom and I were met at the airport in Ho Chi Minh City and driven three hours to the city where the orphanage was located. I was dirty and tired and I really wanted a shower, but instead they took us immediately to the orphanage. I didn't know we would go straight to the orphanage and couldn't find my camera in the short time I had. We were led into the office of the orphanage director and then two caregivers appeared holding babies. I immediately recognized my daughter and knew I was in love with the most precious gift God had ever given me.

Vietnam has a wonderful tradition called the "Giving Receiving Ceremony." We showed up at the Justice Department and our children met us there in the arms of their caregivers. After listening to different officials speak, we were officially presented with our children. Her transition was amazingly smooth; she rarely cried and never seemed to mourn. —*SR, North Carolina* [Vietnam's process may be different under the new laws.]

———

Our son was eight months old when we went to Korea to get him. We got custody right before we got on the plane, and the next thirty hours until we got home were pretty rough. I think he was grieving and I also think he was just plain freaked out—by us, by air travel, by everything. He didn't want to be held, he wanted to be down and crawling around. We simply couldn't allow that, so he cried! Although we felt bad for him, there was nothing we could do other than hold him and sing to him, but neither was effective at soothing him. His crying was something we all had to endure—my son, my wife, me, and the people in the seats around us (unfortunately for them!). He was so exhausted when we finally got home, it took him a while to get caught up on sleep and to reset his body clock to our time. After about a week he was great, and his transition has been smooth ever since. —*JL, Oklahoma*

———

I traveled alone to get my sixteen-month-old son from Ethiopia. I was the only dad traveling alone to pick up a child, and I think all the moms were concerned that I needed help to survive. I was dreading the long flight home since I had heard many horror stories from other families. To make matters worse (or maybe better), I am an airline pilot and was flying standby.

I started the trip home with only three hours' sleep because of last-minute packing and an early flight. Fortunately, my son slept well and continued to sleep in my arms on the drive to the airport. As he slept, I stared at him and wondered what his life would be like in the United States, and what it may have been like if we were not adopting him. I don't know the answer to either question. As we waited to board, an Ethiopian man came up to me and asked if I was adopting the baby. When I replied yes, he said, "One day I hope I can be as big a man as you." I had no idea how to reply, but I had to turn to the window so no one would see my tears. It had been an emotional week.

My son is a terrific traveler. He seldom fussed and ate and slept well. He would only sleep on my chest, which felt really nice but didn't allow me to get much sleep. I'm sure we looked cute, though, a drooling baby sleeping on an airline pilot's chest.

I had these grandiose plans for when we arrived home to change him into new clothes, make myself look respectable, and walk off the plane while videotaping the waiting family and friends. But after twenty-two hours with almost no sleep, I just dragged us off the plane and into the waiting arms of our family. —*GB, Arizona*

I wasn't prepared for the depth of my daughter's sadness, anger, and fear when we first met. It was heartbreaking and exhausting to witness. She screamed for fifteen hours straight. I finally had to give her medication to get her on the plane to come home. She had a really hard two weeks, and then things began to smooth out.

I wished I had asked more questions of the foster mother. I didn't have a list and I forgot to ask most of the things I really needed, like her schedule and what soothed her. It's actually pretty awkward asking these questions, which is probably why I didn't ask many.

I strongly recommend that you not travel alone to pick up your child, even if you are a single parent. There is so much to handle at once: baby, stroller, luggage, and documents. It's a logistical nightmare, plus it is really nice to have emotional support. —*MM, Maryland*

When we were in Guatemala, we were given the opportunity to meet our daughter's birth mother. I had mixed emotions, but my husband was all for it. The birth mother came to our hotel to meet us. It was only the second time she had seen our daughter, who was four and a half months old. Our meeting was very emotional but also very comforting. On some level beforehand I felt a little guilty, as if I was taking a child away from her mother. Although it was sad and there were lots of tears on both sides, it was also very clear that there was no ambiguity on her part. She had five other kids and simply couldn't raise this one. She very consciously made an adoption plan for our child and was at peace with her decision. This made it so much easier for us, and now we have this information to share with our daughter. Since we have been home, we have written to her twice and sent pictures. We hope someday to go back to visit her. —*SG, Washington, D.C.*

We were adopting two children at the same orphanage. The orphanage director met us and said, "Let's go meet your kids." She brought us to the baby room and asked if we thought we could pick out the two that were ours. We had memorized their pictures, so it was easy. We visited the children two times a day for three days before we went to court.

I think meeting the children at the orphanage was a good experience for their caregivers and for us. It was clear to us that their caregivers loved them and were happy for them to be adopted. I think it was good for them to see that we were so happy to be adopting these two children, but it was definitely a bittersweet experience and I was bawling when we left.

Before we left, someone encouraged us to record as a memento for them later in life the meeting with the orphanage director when he was giving us background information on our children. The information he gave us on our daughter was very difficult to hear and certainly not something that I would ever want her to hear in the manner it was told. It is intensely emotional for me even now to listen to it, especially knowing how wonderful she is. I vacillate with whether I should destroy it, and wish now I had never recorded it. —*MS, Virginia*

We took way too much stuff with us to China and had to lug it around the entire trip. The only thing I would definitely recommend is sleeping pills and upset-stomach medicine. Unlike most families who adopt from China, we did not travel with a group, and I really missed that experience. We felt very alone. An interpreter was available only when needed and we were afraid to venture out of our hotel much. On the positive side, we were able to meet our son at his foster family's apartment and ask lots of questions. I was scared to death on the way to meet him—of what, I'm not sure, but I was a basket case. They were very poor (three bio kids and three foster kids in a one-room apartment), but it was clear that the foster mother loved our son and was happy for him. —*MD, Florida*

My husband, my parents, and my precious three-year-old, Jessica, flew to China to pick up our second daughter, thirteen-month-old Ellie. We waited in a cold, dark conference room for the babies. When they finally called our name, the child they handed my husband had bright-red cheeks, and four layer of clothes on top of three soggy bottom layers. She was screaming, and after taking one look at my husband, she literally launched herself into my arms. My father was busily snapping pictures as they herded us to the back of the room so the other babies could be presented.

With this child stuck to the front of me like Velcro, the mother in me kicked in and I tried to comfort her. The first thing I noticed after she stopped crying was that she was not cooling down—she clearly had a fever. The second thing I noticed was an angry, infected-looking sore on her neck. While taking all of this in, Jessica looked at me and asked, "Mommy, we need to sing my Ellie our song." So we started singing a song we had made up about getting Ellie. About halfway through, I realized that I was now the mom of two. It took the simplicity of a child laying claim to her sister to bring that home to my heart.

When we got back to the hotel, we discovered a fiery red rash and three infected open areas on her back. Her skin was hot to touch and the look in her eyes was total misery. There were marks on her hips where her diaper had been tied onto her with a bungee-type cord. I immediately called our coordinator to get someone to look at her back and was told that the orphanage director was a doctor. He told us it was a heat rash, but I wasn't convinced. While he was there, I asked if my daughter had a nickname. He said no. Then I asked why she was named what she was and if there was a special meaning behind her name. He spoke to our coordinator for translation, trying not to look at me as he answered, but it was as if he could not help but look at me when he answered, "No, there is no special reason for her name. She was just named. There are just so many children." There was such sadness in his eyes and fatigue in his face.

This was not the beautiful "Gotcha Moment" that we had experienced with our first daughter. I was terrified of how sick this child looked and acted. I was also scared of my lack of connection to her. All I felt was the weight of the responsibility of taking care of her. The only thing I could do was let her cling to me and pray.

That night, the only way we could get her comfortable enough to sleep was to give her Tylenol and Benadryl. I lay awake that night troubled by my own thoughts. I was not sure I even wanted to continue this—we had a very happy family with just Jessica. Was I doing the right thing bringing this very sick and needy child into it? What effect would it have on our daughter? Was I capable of meeting the needs of everyone?

The next morning, even with all the doubts in my heart, we finalized the adoption and gave her our name. She was now officially part of our family. But my feelings of dread and anxiety did not lift. She continued to let only me hold her and demanded that I do so all the time. She was extremely jealous of any attention that I showed Jessica. I was sinking deeper and deeper into fear of what we had done. The weather did not help—it was cold, damp, and foggy, which matched my mood.

During our six days in Nanchang, new lesions continued to form on Ellie's back, she was not eating well, and to increase the tension, she started having diarrhea stools. I also noticed during one screaming fit that she had eight teeth trying to come in. She continued to demand my undivided attention and would not even look at her dad. During one thirty-one-hour period she would not allow me to put her down, and would scream if I moved out of anything other than three positions that she found comfortable. I had made a commitment to this child, and that was the only reason that I continued to meet her needs. I still did not feel any emotional connection to her at all. I was at my wits' end.

I finally called back to the States to speak with our pediatrician, who recommended starting her on the oral antibiotics I had brought. Within forty-eight hours she was obviously feeling better, but by this time I was so physically and mentally exhausted that I could not appreciate the strides she was making. All I could do was feel intense gratitude that she would allow my parents to hold her.

Finally, we headed to Guangzhou. We landed to warm temperatures and familiar sites from our first adoption. I was so ready for the familiar. We met an American pediatrician traveling with another group who diagnosed Ellie with an unusual case of scabies. We began treatment that night, and by the end of the three days of treatment Ellie became a new child. Once again, I missed the transformation because by this time I was just too tired and overwhelmed by emotional stress to care.

I had been looking forward to Guangzhou for so long but now found myself too tired and strung out to do all the things we had planned. I was frustrated and angry at everyone. The reason for my anger was Ellie, but I took it out on everyone else because I could not admit to myself that I really did not like this child that we had adopted.

The trip home was long and arduous—three hotels and four flights. When we finally arrived home, all I wanted to do was sit down and cry. I was so thankful to be home. One of my friends came running up to us and threw her arms around me and Ellie. I just sobbed into her shoulder. I can never explain how wonderful it was to see those faces when I thought I could not take any more.

Our story has a happy ending. [See a continuation of this story in Chapter 10.] After a rough first month, we began to adjust. However, the memory of our trip and my reaction when faced with the reality of my daughter's needs was both scary and humbling—it was emotionally brutal. But the end result was oh so worth it! —*NA, Indiana*

BACK HOME

From Wishing to Becoming

Molly Ann-Zhen was born in China on December 9, 2004, and joined her forever family in November 2005. She is pictured here with her brothers, Sam and Eli. Lincoln Wondimu and Abigail Birhanesh were born in Ethiopia on September 23, 2000, and December 18, 2002, respectively. They joined their forever family in June 2005. They are pictured here with their parents, Paul and Susie, and their siblings, Tyler, Marcus, and Joshua.

Katherine and Brett's preparation came in handy when they first brought Jessica home. They had read extensively about the typical growth and developmental delays of children who spent their first year in an orphanage, and they were prepared to give her time to develop. "I'm the type who worries over everything, so it's a minor miracle that I was fairly relaxed about her developmental delays," notes Katherine. They had Jess evaluated by an early-intervention specialist who gave them suggestions to help her catch up. They decided to wait before starting therapy to see if it was really needed. Within six months Jess was on target developmentally without specialized therapy. "Although we were well prepared for the developmental delays, we were a bit caught off guard by some of her behaviors, especially her intense clinginess those first few months," notes Brett. "We probably could have been more prepared for the emotional aspects of the transition."

You are finally back home. The long journey that began with a dream many months or years ago is now over. You've finally found your child. Now you can get on with the life you dreamed of and put all this behind you. Right? Wrong! The real journey—parenting—is just now beginning, and parenting through adoption is both the same as and different from parenting through birth.

You've had to work hard to get to this point. By the time you walk through your front door with your child in your arms, you have handled a forest's worth of paper, asked and answered thousands of questions, agonized over money, worried over political or bureaucratic instability, waited patiently and impatiently, and traveled halfway around the world and back. Up until this point you've been a bit preoccupied with just finding your child, but now that she's home you must shift your focus to raising her.

This chapter will be a starting point—the first months home. I will share with you what the experts say and what I know as a mother who has been there and done that. Both parents, if you are married, must read this chapter. If you are single, ask your primary support person to read this chapter as well.

The recurring theme throughout this chapter is to be flexible in your expectations and look for slow and gradual improvements. Give yourself the gift of time: time for you and your child to adjust, time to feel like a family, time to grow in love, time before you start to worry. Parents report a big improvement in three months and an even bigger one in six months.

My attitude throughout parenthood has always been "progress, not perfection." At no time is that more important than in the first months home.

THE FIRST WEEKS

Parents who have had to work so hard to become parents may expect bliss. And while I wish for you nothing less, at best it will be fleeting emotion and at worst it will elude you like a recalcitrant toddler. You are jet-lagged and adjusting to a significant, albeit welcome, change in your life. Your child is jet-lagged and adjusting to an even larger, and probably not welcome, change in her life. Throw in unpaid bills, unanswered calls, and visitors at the door and you've got the makings of something, but it's probably not bliss.

It generally takes about two weeks to get over jet lag. Exhaustion and interrupted sleep should be expected during this time. The best way to get over jet lag is to get on a normal sleep cycle, even if it means going to bed when you're not tired and waking up when you are. During the day, get as much sunshine as possible to help reset your internal clock. Ask for help with meals and cleaning. Lower your expectations of what you can get done. A successful day during the first weeks is one where you and your child survive until the end of the day. Anything more is a gift.

ADJUSTING FROM THE CHILD'S POINT OF VIEW

There is no way to predict how your child will respond when you bring her home. The transition to your family will be amazingly smooth for some and agonizingly rough for others, with most falling somewhere in between. Ease of adjustment is influenced by factors unique to your child (age, health, early-life experiences, and temperament) and factors unique to you (temperament, preparation, and expectations). Given the variables, it's impossible to generalize, but once again my grandmother's advice rings true: Prepare for the worst, hope for the best, and settle for anything in between.

Change is stressful, even positive change, and from your child's point of view, adoption is the total change of everything he knows. He faces new caregivers, new environment, new smells, new sounds, new foods, new bed, new schedule, new expectations, and the list goes on and on. When you think about it, it's a miracle the poor kid is even functioning. And this explains the times when he isn't.

While you have been planning and preparing for this event for months or years, your child likely had no advance preparation. Babies and toddlers have no comprehension of adoption, and even older children have a limited understanding and often poor preparation. They may not be told until shortly before they are to leave with you, and frequently they are given misleading information. They may have been told that if they don't behave you will send them back, or they may have had an unrealistic portrait painted of the glories of life in rich America.

How she behaves in the first couple of months is no indication of how she'll be in the future. None of us is at our best (or even at our *normal*) when we are frightened and stressed. I would certainly hate to be judged at that time. Under these circumstances, I might appear to be a controlling witch (choose your own beginning consonant); and while I may be that some of the time, I hope that you'd give me a chance to find out that I'm not that most of the time. Your child deserves the same.

Your child may be terrified by all the changes in her life. She might withdraw, avoiding eye contact and interaction, or she might go to the other extreme with tantrums and long crying jags. She may cling to one parent while actively rejecting the other; either parent can be on the receiving end of the rejection. Developmental regression is common.

THINGS TO DO WITHIN THE FIRST COUPLE OF MONTHS

- Take your child to the pediatrician. Postpone any tests that will require drawing blood for at least a few weeks unless it is a medical necessity. Suggested testing is outlined in the American Academy of Pediatrics' *Red Book*. Testing for parasites, anemia, vision, and hearing should be routine. Call your doctor before the first appointment to find out how to collect a stool sample for parasite testing. Depending on the birth country, your doctor may suggest redoing the immunizations. Postpone these shots for a while, but keep in mind any immigration waiver you signed promising to complete the immunizations.
- Add your child to your benefit plan. It may be necessary to do this before your first pediatrician visit.
- If your child had an IR-3 visa (both parents saw the child and adoption was finalized in country), you will receive his U.S. Certificate of Citizenship (COC) in the mail automatically, usually within forty-five days. If he had an IR-4 visa, you must apply for his COC through the USCIS Web site after you readopt.
- Register your child with his birth country's embassy if required.
- Contact the home-study agency to schedule the first post-adoption report visit.
- Update your will to make sure your child is included and guardianship is determined.
- Postpone visits to the dentist for a few months unless absolutely necessary.
- Pay back the help you received or wish you had received by posting an evaluation of your agency experience on the Inter-Country Adoption Registry (ICAR) at www.adoptachild.org and on any of the agency research forums you used.
- If you are concerned about your child's development, contact your local public school system to have her evaluated by the early-intervention program. The evaluation and services are usually free.
- Send pictures back to the orphanage and government officials through your agency.

Regardless of how your child behaves, remember that she is not being bad; she is not trying to ruin your life or your home or your family. She is coping the only way she knows how. However hard it is on you, it is harder on her. Tell her how brave and capable she is to handle all that has been thrown at her. Even if she doesn't understand you, she'll pick up on the tone and it will remind you as well.

HOW TO APPLY FOR A SOCIAL SECURITY NUMBER

Bring the following to your local Social Security Office. Office locations are listed at www.ssa.gov. You can also mail the documents to the office, but I don't recommend that since some are originals. You will receive your child's social security card in the mail.

- Completed application form SS-5 (download from www.ssa.gov).
- Original copy of your child's foreign or U.S. birth certificate and adoption decree.
- A picture ID for you.
- You do not have to have your child's Certificate of Citizenship (COC) in order to get her SSN, but it will save you an extra trip to the Social Security Office if you do. Your child's COC is mailed automatically if your child arrived with an IR-3 visa. If your child arrived with an IR-4 visa, you will need to readopt before you can apply for her COC. Unless you need her SSN immediately for filing your tax return, wait until you get her COC. If tax season is upon you and you can't wait, call the local Social Security Office and find out what document they require to issue an SSN without proof of citizenship, such as her passport and immigration card. Once you receive the COC, you must take it to the local Social Security Office and they will update their file to show your child as a U.S. citizen.

Some families go through an initial honeymoon phase when both the child and parents are on their best behavior. This is especially true with older kids. Toys are picked up with a smile and teeth are brushed without a reminder. Parents play with their freshly scrubbed cherubs each night instead of watching TV, while the smell of fresh-baked cookies wafts through the house. You feel like you are living in a Norman Rockwell painting and it feels good. I always felt a little cheated that my family never went through this stage. Unfortunately, all good things must come to an end, and at some point your child and you will feel comfortable enough to start being yourselves.

Children experience the disruption caused by adoption regardless of their age. Some parents and experts tell us that preschool-aged children have the hardest adjustment because they are old enough to know what is going on and retain memories of their prior life, but aren't old enough to understand the reasons behind the changes and to understand that life in a family has advantages. The same basic strategies of flexible parental expectations, time, and consistency work for all ages of children.

A number of common issues can surface in the first couple of months home. Give your child and yourself time to improve with love and consistency.

If things don't improve with time, seek help from a professional trained in working with post-institutionalized kids.

Sleep Issues

The number-one issue facing newly adoptive parents is sleep. Actually, in my experience, the number-one issue facing all parents of children under the age of five is sleep, but adoptive parents may have a double dose of sleep problems in the first several months. Stress and anxiety have a nasty habit of coming out at night to wreak havoc on the unsuspecting. Experiences from the past can also disrupt sleep. It will take time before your child feels safe in your home.

Regardless of the age of the child when adopted, consider them to be newborns when it comes to putting them to bed and keeping them there. No one expects a newborn to fall asleep easily or stay asleep for long. Parents do whatever it takes for the newborn (and his parents) to get some sleep, and you should expect to do the same for newly adopted kids. But this "doing whatever it takes" stage shouldn't last forever.

Your goal is to have a simplified and mutually satisfying bedtime routine within about six to eight months. Everything you do during the day and at bedtime to help your child feel safe will move you toward this goal. You will have to decide how fast you should move in this direction, depending on how secure and attached your child is feeling. But move you must if you are going to enjoy being a parent.

Most children from orphanages have never slept alone, and now is not the time to start. If your child does not want to sleep alone, don't make her. Some parents and experts recommend letting the child sleep in your bed with you. Each family has to decide, based on their circumstances, if this is the best decision for them. It can provide security and a wonderful bonding opportunity, but it may further disrupt your sleep. Also, parents may need a break from a child struggling with the transition from orphanage to home, and nighttime may be their only chance. Some families are not comfortable giving up this time for parental quiet and intimacy.

If sharing a bed with your child is not the best decision for your family, there are alternatives. One parent can sleep part or all of the night in the child's room, or the child's bed can be placed in the parents' room. The child may like sleeping with a sibling. Depending on the age, the child can perhaps start the night in his room and then move to a sleeping bag in your room if he wants to be closer to you in the night. No shame should be associated with his decision to move in the night. My son did this for many years. He always brought his flashlight, stuffed animal, and favorite toy with him, and in the morning, he simply tucked the sleeping bag away and carted his treasures back upstairs. When he was ready to stop, he did.

Even if you decide to have your child sleep with you, unless you plan on going to bed at the same time, you still must put your child to bed. I can't offer you a quick fix, but remember that your goal is gradual, not quick, progress.

Set a bedtime. Although there are normal variations, consider the following when deciding on a bedtime:

- Nine- to twelve-month-olds usually need a total of ten to twelve hours of sleep at night and two naps during the day.
- One- to three-year-olds usually need ten to twelve hours of sleep at night with one nap in the afternoon. The transition from two naps to one nap was a bumpy one for all my kids. We seemed to go through a prolonged period where one nap wasn't quite enough but two naps were too many.
- Three- to six-year-olds usually go to bed between 7:00 and 9:00 at night and wake up between 6:00 and 8:00 in the morning. Most three-year-olds nap; most five-year-olds don't. A small minority of kids stop napping very young. If you have one of these, your goal should be a quiet time alone with or without a nap.

Establish a bedtime routine. Choose activities that both you and your child will look forward to. Don't let it get too cumbersome, since you'll be repeating it every night. A routine that takes an hour might be fun the first night, but at the end of a long day I'm ready to punch off the parenting clock and don't want to spend an hour putting my little angel to bed. The routine for a toddler might look like this: brushing teeth, laying out clothes for the next day, reading two books, saying prayers, singing one song while rubbing his back, and then five kisses (four around the outside and one for the lips, or if your child is not comfortable with that yet, try the nose).

With toddlers and older children, be vigilant about bedtime creep caused by the "one mores": one more drink, one more trip to the potty, one more book, and the most cunning of all—one more kiss. (Actually, my kids soon realized that this one always worked, but then, I got the extra kisses I wanted, so it was a win/win.) Kids are born with a natural ability to stall. I'm sure there is some biological purpose to this talent, but they don't need to practice it at bedtime.

About a half hour before you start putting your child to bed, slow down the activity level in the house. Don't roughhouse or play active games. Your child might enjoy a long, soothing bath or a gentle massage.

Tell your child a few minutes before you will start the routine. "It'll be time for bed after we finish this game or when the kitchen timer goes off." Use the words even if your child doesn't understand them at the beginning because of age or limited English. Nonfluent kids may need other cues as well, such as their picture board (see discussion later) or playing soothing music with the routine starting when the music ends.

Conquering the pop-ups. Ahh, if only it was so simple as going through the bedtime routine and walking out of the room. Kids are like that blow-up doll weighted on the bottom—you lay it down, but it pops right back up. This very common situation is especially difficult with newly adopted kids, because parents are concerned about creating a secure bond and much of the advice on attachment seems to contradict typical parenting advice for training a child to stay in bed. There are no easy solutions, and only you can figure out the balance between your desire for time off and your desire to create a well-attached child. In deciding how to strike the balance, don't shortchange your own needs. A well-rested parent is a happier parent, and a happier parent is better able to do all the things the next day to help the child feel secure and attached.

Encourage the use of a transitional object, such as a blanket or stuffed animal. Use a night-light. Play a music or story CD when you leave the room. (Several great bedtime story CDs are listed in the Resource Guide.) Or leave your child with the beginning of a happy story for him to finish: "A little black kitten is playing with his tail. What will he do next?" Don't rush to move your child from the crib to a bed. Even though she can climb out of the crib, for some children the sides of the crib make it less likely that they will pop up and leave the room.

Teach him how to relax if he is old enough. Start by teaching him to slow and deepen his breathing; later, add progressive muscle relaxing. See the Resource Guide for books on using this technique with kids. Massage can help any age child relax.

At the beginning, consider lying with the child until he falls asleep. Look for ways to make this an enjoyable part of your evening. Listen to music, daydream, nap, and if you are married, enjoy the fact that you are getting out of cleaning the kitchen. Do not talk or interact with your child during this time. If you don't want this to become a permanent part of your routine, over several months gradually shorten the time you spend lying with your child. Switch to sitting on the floor or a chair close to his bed, and each night gradually move toward the door and decrease the time. Your goal is to be able to go through his routine, tuck him in, and leave the room.

If after you leave the room your little darling gets back up, take him back to bed without fanfare, tell him you love him, and leave. Keep it short and sweet. Try setting a timer for a couple of minutes and promise to come back in before it rings. Follow through with praise and a quick back rub. Gradually increase the time you are out of the room. This can be exhausting, but it won't last forever.

Give it some time, since it will take a while to help her understand what is expected. After a few months, if it is still a problem and your child is old enough, try a reward chart. The basic principle is that the child gets a reward the first morning she stays in bed after being tucked in. The child then has to stay in bed two nights to get a reward, and so on. Be very clear about what you expect the child to do to earn the reward. Use pictures and a chart. The younger the child, the more concrete you have to be. When one of mine was three, I taped the rewards to the chart itself (little cars, zoo animals, lollipops) so he would understand what was expected.

One parenting trick with reward charts is to have the whole family share in some of the rewards, such as a trip to a fast-food place to celebrate. Without their knowing it, you will have conscripted your older children to help their younger sibling succeed, and they may be more successful than you. We jokingly say that our first potty-trained our second in a day because she wanted her share of his reward.

Parental attitude is crucial in resolving sleep issues. Your child is not being bad; she is just struggling to adjust. Sleep problems are common, but they will improve by taking little steps each day. Set a goal of having a well-established routine in six months. Having a time period in mind takes the immediate pressure off when you seem stuck, while keeping enough pressure on to ensure movement. Remind yourself of the progress you have made rather than focusing on how much further you have to go. After a few months of little progress, read one of the general parenting books on sleep issues listed in the Resource Guide. Make a commitment with your spouse or support partner that neither of you will go more than one night without sleep. See the discussion under the "Self-Care" section of this chapter.

Food Issues

Typical food issues can run the gamut from the child not wanting to eat to the child always wanting to eat. It helps to understand how food was handled in her life before she came to you, but unfortunately you may never know this.

A poor appetite can be caused by depression and stress. If your child is eating and drinking enough but not as much as you would like, talk with your pediatrician and give it some time before you start worrying. Some older babies and toddlers who have been fed only with a bottle are very orally sensitive and may resist strongly the attempts to introduce solid foods.

There is no magical solution. Continue to focus on the parenting techniques described in this chapter. Use the formula and foods from her birth country and only gradually introduce American formula and foods. Try varying the temperature of her formula, since it is the custom in some countries to prepare formula much hotter than we do. Keep meals calm. Don't try to force her to eat, but play games to get her to try putting food in her mouth (for example, let her feed you and then you feed her or have the airplane spoon flying in for a landing). Subtly increase the calorie and nutrition of what he will eat (fruit smoothie with wheat germ, extra egg in the muffin, and use formula instead of milk in anything you prepare). If problems continue, seek feeding therapy to desensitize her to food textures.

A baby who was usually fed with a propped bottle may resist cuddling while feeding. It is crucial for you to introduce this form of nurturing, but if your child resists, go slowly. Avoid eye contact or even let your hair hang to obscure your face while you feed her at first. Slowly move toward eye contact and more touching.

Overeating is a common problem for some kids raised in an institution. Food was served according to the clock, not individual hunger, and in some orphanages, food was neither plentiful nor nutritious. A well-stocked pantry and refrigerator may be a temptation too strong to resist. Some kids make themselves sick at first by eating too much. When they become accustomed to having enough food, overeating usually lessens. Until that time, consider not serving family-style. Avoid buying junk food, since many parents report that their children have a tendency to fixate on this type of food. Keep healthy foods readily available, such as a bowl of fruit or a plate of cut-up apples and carrot sticks that your child can access whenever he wants. It's hard to overeat on healthy food, and even if he does, now is not the time to worry about contributing to the childhood obesity epidemic.

Kids who have never had enough may hoard food for the future by hiding it in their rooms or carrying it around with them in their pockets. Although worrisome, this phase most often passes once the child feels secure that you will always provide enough food. Until that time, make sure food is readily available, provide a bug-proof storage option for her stash, and look for opportunities to reassure her that you will always take care of her. Some parents have had success gradually moving the stash of food from the child's room to a shelf in the pantry. Go slowly and follow your child's lead.

Sibling Issues

The addition of a child changes the family dynamics for everyone, and especially for the children already in the home. Pay attention to which of your existing kids is being displaced from his position in the family. For example, if you are adopting a child older than your eldest child, pay special attention to how your former eldest child adapts and seek ways to reinforce her position. The same care should be given to any child who is being displaced from his position as the only boy, the only girl, or the youngest. Preparation, forethought, and individual attention are needed to smooth these adjustments. Parents can be sensitive and sympathetic but may not be able to prevent the sometimes rocky adjustment.

If your children are old enough, it helps to prepare them in advance for the myriad of ways their new sibling may react. Remind them of times they had to adjust to a new situation and how they reacted. Explain that their new sibling may be scared and reject them or go to the other extreme and become their shadow. Unfortunately, their new sibling may be mean. Some toddlers and older kids have learned to aggressively compete for the limited attention of caregivers in the orphanage, and while these behaviors might be effective and necessary in that setting, they are inappropriate at home. Although it helps to explain to your older children why their new sister is behaving this way, you also must protect them while gently but firmly retraining your new child in better coping techniques. See parenting strategies later in this chapter.

Explain to your children in advance that your new child may be overwhelmed at first and that you will be staying close to home for a while after she arrives. Brainstorm with them for ideas about things they would look forward to doing at home: Maybe you need to replenish your art supplies or buy the really large Lego set that will take weeks for your child to assemble.

You can expect sibling rivalry on both sides. The new child may get a disproportionate share of the attention, or at least it will seem disproportionate to your existing child. Keep your children's routines as regular as possible during the transition and set aside one-on-one time with your older kids.

A nice gesture is for the new child to bring a gift for the other children when she arrives. You can shop for these gifts when you are on your adoption trip or you can buy them before you leave. If family or friends bring a present for the new child, gently suggest that they bring something small for your other children. Since we adopted an infant who wouldn't know the difference, if someone told me they wanted to bring a gift for the baby, I requested something for my older kids instead and then gave them a suggestion of something small and inexpensive.

Parents of children who have been in foster care sometimes report that their child is accustomed to being the center of attention. Often foster children are the only or the youngest child in the foster family, and I suspect that some foster parents may view their role as that of doting grandparents. This is what I call "a high-class problem," something akin to deciding how to spend your lottery winnings. Your child was well attached and loved and just a bit (or a lot) spoiled. Understand that he's simply behaving as he was trained and is undoubtedly grieving for his foster parents. Give him some time to adjust and learn to share the center-of-the-universe spot.

On the bright side, your older children can be wonderful models for your new child of what it means to be a member of a family. The new child will take her cues from the other children on the fun of being hugged and cuddled. She can learn your family routine from watching the other children. And one of the greatest joys in my life is watching my children becoming friends.

ROUTINES/TRANSITIONS

Children thrive on predictability, and though we may be loath to admit it, most adults do too, especially when we are stressed. After all the change your child has been through, he is in a state of constant alert trying to anticipate what will happen next. A daily pattern will allow him to relax, and knowing what to expect reinforces the trust that is the foundation of attachment.

Toddlers and older children with limited English may benefit from a picture chart with the day divided into sections. You can change the pictures to reflect any changes to his routine. But, especially at the beginning, don't vary from your routine much until your child and you settle in.

Transitions are the tipping point for many a child. A transition is any change from one activity to another or from one place to another. Shifting gears is often tough for newly adopted kids, especially those who spent much time in an orphanage, and meltdowns often occur at these times. If you can smooth out the transitions a better day will be had by all.

The first step is to recognize how often you are asking your child to change from one activity or place to another. Scaling back your activities will help you eliminate many transitions. When a transition is necessary, prepare your child in advance by cueing her in with words and pictures. Do this even with a baby. Don't tell a young child that they'll have to stop in five minutes, since they have no concept of time. Be concrete: "You can throw the beanbag three more times and then we'll clean up." "When you finish breakfast, we'll go to the store." "When the timer goes off, it will be time for your bath."

If your child is struggling, notice if there is a pattern. For one of my children the transition home from first grade was rough. He would come home each day spoiling for a fight, and usually found one with me or his brother. Running errands on the way home was a disaster. Once I realized he was transitioning poorly, I made changes. We came straight home from school and straight into a bubble bath. He soaked and played with his bath toys by himself for an hour every afternoon for most of that year. His after-school snack was even served tubside. He emerged wrinkled but in a decidedly better frame of mind. I lost my favorite errand-running time, but the trade-off was well worth it.

At the end of the day, analyze what went well and what needs a bit of tweaking. Notice when your child fell apart and when you fell apart. Consider what you could do differently tomorrow to avoid or smooth those rough patches. You are educating yourself, not judging yourself. Celebrate your successes and most days will have some, even if you have to search hard for them.

PARENTING TECHNIQUES TO ENHANCE ATTACHMENT AND SMOOTH THE TRANSITION

Attachment is a two-way street. Your child must attach to you and you must attach to your child. The process is cyclical. At first you may just be going through the motions, but as you care for her, you start the process of claiming her as your own; and as her needs are met, she starts to trust and depend on you. Her growing attachment to you serves as a reward for your efforts, thus increasing your feelings of attachment toward her. And the circle of attachment continues, with the bonds deepening each time around. Attachment and love are not the same thing; you have to *grow* rather than *fall* into attachment.

In a nutshell, to enhance attachment try to re-create the environment of a typical well-loved newborn. Unfortunately, we are talking about kids, not nuts (although there are times . . .), so it's not as simple as it sounds. Not for the first time, I will tell you that how soon and well your child and you bond depends on the age, health, early-life experiences, and temperament of the child mixed with the expectations, preparation, and temperament of the parents.

At the heart of creating attachment is meeting the child's needs promptly, with lots of hugs and cuddles along the way. Do not worry about spoiling your child for the first six months. Your child may not be accustomed to this form of nurturing and may resist. Don't worry. As with the tortoise, slow and steady usually wins the race.

- Parents should be the primary ones to care for the child at the beginning. Before your child arrives, explain the theory behind attachment to grandparents and friends who are eager to feed, bathe, and diaper your child. Some parents write a letter to explain this to family and friends before the child arrives. Encourage other ways they can help, such as cleaning, cooking, and listening.

- Strive for a calm environment when you first get home. Discourage visitors at first. This is important even if (especially if) your child seems to love all the stimulation.
- Delay your return to work as long as possible and make the transition gradual. See FUAQs in this chapter for ideas on gradually returning to work.
- Carry your child using a front pack or hip sling. Carry him while you are picking up around the house, at the grocery store, and walking through the mall. Carry him whenever and wherever you can until your back says it has had enough. See the Resource Guide for suggestions. If your child is simply too big for you to carry in a baby carrier, look for every opportunity to cuddle and hold him.
- Encourage bottle-feeding even if your child has moved on to a cup. Snuggling up with a bottle enhances bonding for toddlers and preschoolers, as well as for babies. Encourage skin-to-skin and eye contact during bottle feeding. Go slowly if your child resists. If he won't take a bottle, hold a sippy cup while he snuggles on your lap.
- Look for every opportunity to make eye contact.
  - ~ Reward your child for eye contact (a smile or a tickle).
  - ~ Use a backward-facing stroller.
  - ~ Put a sticker on your face near your eyes. Make it a silly game for him to pull off the sticker.
- Look for every opportunity for skin-to-skin contact.
  - ~ Baby massage.
  - ~ Bathe or shower with your young child. Parents can wear a swimsuit if more age-appropriate.
  - ~ Stroke and touch your child often.
- Play interactive games that encourage touching and eye contact.
  - ~ Peekaboo.
  - ~ Great Big Buzzard. Horrible name, cute game. With your finger circling above your child, chant, "Great big buzzard flying in the air, gonna get Emma right about [pause for effect] THERE." Vary "there," starting with the belly button and moving upward to under the chin and tip of the nose.
  - ~ Little Mousie. With fingers walking up your child's arm, chant, "Little Mousie went upstairs to see if Emma said her prayers. If she didn't say

them right, little Mousie will bite, bite, bite" as you tickle her in the sweet spot under her chin.

- Don't overwhelm your child with toys. He is not accustomed to having many toys, so rotate toys, keeping only one or two out at a time. Toys retain their entertainment value longer if children do not have access to all their toys all the time. You want to have some toys they can only play with at quiet time in the afternoon, some toys that are for quiet play when they first awaken in the morning, and a toy basket that comes out when you absolutely must have uninterrupted time on the phone or preparing dinner. A toy he hasn't seen for a few days will keep him occupied longer than one that he can play with at any time. A side benefit is that pickup is faster with fewer toys.

- Limit the number of choices your child has on clothes, food, or toys. After she has been home awhile, gradually introduce more choices.

- View success in terms of time with your child, not a clean house or jobs checked off your "to-do" list.

- Be prepared to handle your pets differently, depending on how your child and pets respond to each other. Your child may have never seen a domestic pet before, and his reactions can vary from fear to being overly affectionate. Fido may need to spend more time in the crate or outside for the first few months. Gradually increase the time the two have together. Read a book on harmonious living with pets and kids. See the Resource Guide.

- If possible, stay with your child through a tantrum. As she becomes more secure and attached, you will be able to tell the difference between when she is out of control and when she is crying for the effect it has on you. At the beginning, err on the side of assuming she is scared and needs your presence.

- Have few rules, but consistently enforce those you have. Since you are limiting your child's environment at the beginning, you will need fewer rules. One friend closed off all rooms except two for her newly adopted toddler. Her only rules for this period were no climbing on the bookshelves and no throwing toys. Had the whole house been open to her little bundle of energy, she would have had to add no hanging off the upstairs banister, no playing with the cat litter, and no fishing in the toilet. She gradually expanded his environment and added the new rules.

- Choose your battles carefully, and choose only those you can win. (Or, stated another way, make darn sure you win any battle you choose.) Let the others slide for a while. You have many years to correct bad habits.

- No matter what your opinion on spanking, it should not be used for disciplining a child who has not formed the bonds of attachment. Spanking may have a place in child rearing, but it does not have a place with a child who is not attached or who may have experienced abuse in her past.
- Don't worry about potty training until your child has been home for a while, even if she is at an age where other children are out of diapers. Diapering provides another opportunity to nurture your child. Besides, this is a battle you can't win.
- Your child is not a guest in your home and shouldn't be treated like one. Older children should be expected to help out with age-appropriate chores.
- For toddlers and older kids, have someone who speaks the language come over as often as possible at the beginning to act as a translator. At the very least, have someone available by phone. There are things you need to make sure your child understands and things your child needs you to understand.
- Try to speak to your child in her native language, even if you know only a few words.
- Create a picture board to use with toddlers and older kids to help you both communicate. Cut out or draw pictures of things he may want to tell you or you want to tell him. For example, have a picture of the car for you to point to a couple of minutes before you will leave for the store to help prepare her for the transition. If she resists the car seat, include a picture of a child in a car seat and point to it and then to the car to help get her primed. Include pictures of things your child might want to ask for, such as favorite foods, toys, or activities. You can also use these pictures to teach English.
- Talk to your child. Talk slowly, simplify your language, but mainly just talk, even if your child is a baby.
- Use hand gestures or basic signs from American Sign Language (ASL) with your child, from infants through school age, as a way to transition to English with less frustration and tantrums. See the Resource Guide for simple books to use with your child to learn ASL.
- If the child rejects one parent, create a fun routine just for that parent (for example, giving a bath, feeding the applesauce at the end of the meal, or reading her favorite book).

Parents often ask what healthy attachment looks like. I think it is like the famous Supreme Court quote on pornography: You'll know it when you see it. Eventually, your child should seek you out for comfort, prefer your company to others, enjoy closeness with you, and be more cooperative. Rely on your instinct. Progress is seldom smooth and regressions are common, but if you are not seeing progress after six to eight months (remember, progress, not perfection), start reading the resources on attachment listed in the Resource Guide. Get help from a counselor experienced in working with post-institutionalized kids. This counselor should support you as well as help your child, because it is discouraging to parent an unattached child. It's hard for others who have not been in this situation to understand just how emotionally draining it is to try so hard to connect with a child but get so little in return. It is worth finding a therapist who understands attachment, since a different approach may be needed. See the Resource Guide. Attachment issues can and do improve with help.

SCHOOL

If you adopted a preschooler or school-age child, you will face the question of when to start her in school. Opinions vary on the best approach. Some people recommend starting the child immediately to help with their adjustment and language acquisition. They report that children feel very comfortable in school since it is similar to their previous environment. Others recommend delaying school for as long as possible to give you more time to bond and to establish yourself as the primary person in her life. A middle ground is to start the child in school within a few weeks, with a parent staying in the room with the child, and gradually decrease the amount of time the parent stays. There is something to say for establishing the patterns of her new life (school, day care, babysitter, church) early but gradually.

One problem you may face is determining the proper grade. Your child's age and emotional maturity rather than educational level should be your guide. Since both size and social maturity are probably delayed, consider one grade level behind her age group. Talk with the school about English as a Second Language classes. Some parents swear by them and others swear at them.

Most children do not need preschool, so decide what is best for your child based on his emotional needs rather than educational needs. Also consider what is best for you and your family. Do you want more time together or could you use a few hours off each day?

An increasingly popular option for adoptive parents is to homeschool their child at the beginning to facilitate bonding and to better customize her schooling to fill in the likely gaps. Most areas have local homeschooling support groups. Talk with these groups before you make this decision. They can tell you what is required in your state and can paint a realistic picture of what is involved. See the Resource Guide for suggested readings on this option.

Adjusting from the Parent's Point of View

A whole range of emotions is typical for newly adoptive parents. Many feel a deep contentment at finally being parents. Others report that Christmas-morning feeling of tingly excitement. They feel grateful to their child's birth parents and birth country for allowing this child to become theirs. They feel blessed to be the parents of this one practically perfect child. Many wonder why it took so long to decide to adopt and laugh at their earlier worries and anxieties.

Alongside these pleasant feelings parents frequently feel overwhelmed, scared, and just plain tired. After having worked so hard to get this child, you may feel a bit (or a lot) let down. Many a parent has wondered what in the world they have gotten themselves into during the first couple of months home. The enormity of the responsibility can feel debilitating. You may be afraid of messing up and permanently ruining your child. You may feel like a failure because you can't soothe your child quickly or because your child rejects your attempts. You may dislike your child more often than you care to admit. Our society has a romanticized notion of parenthood, especially motherhood, which doesn't always jibe with reality.

You are beginning your parenting career with a child who has a history and baggage. The meeting of your settled ways with your child's settled ways is bound to create turmoil. It is typical to feel like an alien in diapers has invaded your life. (In fact, one has!) Your former competence is laid to waste by this little whirlwind. You are used to being successful and in charge, and it's disconcerting to not be able to "solve the problem" through hard work and determination. Just plugging away and allowing time to work its magic is hard. I personally find *being* infinitely harder than *doing*.

Parents who are staying home for the first time have to adjust to a whole new lifestyle with a new code of conduct and new expectations. Most of the free time they thought they would have is taken up with the details of caring for a young child. Although I love parenting, the day-to-day tasks are often repetitive, frustrating, and—well, to be honest—boring. It helps to develop a support system of other moms or dads as soon as possible.

While most adoptive parents feel tired and scared at times, for some parents these feelings are severe enough to warrant professional help. Post-adoption depression is surprisingly common and parents report feelings of intense anxiety, exhaustion even if they are getting enough sleep, weight gain or loss, and periods of unexplained sadness or crying. If these feelings don't respond quickly to the self-care techniques in this chapter and a few nights of sleep, seek help from your doctor. If you are having thoughts of harming yourself or your child, tell someone and get help immediately.

New adoptive parents can be so hard on themselves. They want to be perfect because they believe their child deserves nothing less. They may think they are supposed to be perfect because, after all, they have received the adoption "seal of approval" by passing their home study. There are no perfect parents, even those you think look perfect from the outside. If I could give you just one piece of advice, it would be to be kind to yourself, especially the first months home. Parents sometimes fail to take care of themselves in the name of fostering attachment. They wear themselves out trying to do all the things this and other books recommend to bond with their child. While bonding with your child is important, you must strike a balance between taking care of yourself and taking care of your child.

SELF-CARE FOR NEW ADOPTIVE PARENTS

Research clearly suggests that the security of attachment is dependent on the interplay between the characteristics of the specific child and the specific parent (Judge, 2004). The best predictor of poor attachment is the unique mix of the behavior style of the child and the coping and stress style of the parent. There is a bit of the chicken-and-egg problem here. The more difficult the child, the more stressed the parent; the more stressed the parent, the less effective they are at parenting in a way that will help change the child's behavior. Nonetheless, what this research does underline is the importance of taking care of yourself in order to care for your child. Martyrs make interesting biographies but lousy parents.

Treat yourself as if you had just given birth. Birth parents are given six to eight weeks off from the demands of life, and any new parent will tell you that the physical recovery is the easy part. The real reason time off is necessary is to adjust to parenthood, and adoptive parents have the same need. Don't expect to bounce right back into your former activities. Don't expect to serve coffee and pastries to visitors. Say "no" to other obligations and "yes" to offers for help.

Schedule breaks into your day if you are staying at home.

- Everyone in the house should have a quiet time during the afternoon for napping or quiet play alone. Have special toys for this time and rotate them every few days. If she can't tolerate being alone, even for a short time, gradually work toward this and in the meantime rely more on the other techniques for getting a break.

- Look for opportunities where your child will entertain himself. Many children are content to play in their crib or bed when they first wake up in the morning or from a nap. Don't rush into his room the moment you hear him awaken. If your child does not do this naturally, encourage this behavior once he has been home for a while. Install crib toys or mirrors. Before you go to bed, leave a toy in or near his bed for him to discover when he wakes up. Rotate this toy daily.
- See my discussion on television later in this chapter.
- If getting a break is particularly difficult with your child, consider hiring a sitter to come to the house while you are there. Use this time to do something for yourself but still be available if needed. Since you will be in the house, you can hire a teen babysitter.

Break/nap time should be reserved for your wants, not shoulds, whenever possible. It is far better to use this time to recharge with a good book or a nap than to scrub a toilet, no matter how dirty the toilet. If you work full-time, use your lunchtime to do something you enjoy, such as meet a friend for lunch, eat at your desk while chatting online, or shop.

Hire housecleaning help for the first few months if possible. If you can't afford it weekly, try every other week. In between cleanings, focus on keeping the house picked up rather than clean. Develop the routine of picking up each evening so you start the day with a clean slate.

Develop a support system. Seek out people who will listen to you in triumph and despair with praise and encouragement, not judgment. It can feel lonely, because your friends and family probably haven't gone through the adjustment period with a newly adopted child. Have them read this chapter so they will be better able to support you. To talk with people who have been there, done that, and bought the T-shirt, join an adoption support group either in person (preferably) or online.

If you have a child who is difficult to take out of the house you must be especially proactive in getting support. Call friends often and ask them to call you regularly. Set aside time each day to go online for support. This time will pass, but while you are in the thick of it you need lots of help.

Find other mothers of young children to hang out with. You need this regardless of whether you work full-time, stay at home full-time, or some combination of the two. Finding the right mother/child pair is a bit like finding a couple to double-date with, although at least while your kids are young it's more important that the moms get along and have similar schedules.

Figure out the little things that recharge you and make these little things happen regularly. Look for win/win opportunities where you are being recharged while your child is having fun. Spend a rainy morning at the mall with your child in the stroller munching on a cookie while you window-shop sipping on a cappuccino. Meet a friend at a park where you can visit while your child burns off energy. Run or walk, pushing your child in a stroller. Play on the floor with your child while *The View* or *Oprah* entertains you in the background.

Don't compare yourself to other parents of children of similar age. It will seem that they instantly know how to soothe or distract their child while you are still going through the list searching for something that will work this time. They bumbled along as well when their child was a newborn, but they've had the time to grow as a parent with their child. The same will happen with you, but until then avoid comparisons.

Give yourself and your child frequent verbal pats on the back throughout the day. "We are doing so well today." "I am a great mom/dad and you are a great kid." "We're both having a bad day, but we'll do better after your nice *long* nap." Your child may not understand you, but he'll pick up on the positive vibes; besides, your real audience is yourself.

Do everything within your power to go only one night with little or no sleep. Both parents, if you are married, should make this commitment. The accumulation of exhaustion saps the joy out of life and makes it almost impossible for you to be the parent you want to be during the day. To the extent that this advice conflicts with what you think is necessary to create attachment, so be it. The best thing you can do to foster attachment is to avoid exhaustion. After a sleepless night, take the following steps:

- Your spouse should take over on the second night, regardless of whether your child does not respond as well to him, regardless of whether he has a big day at work the next day, and regardless of whether he feels inadequate. If you are single, call on your support team.
- Physical separation is usually required to get uninterrupted sleep. Either the on-duty or the off-duty parent should sleep elsewhere so the sleeping parent will not be awakened when the other parent is up with the child.
- Make certain that the sleeping parent will not hear the child. Use earplugs or a white-noise machine.
- If sunlight is a problem, use a sleep mask.

- Establish a soothing routine before you go to sleep (for example, soak in a hot bath or read a calming book).
- Both parents should promise each other that the sleeping parent is not allowed to check on the child.

Getting sleep is harder for singles. Don't hesitate to use your support system. Many singles want to keep their support person in reserve for when they really need them, but trust me, lack of sleep is when you really need them. Sleep issues will resolve and you won't need to ask so much of your team in the future. You may want to give it a second night before you call, but don't let it go any further than that if at all possible. Also, nap during the day if you can and if it won't disrupt your sleep at night.

Refuse to play the "what if" game. What if he continues to be this wild? What if she never attaches? What if I never feel like a mom? Hypotheticals are not reality and serve only to make you nuts. The things you are obsessing on will probably never happen, and if they do you will deal with them. For now, stop yourself the second you start down the "what if" path.

I hope you chose an adoption agency that can support you through this transition. Don't hesitate to call them for advice or just a listening ear. They won't think less of you for the call.

Pray or meditate. Pray for your child, pray for your family, and if you had a hard day, pray for the understanding that this too shall pass.

TELEVISION

I am devoting an entire section to television in order to sing the praises of this much-maligned box. Adoption and parenting gurus have given TV an undeservedly bad reputation. Some recommend that parents prohibit all TV for a year in order to promote healthy bonding. No TV, ever, for any reason. They reason that (1) TV will overstimulate your child, (2) it is bad for brain development, and (3) you should be the one interacting with her, not the boob tube. I have one word to say to this: baloney! Chances are very good that the "experts" recommending this have never been the primary caregiver on duty 24/7 with a child, any child, much less a newly adopted child. Anyone who follows this advice is either a saint or a masochist. I am neither. In my humble opinion, TV has one function and one function only—babysitting. And I for one embrace it wholeheartedly.

Lest you discount my point of view because you think I am a TV-addicted couch potato, let me set you straight. In our house, we watch very little TV other than when I want a break (although as my children age I am less in control). We are one of the few families left in America that still use an antenna, because we don't want our family tempted by all the shows coming in on cable or satellite. However, I think TV has its place, and I'm not sure I would have survived my children's younger years without it.

Every parent needs a break now and again; the more difficult the child, the more necessary the break. TV's role is to provide you with this break. In order for TV to be an effective babysitter, it must be used selectively. The rules of selective viewing are as follows:

- Use it only when you really need it.
- Use it for a limited time.
- Use carefully selected shows or DVDs.

The key to successful electronic babysitting is to use it when you want a break and not at other times. In my house, this time has varied with the ages of my children and my needs. It's almost never in the morning, since we are all fresh. It's seldom in the afternoon, since we have naps or quiet time. It's infrequently at night, since there are usually two of us to handle the chaos. But there is this time in the late afternoon, usually between 5:00 and 6:00, called "the arsenic hour" or "the witching hour." It's not a coincidence that this is the same time bars have happy hour with free drinks. There is no quality parenting going on in my house during this time; actually, there is no quality of any sort going on in my house then. At this point in the day, I am basically just killing time until reinforcements or bedtime arrives, whichever comes sooner. This is the perfect time of day to plug your kids in to the magical babysitting box.

At other times in my life as a parent, this time has changed. When I worked full-time, the first thirty minutes home was the time I needed a diversion, since it allowed me time to decompress and start dinner. Then there was a brief, but wonderful, period of time following the arrival of our second child. While the youngest napped on Saturday, we'd plug in a *Barney* tape for our eldest, and Peter and I enjoyed some uninterrupted adult time behind the locked bedroom door. To this day, the Barney song brings a smile to my face. It gives a whole new meaning to "I love you, you love me, we're a happy family . . ."

The time I needed a break shifted again after our youngest arrived. Peter frequently worked late, and I was struggling to cope with four young kids. On more than one night, I sat a small TV on our kitchen table and the kids and I ate in silence while watching life and death play out on *Animal Kingdom*. This was certainly not the scene I envisioned when I dreamed of parenthood, but on some days I swear it saved my life or at least my sanity. (Watching this show while we ate is the reason, no doubt, that my eldest became a vegetarian and my third became a devoted carnivore.)

For TV to be effective as a babysitter it has to be used sparingly. For most kids, the more they watch the less it works to give you the guaranteed break you so desperately need. It's also bad for brain development, but that reason is secondary in my book. One hour a day is the most mine watch, and when they were younger or when I worked full-time, it was sometimes less.

Choose your programs carefully. A steady diet of inane cartoons or play violence is not good for kids. Children like repetition, so you are going to be seeing or at least hearing this show a lot. We almost always watched a prerecorded show, a tape, or a DVD. The TV should fit around when you need a break, not the other way around. Choose shows where you approve of the message, and for newly adopted kids they should be calming with low stimulation. Deborah Gray, in *Attaching in Adoption,* recommends making a video of you and your child playing, eating, and singing together. This could be the perfect video for your electronic babysitter, although hearing myself sing might seriously interfere with getting a relaxing break.

I'm sorry to say that there are children for whom the TV is not a good babysitter. These kids may be very sensitive to any stimulation, can't focus long enough, or simply are not interested. Also, most videos are ineffective for entertaining babies and very young toddlers. For these children you need to find other ways for you to get a break, because in my experience breaks are what make a content parent.

ADJUSTING AS A COUPLE

The addition of a child can strain marriages or relationships, regardless of how the child joins the family. Parents can become so wrapped up in being a mom or dad that they lose sight of also being a wife or husband. Fight this tendency! You may have always wanted to be a parent and are reveling in your new role, but unless you want to be a single parent you must nurture your marriage as well as your child. Singles need time for their adult relationships as well.

Emotional support is necessary for both partners. You need time to talk and listen, time to laugh and love, and time to remember why you married each other in the first place. If you leave it to chance, this time won't happen. Once you get over the just-surviving period, it's time to start date night. Singles need date night as much as, if not more than, couples, and the date doesn't have to be romantic.

Once a week, without fail, you should go out as a couple. Some couples say that they can have this couple time at home, but I know very few who succeed. When you are at home, there are too many distractions. Between the kids, the TV, and the dirty dishes it is impossible to focus just on each other. You need to get out of the house for a couple of hours once a week and do something that is fun for you both. Peter and I have gone out every Friday night since the arrival of our first child. Only illness has kept us at home, and that has been seldom. We usually just go to dinner and talk. Others might want to go for a Saturday-morning run followed by a chat over coffee.

Attachment enhancement theories on parenting often recommend not letting anyone else touch your child, let alone care for him. But in the balancing act that is parenting, I humbly suggest that it won't kill your kid or cause major attachment problems if someone else cares for him for a couple of hours once a week. If grandparents are nearby and want some grandkid time, there is no better time than date night. Neither my parents nor my in-laws lived nearby or were the babysitting type, so we hired babysitters.

I recommend you find an adult who wants a steady job one night a week. Date night will not happen if you have to go through the hassle of finding a sitter each week. Parents are often reluctant to hire a *stranger,* but if they use the same person each week, they will only be a stranger the first night. Also, it is easier for your child if he has the same sitter each week. My experience is that teenagers will dump you in favor of their own date if they have a chance; besides, they are probably not experienced enough for you to feel comfortable. Nothing takes the romance out of an evening faster than anxiety. Ask friends and other parents in your area for recommendations of an adult who might want a steady babysitting job. Ask for and call references. Pay well—it's worth it.

At the beginning, you may have to be flexible on timing. If you are absolutely sure that no one other than you can put your child to bed, schedule your date so you'll be home in time. Don't be too quick to decide this is necessary. I was shocked when our grandmotherly sitter put my little darling to bed easily the first night I gave her a chance. She actually taught me a trick or two—imagine that! Even though it may be tempting to go out once your child is asleep, do so only if you are sure she won't wake up while you are gone. It can be very frightening to wake up to a stranger. And remember, dates don't have to be at night if this time is too hard on you or your child.

Make date night special for your child, too. In our house, date night means the rules are relaxed: junk food is allowed, a movie is rented, and bedtime is later. With a little careful planning, your children will look forward to date night as much as you. Although you may not like to think about it, they need a break from you as much as you need a break from them.

BECOMING A MULTICULTURAL FAMILY

Not all adoptive parents are white and not all international adoptions are transracial; however, all international adoptions are transcultural and many are also transracial. Although more obvious with transracial families, similar issues exist with transcultural families as well.

Our children have a dual heritage. It's easy to forget this when they are young. They grow and thrive within the protective umbrella of our family. People know of them as our children and that is their identity. But as they grow, their universe expands beyond our protective reach and the world will make assumptions based on their appearance. If they are not white, they will be seen as and treated as a minority. If they look Asian, the world will see them as Chinese or Japanese (seldom will the first guess be Korean or Vietnamese). If they look Hispanic or East Indian, the world will see them as Mexican or South American. Our children need to know what it means to be members of this race or culture and to be proud of what it represents. Instilling this pride may seem obvious when your child is of a different race but no less important if your child looks just like you.

Transracial families confront this issue head-on. White parents with Asian, Latino, or African kids stand out. When out in public as a family, there is no hiding the fact that this family was created by adoption. Sometimes this is a source of pride and sometimes an intrusion, but it is always present. When you are out with only one parent or a single parent, others will assume you are married to someone of the child's race. Again, this may be a source of pride or an intrusion, but either way, it is there.

Many a white adoptive parent is caught off guard by the prevalence of racial stereotypes. Latinos are lazy; black adolescent boys are dangerous; Koreans are smart; Chinese women are passive. This is hard for us to hear. We want so much to believe that if we just love them enough, we can protect them forever from these stereotypes. While I will never underestimate the power of love in armoring our kids with the self-confidence to face whatever life throws at them, I know it is likely not enough.

Stereotypes, both positive and negative, are limiting. Your Chinese tomboy drama queen who hates math may face resistance by breaking the stereotype of the ultrafeminine quiet Asian scholar. Strangers often praise Asian or Latino girls for their "exotic" beauty. While most parents enjoy hearing their children praised, too much focus on beauty alone presents its own set of challenges. Our daughters are more than their looks, and I want my daughter to know that she is capable, strong, and smart, as well as pretty.

We are fortunate to be following in the footsteps of the first wave of children adopted from Korea over fifty years ago, and we can learn much from their experiences. The message many adult Korean adoptees send loud and clear is that race matters. As parents who choose to adopt across racial and ethnic lines, we believe that race shouldn't matter and innocently extend this to the belief that race doesn't matter. But it does, and someday our children will know it.

Adult adoptees are not a homogeneous group and little research had been done on their experience. Some report no racial-identity issues, while others remember confusion and anger. They felt Caucasian but looked Korean, a white person trapped in an Asian body. (The racist label is Twinkie or banana: yellow on the outside, white on the inside.) Not surprisingly, by the time they were adults the majority had transitioned to seeing themselves as Korean Americans rather than Caucasians, but for some this was a rough passage.

The majority of adult adoptees reported some form of discrimination based on their race. The banal singsong accompanied by eye-slanting hand motions of elementary school makes way for the relationship issues of adolescence. One friend said of the experience with her South American son, "Other parents thought it was okay for their children to play with him, but not to date him." But others report that their race was no hindrance to their love life, and one friend assured me that it was an asset to hers (a prospect that makes my husband shudder). Another friend, a male now in his thirties, says that discrimination and relationship issues are harder for adolescent boys than for girls, since their looks and body type are far from the American ideal, and they can't fall back on being exotic.

And sometimes what they experienced was less outright discrimination than just standing out as being different. Many report the surprise at first meetings when someone had heard only their name or spoken with them over the phone. The looks they receive clearly say, "You are not what you seem or what I expected." Most stress that this is not necessarily a bad thing but it does make them stand out. As one told me, this can be an advantage or a disadvantage, depending on how you play it. Some reported having to work harder to fit in with others of their ethnicity because they don't share the same cultural base; others feel a natural affinity with second- and third-generation kids of immigrants since they share the situation of having the looks but not the culture or language of their birth country.

The adult adoptees I have spoken with and the limited research that has been done on transracial adoption indicate that most adoptees traverse the minefield of adolescence and enter adulthood strongly attached to their families and with a strong racial identity as both American and Korean. As parents, we can help smooth the transition by honoring and educating them on their dual heritage. I want my daughter to feel proud of both the first and second part of the Korean American label. They will naturally get lots of exposure to being American, but we will have to work harder to give them exposure to the culture and heritage of their birth country. Consider the following:

- Join a local country-specific adoption support group.
- Join or start a play group of moms and kids adopted internationally. Even if the children are not the same race as your child, it's good for kids to see other transracial families.
- Attend culture camps and programs with your child as he ages. Being in the majority every once in a while is affirming. Start young so your child is more willing to go as she ages. Some kids resist attending when they reach the tween years, around ten to twelve. You'll have to decide on your own how hard to push. For the record, I tried veiled bribery and then caved.
- Expose your child to role models from his country or race. The best place to find them is through language schools, churches, dance groups, and civic organizations. These groups often have programs designed for first-generation kids from this country and are open to adopted kids as well. Even though you may feel awkward, volunteer to help. Exposure to adolescents and adults of his race is the best way to prepare your child to become an adult of his ethnicity.
- Although you can't manufacture friendships, you can look for opportunities at these activities to meet adults from your child's birth country and fan the flames of friendship if a spark develops. These friendships can provide you with inside information on racial issues your child may face.
- Read fiction and nonfiction books for adults and kids about your child's birth country. Also read about children and adults of that ethnicity who live here. Read them yourself and read them to your child.
- Buy a coffee-table book on your child's birth country and do the unthinkable—open it.
- Offer to make a presentation on your child's birth country to his class at school each year. Collect pictures, maps, money, trinkets, and other information for use from year to year. Bring toys, books, and a child-friendly

dish or dessert from the country to share with the class. Include a discussion of the contribution of Americans of this ethnicity.

- Incorporate a few dishes from his country into your family's regular diet. Experiment until you find one or two that are family favorites.
- Learn some phrases such as "I love you," "hello," "good-bye," and "I'm sorry" in her birth language and use them frequently as a family.
- Regularly eat at a restaurant specializing in her birth country's food.
- Live in a racially diverse neighborhood.
- Send your child to a school where there are other kids of his race.
- Attend a racially diverse church, especially one that has members from your child's birth country.
- If you can afford it, take a family trip to her birth country.

With all this talk about honoring differences, don't forget that first and foremost your child is yours and a member of your family. You may be of different ethnicities, but you are all Joneses or Smiths, and as such, you share much in common. Look for opportunities to point out how you are alike. The Johnson clan can play a mean game of gin rummy and everyone has a specialty dish they can prepare. I like the one-to-two rule: For every one difference that is raised, point out two similarities. I don't like highlighting the similarities in the same conversation, since it seems to dishonor the spirit of what my child wants to talk about at that time, but I make a mental note to find a time later that day to highlight a way in which we are alike. For example, when your son notes that he is darker than you, you could acknowledge that difference, but after dinner you could point out how you all love ice cream, and then as you are putting lotion on him at bedtime you could talk about how you both have dry skin that soaks up lotion.

When my daughter went through a stage of focusing on differences, I joined her where she was but tried to expand her ideas. We made a chart of all the different hair colors in our family. When we looked at the chart, she saw that she was in the majority on hair color since four of us have varying degrees of dark brown hair. She really liked the idea of charts, so we also made one for our favorite flavors of ice cream and favorite seasons. Again, the subtle message was that there were lots of differences in our family but similarities, too, and the grouping changed depending on the issue.

We had similar discussions on skin color. Using a globe and my limited understanding of the science, we talked about why different people had different amounts of melanin in their skin. We compared our family's skin coloring as well. Yes, she had the most melanin, but each of us had a different amount.

During this period, we also read books about children from all over the world and together pointed out their similarities and differences. I've listed some of our favorites in the Resource Guide. Also, look at the suggestions in the FUAQ section of Chapter 1 for other ideas on building a family despite differences.

Adoption is always a mixed bag of gains and losses: We gain a child, but someone loses one; our child gains a culture, but loses one as well. When I think about the suggestions in this section, each one seems so inadequate by itself and certainly not up to the task of equipping my child to face the realities of growing up different. As trite as it may sound, I fall back on the belief that she was meant to be our child. I pray that the cumulative impact of our efforts combined with our fierce love will be enough. I suspect it will.

TALKING WITH YOUR CHILD ABOUT ADOPTION

Talking about adoption is like the old cliché about voting in Chicago: early and often is best. The same can be said for talking about all the big subjects of life, such as sex and money. Your competence will grow with your child. It's easier to fake a comfort level you don't feel when your conversation is with a one-year-old. "Vagina," "penis," "adoption," and "birth mother" all rolled off my tongue with equal ease when mine were babies. I thought I had succeeded completely when my eldest daughter's preschool teacher told me she was the only child she had ever heard say "mucus" rather than "snot" and "urinate" rather than "pee." (My family's word choice, I'm sorry to say, has degenerated significantly since that time. When my son was having surgery and a nurse asked if he had had a bowel movement that day, he stared at her blankly and didn't respond until his older sister whispered, "She means poop.")

Information is best shared over many mundane talks rather than one big "sit down, we have something important to talk about" discussion. The question of when to tell your child is simply not relevant, since the fact that he is adopted is just a natural part of life. He won't understand what it means to be adopted when he is young, but he will always know that he is adopted, and through the many conversations with you he will gradually understand what this means.

Don't bypass the small windows of opportunity that come up throughout the down times of parenting (while in the car, washing dishes, or—my kids' favorite—on the toilet), thinking that you'll wait for a planned discussion when you're totally prepared. You may reason that only then will you say it right, so she will hear it right. (By *right* you mean that she will leave the conversation feeling affirmed and loved and full of self-confidence, with all her questions answered so completely that she will never need to ask again.) While it may be possible to reach this mythical state of preparedness, it's not likely to happen in this lifetime, so you had best grab any chance you get to share with your child her story and answer her questions. Besides, you don't have to get it right (as if that's ever possible) the first or second time, since you will have this discussion many times over the years. Repetition helps your child process the information as she matures. What rolled off her back at seven will be of great interest at thirteen.

Think through how you want to tell him his story. You and your spouse should agree on the way you will share and shape the information of his journey to your family. It is your child's story and he has the right to hear it all; but while you can't change the facts, you can choose how to tell them.

Sometimes the information we have to share is difficult, and you may be tempted to not tell him that his adoption record said his mother was a prostitute, or his father was an alcoholic, or he was abused by his birth parents, or that he was conceived through rape or incest. Most professionals encourage parents to not lie but to carefully share this information with the child in a way that helps him understand his birth parents' bad choices and the special circumstances that may have led to these choices. It's also important for him to understand that he is not doomed to repeat these mistakes. Talk with a social worker at your adoption agency about suggestions on how and when to share this information. Usually experts recommend mid-childhood, when he is old enough to understand but he has a few years before the turmoil of adolescence to process the information. See the Resource Guide for books on adoptive parenting.

With children who were abandoned, we have the problem of telling their stories when we have little information. It's okay to speculate but not to lie. You can tell her why you think she was abandoned and together you can imagine how her birth mother and birth father may have felt, but it is best not to make up the supporting details. And remember, it's fine to say you don't know when you don't. No matter what you say, make sure you address the common misconception that young children often have that there was something wrong with them that caused their birth mother to choose not to parent. The story you tell should address this concern while still honoring the truth of what you know.

In our family, we include our religious beliefs in these conversations. We believe that her being in our family was one of God's greatest ideas, and we tell her so. She also knows that I thank God for her presence in my life every day.

Answer your child's questions in a developmentally appropriate way. If your four-year-old asks if she grew in your tummy like the baby growing in

Aunt Sarah's tummy, an age-appropriate answer would be "No, you grew in your birth mother's [or another lady's] tummy. Some kids join a family by growing in their mommy's tummy and others join the family by adoption after growing in their birth mom's tummy." It would not be helpful to launch into a discussion of the economic and political environment of her birth country, although that might be appropriate when your twelve-year-old asks why she was abandoned.

Our role as parents is to create an atmosphere of openness where our children feel free to ask questions and express concerns. While it's important to allow your child to lead, in my experience some children are just not the inquisitive type and need their parent to start the conversation or give information that has not been asked. Look for opportunities to do this: A pregnant aunt could be an opportunity for you to start a conversation about how families are formed, doll play could be an opportunity to role-play adoption, and an insensitive remark could be an opportunity to explore how it feels to look different from your parents. Just because your child does not ask questions, doesn't mean that you don't need to talk about it. Children's books about adoption are great conversation starters. Some of my favorites are listed in the Resource Guide.

With a child who doesn't ask questions, a fine line exists between providing information and honoring your child's supposed lack of interest. Trust your parental instincts. I periodically will ask a direct question, such as "Does anyone at school make comments about you not looking like your brother?" or "I always think about your birth mother on your birthday—do you?" I throw it out there and then respect her choice to pick it up or let it drop.

Parents of children adopted at an older age sometimes hope that they can keep the bad memories away by not talking about their children's previous life. It doesn't work that way. Her life before she came to you is a part of her, and she needs your help in understanding it all—the good, the bad, and the ugly. She needs to know that she's not alone and that you are not afraid to listen and talk.

LIFEBOOKS

A lifebook is the story of how your child came to be yours and the story of his life before he came to you. Adoption is only one aspect of your child, and at some point his life merges into your life and a separate book is not needed, since he'll look at the family photo album and scrapbook for that part of his life story. However, he had a life before he came to your family and his lifebook tells this part of his story.

I am not intimidated easily, but I was totally cowed by the idea of creating a lifebook. To put it charitably, I am not the crafty sort and everything I read about lifebooks smacked of clever, crafty creativity. It is much easier for me to be clever, crafty, and creative with words than things, so it stayed on my to-do list for years. As my daughter neared kindergarten, embarrassment over my procrastination and worry over lost opportunities finally propelled me into action. I had to put aside any notion of a masterpiece and aim for utilitarian function.

I wanted to reflect her adoption journey from her perspective and from ours. I started by including all the information we were given on her birth history and birth parents. I put these documents in a plastic sleeve at the front of a three-ring binder so she would have ready access whenever she was curious or whenever I wanted to talk about her birth parents. I opted to make this information available from the beginning, because I reasoned that waiting for the *right* moment when she was older would feel unnatural and would make it seem a monumental *occasion* (now we gather for the sharing of *the* information) rather than a natural part of her life. Include a copy of any note from her birth parent or information on her abandonment as well. Obviously, you may opt for a different approach depending on the information you have to share.

I then included things her siblings and Peter and I had written and drawn in anticipation of her arrival. Most of these also were put in plastic sleeves. You can include anything that you wrote during your wait that showed your feelings of anticipation and excitement. I included the battered photocopy of her referral picture that I carried with me everywhere to show the world. I included the Popsicle-stick puppets with photograph heads that I made for her next-oldest brother to help him understand the idea of becoming a big brother. I included the potential-names list Peter and I wrote on the back of a napkin.

Include all the pictures and paper souvenirs from your adoption trip. Your child will enjoy it all, including the gin rummy scoresheet from the plane trip over. Everything flat went into her lifebook and everything bulky into her keepsake box. I made double prints of travel, arrival home, baby shower, and first-months-home pictures and included one copy in her lifebook and one copy in our family photo album. The pictures and "books" her siblings made describing her arrival and their love were included as well. Her lifebook is plain on the outside, but it has served us well as a jumping-off point for discussion. It is kept in her room for easy access whenever she is curious or I am looking for an adoption conversation starter. I know from questions she asks that she periodically looks through it.

Your child's lifebook will be different, depending on his age and what information you have. Some of you will choose to continue this book as your child grows, making it truly a reflection of your child's life. This was way beyond my capabilities, but I've included resources to help you in the Resource Guide.

HANDLING INSENSITIVE COMMENTS

Most adoptive parents have stories of rude, insensitive, or ignorant questions or comments. They are common enough to be broken into groups:

"Real" questions. (These are my particular pet peeve.)

- "Are you her *real* parents?"
- "Are they *real* sisters?"
- "Do you have kids of your own?"

Payment questions.

- "How much did you have to pay for him?"
- "How much did he cost?"

None of your business questions.

- "Why didn't her parents want her?"
- "What do you know about her *real* parents?"

"You should have adopted kids here at home" comments.

Funny/Stupid questions.

- "Does he speak English?" (Asked when they knew he was adopted as an infant.)
- "Did you have to teach him to use a fork?" (Again, asked when they knew he was adopted as an infant.)

"You're so wonderful" or "She's so lucky" comments.

Unnecessarily referring to the child's adoption comments.

- "This is Dawn and her adopted daughter Betty." (The following story is gleefully repeated in adoption circles: When an adoptive mom and child were introduced this way, the mom responded to the introducer, "And where is your vaginally delivered daughter, Sue?")

- Tom Cruise was spotted around town with his children whom he adopted with Nicole Kidman. (Oh, how I hate it when journalists include the adoption status of a celebrity's child or that of an ax murderer. If the adoption is relevant to the story, then it's fair to include; otherwise, Tom was simply spotted around town with his kids, period, and no adjective is necessary.)

Getting-pregnant comments.

- It's a good thing you adopted, because you'll get pregnant now.

How should you handle these types of questions? The answer depends on the tone of the questioner and the situation. I think it is important to distinguish comments that are rude from those that reflect ignorance or those that reflect kind but ill-timed curiosity. I usually ask why they want to know to determine their motive. If they are asking out of idle curiosity, their nosiness will be obvious. If they are asking because they are interested in adoption, I give general information about international adoption but no personal details. Or, if I feel comfortable, I offer to meet them later to talk about adoption.

Although comments can be intrusive, I find that some parents wear their adoption on their sleeve and immediately assume ill intent. I was being interviewed on a radio show on this topic once and someone called in to the show to proudly tell of the time she responded to a question about where her infant, adopted from South America, was from with "You mean to tell me you don't know where babies come from?!?" This struck me as gratuitously mean or overly sensitive to the fact that her child was adopted. For all she knew, the questioner was someone who was interested in adopting, or had someone in their family who was adopted and was looking for a conversation starter. Or perhaps the person was from her child's birth country. An Asian woman once asked me if my daughter was adopted. When I responded that she was adopted from Korea, the woman smiled and told me she was also adopted from Korea. We have since struck up a friendship that has been nice for both of us. No doubt there are situations that call for a cutting reply, but don't make this your automatic response. In my experience, most comments are well meant.

Many times people are asking for legitimate reasons and simply don't know the correct language to use. In that case, a response that includes the politically correct language and general information without putting down the questioner is appropriate. Like it or not, you are a spokesperson for adoption.

Hypersensitivity to politically correct language serves only to stop others from talking about adoption and leaves the impression that adoption is something to be ashamed of. In the long run, this serves no one, especially not our kids.

The problem is that sometimes we just want to be a family and not a spokesperson for the glories of international adoption. Or there are times when our children don't want to be singled out or don't want their time with Mom or Dad consumed with talking with another adult, regardless of the topic. I don't have any perfect response that will spare you this burden. I find that answering briefly with a smile and then returning my attention to my family usually does the trick. If you are asked an insensitive question in front of your child, remember that your response is always for his benefit, not for the questioner. Think what response will affirm him and protect his privacy, and then make your response one he can model.

Q: *Are they real sisters?*

A: "Certainly. I doubt they'd fight like they do if they weren't." Or "They are now."

Q: *Do you have kids of your own?*

A: "Of course!" said with a confused look. Then I list all four of my children, starting with my adopted child first.

Q: *How much did you have to pay for her?*

A: "Why do you ask?" If they are asking out of idle curiosity, I just look surprised and say children aren't for sale. If they are interested in adoption, I give general information about international adoption, such as "The cost of adoption varies by country. Of course you pay for the services of processing the adoption; it's illegal to pay for a child. If you want more information, buy this great book, *The Complete Book of International Adoption*."

Q: *Why didn't her real parents want her? What was wrong with her real parents?*

A: Some parents suggest responding to the personal-background questions with "That is her private information and she will decide when she is older if and when she wants to share it." Although nothing is wrong with this response, I have never used it because I think it implies that there is something really bad in the child's past that needs to be covered up. I prefer the following: "Why do you ask?" said with a very perplexed look that hopefully makes the questioner squirm. If I feel the need to add anything else, "That's pretty personal, but there are many reasons birth parents make an adoption plan for their child, such as extreme poverty, governmental population-control policies, war, or wanting the child to have a two-parent home. Each situation is unique." And then change the subject.

Q: *She's so lucky.*

A: "Her dad and I are the lucky ones."

From my experience and my interviews with adult adoptees, the comments that will affect your child the most are the comments from other children. Children most often focus on differences in appearance, and the remarks are usually some variation on the "real" parents/"real" family genre. Before you get all huffy, realize that usually no harm is intended; the other child is simply trying to figure out the difference. I think it helps to prepare your child ahead of time. I overheard my daughter respond to a classmate with all the disdain that seven-year-old girls the world over have for seven-year-old boys, "Your *real* mom is the one who raises you, dummy." (Fortunately, the last word was implied by the tone but left unspoken.)

The good news is that the questions become less common over time. You tend to run in the same circles and your *uniqueness* wears off. And for goodness' sake, keep your sense of humor. This is not the worst problem to face. One day I was at a fast-food restaurant with my three younger children. My eldest son looks like me. My second son sports a mop of blond curls and blue eyes that stand in contrast to my dark brown hair and green eyes. Leah, then one, was adopted from Korea. The woman behind the counter did a double take worthy of a sitcom when she saw my family and said with a sly smile, "Law child, you sure like your men different!" It had been a long day and I was not up to educating this woman on international adoption, so, since the kids weren't listening, I responded, with a wink and sly look of my own, "Yep, variety is the spice of life."

OVERDIAGNOSIS SYNDROME

Labels

I have a love-hate relationship with labels. Actually, it is more of a hate-love relationship. I deplore the *acronymization* of our children. (I know it's not a word, but it should be.) Two of my kids have a string of acronyms trailing their names in their school records that would make a mother proud if only they represented their degrees and accomplishments. Unfortunately, the educational powers that be see little reason to give shorthand to their strengths, only to their challenges. I hate it! I hate it when people refer to their child as their ADHD, PTSD, RAD, FAS, LD child. I really hate it when someone refers to my child that way.

A label does not reflect the totality of my kid. It does not reflect the determination of one or the resilience of another. It does not reflect her wit or his kindness or their courage. It does not reflect their successes, which are many. And it certainly does not reflect the immense pride their dad and I feel for their accomplishments.

But, much as it pains me to admit, labels do have a place. They provide a much-needed explanation for the incomprehensible. They serve to normalize what we are going through by assuring us that others have been there before. They help us to coalesce for support and education. If nothing else, they simplify our communication. I grudgingly admit to their usefulness, but I'll give them no more due than is absolutely necessary.

Most children who spent much time in an institution will have a few well-earned labels. These acronyms have their place and you'll have no problem finding professionals to attach them, but your child is much more than the sum total of her labels.

Adoption Paranoia

Peter and I attended an adoption support group when our second birth child was two in anticipation of adopting. While at this meeting, I listened to the parents discuss the adoption-related problems their children faced. One worried over her child's dislike of being cuddled and rocked; another was concerned about his child's thumb sucking; and yet another talked about her child's nonstop motion. I looked at Peter in horror. Here we were with two children from birth that we had obviously screwed up royally, because they were exhibiting most of these same "adoption symptoms." Our son had never liked to be rocked. In fact, he wasn't much for cuddling at any time. He favored motion, the faster the better. Up to this point, I had not realized it was a problem and thought it boded well for his future in sports. Our daughter was the most orally fixated child I had ever seen. Once she got past a very deep attachment to her thumb (no small feat, I might add), she started biting her nails and sucking on her shirts and hair. Up until this point, I just encouraged frequent hand washing and looked for shirts that were hard for her to get into her mouth. I hated to think what it meant that my son preferred to sleep on the floor under his bed or that my daughter hid her clean underwear in the potted plants.

Now, all these years and two kids later, I still don't know why my kids do most of the things they do. I'm not even sure I know why I behave like I do most of the time. What I do know is that not all "weird" behavior is pathologic

---

POST-ADOPTION REPORTS

Most countries require post-placement reports. You knew this going in and you agreed to it; you probably even signed a legally enforceable contract saying you would provide them. Unfortunately, once they have their child some parents fail to follow through, and an increasing number of countries are closing or limiting international adoption because of this. Parents can find lots of reasons to justify their noncompliance:

- I'm mad at my agency and don't want to have any more contact with them.
- I don't want "big brother" looking over my shoulder.
- We are a family now and I don't want to be constantly reminded that we're an adoptive family.
- It's a hassle.
- It's expensive.
- No one can make me.

You may be right that your agency can't or won't legally enforce this agreement, but your real obligation is ethical. You have a moral obligation to your child's birth country, to all prospective adoptive parents who so desperately want to adopt, and, most important, to all the children who will grow up in orphanages if international adoptions are closed. Call your social worker and set up a meeting to start the process.

---

or predictive of future woes. My son has bounced his way through life and started sleeping in a bed when he was thirteen. (When asked why he moved to the bed, he said beds are more comfortable. Duh!) My daughter continues to bite her fingernails, but her shirts and hair are now dry and she hasn't substituted cigarettes. And, sad to say, I haven't been on an underwear hunt in years.

I'm not trying to discount your fears or offer meaningless platitudes about everything turning out okay in the end. You'll get enough of that from others. But in all my interviews and talks with adoptive parents, I've noticed a tendency in some to assume each "problem" their child is experiencing is related to adoption and is an ill omen for the future. I understand the need to try to make sense of our children's behavior and strongly encourage you to get help soon and often. But in our attempt to be proactive, I think we sometimes miss the point that adopted kids are more like birth kids than different. In my experience, all kids can be pretty strange at times and it usually means nothing in the end. As even Freud supposedly acknowledged, "Sometimes a cigar is just a cigar."

THE DIRTY LITTLE SECRET
NO ONE TELLS YOU ABOUT

I'm going to let you in on a secret all parents know but few admit: Kids can drive you crazy. I don't mean the "kids can do the darnedest things" said with a weary smile kind of crazy. I mean the honest-to-goodness "running out of the house in your bathrobe (or less) screaming" kind of crazy . . . or worse, the "hands on her shoulders not knowing if you can stop yourself" kind of crazy. This has absolutely nothing to do with how much you love the little buggers or how much you want them. It has nothing to do with how good a parent you are most of the time. It has everything to do with the nature of kids, all kids, but newly adopted kids can be especially gifted at driving you nuts. (You finally got your gifted child and this had to be her gift?!)

The first piece of good news is that you are not alone. Most parents have these feelings at some time. Listen to me: I am a loving good mother and I have had these feelings. The feeling that I just couldn't cope one more minute with this strong-willed little monster, with all these damn demands, with all the crying, with the inability to even shave my legs in peace. One night when my children were younger I told Peter that the only difference between me and a child abuser was a very small shred of self-control, or more likely, just plain luck. Fortunately, all we need is that one small shred and a little luck.

The second piece of good news is that things will get better—I promise. It's hard to see progress from the trenches—you need a bird's-eye view, but you're stuck in the muck. When you are in the midst of these feelings, remember my words: Things will improve, and usually much quicker than you think. "Improve" doesn't mean that parenting will become easy, but it will become easier and your feelings of despair will lift.

The third piece of good news is that there are things you can do right in the moment when you feel like you are going over the edge. Unless your child is in a dangerous situation, like the bath, get away from her if just for five minutes. Put a closed door between you and your child. Go outside or lock yourself in your bedroom. Don't test your self-control at this exact moment by picking your child up to put him in his room. You are not a bad parent; you are a real parent who is coping the best way you can right now. You will cope better tomorrow, but for now this is the best you can do and it's good enough.

Send up the SOS for help immediately. Call your husband, your mother, a friend, or a neighbor. Tell them you are stressed to the max and need a break right now. I know you are afraid of being judged, but you must take this risk for you and for your child. While you wait for help to arrive, post on your favorite adoption forum asking for help. It will come pouring in, because we have all been there.

The fourth piece of good news is that there are things you can do to lessen the times you feel the need to run away screaming. Show me a parent who has reached the end of her rope and I'll show you a parent who is not taking good care of herself. Reread the "Self-Care" section in this chapter. Critically analyze whether you are trying to be a superparent. Decide on one thing you will do starting tonight or, at the latest, tomorrow that will be kind to you. Tell someone else what you've promised and ask them to check that you followed through. Give them permission to kick you in the butt if you don't.

Listen to your internal dialog. Are you telling yourself that you shouldn't be feeling this way, that parenthood is what you've always wanted, that there must be something wrong with you or your child? If so, change the characters in your dialog. Imagine your daughter or daughter-in-law twenty-five years from now telling you she feels like she is going crazy trying to cope with your grandchild. How would you respond? Would you tell her to buck up and deal with it like a real woman? Or would you put your arms around her and tell her that these feelings are normal and that she needs support to get through this time? You deserve someone to do the same for you, and that someone may need to be you.

Your feelings do not mean you are nuts, but you are facing a difficult period and you could benefit from professional support to help you along the way. I'm not talking about long-term psychotherapy but short-term counseling. I know money is tight; I know it is hard to get away; I know some people will judge you; I know that you may even judge yourself. So what? You need this right now. Your child needs this right now. There are times in your life when you fly high and there are times when you slog through the swamp. This may be your slogging time, but later you will soar. I promise.

PARTING WORDS

You have worked very hard to finally become the parent of this beautiful child that is now yours. My final piece of advice is to relax and enjoy being a parent. Don't fret over your mistakes. We all make them, and our kids are not as fragile as some would have you believe. The best you can do is acknowledge your screwups, ask your child's forgiveness, and get on with parenting.

As I look over adoption literature and discussion on some of the adoption forums, I am struck by the focus on the negative. I realize that this book falls into that trap as well. In our attempt to prepare you for the worst that might happen, we fail to celebrate the best that usually does happen. And celebrate we should: celebrate the coming home of a child; the becoming of parents; the forming of a family. So by all means take the time to celebrate and drink deeply of the laughter and joy that is parenting.

FUAQs

Should we circumcise our fifteen-month-old son? My husband is circumcised, but we do not have religious reasons to do so.

This is a surprisingly hot topic on some adoption and parenting forums. It seems that parents, usually mothers, care deeply one way or the other about this issue. I should disclose up front that we did not have either of our sons circumcised. It was a relatively easy decision for us. The American Academy of Pediatrics (AAP) did not recommend it and most of our friends were not doing it. We figured our boys could make this decision for themselves if it was important to them when they were older.

The American, Australian, Canadian, and British pediatric organizations do not recommend routine circumcision of male newborns. Circumcision has some health advantages and disadvantages, but on balance the pediatric associations think that the benefits "are not sufficient to recommend routine neonatal circumcision." You will have to weigh the risks and benefits and decide for yourself.

Other than medical concerns, parents often give two reasons for wanting to circumcise their son—one freely talked about and one only acknowledged among friends. The most often cited reason I hear when I interview parents is that they want him to look like his dad and friends. Having this similarity may be more important to adoptive parents, since it further claims him as their own.

Circumcision is uncommon in most of the world, including Asia, South and Central America, and most of Europe. Circumcision rates in the United States vary greatly by geographic region, with 2004 estimates (the last year statistics were available) ranging from a low of 31.7 percent for the western United States to a high of 79.5 percent for the midwestern United States. The combined estimate for the United States is 57.4 percent of newborn males circumcised in 2004.

I decided to get an expert opinion on this subject. The following conversation took place last night with my seventeen-year-old son:

Me: Hey, bud, I want to talk with you about circumcision.
Son: No, Mom, you really don't.

Me: Did it ever bother you that you don't look like your dad?

Son: Do we have to have this conversation?

Me: If you want me to leave your room, yes.

Son: (Sigh) It seems to me that there are a lot more obvious differences down there between a grown man and a little kid than that one little (ha, ha) area. I can't remember focusing on that one specific difference.

Me: Well, what about looking different from other guys your age?

Son: (Deep sigh) When I was little it didn't bother me at all, but when I got to middle school, I was worried that someone would tease me about being different, but I worried about a lot of stuff in middle school. It didn't happen, and now I don't care. It's not like we have open showers in school or anything, and it's not like you look at someone when you're at a urinal. I really don't know who is circumcised or not and I don't think anyone cares who is or isn't. It's just not something that comes up very often. (Doubled over laughing)

Me: (Ignoring the obvious and looking for a graceful exit) What would you recommend for parents who are trying to decide?

Son: I can't think of any reason why they'd want to do it, but whatever they decide, tell them that they should definitely not discuss it with their son when he's seventeen.

Me: Amen!

When talking about this subject with friends who are deciding, the subject of—hmmm, how to delicately put this—*looks* will come up. As one friend said, "I've never seen an uncircumcised male and I'm afraid he, or it, will look weird." Another friend told me she and her husband were going to make the decision after they saw what their son looked like. I understand completely. For our generation, circumcision was the norm and things outside of the norm can seem *weird*. But from my experience, after changing a few diapers, what you see is what will be normal for you and anything else will look unusual. Uncircumcised males are about half of your son's generation, so if you decide to not have him circumcised, his appearance will be normal to anyone who sees him undressed as a man.

If either the spoken or unspoken reason for circumcision is a big deal to you, then go ahead and have him circumcised, but postpone your decision until your son has been home awhile to allow you time to reassess whether it is still important to you. It's a very good idea to wait for all elective invasive procedures until your child is firmly attached. General anesthesia will likely be required, so your child must be medically and nutritionally stable. Of course, sometimes circumcision is suggested for medical reasons specific to your child, but always get a second opinion by a pediatric urologist. If you decide to have your son circumcised, you don't have to justify your decision to anyone. Most parents report that their son got over it faster than they did.

Do I need to readopt my child in the United States?

Readoption is the process of obtaining a new adoption decree from your state that is independent from the adoption decree issued by your child's birth country. Whether you are required to readopt depends on what type of visa your child was issued when she came home. See the information box in Chapter 6 for a discussion of visa types. If both parents (if married) or the only parent (if single) saw the child prior to the adoption being finalized in the birth country, your child was issued an IR-3 visa and readoption in the United States is not required for your child to become a U.S. citizen and for you to get the adoption tax credits.

In all other cases, your child entered the United States on an IR-4 visa and readoption will be required for your child to become a U.S. citizen and for you to get the adoption tax credits. For example, if only one parent saw the child before the adoption was finalized in country (as can happen in China), then your child was issued an IR-4 visa. If neither parent saw the child before the adoption was finalized in country (as can happen in Guatemala), then your child was issued an IR-4 visa. If the laws of the birth country do not allow adoption before the child comes home (as in Korea and India), then your child was issued an IR-4 visa.

Each state has different rules for readopting. Whether you need an attorney depends on the complexities of your state's laws. To get information about your state, ask your home-study agency. Another good source of state-specific adoption information is the state adoption group on yahoo.com. The laws for readoption for each state are listed by the Child Welfare Information Gateway at www.childwelfare.gov (under General Resources, click on State Statutes Search, and look under adoption for a document titled "International Adoptions Finalized Abroad").

Readoption has advantages even if it is not required to establish citizenship and get tax credits. In some states, you must readopt (or follow a simplified recognition procedure if allowed) to get a state-issued birth certificate. Although the foreign birth certificate is legal, you may prefer a state-issued birth certificate because:

- It will be easier to get multiple copies. You will be amazed at the number of times you will need your child's original birth certificate. If you have only one copy, you will want to keep it safely in your lockbox. Retrieving it to register your child for peewee soccer and returning it the same day for safekeeping will be a major hassle.
- It will be easier for others to read (usually they are just looking for the birth date), since it will be in English.

Another advantage of readoption is that it gives you an opportunity to legally change your child's name if her new name is not reflected on her foreign birth certificate or adoption decree. A state-issued adoption decree will also be easier to replace if ever you lose the original. Additionally, the new adoption decree will be in English, which will be beneficial if you ever have to prove the legality of the adoption, but I doubt this comes up very often.

Finally, readoption provides a good excuse to celebrate and throw a party. Family and friends are usually allowed to attend the actual hearing in front of the judge, and even if your state simply recognizes the foreign adoption decree without a court hearing, you can still have a party. We need more celebrations in our lives, and what better reason to bring family and friends together than to celebrate the forming of a family.

I am just home with my daughter and she cries all the time and doesn't want me to comfort her. I feel horrible saying this, but I am really questioning our decision to adopt. This is not at all what I expected.

If you haven't already done so, take her to the doctor to see if she is ill. Parasites and ear infections are very common in kids when they first arrive.

Your feelings of inadequacy and despair are not unusual. Rejection stinks, and it's particularly hard to take from this child you have longed and worked hard for. Remind yourself constantly that this is not personal. She is not rejecting you; she is rejecting the situation. She is confused and frightened and has no other way to show it. This spunkiness will serve her well someday.

Don't expect to love her right away; trust that this will come. Look for small signs of improvement. Be kind to yourself and make sure you have plenty of support. Post online in your favorite adoption forum and ask to correspond with others who had a tough adjustment.

Run through the list of classic soothers: rocking either in a chair or standing up, a car ride, walking fast or jogging with her in the front pack, massage. If none of them works, just put her in her crib and sit nearby and sing a gentle lullaby over and over.

This too shall pass. Believe it or not, you and she will probably reminisce someday over her rough adjustment and what a little toot she was.

My son seems very immature. How long should I wait before I start to worry?

Children who have spent time in an institution almost always arrive home with physical, cognitive, and emotional delays—the rule of thumb is one month's delay for every three months in an orphanage. Most children make up these delays with time. A good approach in the first months home is to note any concerns but postpone worry for a couple of months, since many issues resolve themselves within that time. If your instinct continues to tell you that something is wrong, contact a pediatrician specializing in international adoption medicine to discuss your concern. In the meantime, have your son evaluated by your local school system's or county's early-intervention program. It is usually free and available for children up to three years of age, as well as older preschoolers.

I am a single adopting mom. Do you have any ideas for maximizing my time off work so I can be at home longer with my child?

First check the parental-leave policy your employer already has in place. You may be able to take vacation and sick leave in addition to parental leave to extend the time you have home with your child.

If your company does not have an adoption-leave benefit, you may be eligible for twelve weeks of unpaid leave under the federal Family and Medical Leave Act (FMLA) without losing your job or group health benefits. FMLA applies to public employers and private employers of fifty or more people, depending on your length of employment. Some states have family-leave statutes that are more beneficial than FMLA, so check with your state's government offices.

Since you are the sole wage earner in the family, twelve weeks of unpaid leave may be a problem. One option to consider is working a reduced schedule so you would still be earning some money. It never hurts to ask your employer, but they are not required to allow you this option under FMLA unless it is being requested to care for certain medical conditions. Some parents have reported that the typical delays of post-institutionalized kids can be qualified as a medical condition under FMLA, requiring your employer to allow you to work a reduced schedule. Discuss this option with your child's doctor.

FOR EVERY ADOPTION, A DIFFERENT STORY . . .

Our first daughter was three months old when she was escorted to us from Korea. We were prepared for her to grieve and struggle some, but her adjustment into our family was amazingly smooth. From the beginning, she was happy and healthy and it felt like she had always been ours. She immediately bonded to both my husband and me. Her sleeping was not disrupted by jet lag or the changes in her life: She napped frequently and slept well at night. Maybe it was her young age or her personality or both, but she was a happy, content child right from the get-go and our whole family was totally taken by her.

Two years later, we adopted another daughter, this time from China. She was ten months old when we traveled to get her. Our transition home with her was rough at first. She was older, and that made it more difficult since she was more aware of what was going on around her than our first daughter had been. Also, she showed a strong preference for me and only me.

When we got home from our adoption trip, we had been away from our older two children for eighteen days and they wanted and needed our attention, but our new child was very jealous when one of the other children came near me. She didn't want me to put her down—ever. My son took it in stride, but our older daughter did not. It took a couple months for our new daughter to feel comfortable with me setting her down around the house or holding another child. We've been home six months, and although she's still a mommy's girl, she is beginning to warm up to her dad. She caught up completely developmentally in two months. Even though it was a little rough, we can't imagine our family without her. —*CH, North Carolina*

Two months home with a three-year-old from Ukraine:

It's funny that you should ask me about transitioning today, since we have had a rough day! I think patience is the key. I forget at times he has only been home for two months—it's like he has been here longer. Right now I am working on not taking things so personally! Any child new in a situation is going to test the boundaries, no matter what. As the primary caregiver, I find myself the one who is tested the most, especially as he begins to attach to me. It is hard not to take that personally. I know the road has just begun for us, and that ultimately we will find our balance, but until then, my goal is to keep focusing on the little things that go well each day.

When I can be objective and see it from the outside, I am surprised at how well he has transitioned, and how well my daughter has adjusted emotionally to having a brother the same age as her. My son definitely bonded to her first, and their bond is still the strongest. —*AC, Ohio*

———

I had some form of post-adoption depression after we got home. I had always been a career woman, and being stuck at home drove me nuts. I had wanted to be a mother most of my adult life, but now that I was one I didn't feel very fulfilled. I guess I thought I'd be a lot happier than I was. My feelings were compounded by a real sense of isolation. I didn't know many stay-at-home mothers, and I was older than the ones I did meet. One day after we had been home a couple of months, I looked at my son and truly did not feel any love. All I could think was "Who are you? I know nothing about you." I had no one to help me figure out if these feelings were normal or an indication of major problems. Reading books on adoption didn't help. They all scared me to death: Was this a sign of an attachment problem, was that a sign of a learning disability, and on and on. The first six months were hard. But it got better, especially after I started to network and find other first-time moms my age and other adoptive moms. Now my son and I are totally bonded. He is the most amazing kid. I know you think I'm saying that because he's mine, but he really is pretty great. —*RM, Virginia*

———

My daughter was thirteen months old when she came home, and our adjustment to becoming a family was much easier than I thought it would be. She and I bonded to each other very quickly; she seemed to know I was her mom almost from day one, and I felt like her mom just as fast. Her outward signs of adjustment only took a couple of weeks— three days to sleep through the night and a couple of weeks of staying pretty close to me. Her personality began to blossom once she was away from the orphanage. Now that I am about to do it all again, I am afraid that my second experience can't be this good. —*SR, North Carolina*

Two weeks home with a one-year-old from China:

Our rough transition that began in China has continued. For the first week, none of us got much sleep, and it seemed that Ellie (thirteen months) did nothing but cry. She was still totally rejecting my husband and was intensely jealous of our older daughter. I am just now able to put her down for a moment to play on the floor. Her back is beginning to heal from a bad case of scabies, and we have started treating her for *Giardia* (a parasite). But during that first week, I was still not feeling anything close to maternal love for this child.

Earlier this week, two weeks after being home, I was playing with her on the floor when she came up to my face and placed her open mouth next to mine in a baby kiss. She pulled back and grinned at me. Finally, my heart opened. I felt that wall of resentment and anger regarding the entire situation begin to melt. And yesterday she finally let her dad hold her and give her a bottle! This is a big deal, because it gave me a few minutes to cuddle with my older daughter without Ellie trying to compete for my lap. It feels like the pieces of our family are finally fitting together. I know we are not totally there yet, but we are on our way. And today as I rocked her before her nap, I could look her in the eye and say with all of my heart, "I love you."

I wish I could say that this adjustment to being her mom was grace, but it was more a case of scooting along on my rear end and hoping and praying that it would work out. It has. I looked at her today and wondered how I could have ever not liked her—in fact, if they had offered me another child while we were in China, I probably would have given her back. But I am so glad no one gave me that option. I think what we went through will make our relationship that much stronger and sweeter.

One year later:

It has now been a year since Ellie came home. She has become a precocious, ornery, loving two-year-old who is an integral part of our family. Life has settled into a wonderful routine (most of the time) of sibling rivalry, family teasing, and loving embraces. Once Ellie let her guard down and gave her daddy half a chance, there was nothing that could come between them. Tonight when I came home she ran squealing up to me and threw herself against me until I picked her up. She melted into my arms and patted my back, saying, "Mama home, Mama home." I held her tight and, thinking of our difficult beginning together, said, "Ellie's home, Ellie's home" and my heart is complete. —NA, *Indiana*

———

I had wanted to be a mother for so long, but my image of motherhood was completely different from the reality. I quit work just before we went to Russia to pick up our two babies. We came home so excited, and then reality set in. For the first six to nine months I felt like my life was in indefinite suspension—just finding time to shower was a major ordeal. I couldn't do anything that I wanted to do at all. I always felt love and gratitude to have them, but adjusting to being with them all the time and having to readjust my identity was a rude awakening. I desperately needed a network of support, but it is hard to establish, especially with two babies.

If I had it to do over again, I would do things a little differently. I would allow others to share the night duty so I could get more sleep. I was so worried about attachment that I wouldn't allow anyone else to help much with the kids. I would limit visitors much more and would postpone any welcoming events until we had been home a few months. The biggest mistake I made was comparing myself to other moms. I felt so inadequate by comparison, especially in public. I thought people were judging me because I didn't handle them as well as other mothers who had been with their babies since birth. If I had it to do over, I would be nicer to myself. —MS, *Virginia*

———

It has been really wonderful to see how my family has warmed up to my daughter. I wasn't sure this would be their reaction because they were cool to the idea of me adopting a Guatemalan child, but now that she's home they are all thrilled and ask why I waited so long. At first it bugged me that my dad introduces her as my "adopted daughter," until I realized he was trying to protect my reputation by making certain everyone knows I'm not some floozy who got pregnant outside of marriage. I can tell how proud he is of her, and it touches me deeply. —MM, *Maryland*

———

The first weeks home with our second child were very difficult, so much more difficult than our adoption trip had been. Everyone was stressed in some way (jet lag, transition, separation anxiety, and sibling rivalry), and no one was sleeping well. I had two insecure children clinging to me at all times and mountains of luggage everywhere. I carried our new child as much as possible and tried to comfort our first daughter as best I could. She really needed emotional support and showed strong flashes of sibling rivalry toward our new child, who at eleven months was big and strong—a definite threat to her. We sent our laundry out and ate takeout as much as possible. My hygiene really suffered until I started bathing with the girls, partly so I could get clean and partly to separate them in the bath. I didn't suffer from post-adoption depression, but I can really see how it could happen during those first few weeks at home. You have to grit your teeth and just get through it as best you can, scheduling breaks for yourself whenever possible. Sleeping pills helped me shake the jet lag, since we returned home in the winter and had little natural sunlight to help reset our internal clocks. I realize now that exhaustion made the transition much worse. The good news: It all got a little bit easier after the first month and a lot easier after the first six months.

International adoption is not for the faint of heart, but the rewards are many. Today, our daughters are beautiful, loving girls who are doing very well. We have found a new community of adoption-related friends, and learning about our children's culture has enriched our lives. Our adoptions were the high points of our twenty-year marriage, but it is not easy for either you or the child; it is transformative, which is always painful and awkward. You will all come out of this experience as different people than you were before. During the first months home, I thought of our family as a caterpillar getting ready to morph into a butterfly. —*JF, New York*

My husband and father-in-law traveled to get our daughter. When they finally came home, my overwhelming emotion was elation. I had worried that my daughter would not respond well to me since I had not traveled, but she immediately seemed to accept me as her mom. Everything seemed to be falling into place, so I was completely taken by surprise when a huge wave of anxiety washed over me in the middle of the night. For me, it wasn't about being able to love my daughter, since I thought she was completely endearing and sweet; however, I suddenly had huge doubts about my parenting skills. In my mind, my daughter deserved so much—she had lost so much, she had gone through so much. She deserved the best now.

How could I ever live up to it all? I honestly felt like a fraud. During the whole paper chase, I promoted myself as a good future parent. Then, all of a sudden, I'm a mom and I'm just not sure I'm going to be good enough. On my husband's first day back to work, I smiled and waved good-bye, while deep down thinking, *Holy Cow! Why did I ever think I could do this?*

I'm happy to report that we got through those first weeks despite my clumsiness, my mistakes, and my millions of calls to my mom. A year later, my daughter and family are thriving, and when I've shared these feelings with other moms (both through birth and adoption), I learned that everyone has these "Holy Cow!" moments. —*MC, Ohio*

———

I have learned something important about myself in these first weeks home: I need to be more open to help. Most people haven't adopted and won't understand unless I become an open book so they can share in the experience. I think people assume because my son is a toddler that I don't need much help, but because he's older, I do need more help. Dinners and bedtimes are hard. I have basically held down the fort with all three kids for weeks now because my husband has been out of town, and I'm really tired. And yet, when a lady from church showed up at my door at 7:00 P.M. offering to help, I politely declined because, well, I guess because I didn't know how to accept and I didn't want to appear needy. As she backed away, I could tell that she was embarrassed she had even stopped by, so I swallowed my pride and asked her to read them stories while I picked up. It was so nice, and to think I almost turned her down out of silly pride. She came back and helped the next day. The word is getting out since I've let down my guard. Someone is bringing dinner tonight, and friends are planning a shower for us. —*KB, Arizona*

———

Our first daughter had oral defensiveness, which is when children will not allow you to put solid food or medicine in their mouth. They clamp their mouth very tightly shut and will only accept a narrow range of food or drink; in our daughter's case, she would gag on anything except scalding-hot Chinese formula in a bottle with a widened nipple. Oral defensiveness occurs when solid food is not introduced on time; it can result in atrophy or lack of development of important muscles in the mouth and face, causing or exacerbating speech delays and sensory-integration disorders.

Our daughter was young enough when we adopted her that her oral defensiveness eventually resolved with no lasting effects. Fortunately, we brought home a whole suitcase full of Chinese formula and gradually, I managed to switch her over to half-Chinese, half-American formula in an American bottle with the nipple widened. Within a few months, she began eating some solid food, and now, four years later, shows no ill effects.

We've now learned oral defensiveness is extremely common in children adopted from her institution (and from many others in the same region, I have heard). I would strongly advise people to check out the Yahoo group for the social welfare institution their child is in to get information about challenges associated specifically with that institution. —*JF, New York*

I think what surprised me most about the transition both times was how easy it was. We were prepared for the worst, but it didn't happen— maybe because we were prepared. When we brought the twins home, they were almost five months old, and they did great from the beginning. They slept well, ate well, and adjusted wonderfully overall. When we brought our two-year-old home last year, we were expecting a rougher transition since he was older, but he adjusted quickly. I think having other children in the house helped. I know it doesn't always happen this way, but he fit right in and felt like a part of our family from the very beginning. Life now, with three two-year-olds, is hectic but exactly what I want. —*RM, Pennsylvania*

Two weeks home with a seventeen-month-old from Ethiopia:

It's hard to find one word to describe how I feel right now: swamped; yes, that's a fitting word, but drowning might work too . . . and also blessed and happy and tired. So far our adjustment has been relatively easy, with our biggest problems being some fairly minor health and medical insurance issues. But around 5:00 in the afternoon, when all three kids start screaming, it can get pretty hairy.

J is a very easy baby—quiet and content most of the time. He is beginning to trust me more and more each day. He said "mama" for the first time today, and I can feel tears welling up right now as I talk about it. I was so excited, but I don't think other people understand what a big deal these little moments are, and sometimes that makes me feel so alone.

I find that I call him "son" and "my boy" a lot, and I incorporate the word "brother" when I talk with the other kids. "Go help your brother" or "It's your brother's turn." I think if we say it, it will become more real, and so I say it a lot.

One thing that surprised me is that he doesn't know how to play. He's not a little carefree Americanized child who is used to everything we have. He's never seen a playground or had many toys. Daily, I realize anew that I missed out on the first part of his life, and that makes me sad. The only background information in his referral was the date and place he was found abandoned. He's got scratches all over his little bottom and a pretty big scar on his elbow, and I have no idea how he got them. They are little reminders that we don't know anything about him except what we have figured out in the last two weeks.

It has been a bit of an adjustment for my husband and me, but no different from what we went through when we had our first two kids. We are experiencing the standard new-baby stuff: loss of sleep, bickering over who does what and how, and just trying to figure things out.

Two months home:

Well, it turns out we were in the honeymoon phase when we last spoke. The honeymoon is definitely over and life is both harder and easier. J was more like a baby when he first came home. Even though he was seventeen months old, he was at the size and developmental level of a nine-month-old. He was not walking and was content just to be carried around. He was so full of fear; everything scared him: balls, stuffed animals, cars, dogs; you name it, and he was afraid of it. Although he is still small, in the last two months he started walking—no, he skipped walking and went straight to running, jumping, and climbing. He has not quite caught up to his age developmentally, but he is close. His personality has also changed. When he first came home I realize now he was in shock, and what we saw was a quiet, solemn, timid, and shy little guy. Now that he is comfortable with us, he's become a regular little boy, which means he feels safe to throw tantrums—full-fledged, throwing himself on the ground with arms flailing tantrums. But it also means that he feels safe to dance, sing, laugh, and smile. He is now fearless, which is both good and bad. It's like we see the whole of him now rather than just one tiny good little part.

Every once in a while I will look at him and think, *I know nothing about him or where he came from.* I can't let myself go there; all the unanswered questions are too overwhelming. I fantasize about flying to Ethiopia and searching until I find out more, but I know I have to make peace that I will never know his past.

An issue I had not anticipated was that in public people fawn over J while ignoring my older two kids. I haven't figured out how to handle that, but I need to before it becomes a problem for my older children.

The reality of my life right now is that I am stretched very thin. Before he came, I thought adding one more kid couldn't possibly add that much more work, since we already had a two- and four-year-old. I was wrong— very wrong. I don't have time to spend alone with my older children, I don't have time to clean my house, I don't have time for my husband, and I don't have time for myself. It is as if everyone wants a piece of me: my children, my husband, my animals, my friends, and my extended family. And then there are the things I am supposed to be helping with, like church, preschool, and my son's sports team. I feel very pulled. But I know this is only temporary, and believe it or not, we are starting the process to adopt again since we want four children close in age. —*KB, Arizona*

We have only been home two months, but so far the transition has been easy—joyous actually, and we both felt instantly bonded and connected to our son. Although this was our first international adoption, it was our third adoption, so we knew what to expect.

The only difficult part was dealing with some minor but puzzling medical issues. We spent a lot of time in and out of the pediatrician's office the first six weeks, dealing with scabies, chicken pox, an infected cyst, and an ongoing and puzzling rash that finally responded to antibiotics. If we could have a "do-over," I would take our son to an international adoption specialist. Our pediatrician felt confident that with some additional reading he could handle any issues our son had, and we trusted his judgment. But now I think it would have been a lot less stressful, and our son probably would have been "cured" of his rash sooner, if we had gone immediately to a doctor who had experience with children adopted internationally. —*HMJ, California*

One month home with a two- and five-year-old from Haiti:

Our first month home has been very difficult. We adopted two girls

who were nine months and three years old when we accepted the referral, but it took almost eighteen months to get them home. The extended
time in the orphanage was especially hard on our oldest daughter. I now
have five children, ages two to ten, and make it each day, moment by
moment, by the grace of God.

The three that are at home (five, three, and two) are like triplets. The
five-year-old is in many ways like a two-year-old. The two-year-old is
somewhat like a two-year-old, with some of the challenges of a much
younger baby. My three-year-old bio son is as much trouble as the five-
year-old, because he is defending his position as the baby with all of his
might. At times, I sit with all three while they all cry and jockey for position on my lap. I wake up at 5:00 every day to prepare breakfast for
everyone and lunches for my school-bound kids, and after that, it is nonstop. I am exhausted all of the time.

I am juggling so many appointments with doctors and specialists to
meet the girls' needs that I have no time for me. I can no longer go to the
gym because I can't leave the baby in child care yet, and it is impossible
to get up any earlier to exercise. Can you imagine my laundry or the state
of my home under these conditions? That wouldn't be so bad, except I
am one of those people that disorder makes CRAZY! I don't have time to
eat, and when I do, sometimes I am too tired to be hungry. I have lost a
lot of weight and most of it is muscle. What little time I get to myself, I
read the Bible, journal, and pray—without prayer I would not survive.

The five-year-old is a bundle of contradictions: she alternates between
telling me she doesn't want me and then the next moment asking me to
carry her like a baby. She is grieving for her old life—at times, she tells
me I am not her mother and she is going back to her house mom. She
does this and yet she needs me desperately.

They all need me—all of the time.

My husband is working a lot right now and he is my only help. I am
very isolated. One close friend just moved, and another doesn't understand our adoption, and somehow this whole thing has separated us. My
church is great and brought meals after we brought the girls home, but
my day-to-day, moment-to-moment existence is very alone.

When I am out, people stare at me everywhere I go. Most of the time I
ignore it, but sometimes people ask lots of questions I would really
rather not answer. If the family is together somewhere at the same time,
we are the focus of the entire setting. I told my husband recently that

restaurants should give us free meals for being the "entertainment." My girls are very light-skinned, and my five-year-old daughter is the exact same size as my three-year-old bio son, so you can tell people are thinking, *How did they do THAT?*

I keep telling myself it won't always be this hard, and I know it is true. I am trying to practice asking the Holy Spirit for help when I have no answers or strength. Just last night I said, "Jesus, you said you are a very present help in time of trouble, and I am in trouble. Help!" Anytime I have prayed that prayer, he has shown me practical help. He is faithful. Always.

But I am still tired.

My agency has not done anything to help. I called and gave them an update when I got back, but they don't really check to see how I am doing or anything. They sent us a card and a packet of paperwork to complete, along with their requirements for home visits with the social worker (who has not bothered to call to schedule).

I have to say (somewhat to my own astonishment) that throughout this whole adoption, I have never, ever said, "Why did I do this?" I know God called me to this. He gave me very specific and powerful confirmations of that calling. This knowledge has sustained me, but my day-to-day existence is still very difficult.

Three months home:

Well, things are getting better—at least I have time to eat now. I feel less isolated and exhausted. I still really, really miss going to the gym, and some days I think I just can't bear it unless I can do that more regularly. But on the whole, things are definitely better.

The two-year-old is doing well. She still has some challenges developmentally and easily becomes nervous in new situations or around non–family members. But overall she has adjusted very well.

Our five-year-old, on the other hand, is still struggling. She loves me and has attached strongly in some ways, but just when I think things are getting easier, she will hit me with something out of the blue that takes my breath away. She will tell me she would rather be in Haiti with her house mom and that I don't love her and she doesn't love me. She has built a fantasy world around her house mom: Her house mother took care of only her and no one else, her house mom let her do whatever she wanted, her house mom did not hit her hard with a hairbrush, her house mom loved her best. I just say, "Yes, she loves you. We both love you. She took good care of you, but I am your mother and I will also take good care of you." Still she struggles. I understand these behaviors rationally, but somehow it still hurts when I am trying so hard to love her.

When they first came home, our five-year-old had this deeply ingrained sense that she was responsible for her younger sister. I had to claim my position as the mother by literally telling her, "I am the mother. You are the little girl. Taking care of you both is my job, not yours. You can trust me. You can be a little girl." She has really improved in this area, but when we left the kids with my in-laws for an evening last week, she became the "little mama" again. This makes me very sad, because I realize she carries some deep burden of responsibility for her little sister in case they are ever on their own again. I grieve for the loss of her carefree childhood.

One thing I was not prepared for when adopting "older" children from an orphanage was the negative social behaviors that they learned. Both girls are very selfish and have a "dog eat dog" mentality. Our five-year-old hoards her possessions in her hiding spots. She clings to her things rather than to us. It is getting better, but it takes a tremendous amount of work.

I do see a light at the end of the tunnel, but I am also very realistic; this life God has called me to is a life of hard work. It reminds me of a plant growing. Plants grow so slowly that they appear to be making no progress at all when in fact a miracle is happening. Adoption of older kids is miraculous and beautiful, but sometimes progress is extremely slow and hard won.

Six months home:

Wow, it seems like an eternity since I felt those feelings I described. I can't say for certain when things started to improve, but I am certainly in a different place now than I was even three months ago. There are days when it is still hard, but now I can also see that it is miraculous on so many levels. Looking back, I see that the first months home are very similar to the post-partum feelings I had after giving birth, and they fade just the same. The improvement was gradual. The children learned the routine while I learned how to best parent them, and slowly things calmed down for all of us.

My advice to other parents who are struggling at the beginning is to find some way of being good to yourself. For me, I had to make it a priority to go to the gym. It was amazingly hard for me to leave our two new children in the gym child care even for an hour. I wasn't sure if it would be good for them or how they would react, but I needed to do it for myself. I realize now that doing things for me is the opposite of being selfish. It refuels me and allows me to be a better mom.

Another thing that has helped me immensely is connecting online with someone who is at the same stage in adopting. People who have not adopted older kids don't understand what it is like, and even though they mean well, they really aren't able to support you and understand you like someone who is in the same place. I have become close to a woman I "met" on my agency's adoption forum. We found that to really communicate we needed to use private e-mail rather than the forum since we were too guarded in the forum setting. She lives half a country away, but we feel so close to each other because we understand what the other one is going through.

And of course, my faith has given me the most strength. God has truly sustained me on this journey. —*SG, Tennessee*

———

I have been caught a bit off guard by my reaction to the whole race issue. I have had a few moments I haven't shared with many people. When I first saw him, I was shocked at how black he was. Yes, I knew he was African, and yes, I had spent months staring at his picture, but when I actually saw him it hit me just what we were doing. I have had moments when I realized how different we looked from each other and I grieved again for the blond-haired, blue-eyed biological baby I would never have.

The other day I was holding him in front of a mirror and realized, "Wow, I'm so white!" I felt bad, sad, and almost ashamed for some reason of my whiteness. I wish our whole family was black. When I see my very blond son holding my very black son, it strikes me as both beautiful and strange.

My dear friend, who is black, held J to her face and I felt a stab of jealousy because he looked more like her than me, and I'm his mother. I felt so distant and so removed from her struggles and so outside of the whole color minority thing. I want my son to be proud to be black. I have the responsibility to raise a strong black man, and I'm neither a man nor black. Sometimes the responsibility of it all makes me cry, which is what I'm doing right now.

When we go out in public, I am so proud of my family—we are beautiful individually and as a family. And that's what we are, just a normal family. By being an obvious adoptive family we redefine what a family looks like and challenge the way people think.

Two months later:

I don't know if he's gotten whiter or I've gotten blacker, but I don't notice the difference much anymore. All three kids sound and act alike now; he's picked up their mannerisms and they've picked up some of his, so that now they all just seem like mine. Every once in a while something will happen that makes me realize the difference. The other day, the kids were eating blueberries and my older two had blue stains all over their hands and faces, and it struck me that I couldn't see the stains on J. But then later, when they were all three eating yogurt, the whiteness stood out on him but not on the other two. The image in my head of blue- and white-stained kids struck me as funny and beautiful. —*KB, Arizona*

———

I am thirty-four years old and was adopted from Korea when I was three years old. My family is Caucasian, and I have three brothers (one older and two younger) who were born to my parents. I am immensely glad I was adopted—I feel blessed actually, which, I might add, is very different from feeling appreciative. For me the thought that I am supposed to be appreciative has negative connotations, because shouldn't everyone (adopted or not) appreciate their family? My family is my family. I know no other and I love them all dearly.

Being a different race from the rest of my family wasn't really difficult, it was just different. Funny as it sounds, I never really noticed the difference and neither did my brothers. They would notice other people as Asian, but not me. We still laugh about that. I do remember as a child not wanting to stick out like a sore thumb—within my family or with my peers. I wanted to be known for being me and not for being "adopted." I didn't want that label or any label.

As you grow older you tend to embrace your uniqueness, and I definitely did. I learned to appreciate my differences and value them as an asset. Dating was absolutely never a problem, and I am now married with two children. But as you get older, you start to understand that children inherit certain traits from their parents. As an adopted child you miss out on that. If you are not adopted you take that for granted; it's just a part of you—your history and your future. I think most adopted people feel as though there is something missing . . . just a little part of you. If you're lucky to have children, it fills you up and provides that missing puzzle piece. The first time I saw my firstborn was the first time I saw someone who looked like me and was related to me by blood. That was an amazingly wonderful feeling.

After the birth of my first child, I had to work through some anger I had pent up related to being adopted. I wondered how anyone could give up such a beautiful, helpless baby, and I was mad that someone had done that to me. The generic reasons (oh, your mom couldn't afford you . . . she just wanted the best for you) were all offensive to me. The idea that people would assume only positive reasons for abandonment made me feel like they were washing over the possible truths behind my "beginning" (as if the truth really didn't matter). I just had to work through these feelings—which I did.

I hear of some adult adoptees who are angry that they were adopted. This is not my experience, but I try to understand where they are coming from. It's hard not knowing your own history. This can create a feeling of always having to prove your self-worth. Also, not everyone was adopted into a nurturing, loving family that was willing to love unconditionally. I think the angry outcry of these adoptees is a cry for attention and validation. They get a lot of attention because they vent their hurt publicly. The reason that the rest of us contented adoptees don't get as much attention is that we are busy living our lives. We're focused on living, rather than on the past and playing the blame game. I imagine and hope that those that are angry will eventually get there as well.

Obviously, there is no right or wrong way to raise your children. Adopted children just want to be loved and accepted. As they grow older they want answers, so it is important to provide the answers when you can and to give them the support and tools to find those answers you can't provide. Take your cues from your children.

I would encourage anyone to adopt. If you've got the love to share, go for it. My family is continuing in this tradition. One of my brothers just adopted a son from Korea last week, and as I held this beautiful little baby whose experience will mirror my own, it was like coming full circle. My other two brothers and I all hope to someday adopt as well. —*LW, North Carolina*

I was adopted from Vietnam when I was four months old (I am now thirty-one). I arrived weighing just six pounds, with a high fever and tuberculosis. I feel very blessed to be given a second chance at life. I am convinced that if I had not been adopted I would not be alive today. With my parents' love and proper nutrition, I thrived and I feel very grateful.

I was very loved growing up—both by my family and my extended family. I was theirs, and I knew I was totally loved and accepted. The fact that I was a different race didn't matter to them and it didn't matter to me. My mother always told me I was beautiful, and I believed her. When I was around six, I told her I wanted to look like her, but she told me to be proud of my features because they made me beautiful.

I don't remember any negative comments by adults, but I had a hard time with the kids in elementary school. I was the only Asian and one of the few minorities at my private elementary school. I had to put up with that stupid Asian eye song, but what really hurt me was when kids would say that my mom and dad weren't my "real" parents. I absolutely hated that.

I moved to a public middle school with much more diversity—only a few Asians, but lots of different races. This was a good move for me. I became more confident, with a stronger sense of myself.

I was comfortable with my looks when I was younger, but when I was in college I began to truly value them. I embraced being different and *exotic*.

As an adult, I think of myself as American rather than Vietnamese. The only irritating part of being Asian in America is that most Americans assume all Asians are Chinese and that all Asians look alike, when in fact we don't.

I don't fit the cultural stereotypes of an Asian woman, probably because I was raised in an Italian family. I have Asian friends and the cultural differences aren't important when we are together because we are all Americanized. I'm sure they are more Chinese, Japanese, Vietnamese, or whatever when they are with their parents, but when we are together these differences don't matter. I really didn't think much about ethnic differences until I started dating a first-generation Chinese man two years ago. Our families are very different. He says he was raised traditionally Chinese, which is quite different from my wild, loud, and loving family. I think he is a little envious of the way I was raised.

My advice to anyone thinking about adoption is that it is great as long as you can love the child unconditionally as your own. My mother always told me that I was born in her heart, not under her heart, and that is how I always felt—surrounded by all the love in my family's heart. —*MO, Florida*

I was abandoned at a police station when I was five weeks old and was adopted when I was six months old by a white family with two biological boys. My parents later adopted my sister from Korea and my younger brother domestically. I am now twenty-four years old and live about four hours away from my family.

Growing up looking different from my parents and brothers really wasn't a big deal for me or for my sister. My dad has dark hair and eyes, and we always said we looked alike. When I look in the mirror today, I don't see Korean or American—I see me, and I'm both.

My parents always talked openly about adoption—celebrated it, really. We called the date they brought me home my Anniversary Day, and I always brought cookies to school to celebrate with my class. I never remember not feeling confident about myself or concerned about being adopted. It was just not a big deal at all to anyone in my family; it was simply a part of life. I sometimes heard comments from other kids, but my confidence helped me to blow them off.

Now that I am an adult, I realize that not all adopted kids are raised this way. I think some families are a little ashamed of adoption, maybe because they weren't able to have children biologically. They don't talk about it openly and they send the message to their kids that adoption is second best and something to be ashamed of. I think this is why some adoptees have a bad feeling about being adopted.

After high school, I decided to search for my birth mother because I was curious. I know I am loved and have a great family, but I wanted to know who I looked like, whose mannerisms I may have inherited. My parents were very supportive and helped me with my search. I eventually found my birth mother and was able to meet her after I received a scholarship from our adoption agency to study the Korean language in Korea for the summer.

The meeting was everything I had hoped for. I was able to ask her questions, and we continue to write to each other. My mother has also written to my birth mother to tell her how much I am loved and to thank her.

My parents were never threatened by my desire to meet my birth mother. Why would they be? Again, I think it is because we are all so comfortable with adoption. They had no reason to worry that I was going to up and leave them for someone else. We are a very close family, and they knew that nothing would ever change that. Reconnecting with my birth mother was an answer to a prayer. —*MD, Ohio*

RESOURCE GUIDE

International adoptive parents are a diverse group of folks—it's part of what makes us such an interesting community, but it makes it difficult to recommend resources. What speaks to me may not speak to you; what I need may not be what you need. I encourage you to pick and choose your way through this list to find the best resources for your situation. This is an ever-changing field, and my Web site (www.findingyourchild.com) will be continually updated with new resources.

NATIONAL SUPPORT GROUPS AND FORUMS

- Families with Children from China—Fantastic source of information and support. Join both the national organization (www.fwcc.org) and a local chapter, which are listed on the national Web site.
- Families for Russian and Ukrainian Adoptions—Despite the name, this wonderful organization is the place to go for information on adopting from all countries of the former Soviet Union. The national organization and an active forum can be found at www.frua.org. This site also lists local chapters.
- Eastern European Adoption Coalition—(www.eeadopt.com).
- Latin America Parents Association—(www.lapa.com). This group uses an e-mail listserve discussion format.
- Adopting from Korea—(www.adoptkorea.com).
- IChild Indian Adoption Resources—www.ichild.org.
- Adopt Vietnam—www.adoptvietnam.org. A print newsletter is also available.
- Families with Children from Vietnam—www.fcvn.org.
- There is a Yahoo group for almost every country—www.groups.yahoo.com.

- Forums are available for most countries at www. adoption.com.
- Forums for international adoption at www.ivillage.com.

GIVING BACK

I believe those of us who have been blessed by international adoption have an obligation to give back.

Rather than giving perfume, ties, or knickknacks for birthdays or other gift-giving occasions to the adults in your life, consider making a contribution to one of these organizations in their name. The charity will send a note to this person acknowledging the gift. Do your own research before giving to any charity.

- Most good agencies have foundations or funds for supporting the children left behind or for providing grants to aid families in adopting. Support your agency's fund.
- Joint Council on International Children's Services (www.jcics.org) has a Global Awareness Campaign to promote international adoption as a positive option to policy leaders and the global community.
- Half the Sky Foundation (www.halfthesky.org) establishes early-childhood education and infant-nurture programs in Chinese welfare institutions.
- Worldwide Orphans Foundation—www.orphandoctor.com/wwo.
- Families with Children from China Orphanage Assistance Programs—www.fccny.org.
- Foundation for Chinese Orphanages—www.thefco.org.
- The Grace Children's Foundation—www.gracechildren.org.
- PLAN International—www.planusa.org. This is a good site.
- CARE—www.care.org.

GENERAL ADOPTION

- Evan B. Donaldson Adoption Institute—www.adoptioninstitute.org. Great resource for information on all types of adoption, including abstracts of research.
- *Adoptive Families* magazine—www.adoptivefamilies.com.
- *Adoption Today* magazine—www.fosteringfamiliestoday.com. (The magazine is buried on this site. To find, click on Subscribe.)
- Karen's Adoption Links—www.karensadoptionlinks.com.
- www.adoption.com.

- Ethica, an impartial voice for ethical adoption practices worldwide— www.ethicanet.org.

FUN/INSPIRATIONAL/INTERESTING READS

- *Lost Daughters of China* by Karin Evans
- *Adoption Nation: How the Adoption Revolution Is Transforming America* by Adam Pertman
- *Wanting a Daughter, Needing a Son: Abandonment, Adoption, and Orphanage Care in China* by Kay Ann Johnson
- *Mei Mei* by Richard Bowen. A collection of portraits of children growing up in Chinese orphanages. Proceeds go to support the Half the Sky Foundation if bought through their Web site, www.halfthesky.org. These are truly stunning and touching pictures.
- *Love in the Driest Season: A Family Memoir* by Neely Tucker
- *Welcome Home! An International and Nontraditional Adoption Reader* edited by Lisa Schwartz and Florence Kaslow
- *Moving Heaven and Earth: A Personal Journey into International Adoption* by Barbara Birdsey
- *A Love Like No Other: Stories from Adoptive Parents* edited by Pamela Kruger and Jill Smolowe
- *The Exact Same Moon: Fifty Acres and a Family* by Jeanne Marie Laskas
- *Daughter from Afar: A Family's International Adoption Story* by Sarah L. Woodard
- *The Waiting Child: How the Faith and Love of One Orphan Saved the Life of Another* by Cindy Champnella
- *Love You Forever* by Robert Munsch. This is a children's book, but it always struck me as more for the parents than the kids. My kids hate this book because it always makes me cry, but I love it.
- *China's Lost Girls,* a DVD by National Geographic

ADOPTIVE PARENTING/TALKING WITH KIDS ABOUT ADOPTION

- The Child Welfare Information Gateway (www.childwelfare.gov) has wonderful fact sheets for parents for free (type titles under Publication Search), including:
  - ~ Adoption and School Issues
  - ~ Adoption and the Stages of Development

- ~ Explaining Adoption to Your Children, Family, and Friends
- ~ Helping Classmates Understand Adoption
- ~ Parenting the Adopted Adolescent
- ~ Talking to Your Six- to Eight-Year-Old About Adoption
- ~ Talking to Your Three- to Five-Year-Old About Adoption

- *Real Parents, Real Children: Parenting the Adopted Child* by Holly van Gulden and Lisa M. Bartels-Rabb. This is a great resource.
- *Raising Adopted Children, Revised Edition: Practical Reassuring Advice for Every Adoptive Parent* by Lois Ruskai Melina. Another great book.
- *Making Sense of Adoption: A Parent's Guide* by Lois Ruskai Melina
- *Talking with Young Children About Adoption* by Mary Watkins and Susan Fisher
- *Twenty Things Adopted Kids Wish Their Adoptive Parents Knew* by Sherrie Eldridge
- *Secret Thoughts of an Adoptive Mother* by Jana Wolff. Although written by a mother who adopted transracially in a U.S. open adoption, this book addresses hard issues parents who have done transracial adoptions may also face.
- *I Wish for You a Beautiful Life: Letters from the Korean Birth Mothers of Ae Ran Won to Their Children* edited by Sara Dorow
- *Adoption Is a Family Affair! What Relatives and Friends Must Know* by Patricia Irwin Johnston
- Adoption Learning Partners (www.adoptionlearningpartners.org) has online courses titled "Let's Talk Adoption," "Finding the Missing Pieces," and "Becoming Your Child's Best Advocate." There is no fee unless you want a certificate of completion.

INFERTILITY

- *Adopting After Infertility* by Patricia Irwin Johnston. A truly invaluable resource.
- *Conceive* magazine (conception, infertility, and adoption). Great magazine that is available in all major book and magazine stores. Ask them to order if they don't carry it.
- RESOLVE: The National Infertility Association—www.resolve.org.
  - ~ *Family Building* magazine (infertility and adoption). Order through RESOLVE.
  - ~ *Resolving Infertility* by Diane Aronson and RESOLVE

GENERAL CHILD DEVELOPMENT/PARENTING

- *The Attachment Parenting Book: A Commonsense Guide to Understanding and Nurturing Your Baby* by Martha Sears and William Sears
- *The Fussy Baby Book: Parenting Your High-Need Child from Birth to Age Five* by Martha Sears and William Sears
- *What to Expect the First Year* by Heidi Murkoff
- *What to Expect the Toddler Years* by Arlene Eisenberg
- *Parenting with Love and Logic* by Foster W. Cline and Jim Fay. Great practical resource for raising responsible kids.
- *Siblings Without Rivalry: How to Help Your Children Live Together So You Can Too* by Adele Faber and Elaine Mazlish. An oldie but goody.
- *Raising Your Spirited Child: A Guide for Parents Whose Child Is More Intense, Sensitive, Perceptive, Persistent, Energetic* by Mary Sheedy Kurcinka. This was one of the best books I read that seemed to fit my "high maintenance" kid.

BOOKS FOR THE SERIOUSLY SLEEP DEPRIVED

If you have given your child some time to adjust and for the dust to settle and you are still having sleep issues, it's time to start reading. There are various theories on how to best deal with sleep problems, ranging from letting them cry it out to praying they'll outgrow it. The books below cover the various theories, and I suggest you read a few and then pick and choose the suggestions in each that feel right for you and your child. These books are for the fairly run-of-the-mill (although very frustrating) sleep problems. If you think your child may have serious attachment issues, I would work on that before I tackle the sleep problems.

- *The No-Cry Sleep Solution: Gentle Ways to Help Your Baby Sleep Through the Night* by Elizabeth Pantley and William Sears
- *Solve Your Child's Sleep Problems* (New, Revised, and Expanded Edition) by Richard Ferber. Parents either love or hate Ferber's approach, but it is often misrepresented as simply a "let them cry it out" approach, which it is not.
- *Healthy Sleep Habits, Happy Child* by Marc Weissbluth
- *Helping Your Child Sleep Through the Night* by Joanne Cuthbertson and Susanna Schevill. Although this is an older resource, I think the advice has stood the test of time, even if you have to update the "put babies to sleep on their stomach" advice.

POTENTIAL ADOPTION ISSUES

Although some of these books and resources were written for therapists, they are not too dense for most parents. Pick and choose the ones that suit your needs, your child, and your personality.

- Parents Network for the Post-Institutionalized Child—www.pnpic.org.
- www.attachment.org. Provides suggestions on finding a therapist trained in attachment issues.
- *The Out-of-Sync Child: Recognizing and Coping with Sensory Processing Disorder, Revised Edition* by Carol Stock Kranowitz
- *Adopting the Hurt Child: Hope for Families with Special-Needs Kids: A Guide for Parents and Professionals* by Gregory C. Keck and Regina M. Kupecky. Focused on families adopting children who have experienced abuse or neglect prior to adoption.
- *Parenting the Hurt Child: Helping Adoptive Families Heal and Grow* by Gregory Keck and Regina M. Kupecky
- *Fantastic Antone Succeeds!: Experiences in Educating Children with Fetal Alcohol Syndrome* edited by Judith Kleinfeld and Siobhan Wescott. A helpful and hopeful look at FAS.
- *Adoption and Prenatal Alcohol and Drug Exposure: Research, Policy and Practice* by Richard P. Barth, David Brodzinsky, and Madelyn Freundlich. This is a little dense, but the summaries are good.
- *When Love Is Not Enough: A Guide to Parenting Children with RAD—Reactive Attachment Disorder* by Nancy L. Thomas
- *Attaching in Adoption: Practical Tools for Today's Parents* by Deborah D. Gray
- *Building the Bonds of Attachment: Awakening Love in Deeply Troubled Children* by Daniel A. Hughes
- *Facilitating Developmental Attachment: The Road to Emotional Recovery and Behavioral Change in Foster and Adopted Children* by Daniel A. Hughes
- *Attachment, Trauma, and Healing: Understanding and Treating Attachment Disorder in Children and Families* by Terry M. Levy and Michael Orlans
- Attach-China/International; www.attach-china.org. Great ideas for games to play to enhance eye contact and attachment.
- Adoption Learning Partners (www.adoptionlearningpartners.org) has an online course titled "The Journey of Attachment." There is no fee unless you want a certificate of completion.

- *The Post-Adoption Blues: Overcoming the Unforeseen Challenges of Adoption* by Karen J. Foli

ADOPTION BOOKS FOR KIDS

These books are great for explaining adoption or for conversation starters. I've given the suggested ages, but I recommend expanding the age range upward to fit your child's emotional age and downward to allow your child's understanding to grow with the book. Don't limit yourself to books just from your child's birth country or books aimed at international adoption.

In addition to your local or national bookstores, other great resources for adoption books for kids and parents are: Tapestry Books (www.tapestrybooks.com), Adoptive Families (www.adoptivefamilies.com/books), Adoption Shop (www.adoptionshop.com), and AdoptShoppe Books (www.adoptshoppe-books.com).

General

- *Little Miss Spider* by David Kirk (2–8)
- *A Mother for Choco* by Keiko Kasza (2–6). This was our very favorite when mine were little.
- *Horace* by Holly Keller (2–6). Another one of our favorites.
- *My Family Is Forever* by Nancy Carlson (4–8). Child is Asian, but this is a great general book.
- *A Blessing from Above* by Patti Henderson (4–8)
- *Amy Angel Goes Home: A Heavenly Tale of Adoption* by Kathleen Lathrop (3–9). This book approaches adoption as part of God's plan for our children.
- *A Koala for Katie* by Jonathan London (2–6)
- *You're Not My REAL Mother!* by Molly Friedrich (4–8). Discusses what being a real family means.
- *How I Was Adopted* by Joanna Cole (4–8). Explains adoption but is not specific to international adoption.
- *All About Adoption* by Marc Nemiroff and Jane Annuziata (4–8). Explains adoption but is not specific to international adoption.
- *Mr. Rogers—Let's Talk About It: Adoption* by Fred Rogers (4–8). Explains adoption but is not specific to international adoption.
- *The Family Book* by Todd Parr (2–6). This book covers all types of families, including traditional, step, single, gay, and adopted.
- *Giant Jack* by Birte Muller (4–8)

- *The Colors of Us* by Karen Katz (3–8). Great for transracial families of any hue.
- *We're Different, We're the Same* by Bobbi Jane Kates (2–6). Not specifically about adoption, but the Sesame Street characters talk about differences.
- *The Best Single Mom in the World: How I Was Adopted* by Mary Zisk (3–8)
- *The Mulberry Tree* by Anne Braff Brodzinsky (6–12)
- *Anne of Green Gables* by Lucy Maud Montgomery (6–12)
- *W.I.S.E. Up Powerbook* by Marilyn Schoettle (6–teens). Great resource for helping older kids handle personal and general questions about adoption.

China

- *The White Swan Express: A Story About Adoption* by Jean Okimoto and Elaine Aoki (4–8). Tells the Chinese adoption story of both couples and singles.
- *I Don't Have Your Eyes* by Carrie Kitze (2–5)
- *The Red Blanket* by Eliza Thomas (2–6). Single mom adopting little girl from China.
- *Mommy Far, Mommy Near—An Adoption Story* by Carol Peacock (3–8). Great conversation starter to talk about birth mothers.
- *I Love You Like Crazy Cakes* by Rose Lewis (4–8). Story of a single mom adopting from China.
- *When You Were Born in China* by Sara Dorow (6–teens). Photo essay of a Chinese adoption.
- *At Home in This World, A China Adoption Story* by Jean MacLeod (4–10)

Eastern Europe

- *Borya and the Burps: An Eastern European Adoption Story* by Joan McNamara (3–6). Cute tale from the child's perspective written by my friend Joan, a kind, compassionate woman who is both an adoptive mom and an adoption social worker.
- *Adoption Is Okay* by Sylvia Rohde (3–10). Tells the story of a Russian adoption.
- *When I Met You* by Adrienne Ehlert Bashista (3–8)

Latin America

- *We Wanted You* by Liz Rosenberg (4–10). Story of a little boy from Latin America growing up.

- *Carolyn's Story: A Book About an Adopted Girl* by Perry Schwartz (4–10). Story of a girl adopted from Latin America.

Korea

- *When You Were Born in Korea* by Brian Boyd (6–teens). Photo essay.
- *We Adopted You, Benjamin Koo* by Linda Walvoord Girard (4–8)
- *Chinese Eyes* by Marjorie Waybill (4–8). Addresses how to handle hurtful comments.
- *I Wish for You a Beautiful Life: Letters from the Korean Birth Mothers of Ae Ran Won to Their Children* edited by Sara Dorow
- *Land of Morning Calm: Korean Culture Then and Now* by John Stickler (7–teens). This is the best culture book I've found for elementary-age kids.

Vietnam

- *When You Were Born in Vietnam* by Therese Bartlett (6–teens). Photo essay.

Don't limit yourself to adoption-related books. Our kids are kids first, and you should read the same books that enrich and sustain all kids. Hands down the best review of quality children's books I have found is the Chinaberry catalog: www.chinaberry.com (1-800-776-2242). They also review parenting books and all-around good adult reads. Just reading the catalog nourishes my soul.

Books to Help Prepare Children for the Adoption of a Sibling

Many of the books written to explain adoption to adopted kids can also be used to prepare kids already in the family for the arrival of an adopted sibling. Also, your library has many general books on preparing kids for becoming a big brother or sister. These books specifically address adding a sibling through adoption.

- *Seeds of Love: For Brothers and Sisters of International Adoption* by Mary Petertyl (2–8)
- *Things Little Kids Need to Know* by Susan Uhlig (2–6)
- *Is That Your Sister* by Catherine and Sherry Bunin (5–10)

- *My Special Someone* by Brittany and Sherry Kyle (2–7)
- *Just Add One Chinese Sister: An Adoption Story* by Patricia McMahon and Conor Clarke McCarthy (4–8)
- *My Mei Mei* by Ed Young (2–8). Fantastic artwork. Both girls are adopted from China.
- *Jin Woo* by Eve Bunting (4–10)
- *Emma's Yucky Brother* by Jean Little (5–10). Great for families adopting a toddler or older child to help prepare the older siblings. The family is adopting from the foster-care system in the United States, but this book could be adapted for a family adopting an older child internationally.

Toddler/Older Child Adoption

- *Toddler Adoption: The Weaver's Craft* by Mary Hopkins-Best. Great information.
- *Our Own: Adopting and Parenting the Older Child* by Trish Maskew
- *Adopting the Older Child* by Claudia L. Jewett. Written in 1979 but still relevant.
- www.olderchildadoption.com. Great Web site with lots of articles on older-child adoption written by a mom who adopted an older child.
- AOK-China-2 (Adopt Older Kids from China-2) at www.groups.yahoo. com. For parents considering or adopting a child over three from China.

Older Parents

These books are not specific to parenthood through adoptions.

- *Hot Flashes Warm Bottles: First-Time Mothers over Forty* by Nancy London, MSW
- *Midlife Motherhood: A Woman-to-Woman Guide to Pregnancy and Parenting* by Jann Blackstone-Ford.
- *You Make Me Feel Like an Unnatural Woman: Diary of a New (Older) Mother* by Judith Newman. Funny and enjoyable read.
- *But I Don't Feel Too Old to Be a Mommy! The Complete Sourcebook for Starting (and Restarting) Motherhood Beyond 35 and After 40* by Doreen Nagle.
- GAARP: Gracefully Aging Adoptive Refined Parents. Yahoo group at www.groups.yahoo.com. A supportive forum for adoptive or would-be adoptive parents over the age of forty.

Single Parents

- *Adopting on Your Own: The Complete Guide to Adoption for Single Parents* by Lee Varon
- Single Parents Adopting Children Everywhere (SPACE); www.geocities.com/odsspace.
- single-adopt-china. Yahoo group at www.groups.yahoo.com/group.
- *The Single Parent Resource* by Brook Noel and Arthur C. Klein. Not specific to adoption.
- SingleMom.com—www.singlemom.com. Information and forum geared to support women who choose to become single moms either through birth or adoption.
- Single Moms by Choice—www.singlemothers.org. National Organization of Single Mothers, Inc. Forums and quarterly publication. Not specific to adoption.
- Parents Without Partners, Inc.—www.parentswithoutpartners.org. Not specific to adoption.

Medical Issues for International Adoption

- www.cdc.gov (Click on Travelers' Health, click on Yellow Book, click on Table of Contents: Outline format, scroll down to chapter "International Travel with Infants and Young Children," and click on International Adoptions.)
- www.orphandoctor.com
- *The Handbook of International Adoption Medicine: A Guide for Physicians, Parents, and Providers* by Dr. Laurie C. Miller

Early Intervention

- *National Dissemination Center for Children with Disabilities*—www.nichcy.org
- Early Intervention Solutions—www.earlyintervention.com
- Zero to Three—www.zerotothree.org

Becoming a Transracial family

- The Child Welfare Information Gateway has good publications for transracial families—www.childwelfare.gov (click on Publication Search, type in the keywords "transracial adoption").

- The Gathering of the First Generation of Adult Korean Adoptees. Can be found at the Evan B. Donaldson Adoption Institute—www.adoptioninstitute.org. Very insightful and balanced.
- *A Single Square Picture* by Katy Robinson. Memoir by an adult Korean who was adopted at age seven and returned to Korea to search for her birth family.
- *After the Morning Calm: Reflections of Korean Adoptees* edited by Sook Wilkinson and Nancy Fox. Collection of essays by adult Korean adoptees expressing a range of emotions and experiences.
- *Beyond Good Intentions: A Mother Reflects on Raising Internationally Adopted Children* by Cheri Register. Interesting viewpoint of a mom of two children adopted from Korea who are now adults.
- www.alsoknownas.org. Organization of adult adoptees formed to recognize and celebrate people whose lives bridge nations, cultures, and races through adoption.
- PACT—www.pactadopt.org. Although primarily geared to domestic adoption of U.S. children of color, this site contains good information on transracial adoption.
- *Inside Transracial Adoption* by Gail Steinberg and Beth Hall. Written primarily from the perspective of Caucasian parents adopting African American children domestically, but still useful information.
- Adoption Learning Partners (www.adoptionlearningpartners.org) has an online course titled "Conspicuous Families." There is no fee unless you want a certificate of completion.

Adoption Agency Research

- Inter-Country Adoption Registry (ICAR) at www.adoptachild.org
- The Adoption Agency Research Group at www.groups.yahoo.com. Safe place to ask specific questions online and research archives about international adoption agencies.

Funding Adoption

- Affording Adoption—www.affordingadoption.com. Do your own research on grant and loan opportunities.
- The Adoption-Friendly Workplace Guide is available at www.adoptionfriendlyworkplace.org and is an excellent resource for how to get your employer to fully support adoption.
- Child Welfare Information Gateway—www.childwelfare.gov. Good infor-

mation, although not specific to international adoption. Go to Adoption, then to Prospective Adoptive Parents and click on Funding.

- Adoption benefits for federal employees. Office of Personnel Management—www.opm.gov. Search for "adoption benefit" and you will find the Adoption Benefit Guide.
- Adoption benefits for military families—www.nmfa.org
- www.karensadoptionlinks.com. Lists possible grants and fund-raising ideas on the Funding and Benefits page. Do your own research on these possibilities.
- Although not specific to international adoption, the Adoption Exchange Association (www.adoptea.org) has the following books available for the cost of postage:
  ~ *How to Make Adoption an Affordable Option*
  ~ *You Can Adopt! A Guide for Military Families*
- *How to Make Adoption an Affordable Option* is a comprehensive booklet from the National Endowment for Financial Education—www.nefe.org/adoption.
- Adoption Learning Partners (www.adoptionlearningpartners.org) has an online course titled "Understanding the Adoption Tax Credit." There is no fee unless you want a certificate of completion.
- *You Can Afford Adoption* by Kari Hunt and Ruth Ellen Heaton. You can order from www.motherscharm.org.
- Frugal_Adoptions (www.groups.yahoo.com/group)
- Fundraising for Adoption (www.groups.yahoo.com/group/fundraising-foradoption)

Books on Teaching Children to Relax

- *The Goodnight Caterpillar: Muscular Relaxation and Meditation Bedtime Story for Children, Improve Sleep, Manage Stress and Anxiety* by Lori Lite, as well as other relaxation books by the same author.
- *Good Night: Story Visualizations with Sleepytime Music,* a CD by Jim Weiss. This doesn't really teach relaxation as much as induces it. My family has loved this for years, and we own both the cassette and the CD version. I ordered ours from www.chinaberry.com.

Bedtime Story CDs

Any story CD that your child likes is fine, but you want it to be long enough that your child will fall asleep before the CD is finished. Otherwise, I find that once the CD is finished the child will feel the overwhelming need to get out of bed to share this information. Again, I love the suggestions in the Chinaberry catalog—www.chinaberry.com (1-800-776-2242).

Baby Massage

- *Infant Massage: A Handbook for Loving Parents* by Vimala McClure
- *Baby Massage: The Calming Power of Touch* by Alan Heath and Nicki Bainbridge
- *Hands on Baby Massage* by Michelle Kluck-Ebbin

Books on American Sign Language

- *Signing for Kids* by Mickey Flodin
- *Signing Is Fun* by Mickey Flodin
- *Baby Sign Language Basics* by Monta Briant

Lullabies

- *Lullaby Favorites: Music for Little People* sung by Tina Malia. Produced by Music for Little People. This is the best for learning traditional lullabies. Can be found on Amazon.com.
- For the more contemporary minded, try *Hand In Hand (Songs of Parenthood)* with songs sung by Joni Mitchell, Bobby McFerrin, John Lennon, Jackson Browne, and others. Produced by Music for Little People. Can be found on Amazon.com.

Babyproofing Your House

- The American College of Emergency Physicians has a good list of things to do—www.acep.org.

Books on Pets and Kids

- *Living with Kids and Dogs . . . Without Losing Your Mind* by Colleen Pelar
- *Childproofing Your Dog: A Complete Guide to Preparing Your Dog for the Children in Your Life* by Brian Kilcommons and Sarah Wilson

Baby Name Books with an International Flavor

- *The Best Baby Names in the World, from Around the World* by J. M. Congemi
- *A World of Baby Names* by Teresa Norman
- *Baby Names Around the World* by Bruce Lansky

Books on Taking Pictures of Your Kids

- *Capture Your Kids in Pictures: Simple Techniques for Taking Great Family Photos with Any Camera* by Jay Forman
- *Picture-Taking for Moms & Dads* by Ron Nichols
- *The Art of Photographing Children: Creative Techniques for Taking Amazing Color, Black & White, Handcolored and Digital Pictures* by Cheryl MacHat Dorskind

Baby Carriers

- www.thebabywearer.com. For everything you ever wanted to know (plus some) but were afraid to ask.

Lifebooks

- *LifeBooks: Creating a Treasure for the Adopted Child* by Beth O'Malley
- See other books listed at www.tapestrybooks.com.
- Adoption Learning Partners (www.adoptionlearningpartners.org) has an online course titled "Lifebooks: Creating and Telling Your Child's Story." There is no fee unless you want a certificate of completion.

COUNTRY CHARTS*

China • Russia • Guatemala • South Korea • Ukraine • Kazakhstan • Ethiopia • India • Colombia • Philippines • Haiti •
Liberia • Taiwan • Mexico • Poland • Thailand • Vietnam

China

Parental age	30–55 (age of youngest spouse). Over 55 considered on case-by-case basis.
Length of marriage	No country requirement, but some agencies have limits.
Divorce	No country requirement; but tell your agency before you apply if you have more than 3 or 4 divorces between you and your spouse to make certain it will not be a problem.
Children in family	No more than four birth or adopted children in the home.
Single applicant	China has set a quota per year, although the quota does not apply for singles adopting special-needs children. Accepted on case-by-case basis, depending on the agency. For some agencies there is an advantage to submitting application in the fall of the year to take advantage of an unexpected opening in their singles waiting list that must be filled by the end of the year.

(continued on next page)

(continued on next page)

*Country requirements change; look for updates of the country charts at www.finding-yourchild.com.

China *(continued from previous page)*

	Single males adopting a girl must be 40 years older than child. Singles must sign a statement that they are not homosexual.
Sexual orientation	Specifically prohibits placement with homosexuals; single applicants must sign statement attesting to their sexual orientation.
Children available	8–30 months at time of coming home to the United States; average age is 10 months. Older children and correctable special needs available. Sibling groups rare.
Race/Ethnicity	Asian.
Gender	Mostly girls; boys becoming more common.
Adopting more than one unrelated child at same time	Not allowed.
Travel in country	Required. One parent, although many agencies strongly recommend both travel. 10–14 days. Parents travel in groups with bilingual guide.
Referral method	Standard; governmental agency assigns referrals to families.
Wait for referral (after dossier submitted)	10–12 months. Times have been increasing; ask your agency. Quicker for families of Chinese heritage.
Wait after referral	6–8 weeks.
Approximate cost	$14,000–$18,000 plus travel.
Adequacy of medical reports	Standardized medical and developmental forms, with all boxes usually checked as normal unless child is classified as special needs. Information may be dated. In the 1990s, one study found that approximately 18% of children had undiagnosed medical problems upon arrival home (Miller and Hendrie, 2000). Usually only a single set of growth and developmental measurements are given. Lab reports considered fairly accurate. No birth family or prenatal history. Additional information and testing not usually available unless child is special needs.

Youngest age upon arrival home	8 months, but average is 10 months.
Orphanage/foster care	Usually orphanage, but foster care becoming more common in some provinces.
How children enter government care	Abandonment. The assumption is that babies are abandoned due to legal restrictions on family size and a societal preference for boys. Children with special needs are also abandoned.
Prevalence of FAS	Historically, there has been little alcohol use among pregnant women in China, although social conditions are changing. The assumption is that most were wanted pregnancies, which may indicate better prenatal habits. IA doctors generally report seeing very few children with a concern for FAS.
Number of children placed in the United States, 2002–2005	26,862
Program stability	Stable.
Growing/declining	Increase of 56% from 2002 to 2005.
Post-adoption reports	Required at 6 and 12 months after returning home. Must be prepared by home-study agency.
Hague Treaty	Yes.
Additional information	IA doctors note that although developmental delays are common when children first arrive home, most children are otherwise in good health. IA doctors note that head circumferences are generally average. Adoption finalized in China. Income-requirement guidelines: $30,000 per family plus $10,000 for each child in home, including adopted child. Check with agency if investments or self-employment affects these numbers. Parents are required to make a "donation" to the child welfare institution that cared for the child. Most agencies include this cost in their program fee, and this money was included in the cost estimate in this chart. Parents must carry $3,000–$4,000 in U.S. dollars to hand to orphanage director at time they receive the child, although some agencies allow money to be wired.
Useful links	U.S. Department of State, www.travel.state.gov; click on Children ϴ Family, click on Country-Specific Information

(continued on next page)

China *(continued from previous page)*

Joint Council on International Children's Services,
www.jcics.org; click on country information
Families with Children from China, www.fwcc.org
Yahoo group a-parents-china, www.groups.yahoo.com
China Connection—bimonthly print newsletter for adoptive families; order from www.chinaconnectiononline.
com

Russia*

Parental age	Russia has no specific age requirements, but generally agencies have found that Russian judges expect the mother to be no more than 45 years older than the child; there are exceptions depending on the region. In general, Russia doesn't make an issue of the father's age.
Length of marriage	No country requirement, but some agencies and some Russian judges have limits.
Divorce	No specific requirement, but some Russian judges have not looked favorably on more than 2 divorces per person.
Children in family	No restrictions in most regions; income must be sufficient for support.
Single applicant	Single women are allowed to adopt, and in a few regions, single men may adopt. Must show above-average financial resources. Look for evidence of extended family support and opposite-gender role models. Singles must submit a psychiatric evaluation. More documents in dossier required of singles.
Sexual orientation	Does not knowingly place children with homosexuals.
Children available	9 months to teens at time of coming home to the United States; special needs also available; sibling groups.
Race/Ethnicity	Caucasian; some Asian, Roma (Gypsy), and other minorities.
Gender	Girls and boys; families may request gender in most regions and with most agencies; longer wait for girl.
Adopting more than one unrelated child at same time	Allowed.

* The only thing consistent about Russia is its inconsistency; therefore, ask your agency for the most current information.

Travel in country	2 trips usual: first trip to meet child, second trip to finalize adoption. With some regions, only one parent need travel on first trip. Both parents must be present for court date on second trip. Length of each trip varies with region; check with agency. Parents usually do not travel in groups, although may be possible with largest agencies.
Referral method	Standard, semi-blind, or blind; referrals are assigned by regional governmental agency.
Wait for referral (after dossier submitted)	A great deal of variation at this time; therefore, ask your agency. Infant and toddler girls: 3–10 months. Infant and toddler boys: 2 weeks to 8 months. Older children, sibling groups, or special needs: varies, but usually shorter wait.
Wait after referral	A great deal of variation at this time; therefore ask your agency. Wait between trips varies greatly due to court schedule and region.
Approximate cost	$22,000–$28,000 plus travel for two trips.
Youngest age upon arrival home	9–12 months.
Orphanage/foster care	Orphanage. Quality varies considerably.
How children enter government care	Relinquishment, removal, and abandonment. Removal more common than in many other countries due to abuse and neglect, often related to alcohol.
Prevalence of FAS	Alcoholism is a serious social and medical problem in countries of the former Soviet bloc. The IA doctors interviewed reported seeing a higher incidence of FAS than with other placing countries. One report estimates the FAS rate in Russian orphanages is 8 times the worldwide average; approximately 15 per 1,000 births (Aronson, 2003b). One recent large study of all the orphans (234) in the baby homes of the Murmansk region of Russia found that over 50% had a high to intermediate score (13% high, 45% intermediate) on an assessment tool, suggestive of prenatal alcohol exposure, and these children showed significant developmental and growth delays compared to the other orphans in these baby homes (Miller et al., 2006). Russian orphans are at an increased risk for FAS and FASD.

(continued on next page)

Russia *(continued from previous page)*

Adequacy of medical reports	Fairly good. Some diagnoses may be confusing to Western-trained doctors. In the 1990s, one study found that approximately 20% of children had undiagnosed medical problems upon arrival home (Albers, 1997). Lab results fairly accurate. Can usually get growth records over time. Usually little birth family or prenatal history available. Usually not much developmental data. Additional data and testing may be available if not too costly.
Program stability	Unstable.
Number of children placed in the United States, 2002–2005	20,652
Growing/declining	Decreased 6% from 2002 to 2005.
Post-adoption reports	Required at 3, 6, 12, 24, and 36 months after returning home. Must be prepared by a home-study agency. Occasionally, a judge will require additional post-adoption reports to be prepared by the family.
Hague Treaty	Russia signed the treaty but has not taken the steps necessary for the treaty to be in force; therefore, the Hague rules do not apply.
Additional information	Low birth weight common. 40–50% of referrals have a small head circumference. Adoptions finalized in Russia. Adoptions vary considerably between regions within Russia, just as adoption laws vary considerably between states within the United States. Interpretation of adoption laws can vary with different judges within the same region. Different agencies work with different regions, so if you don't like what you hear from one agency, check with a different agency. Russia accredits agencies that are allowed to place children for adoption. For current status of accredited agencies, go to Joint Council on International Children Services at www.jcics.org, click on Country Information, and then click on Russia. Certain medical and psychological illnesses of adoptive parents may preclude adoption. Discuss any issues with agency at the beginning. Many Russian judges now require adoptive parents to submit a psychological evaluation as part of the dossier.

Useful links	U.S. Department of State, www.travel.state.gov; click on Children & Family, click on Country-Specific Information
	Joint Council on International Children's Services, www.jcics.org; click on country information
	Families for Russian and Ukrainian Adoption, http://frua.org. Active forum.
	Eastern European Adoption Coalition, http://eeadopt.com.

Guatemala

Parental age	25–55; some agencies prefer to place infants with parents under 50, but others place infants up to age 55.
Length of marriage	No country requirement, but some agencies have limits.
Divorce	No country requirement, but some agencies have limits.
Children in family	No restriction.
Single applicant	Single women and men allowed, although some regions only place with single females; preferred living alone; look for evidence of extended family support and opposite-gender role models.
Sexual orientation	Does not knowingly place with homosexuals.
Children available	Most referred at 1 month and arrive home between 5–8 months; some sibling groups, older children; and special needs.
Race/Ethnicity	Hispanic; Indian
Gender	Girls and boys; families may request gender; longer wait for baby girl.
Adopting more than one unrelated child at same time	Allowed, but infants will usually not be ready to come home at the same time, since each infant is usually relinquished by the birth parents at birth and progresses on a separate timeline for adoption. May be able to adopt more than one older child at the same time from an orphanage.
Travel in country	Parents can travel to pick up their child or child can be escorted. Most agencies encourage at least one parent to travel to pick up the child.
	Only one parent must travel if child is not escorted.
	Time in country is usually 3–4 days.
	Parents usually do not travel in groups.

(continued on next page)

Guatemala *(continued from previous page)*

Referral method	Standard; referrals are assigned by attorneys or orphanage director in Guatemala.
Wait for referral (after dossier submitted)	0–3 months for infant boy (usually about 1 month). 2–5 months for infant girl. Variable waits for toddlers and older children.
Wait after referral	5–7 months if travel to pick up child. 7–9 months if child is escorted. Families can go to Guatemala to visit child after the referral while they wait, or can temporarily move to Guatemala to foster the child later in the process.
Approximate cost	$25,000–$31,000 plus travel or escort fee (usually around $2,000).
Youngest age upon arrival home	4 months, but average is 6–8 months.
Orphanage/foster care	Foster care, although some agencies place children from orphanages.
How children enter government care	Relinquishment due to poverty for infants; older children in orphanages can be relinquished, abandoned, or removed from the home.
Prevalence of FAS	Historically, drinking among pregnant women has been low, but that may be changing. Most IA doctors report seeing few children from Guatemala with concerns for FAS, but one small study suggests otherwise (Miller et al., 2005).
Adequacy of medical reports	Good medical reports; reliable test results. Opportunity to communicate directly with Guatemalan doctor. Monthly updates during the waiting time on development and health. Children are young at referral, so not much developmental data is available, but usually included in monthly updates. Not much birth family or prenatal information usually included, but may be possible to get more since birth mothers are known. Additional testing available if parents are willing to pay.
Program Stability	Variable.
Number of children placed in the United States, 2002–2005	11,594
Growing/declining	Increased 70% from 2002 to 2005.

Post-adoption reports	None required by Guatemala, but many agencies require.
Hague Treaty	This situation is complicated. Although Guatemala is a party to the Treaty, its adoption procedures do not comply with the Treaty requirements. The U.S. State Department has stated that if Guatemala is not in compliance with the Treaty when the United States becomes a party, it would be difficult for Americans to adopt from Guatemala. For a current update, check the U.S. Department of State Web site at www.travel.state.gov, click on Children & Family, go to the Hague Convention or Country-Specific Information or check the Joint Council on International Children's Services, www.jcics.org, click on Guatemala in-country information.
Additional information	It is possible to visit your child in Guatemala during the waiting time. May be able to live in Guatemala and foster the child until adoption is finalized. Adoption finalized in Guatemala. Readoption is required in the United States unless both parents make an additional trip to Guatemala to see the child prior to the final trip to pick up the child. Good medical care for infants in foster care. Fewer children have developmental delays on arrival than is the case with many other major placing countries. May be required to pay for child's foster care and medical care after referral. Ask agency. It may be possible for you to meet your child's birth parents and for your child to search for them later in life.
Useful links	U.S. Department of State, www.travel.state.gov; click on Children & Family, click on Country-Specific Information Joint Council on International Children's Services, www.jcics.org; click on country information Latin America Parents Association; www.lapa.com. www.guatadopt.com Yahoo group Guatemala_Adoption; www.groups.yahoo.com.

South Korea

Parental age	25–44 for healthy infant. Exceptions may be considered if one parent is under 45, the family has already adopted from Korea, or the family is adopting a child with special needs. Need preapproval from Korea for exceptions. No more than 10 years between husband and wife.
Length of marriage	3 years.
Divorce	1 divorce each.
Children in family	Up to 4 biological or adopted children in home.
Single applicant	South Korea does not place with singles.
Sexual orientation	Does not place with homosexuals.
Children available	Infants; some toddlers with special needs; babies usually between 5 and 8 months when they arrive home in the United States.
Race/Ethnicity	Asian.
Gender	Boys and girls; agencies have different policies on allowing parents to select gender; longer wait for girl.
Adopting more than one unrelated child at same time	Does not allow.
Travel in country	Parents may travel or child may be escorted to nearest U.S. port of entry or to home airport. If parents travel, one trip of 3–4 business days; one or both parents may travel. Parents do not travel in groups, and guide and driver usually not provided; interpreter available when needed. Will be able to meet child once or twice, but will not be given custody until ready to return to United States. Usually able to meet child's foster family.
Referral method	Standard; agency receives the referral and matches it to family on their waiting list.
Wait for referral (after paperwork submitted)	Since referrals are made to the agency to match with families on their waiting list, there is a fair amount of variation between agencies, depending on how many parents are on their list (2–15 months). Shorter wait for child with special needs.
Wait after referral	3–6 months before travel or child escorted.
Approximate cost	$17,000–$22,000 + travel or escort fee + adoption finalization fee.

Youngest age upon arrival home	3 months, although usually closer to 5 months.
Orphanage/foster care	Foster care. Every IA doctor I interviewed rated the care after birth to be the best.
How children enter government care	Relinquishment due to social stigma and lack of support for unwed mothers.
Prevalence of FAS	Birth mothers are interviewed thoroughly, and according to agency and IA doctor interviews, approximately 30–35% say that they drank some alcohol while pregnant. Details are usually included on the type of alcohol, frequency of consumption, and timing during the pregnancy. IA doctors are not generally seeing neurological impacts, which may mean that the type, quantity, and timing of consumption were not of the nature to cause FASD, or it could mean that impairments are subtle and will not be detected until the child reaches school age.
Adequacy of medical reports	Every IA doctor interviewed rated the Korean medical reports as the best. Usually fairly detailed information on birth-family medical and background information. Usually fairly detailed information on prenatal history. Excellent medical care. Updates on child's development usually given to families while they wait, although not monthly. Additional information and medical testing are readily available.
Program Stability	Very stable.
Number of children placed in the United States, 2002–2005	6,915
Growing/declining	Decreased 8% from 2002 to 2005. Korea has a policy of phasing out international adoptions; therefore, they reduce slightly the number of children they will place abroad each year.
Post-adoption reports	Not required by Korea, but will be required by your state for several months in order to finalize the adoption.
Hague Treaty	No.
Additional information	Children are generally healthy. Children are usually of average birth weight and head circumference and arrive with no developmental delays unless classified as special needs.

(continued on next page)

South Korea *(continued from previous page)*

Most IA doctors said that the Korean program is the model for the world in health of the child, postnatal care, and providing accurate medical and developmental information.

Adoptions must be finalized in the United States.

Korea specifies which agencies may place in each state. To find an agency that places children in your state, go to www.travel.state.gov, click on Children & Family, click on Country-Specific Info, go to Korea. If your state is not listed, call one of the agencies listed and ask who has partnered to place in your state.

Due to the quota system limiting the number of children placed for international adoption, there may be a delay in travel to pick up the child—or have him escorted in the fall of the year, when quotas have been filled. Ask your agency.

No dossier is required; therefore, paperwork is less.

There may be weight requirement of no more than 30% overweight for parents adopting from Korea, depending on which Korean placing institution your agency works with. For a copy of the weight charts, go to www.adoptkorea.com and discuss this with your agency.

Korea expects families to have an income higher than the national average, and $35,000 is often cited as a minimum.

It may be possible for your child to search for and meet his birth parents.

Useful links	U.S. Department of State—www.travel.state.gov, click on Children & Family, click on Country-Specific Information www.adoptkorea.com Yahoo group adopt_Korea, www. groups.yahoo.com

Ukraine

Parental age	The only country requirements are that parents be at least 18 years old and there is at least a 15-year age difference between the child and the parent. Agencies may have additional requirements.
Length of marriage	No country requirements, but agencies may have limits.
Divorce	No country requirements, but agencies may have limits.
Children in family	No country requirements.

Single applicant	Allowed, considered on case-by-case basis. Ukraine prefers to place with couples.
Sexual orientation	Does not knowingly place with homosexuals.
Children available	Uncertain at this time—ask agency. Many special-needs children available.
Race/Ethnicity	Caucasian; children may be of Roma (Gypsy) heritage.
Gender	Girls and boys.
Adopting more than one unrelated child at same time	Ukraine prefers that families adopt only one child at a time unless it is a sibling group, but may still be possible.
Travel in country	Both parents are required to meet the child and be at the court hearing, but one parent can then leave. Approximately 3–5 weeks in country. Parents do not travel in groups.
Referral method	Blind.
Wait for invitation to travel (after dossier submitted)	Uncertain at this time—ask agency.
Wait after referral	See above under Travel in country
Approximate cost	$22,000–$32,000 + travel.
Youngest age upon arrival home	Uncertain at this time—ask agency.
Orphanage/foster care	Orphanage. Quality varies considerably.
How children enter government care	Relinquishment, removal, and abandonment. Removal more common than in many other countries due to abuse and neglect often related to alcohol.
Prevalence of FAS	Similar to Russia.
Adequacy of medical reports	Similar to Russia.
Program Stability	Very unstable.
Number of children placed in the United States, 2002–2005	3,352
Growing/declining	Decreased 26% from 2002 to 2005.
Post-adoption reports	Required once a year for the first three years after adoption prepared by a home-study agency. After the first three years, one report prepared by the parents must be submitted every three years until the child turns 18.

(continued on next page)

Ukraine *(continued from previous page)*

Hague Treaty	No.
Additional information	Adoptions finalized in Ukraine.
	Ask agency if the translators used are competent to translate and explain complex medical information.
	Parents should include one or two prepaid, self-addressed international express delivery envelopes with their dossier. The Ukrainian government uses these envelopes for mailing registration and appointment letters to U.S. families. Unless these are included, all notification is by regular mail and can take up to 3 weeks.
	Child must be registered with the Consular Office of the Ukrainian Embassy within one month of returning home.
	Child must maintain dual U.S./Ukrainian citizenship until age 18, when child can decide to drop the Ukrainian citizenship.
Useful links	U.S. Department of State—www.travel.state.gov; click on Children & Family, click on Country-Specific Information
	Joint Council on International Children's Services—www.jcics.org; click on country information
	Families for Russian and Ukrainian Adoption—www.frua.org. Forums are active.
	Eastern European Adoption Coalition—http://www.eeadopt.org.

Kazakhstan

Parental age	No country requirements, but there may be agency requirements. Parent must be 16 years older than the child being adopted.
Length of marriage	No country requirements, but individual judges may prefer parents to have been married one year. Agencies may have limits.
Divorce	2 divorces per person.
Children in family	No limit, but country looks for evidence of ability to support.
Single applicant	Single females.
Sexual orientation	Does not knowingly place with homosexuals.

Children available	Infants from 6 months (although usually closer to 12 months), toddlers, older children, special needs. Sibling groups not common.
Race/Ethnicity	Most children available are mixed Caucasian/Asian or Asian. Some Caucasian children available.
Gender	Girls and boys; can specify gender; longer wait for girl.
Adopting more than one unrelated child at same time	Allowed in some regions.
Travel in country	One long trip of 50–60 days or two shorter trips; first trip 2–3 weeks, second trip 4–14 days; about 1 month in between trips; both parents must go on first trip only. Both parents must visit with the child for a minimum of 14 days at the child's place of residence prior to the adoption (the "bonding period"). Parents do not travel in groups.
Referral method	Blind or semi-blind.
Wait for invitation to travel (after dossier submitted)	Usual wait after submitting dossier until permission to travel is received is 2–8 months, with longer wait for baby girls.
Wait after referral	See above.
Approximate cost	$20,000–$28,000 plus travel for 2 trips or 1 long trip.
Youngest age upon arrival home	6 months, but average is closer to 12 months.
Orphanage/foster care	Orphanages. IA doctors and adoption professionals report that the quality is generally better than that found in Russia and Ukraine.
How children enter government care	Primarily relinquish rights due to poverty or mixed Kazakh/Russian child not accepted by extended family; parental rights terminated due to abuse or neglect.

(continued on next page)

Kazakhstan *(continued from previous page)*

Prevalence of FAS	Some adoption agencies tell parents that there is less risk of FAS because of the Islamic influence. However, the Islamic faith prohibits adoption; therefore, children of Muslim birth mothers are not likely to be placed for international adoption. It may be true that there is less drinking as a whole due to the Muslim influence, but I have seen no evidence to support that. Some agencies that place children from Kazakhstan tell parents that the children of Russian descent (Caucasian) in Kazakhstan have similar risk as in Russia, while the children of Kazakh descent (Asian) have similar risk as in China. The IA doctors who had seen enough children from Kazakhstan to have an opinion report that the prevalence of FAS in Kazakhstan is similar to Russia. Kazakhstan is relatively new to international adoption, so we will likely know more in the future.
Adequacy of medical reports	Reports are very similar to what is received with children from Russia, so refer to the Russia country chart.
Program stability	Unstable.
Number of children placed in the United States, 2002–2005	3,225
Growing/declining	Decreased 8% from 2002 to 2005.
Post-adoption reports	Required at 6, 12, 24, and 36 months after returning home to be prepared by a home-study agency. Thereafter, annual reports prepared by parents must be submitted until the child is 18.
Hague Treaty	No.
Additional information	Families and IA doctors report that the transition is easier for the children because of the required bonding time before adoption. Adoption finalized in Kazakhstan. Kazakhstan prohibits parents with certain diseases or conditions from adopting. The list of diseases is vague, so check with several agencies that have active Kazakhstan programs if you have any chronic conditions. Flight delays and lost luggage to and from Kazakhstan are fairly common, so plan travel accordingly.
Useful links	U.S. Department of State—www.travel.state.gov, click on Children & Family, click on Country-Specific Information

Joint Council on International Children's Services—
www.jcics.org, click on country information
Kazakh Adoptive Families—http://kazakhadoptive-
families.com
Eastern European Adoption Coalition—www.eeadopt.org
Yahoo group Kazakhstan_Adoption—
www.groups.yahoo.com
Families for Russian and Ukrainian Adoption—
www.frua.org. Active forum.

Ethiopia

Parental age	25–60.
Length of marriage	1 year.
Divorce	No country requirements, but some agencies have limits.
Children in family	No restrictions.
Single applicant	Single women are allowed.
Sexual orientation	Country does not knowingly place with homosexuals.
Children available	5 months to teens; some sibling groups.
Race/Ethnicity	Black.
Gender	Girls and boys; parents may request gender.
Adopting more than one unrelated child at same time	Allowed.
Travel in country	1 trip of approximately 1 week, or child may be escorted. Only 1 parent must travel. Parents do not travel in groups.
Referral method	Standard; referral assigned by orphanage director.
Wait for referral (after dossier submitted)	1–10 months.
Wait after referral	3–5 months.
Approximate cost	Approximately $13,000–$22,000 + travel or escort.
Youngest age upon arrival home	5 months, but average is closer to one year.
Orphanage/foster care	Orphanages or large foster home. Parents and IA doctors report that the quality of care is good in the privately run facilities.

(continued on next page)

Ethiopia *(continued from previous page)*

How children enter government care	Abandonment or relinquishment of rights due to poverty, disease, death of parent, or stigma against single motherhood and lack of social support for single mothers.
Prevalence of FAS	Historically, drinking during pregnancy is not common, and IA doctors report they are not seeing much evidence of FAS.
Adequacy of medical reports	Fairly good. Good doctors. Willing to get additional information and testing if possible.
Program stability	Variable.
Number of children placed in the United States, 2002–2005	970
Growing/declining	Increased 320% from 2002 to 2005.
Post-adoption reports	Report prepared by home-study agency at 3 and 6 months post-placement and then a report prepared by the family annually until the child is 18.
Hague Treaty	No.
Additional information	IA doctors report that the babies being adopted are usually healthy. Adoptions finalized in Ethiopia, but unless both parents have seen the child prior to the adoption, the child must be readopted in the United States. Agencies must be authorized by Ethiopia to place children. For a listing of approved agencies, go to www.travel.state.gov, click on Children & Family, then click on Country-Specific Info, then go to Ethiopia. Ages of the children are usually an approximation, since birth dates are seldom available.
Useful links	U.S. Department of State—www.travel.state.gov; click on Children & Family, click on Country-Specific Information Yahoo group EthiopiaAdopt—www.groups.yahoo.com

India

Parental age	Maximum age difference of 83 years between combined age of parents and child's age. No more than 45 years (some agencies enforce 43) between older parent and child. Neither parent may be older than 55. Some agencies require parents to be between 25 and 40.
Length of marriage	India prefers 5 years, but will consider marriages of 2–3 years.
Divorce	No more than 2 total for the couple; some agencies have stricter limits.
Children in family	Childless or only 1 child given first priority; more children allowed if family is seeking to balance the genders of their children; more allowed for special-needs adoptions.
Single applicant	Single females between ages of 30 and 40 are considered on case-by-case basis. Single women over 40 considered for older children or children with special needs.
Sexual orientation	Does not knowingly place with homosexuals.
Children available	14–18 months when arrive home in the United States; toddlers and older children up to age 12. Many children are premature or low birth weight, likely due to early induction of labor.
Race/Ethnicity	East Indian.
Gender	Girls and boys; parents may request gender.
Adopting more than one unrelated child at same time	Allowed, although agencies may prohibit the practice.
Travel in country	There is a fair degree of discrepancy between agencies for travel requirements, depending on which child-welfare institution they are working with in India. Some require travel for one parent for anywhere from 3–5 days to 5–6 weeks. Some require both parents to travel. It is culturally preferred for single women to have a travel companion. Some allow for escort, but India prefers for at least one parent to travel. Parents do not travel in groups.
Referral method	Standard

(continued on next page)

India *(continued from previous page)*

Wait for referral (after dossier submitted)	9–12 months for girl; wait for boy variable depending on availability; shorter wait for an older child or a child with special needs; shorter wait for families if one parent is of Indian heritage.
Wait after referral	4–8 months to receive Indian legal document and permission to travel to pick up child.
Approximate cost	$13,000–$16,000 + travel + cost of finalizing the adoption.
Youngest age upon arrival home	14 months, but 14–18 months is average.
Orphanage/foster care	Orphanage; quality is reported by parents and IA doctors as good.
How children enter government care	Most infants come into care due to relinquishment or abandonment by single mothers due to poverty and societal pressures against unwed motherhood. Toddlers and older children generally come into care due to termination of parental rights due to neglect or death or illness of parents.
Prevalence of FAS	Historically, drinking during pregnancy is not common and IA doctors report they are not seeing much evidence of FAS.
Adequacy of medical reports	Good, especially with special-needs children.
Program stability	Stable, although significant delays can happen when judges change or the orphanage is being relicensed; therefore, ask your agency about these possibilities for the region and orphanage they work with.
Number of children placed in the United States, 2002–2005	1,667
Growing/declining	Decreased 31% from 2002 to 2005.
Post-placement reports	Required quarterly for the first two years post-placement, then every six months for years 3, 4, and 5 after returning home (total of 14 reports). Must be prepared by home-study agency until the adoption is finalized in your state of residence, and the remaining reports are prepared by parents.
Hague Treaty	Yes
Additional information	Low birth weight is very common. Requirements vary greatly, with each region and judge following their own court rules.

Adoption must be finalized in the United States.
India gives preference to families where at least one
parent is of Indian descent, and some agencies work
only with these couples.

Useful links	U.S. Department of State—www.travel.state.gov, click on Children & Family, click on Country-Specific Information Joint Council on International Children's Services—www.jcics.org, click on country information IChild Indian Adoption Resources—www.ichild.org

Colombia

Parental age	25–45+; younger children are assigned to younger parents. If older than 38–40, generally will be referred a toddler or older child.
Length of marriage	Colombia prefers 3 years; some programs require 4 or 5 years.
Divorce	1 prior divorce each.
Children in family	Priority is given to childless couples or those with only 1 child.
Single applicant	Not allowed, although single women are considered on a case-by-case basis for special-needs children.
Sexual orientation	Does not knowingly place with homosexuals.
Children available	5 months (from private orphanages) to 12 months (from government orphanages); older children, sibling groups, special needs.
Race/Ethnicity	Hispanic; Indian; black; mixed race.
Gender	Boys and girls; some agencies do not allow childless couples to specify the gender; shorter wait for boys.
Adopting more than one unrelated child at same time	Possible if you are flexible about the age of the second child. Strong preference to place sibling groups rather than unrelated children.
Travel in country	Both parents; usually 2 weeks unless adopting from Bogotá, where parents stay with child for 6 weeks. Both parents must be present for the first week to 10 days. After this, one parent may return home. Parents do not travel in groups.

(continued on next page)

Colombia *(continued from previous page)*

Referral method	Standard; referrals are assigned to families by the government (if child is in a government-run orphanage) or the orphanage director (if child resides in a private orphanage).
Wait for referral (after dossier submitted)	0–2 years old: 18–24 months, with the longer waits for girls. 2–6 years old: 18 months. 7+ years: 6–9 months.
Wait after referral	2–4 weeks before you can travel.
Approximate cost	$13,000–$22,000 + travel.
Adequacy of medical reports	Not enough placements to get a consensus from IA doctors interviewed, but agencies report that private orphanages give detailed medical reports.
Youngest age upon arrival home	3 months, but average is 3–5 months.
Orphanage/foster care	Orphanage, group homes, and foster care.
How children enter government care	Relinquishment or abandonment by birth mothers due to poverty or stigma against unwed motherhood. Removal by government for abuse, neglect, or incarceration.
Prevalence of FAS	Not enough placements to get a consensus from IA doctors interviewed.
Program stability	Stable.
Number of children placed in the United States, 2002–2005	1,184
Growing/declining	Decreased 13% from 2002 to 2005.
Post-adoption reports	Most orphanages require 3 post-placement reports written by a social worker at 3, 6, and 10 months after arrival home.
Hague Treaty	Yes.
Additional information	Adoption finalized in Colombia, but Colombian government requires proof of readoption in the United States. The U.S. State Department periodically issues travel warnings for travel to Colombia. Go to www.travel.state.gov to check the current status.
Useful links	U.S. Department of State—www.travel.state.gov, click on Children & Family, click on Country-Specific Information Latin America Parents Association—www.lapa.com

Philippines

Parental age	27–47 for child up to age 2. More flexible with upper age when applicant is of Filipino descent. 16 years' difference required between parent and child.
Length of marriage	Minimum of 3 years.
Divorce	1 divorce each.
Children in family	Childless couples preferred; up to 3 children in family acceptable; larger families considered for special-needs children.
Single applicant	Allowed only for older children or children with special needs.
Sexual orientation	Does not knowingly place with homosexuals.
Children available	10 months to 5 years at time child arrives home in the United States; older children; special needs
Race/Ethnicity	Asian.
Gender	Mostly boys, although girls are sometimes available; some agencies prohibit families from requesting a gender.
Adopting more than one unrelated child at same time	Not allowed. Officially, the Philippines requires a 2-year wait before they will approve second application; however, exceptions are common.
Travel in country	1 parent required; approximately 1 week; do not travel in groups.
Referral method	Standard referral; assignments made by Philippine governmental agency.
Wait for referral (after dossier submitted)	Approximately 2 years. Childless couples may get match sooner.
Wait after referral	2–3 months.
Approximate cost	$13,000–$15,000 + travel.
Adequacy of medical reports	Not enough placements to get a consensus from IA doctors interviewed.
Youngest age upon arrival home	10 months, but usually closer to 12 months.
Orphanage/foster care	Foster care, group home, or orphanage.
How children enter government care	Relinquishment or abandonment due to poverty and social stigma against unwed motherhood.

(continued on next page)

Philippines *(continued from previous page)*

Prevalence of FAS	Not enough placements to get a consensus from IA doctors interviewed.
Program stability	Stable.
Number of children placed in the United States, 2002–2005	902
Growing/declining	Increased 23% from 2002 to 2005.
Post-adoption reports	Reports prepared by home-study agency at 2, 4, and 6 months.
Hague Treaty	Yes.
Additional information	Parents with Catholic or Christian background strongly preferred; atheists likely will not get a placement. Most people in the Philippines speak English, which makes travel easier. Preference given to families of Filipino descent. The U.S. State Department periodically issues travel warnings for travel to the Philippines. Go to www.travel.state.gov to check the current status.
Useful links	U.S. Department of State—www.travel.state.gov, click Children & Family, click on Country-Specific Information adopt-philippines-usa at www.groups.yahoo.com

Haiti

Parental age	30–45, although some agencies suggest 35 as the minimum. One parent under age 30 accepted on case-by-case basis. Exceptions to the 30-year minimum have been made for infertile couples.
Length of marriage	Haiti has a law that requires that the couple have been married for 10 years and have no children together, but does not enforce this law. Haiti prefers parents to be married 5 years, but will make exception for infertile couples. Some agencies report that Haiti has considered the time a couple lived together before marriage when calculating the length of a marriage.
Divorce	No country requirement, but some agencies impose a requirement.

Children in family	No more than 4.
Single applicant	Single women allowed.
Sexual orientation	Does not knowingly place with homosexuals.
Children available	7–12 months; toddlers, older children, sibling groups, and special needs also available.
Race/Ethnicity	Black.
Gender	Boys and girls; parents may request gender.
Adopting more than one unrelated child at same time	Yes.
Travel in country	One parent must travel. 3–7 days. Parents do not travel in groups.
Referral method	Standard; orphanage director or agency matches referrals to families.
Wait for referral (after dossier submitted)	Since referrals are made to the agency to match with families on their waiting list, there is great variation, from no wait to up to 2 years, depending on the flexibility of the family and how many parents are on the list.
Wait after referral	Varies greatly; 6–18 months, with an average of 9–12 months.
Approximate cost	$13,000–$17,000 + travel.
Youngest age upon arrival home	7 months, but most are older upon arrival.
Orphanage/foster care	Orphanages run by charitable organizations, some children in large group homes.
How children enter government care	Abandonment or relinquishment of rights due to poverty or death.
Prevalence of FAS	Not enough placements to get a consensus from IA doctors interviewed.
Adequacy of medical reports	With privately run orphanages, the reports are fairly good, since children get regular medical care.
Program stability	Variable.
Number of children placed in the United States, 2002–2005	1,024
Growing/declining	Increased 24% from 2002 to 2005.

(continued on next page)

Haiti *(continued from previous page)*

Post-adoption reports	No country requirement, but individual orphanages and agencies have their own requirements.
Hague Treaty	No.
Additional information	Adoption finalized in Haiti. The U.S. State Department periodically issues travel warnings for Haiti due to political unrest. Go to www.travel.state.gov to check the current status. Delays are common in Haitian adoptions and are often outside the control of even the best agency. Some Haitian orphanages prefer to place with Christian or Jewish families; others have no restrictions. Adopting parents are required to submit a psychological evaluation, and this cost should be factored into total cost. May be possible to meet birth parents.
Useful links	U.S. Department of State—www.travel.state.gov, click on Children & Family, click on Country-Specific Information Joint Council on International Children's Services—www.jcics.org, click on country information Yahoo group Haitianadopt—www.groups.yahoo.com

Liberia

Parental age	21–60.
Length of marriage	No country requirements, but agency may have limits.
Divorce	No country requirements, but agency may have limits.
Children in family	No restrictions.
Single applicant	Single women allowed.
Sexual orientation	Does not knowingly place with homosexuals.
Children available	Infants to teens (fewer infants are available than for Ethiopia due to greater acceptance of single motherhood).
Race/Ethnicity	Black.
Gender	Boys and girls; parents may request gender.
Adopting more than one unrelated child at same time	Allowed.

Travel in country	One trip of 7–10 days; only one parent must travel; parents do not travel in groups; child can be escorted, and some agencies prefer that child be escorted.
Referral method	Standard; orphanage director or agency matches referrals to families.
Wait for referral (after dossier submitted)	2–6 months.
Wait after referral	2–5 months.
Approximate cost	$9,500–$14,000 + travel or escort fee.
Adequacy of medical reports	Not enough placements to get a consensus from IA doctors interviewed, but agencies report that little information on health or background is included in the report.
Youngest age upon arrival home	Not many babies; average age is 5 years.
Orphanage/foster care	Privately run orphanage or large foster homes.
How children enter government care	Parents killed in war; relinquishment of rights due to poverty.
Prevalence of FAS	Not enough placements to get a consensus from IA doctors interviewed, but historically drinking by pregnant women is uncommon.
Program stability	Variable.
Number of children placed in the United States, 2004–2005	Liberia did not make the list of top 20 placing countries until 2004; 268 children were placed in 2004 and 2005.
Growing/declining	Increased 112% from 2004 to 2005.
Post-adoption reports	No requirement by the government, but some agencies and orphanages require annually until child is 18.
Hague Treaty	No.
Additional information	Adoptions finalized in Liberia. Children speak accented English. The U.S. State Department periodically issues travel warnings for Liberia. Go to www.travel.state.gov to check the current status. Ages of the children are usually an approximation, since birth dates are seldom available.
Useful links	U.S. Department of State—www.travel.state.gov, click on Children & Family, click on Country-Specific Information http://groups.yahoo.com/group/adoptafrica

Taiwan

Parental age	30 to 45–50 preferred, but some flexibility, especially if one parent is within the age range.
Length of marriage	Vary by orphanage; some prefer 5 years.
Divorce	No restriction.
Children in family	Prefer smaller families, but flexible since birth mothers usually choose the family that they want to adopt their child and some birth mothers prefer a family with children.
Single applicant	Single women allowed, but usually birth mothers prefer to select married couples, so wait can be long for singles unless open to a child with special needs or over the age of 5.
Sexual orientation	Does not knowingly place with homosexuals.
Children available	Children arrive home between 6 months and 10 months; older children also available.
Race/Ethnicity	Asian.
Gender	Boys and girls; gender selection allowed.
Adopting more than one unrelated child at same time	No set policy, but in practice does not happen unless there are special circumstances where it is better for 2 children to be placed together.
Referral method	Usually information on several families is shown to the birth mother and she selects the parents she wants to adopt her child; information on the child is then sent to the family. Some orphanages prefer to send medical information for parents to decide before a picture is sent; if birth mother does not want to select or the child has been abandoned or removed from the home, the orphanage matches the child to the parents.
Travel in country	1 trip; 4–7 days; only one parent is required to travel; escort is an option; parents do not travel in groups.
Wait for referral (after dossier submitted)	8–12 months for healthy infant; since birth mothers usually choose the family, this time frame can vary; parents submit only part of the dossier before the referral and complete the remaining dossier documents after a referral.
Wait after referral	4–5 months.
Approximate cost	$15,000–$17,000 + travel.

Adequacy of medical reports	If child is relinquished, birth mother is asked an extensive list of questions on medical history and prenatal care and habits. Children receive excellent medical care after birth.
Youngest age upon arrival home	6 months, average closer to 10 months.
Orphanage/foster care	Privately run orphanages.
How children enter government care	Relinquished by birth mothers due to stigma against single mothers.
Prevalence of FAS	Not enough placements to get a consensus from IA doctors. If child is relinquished, birth mother is asked about alcohol consumption during pregnancy; most report none or minimal use.
Number of children placed in the United States, 2002–2005	Before 2005, Taiwan was not in the top 20 placing countries to the United States. 141 children were adopted in 2005.
Program stability	Not enough information.
Growing/declining	Growing.
Post-adoption reports	Two (6 and 12 months) prepared by home-study agency. Birth mothers or orphanages may require additional updates prepared by the parents.
Hague Treaty	No.
Additional information	Not a government-run program. Each orphanage processes adoptions independently. Requirements vary by orphanage. Adoptions are finalized before parents travel to the country to pick up the child. It may be possible to meet birth mother and for child to search for and meet birth parents.
Useful links	U.S. Department of State—www.travel.state.gov, click on Children & Family, click on Country-Specific Information Adopting from Taiwan at www.groups.yahoo.com

Mexico

Parental age	As in the United States, adoption in Mexico is a matter of state law. Each of the 31 Mexican states has different adoption requirements and each judge within the state can have different requirements; therefore, it is impossible to generalize. Generally the national government's only requirement on parental age is that the parents be at least 25 and at least 17 years older than child. Ask agency what the state and judicial requirements are in the states where they work.
Length of marriage	Some Mexican states have no specific requirement, while others require families to be married up to 5 years.
Divorce	No country requirement, but each state, judge, and agency can impose a requirement.
Children in family	Some Mexican states have no specific requirement, while others limit placement to families with no more than 2 children in the home.
Single applicant	Some Mexican states do not allow, while others do.
Sexual orientation	Does not knowingly place with homosexuals.
Children available	6–12 months upon arrival home in the United States for programs where birth mothers relinquish newborns, toddlers, older children, sibling groups, and special-needs children available from orphanages.
Race/Ethnicity	Latino/Mexican. Hispanic; Indian
Gender	Boys and girls; parents can request gender, although this may extend the wait.
Adopting more than one unrelated child at same time	Allowed.
Travel in country	Both parents travel. 2–3 trips for a total of 3–8 weeks in country, depending on the program and the Mexican state. Some Mexican states require that parents bring 2 witnesses with them on one of the trips. Parents do not travel in groups.
Referral method	Standard. Attorney or orphanage director matches referral to families.
Wait for referral (after dossier submitted)	3–12 months.
Wait after referral	For birth-mother placement programs: First trip within 1–2 weeks for some states and 22 days after birth for

	other states; child arrives home usually 3–5 months after referral. For orphanage programs, waiting times vary by orphanage.
Approximate cost	Birth-mother placement programs: $24,000–31,000 + travel (including travel costs for 2 witnesses for some programs) + foster care. Orphanage based programs: $12,000–$17,000 + travel.
Adequacy of medical reports	Not enough placements to get a consensus from IA doctors interviewed.
Youngest age upon arrival home	6 months, but usually older.
Orphanage/foster care	Foster care (for birth-mother placement programs) and orphanage.
How children enter government care	Relinquishment by birth mothers due to poverty or single motherhood; abandonment; removal by government for abuse, neglect, or incarceration.
Prevalence of FAS	Not enough placements to get a consensus from IA doctors interviewed.
Program stability	Variable; significant differences between Mexican states; depending on the program and state, can be an arduous process.
Number of children placed in the United States, 2002–2005	309
Growing/declining	Increased 61% from 2002 to 2005.
Post-adoption reports	Varies by state, but usually one at 6 months and 12 months prepared by home-study agency. Some judges require parents to submit an annual report until the child turns 18.
Hague Treaty	Yes.
Additional information	Adoption finalized in Mexico. Some Mexican states and judges require a psychological evaluation. Document requirements are greater than those for many other countries.
Useful links	U.S. Department of State—www.travel.state.gov, click on Children & Family, click on Country-Specific Information Latin America Parents Association at www.lapa.com

Poland

Parental age	Poland wants no more than 40 years between the mother and child and 45 years between father and child; more flexible for school-age children and sibling groups of 3 or more.
Length of marriage	Poland prefers 2 years; however, it does consider stability of the marriage if less than 2 years.
Divorce	No specific country restriction, but agency either in the United States or Poland may have limits.
Children in family	No restrictions.
Single applicant	Females allowed.
Sexual orientation	Does not knowingly place with homosexuals.
Children available	12 months to teens on arrival; most are older than 3 years; most infants and young children that are available for adoption are adopted by families in Poland; many sibling groups of 3 and 4 children.
Race/Ethnicity	Caucasian.
Gender	Girls and boys; longer wait for girls; can request gender.
Adopting more than one unrelated child at same time	Allowed by country, but complicated. Agency may have restrictions.
Travel in country	Generally 2 trips (first is 2–3 weeks, second is 3–5 days) Both parents go on first trip to see child; only one parent needs to travel on the second trip Parents do not travel in groups.
Referral method	Standard; referrals are assigned by Polish adoption agency or attorney.
Wait for referral (after dossier submitted)	For 1–2 children under 7 years: 18–24 months. For 1 or 2 children over 7 years: 8–10 months. Sibling groups of 3 or 4 under 7 years of age: 8–10 months. Sibling groups of 3 or 4 over 7 years of age: usually shorter than 8 months.
Wait after referral	3 weeks to 3 months, with the longer wait usually in the summer, when judges take vacation.
Approximate cost	$20,000–$25,000 + travel.
Adequacy of medical reports	Not enough placements to get a consensus from IA doctors interviewed. Additional medical information is usually available.
Youngest age upon arrival home	It is uncommon to get a baby under 12 months; average age is 5 years.

Orphanage/foster care	Orphanage; parents report that quality of care is good.
How children enter government care	Parental rights terminated due to abuse or neglect. Relinquishment or abandonment due to poverty.
Prevalence of FAS	Similar to Russia, although since children are usually older, the facial features of FAS are more easily distinguished and neurological impairment more obvious before the adoption.
Program stability	Stable.
Number of children placed in the United States, 2002–2005	373
Growing/declining	Decreased 28% from 2002 to 2005.
Post-adoption reports	1 report prepared by the home-study agency 3 months after adoption. Each of the Polish agencies that match the children have additional post-adoption reporting requirements and each is different.
Hague Treaty	Yes.
Additional information	The adoption is finalized in Poland. Polish heritage is not required, but in most regions and with most agencies it is looked on favorably. There is a great deal of variance between regions within Poland and with different judges in each region.
Useful links	U.S. Department of State—www.travel.state.gov, click on Children & Family, click on Country-Specific Information www.groups.yahoo.com/group/adoptionpoland

Thailand

Parental age	Minimum 25 years and at least 15 years older than the child. Parents over age 50 must be preapproved, and over 55 are discouraged. Parents in their 40s more likely to be referred a toddler.
Length of marriage	No country requirement, but agency may have a requirement.
Divorce	For married couples, a total of 2 divorces (1 per spouse, or 2 for 1 spouse).

(continued on next page)

Thailand *(continued from previous page)*

Children in family	Up to 2; flexible for older or special-needs children and for families who have previously adopted Thai children. Youngest child in home must be at least 2 years old at time of application.
Single applicant	Single applicants accepted on a case-by-case basis. May be required to accept special-needs child. Prior approval by Thailand government required. Not recommended for singles.
Sexual orientation	Does not knowingly place with homosexuals.
Children available	1–6 years at time of placement. The majority are 14 months to 2 years at time of placement. Children over 2 years may have some special needs.
Race/Ethnicity	Asian.
Gender	Childless couples and families who already have a girl must be open to a child of either gender. Shorter wait for boys.
Adopting more than one unrelated child at same time	May be possible, but is not encouraged.
Travel in country	Both parents required to travel. 8–14 days average. Parents do not travel in groups.
Referral method	Standard; referrals sent to adoption agency, which then matches to family on their waiting list.
Wait for referral (after dossier is submitted)	2–6 months after dossier submission.
Wait after referral	6–8 months.
Approximate cost	$15,000–$20,000 plus travel.
Adequacy of medical reports	Medical and developmental information available, but not extensive. Because the children are often relinquished by their birth parents, it is possible to receive birth family social history.
Youngest age upon arrival home	9–12 months, but average is closer to 18 months.
Orphanage/foster care	Generally orphanage, although a few agencies have set up a foster-care program for the children they place.
How children enter government care	Voluntarily relinquished due to poverty.

Prevalence of FAS	Not enough placements to get a consensus from IA doctors interviewed.
Program stability	Variable. Complex.
Number of children placed in the United States, 2002–2005	281
Growing/declining	Increased 9% from 2002 to 2005.
Post-adoption reports	Reports prepared by home-study agency at 2, 4, and 6 months.
Hague Treaty	Yes.
Additional information	About a year after returning to the United States, the adoption must be finalized under Thai law at the Thai Consulate in Los Angeles, Chicago, or New York, or the Thai Embassy in Washington, D.C. Adds to the cost. Some families do not complete this step. Does not affect legality of adoption in the United States, but can't adopt again from Thailand unless completed. The Thai government has a moratorium on adoptions to certain countries, including the United States and Canada. This has not had the huge impact on U.S. adoptions from Thailand that was expected, since it does not apply to children placed directly from the 3 approved charities that regularly place children with U.S. agencies. These relief organizations include Holt, Thai Red Cross, and Friends for All Children Foundation. Make sure your agency is currently placing children from one of these organizations. Parents report that the quality of care in the orphanages that place in the United States is fairly good.
Useful Links	U.S. Department of State—www.travel.state.gov, click on Children & Family, click on Country-Specific Information thailandadopt group at www.groups.yahoo.com

Vietnam*

Parental age	Couples and singles must be at least 20 years older than the child they wish to adopt. There is no upper limit for adopting from Vietnam, but some agencies have limits.
Length of marriage	No country requirements, but some agencies have limits.
Divorce	No country requirements, but some agencies have limits.
Children in family	No specific limit, but may need special permission if you have more than 4 children at home.
Single applicant	Single women and men are allowed.
Sexual orientation	Does not knowingly place with homosexuals.
Children available	3 months to 15 years; special needs; rarely sibling groups.
Race/Ethnicity	Asian.
Gender	Boys and girls; parents can request gender, although this may extend the wait; some agencies require childless applicants to accept either gender.
Adopting more than one unrelated child at same time	May be possible, but is not encouraged.
Travel in country	1 trip of 2–3 weeks. Both parents need to travel, although 1 parent can leave after 1 week. Parents usually do not travel in groups, but with larger placing agencies may travel in small groups.
Referral method	Standard; referrals sent to adoption agency, which then matches to family on their waiting list.
Wait for referral (after dossier submitted)	1–3 months (time frames are just estimates, since the program is new).
Wait after referral	1–3 months (time frames are just estimates, since the program is new).
Approximate cost	$20,000–$24,000 + travel.
Adequacy of medical reports	Unknown since it is a new program.
Youngest age upon arrival home	4–5 months, although it is too early in the program to know for certain.
Orphanage/foster care	Government orphanages; some children are in foster care.

*Vietnam is implementing a new adoption law; therefore, these procedures may change as more adoptions are processed.

How children enter government care	Relinquishment or abandonment due to poverty or stigma against unwed motherhood.
Prevalence of FAS	Not enough placements to get a consensus from the IA doctors interviewed, but historically, drinking among pregnant women is uncommon.
Number of children placed in the United States, 2002–2005	No historic data available since the program shut down in 2003. In the last few years before the shutdown, Vietnam placed over 700 children per year in the United States.
Program stability	Unknown, since it has recently reopened.
Growing/declining	Unknown.
Post-adoption reports	Required once every 6 months for the first 3 years and then 1 report annually from the fourth year until the child is 18 years of age. It is not clear under Vietnam's new law who must prepare these, but the assumption is that the home-study agency will prepare at least the first 2–4 reports and the parents will prepare the rest.
Hague Treaty	No.
Additional information	Vietnam closed January 2003 and reopened for international adoption in 2005, with placements beginning in 2006. Adoptions finalized in Vietnam, but readoption required if 1 parent traveled.
Useful links	U.S. Department of State—www.travel.state.gov, click on Children & Family, click on Country-Specific Information Joint Council on International Children's Services—www.jcics.org, click on country information Adoptive Parents of Vietnam—www.comeunity.com/apv Adopt Vietnam—www.adoptvietnam.org; a print newsletter is also available Families with Children from Vietnam—www.fcvn.org www.groups.yahoo.com/group/a-parents-vietnam

REFERENCES/RESEARCH

Included is the list of research I found most useful; it is not intended to be an exhaustive list of all that is available. I have included the Web site when the report or study is available without subscription online. Many of these journals are available online by subscription, and local public libraries often have subscriptions or can obtain the article through interlibrary loan. Abstracts of a few of these can be found at the Evan B. Donaldson Adoption Institute at www.adoptioninstitute.org.

If you find this research useful, consider supporting the following projects, which further research in international adoption and disseminate the results to adoptive parents.

- The International Adoption Project, sponsored by the National Institutes of Health, the Minnesota Department of Human Services, and various departments at the University of Minnesota, is a wonderful ongoing research project looking at the complete picture of international adoption. Contributions can be made online at www.giving.umn.edu/foundation (specify "The International Adoption Project Fund"), or by mail to University of Minnesota College of Education and Human Development, International Adoption Project Fund, C-M-3854, PO Box 70870, St. Paul, MN 55170-3854.
- The Evan B. Donaldson Adoption Institute is a not-for-profit organization devoted to improving adoption policy and practice. Their Web site includes the best collection of research abstracts on all types of adoption that I have found, including a great collection of Ph.D. dissertation abstracts. The full dissertations are not readily available, so they have not been referenced here; but they are fascinating nonetheless. Contributions can be made online at www.adoptioninstitute.org, or by mail to the Evan B. Donaldson Adoption Institute, 120 Wall Street, 20th Floor, New York, NY 10005.

Abel, Ernest L. 1995. "An Update on Incidence of FAS: FAS Is Not an Equal Opportunity Birth Defect." *Neurotoxicology and Teratology* 17: 437–443.

Albers, L.H., et al. 1997. "Health of Children Adopted from the Former Soviet Union and Eastern Europe: Comparison of Preadoptive Medical Records." *Journal of the American Medical Association* 278: 922–924.

Alstein, Howard, and Mary Coster. 1994. "Clinical Observations of Adult Intercountry Adoptees and Their Adoptive Parents." *Child Welfare* 73: 261–269.

Altstein, Howard, and Rita Simon. 1977. *Transracial Adoption.* New York: John Wiley and Sons.

American Academy of Pediatrics. 2000. "Fetal Alcohol Syndrome and Alcohol-Related Neurodevelopmental Disorders." *Pediatrics* 106: 358–361.

Andujo, Estela. 1988. "Ethnic Identity of Transethnically Adopted Hispanic Adolescents." *Social Work* 33: 531–535.

Aronson, Jane. 2003a. "Alcohol Related Disorders and Children Adopted from Abroad." www.orphandoctor.com/medical/commondiseases/fas/alcoholrelated.html.

Aronson, Jane. 2003b. "Fetal Alcohol Syndrome in Russian Orphanages." http://www.orphandoctor.com/medical/commondiseases/fas/fas_russian.html.

Bagley, C. 1993. "Chinese Adoptees in Britain: A Twenty Year Follow-up Study of Adjustment and Social Identity." *International Social Work* 36: 143–157.

Bledsoe, Julia, and Brian D. Johnston. 2004. "Preparing Families for International Adoption." *Pediatrics in Review* 25: 242–250.

Boer, Frits, et al. 1994. "International Adoption of Children with Siblings: Behavioral Outcomes." *American Journal of Orthopsychiatry* 64 (2): 252–262.

Bohman, M., and S. Sigvardsson. 1990. "Outcome in Adoption: Lessons from Longitudinal Studies." *The Psychology of Adoption,* edited by David M. Brodzinsky and Marshall D. Schechter. New York: Oxford University Press.

Brodzinsky, David M., and Anne B. Brodzinsky. 1992. "The Impact of Family Structure on the Adjustment of Adopted Children." *Child Welfare* 71(1): 69–76.

Child Welfare Information Gateway. 1994. *Transracial and Transcultural Adoption.* http://childwelfare.gov.

Chisholm, Kim. 1998. "A Three Year Follow-up of Attachment and Indiscriminate Friendliness in Children Adopted from Romanian Orphanages." *Child Development* 69: 1092–1106.

Davies, Julian K., and Julia M. Bledsoe. 2005. "Prenatal Alcohol and Drug Exposures in Adoption." *Pediatric Clinics of North America* 52: 1369–1393.

Edelsward, L. M. 2005. "Challenges Experienced by Intercountry Adopted Children: A Survey of the Issues." Intercountry Adoption Services, Social Development Canada. http://www.adoption.ca/pdfs/ias/IASchall05_e.pdf.

Feigelman, W. 1997. "Adopted Adults: Comparisons with Persons Raised in Conventional Families." *Families and Adoption,* edited by H. E. Gross and M. B. Sussman. Binghamton, NY: Haworth Press, 199–223.

Fensbo, Conni. 2004. "Mental and Behavioural Outcome of Inter-ethnic Adoptees." *European Child & Adolescent Psychiatry* 13: 55–63.

Freeark, Kristine, et al. 2005. "Gender Differences and Dynamics Shaping the Adoption Life Cycle: Review of the Literature and Recommendations. *American Journal of Orthopsychiatry* 75: 86–101.

Gray, Deborah D. 2002. *Attaching in Adoption: Practical Tools for Today's Parents.* Indianapolis: Perspectives Press.

Groze, Victor, and Daniela Ileana. 1996. "A Follow-up Study of Adopted Children from Romania." *Child and Adolescent Social Work Journal* 13: 541–565.

Gunnar, Megan, Jacqueline Bruce, and Harold Grotevant. 2000. "International Adoption of Institutionally Reared Children: Research and Policy." *Development and Psychopathology* 12: 677–693.

Hjern, Anders, Frank Lindblad, and Bo Vinnerljung. 2002. "Suicide, Psychiatric Illness, and Social Maladjustment in Intercountry Adoptees in Sweden: A Cohort Study." *The Lancet* 360: 443–448.

International Adoption Project. 2002a. "First Findings from the International Adoption Project." University of Minnesota. http://education.umn.edu/ICD/IAP/Firstfinding1.pdf.

International Adoption Project. 2002b. *International Adoption Project News.* University of Minnesota. http://education.umn.edu/icd/iap/newsletters/IAPNewsletter2002.pdf.

International Adoption Project. 2003. *International Adoption Project News.* University of Minnesota. http://education.umn.edu/icd/iap/newsletters/IAPNewsletter2003.pdf.

International Adoption Project. 2004. *International Adoption Project News.* University of Minnesota. http://education.umn.edu/icd/iap/newsletters/IAPNewsletter2004.pdf.

International Adoption Project. 2005. *International Adoption Project News.* University of Minnesota. http://education.umn.edu/icd/iap/newsletters/IAPNewsletter2005.pdf.

Jenista, J. A. 2000. "Medical Issues in International Adoption." *Pediatric Annals* 29: 204–252.

Johnson, D. E. 2002. "Adoption and the Effect on Children's Development." *Early Human Development* 68: 39–54.

Johnson, K. A. 1996. "The Politics of the Revival of Infant Abandoment in China." *Population and Development Review* 22(1): 77–98.

Johnson, K. A. 2004. *Wanting a Daughter, Needing a Son: Abandonment, Adoption, and Orphanage Care in China.* St. Paul, Minnesota: Yeong & Yeong Book Company.

Johnston, Patricia Irwin. 1992. *Adopting After Infertility.* Indianapolis: Perspectives Press.

Judge, Sharon. 2004. "Adoptive Families: The Effects of Early Relational Deprivation in Children Adopted from Eastern European Orphanages." *Journal of Family Nursing* 10(3): 338–356.

Kelly, M. M., et al. 1998. "Adjustment and Identity Formation in Adopted and Non-adopted Young Adults: Contributions of Family Environment." *American Journal of Orthopsychiatry* 68(3): 497–500.

Kyskan, Christina E., and Timothy Moore. 2005. "Global Perspectives on Fetal Alcohol Syndrome: Assessing Practices, Policies, and Campaigns in Four English-Speaking

Countries." *Canadian Psychology.* http://www.findarticles.com/p/articles/mi_qa3711/is_200508/ai_n15704706.

Lin, S., et al. 2005. "The Relation Between Length of Institutionalization and Sensory Integration in Children Adopted from Eastern Europe." *American Journal of Occupational Therapy* 59: 139–147.

McGuinness T., et al. 2000. "Risk and Protective Factors in Children Adopted from the Former Soviet Union." *Journal of Pediatric Health Care* 14: 109–116.

McRoy, R. G., et al. 1982. "Self-esteem and Racial Identity in Transracial and Intraracial Adoptees." *Social Work* 27: 522–526.

Meese, Ruth Lyn. 2005. "Few New Children: Postinstitutionalized Children of Intercountry Adoption." *The Journal of Special Education* 39(3): 157–167.

Miller, Laurie C. 2005. *The Handbook of International Adoption Medicine.* New York: Oxford University Press.

Miller, Laurie C., et al. 2005. "Health of Children Adopted from Guatemala: Comparison of Orphanage and Foster Care." *Pediatrics* 115: 710–717.

Miller, Laurie C., et al. 2006. "Fetal Alcohol Spectrum Disorders in Children Residing in Russian Orphanages: A Phenotypic Survey." *Alcoholism Clinical and Experimental Research* 30: 531–538.

Miller, Laurie, and Nancy W. Hendrie. 2000. "Health of Children Adopted from China." *Pediatrics* 105: e76–e87.

Mitchell, Marie A. Sills, and Jerri Ann Jenista. 1997. "Health Care of the Internationally Adopted Child, Part 2: Chronic Care and Long-term Medical Issues." *Journal of Pediatric Health Care* 11(3): 117–126.

Nemtsov, A. 2005. "Russia: Alcohol Yesterday and Today." *Addiction* 100: 146–149.

Norvell, M., and R. F. Guy. 1977. "A Comparison of Self-Concept in Adopted and Non-Adopted Adolescents." *Adolescence* 12(47): 443–448.

O'Connor, Thomas G., et al. 2000. "The Effects of Global Severe Privation on Cognitive Competence: Extension and Longitudinal Follow-up." *Child Development* 71: 376–390.

Rutter, Michael, and the English and Romanian Adoptees (ERA) Study Team. 1998. "Developmental Catch-up and Deficit, Following Adoption After Severe Global Early Privation." *Journal of Child Psychology and Psychiatry* 39: 465–476.

Ryan, Scott D., and Victor Groza. 2004. "Romanian Adoptees: A Cross-National Comparison." *International Social Work* 47: 53–79.

Schulte, J., et al. 2002. "Evaluating Acceptability and Completeness of Overseas Immunization Records of Internationally Adopted Children." *Pediatrics* 109(2): e22.

Simon, Rita J., and Howard Alstein. 1987. *Transracial Adoptees and Their Families: A Study of Identity and Commitment.* New York: Praeger. http://www.questia.com/PM.qst?a=o&d=24656886.

Simon, Rita J., and Howard Alstein. 1992. *Adoption, Race, and Identity: From Infancy Through Adolescence.* New York: Praeger.

Simon, Rita J., Howard Altstein, and M. S. Melli. 1994. *The Case for Transracial Adoption.* Washington, D.C.: The American University Press.

Staat, Mary Allen. 2002. "Infectious Disease Issues in Internationally Adopted Children." *The Pediatric Infectious Disease Journal* 21(3): 257–258.

Streissguth, A. P., et al. 1991. "Fetal Alcohol Syndrome in Adolescents and Adults." *Journal of the American Medical Association* 265: 1961–1967.

Streissguth, A. P., et al. 1997. "Primary and Secondary Disabilities in Fetal Alcohol Syndrome." *The Challenge of Fetal Alcohol Syndrome: Overcoming Secondary Disabilities.* (Streissguth A. P., J. Kanter, eds). pp. 25–39. Seattle: University of Washington Press.

Tan, Tony, and Kofi Marfo. 2006. "Parental Ratings of Behavioral Adjustment in Two Samples of Adopted Chinese Girls." *Journal of Applied Developmental Psychology* 27(1): 14–30.

U.S. Department of State. 2006. "Immigrant Visas Issued to Orphans Coming to the US: Top Countries of Origin FY 2005." http://travel.state.gov/family/adoption/stats/stats_451.html.

Verhulst, Frank C. 2000. "Internationally Adopted Children: The Dutch Longitudinal Adoption Study." *Adoption Quarterly* 4: 27–44.

Watkins, Mary, and Susan Fisher. 1993. *Talking with Young Children About Adoption.* New Haven: Yale University Press.

World Health Organization Department of Mental Health and Substance Abuse. 2004. *WHO Global Status Report on Alcohol 2004.* http://www.who.int/substance_abuse/publications/alcohol/en/index.html.

Zeanah, C. 2000. "Disturbances of Attachment in Young Children Adopted from Institutions." *Journal of Developmental and Behavioral Pediatrics* 21(3): 230–236.

GLOSSARY OF ADOPTION AND INTERNET ACRONYMS

ACR Age of child requested

AD Attachment disorder

AD(H)D Attention deficit (hyperactivity) disorder

AM, AD Adoptive mom, dad

AP Adoptive parent(s)

ARBD Alcohol-related birth defects

ARND Alcohol-related neurodevelopmental disorders

BCG The Bacille Calmette-Guérin vaccine (Used to protect against TB in countries where the disease is more prevalent.)

BCIS Bureau of Citizenship and Immigration Services (formerly INS). Now USCIS.

BH Baby house

BIL Brother-in-law

Bio Biological, birth child, child born to parent (Not politically correct but used frequently on adoption forums.)

BMOM, BDAD or BM, BF Birth mother, birth father

BTW By the way

CAPD Central auditory processing disorder

CCAA China Center of Adoption Affairs

COC Certificate of citizenship

Detsky dom Children's home in Russia

DH, DW, DD, DS Dear husband, wife, daughter, son (At times I imagine the "D" stands for something else.)

DOA Date of adoption

DOB Date of birth

DOE, DoE Department of Education (Governmental agency that oversees adoptions in certain countries, including Russia.)

DOR Date of referral

DOT Date of travel

DTC Dossier to China

EE Eastern Europe

EI Early intervention

ESL English as a Second Language

FAE Fetal alcohol effect (No longer a term that is commonly used.)

FAS Fetal alcohol syndrome

FASD Fetal alcohol spectrum disorders

FIL Father-in-law

FSU Former Soviet Union

FWIW For what it's worth

Gotcha Day Day adoptive parents received custody of their child

HS Home study

IA International adoption/Intercountry adoption

IEP Individualized educational plan

IMHO In my humble opinion

IMO In my opinion

INS Immigration and Naturalization Service (Now called USCIS.)

IOW In other words

IRL In real life

LID Logged-in date

LOL Laugh out loud

Lurker Someone who listens in on a forum without posting

MFA Ministry of Foreign Affairs

MIL Mother-in-law

MOE, MoE Minister of Education (Oversees adoptions in certain countries, including Russia.)

NSN Non–special needs

OP Original poster

OT Off topic; not related to the original post

OTOH On the other hand

PAP Pre-adoptive parent; prospective adoptive parent

PDD Pervasive development disorder

PI Post-institutionalization

PP, PPR Post-placement report

PTSD Post-traumatic stress disorder

RAD Reactive attachment disorder

ROFL Rolling on the floor laughing

SAHM, SAHD Stay-at-home mom, dad

SID Sensory integration disorder or sensory integrative dysfunction

SIL Sister-in-law

SN Special needs

SSA, SSN Social Security Administration, social security number

SW Social worker

SWI Social Welfare Institution (The term used for orphanage in certain countries, including China.)

Troll Someone who posts on an Internet forum with ill intent

TTC Trying to conceive

USCIS U.S. Citizenship and Immigration Services (Previously known as INS and BCIS.)

INDEX

DAWN DAVENPORT is a mom of four through both birth and international adoption. She is an attorney, researcher, writer, and adoption expert. She speaks at many conferences on this topic and is interviewed frequently by national media. She lives in North Carolina. Her Web site is www.findingyourchild.com.